A NATION at WAR
1939 ✦ 1945

Essays from LEGION MAGAZINE, Terry Copp

A NATION at WAR

Essays from Legion Magazine

*Dedicated to the men and women of the Canadian Forces
who fought for the liberation of Europe and the hope
of a better world.*

Copyright © 2004 by the Laurier Centre for Military Strategic and Disarmament Studies
(LCMSDS)

First published in 2004 by the Laurier Centre for Military Strategic and Disarmament
Studies, Wilfrid Laurier University, Waterloo, Ontario, N2L 3C5, Canada,
(519) 884-0710 ext. 4594, mbechtho@wlu.ca

Library and Archives Canada Cataloguing in Publication

Copp, Terry, 1938-
A nation at war : collected essays from Legion magazine / Terry Copp.

Includes bibliographical references and index.
ISBN 0-9688750-5-X

1. Canada. Canadian Armed Forces--History--World War, 1939-1945.
2. World War, 1939-1945--Canada. I. Laurier Centre for Military, Strategic
and Disarmament Studies II. Legion Magazine III. Title.

D768.15.C6625 2004   940.54'0971   C2004-904949-6

Cover design: Mike Bechthold, Cover production: Timm Vera
Front cover: "Infantry Near Nijmegen", by Alex Colville (AN19710261-2079)
Book design and production: Timm Vera
Maps: Mike Bechthold, Kevin Weight, Timm Vera
Printed by the Beacon Herald Fine Printing Division, Stratford, Ontario
Printed and bound in Canada

M. Bechthold

Terry Copp with a battlefield studies tour, Dieppe.

A NATION AT WAR, Collected Essays from Legion Magazine

A few months before the 50th anniversary of D-Day Mac Johnston, Editor of *Legion Magazine* asked me to write a series of articles on the events of the last year of the war. The first essay appeared in the June/July issue of 1994 and the last in August 1995. *Legion* readers wrote to tell us they enjoyed the series and we decided to make "Canadian Military History in Perspective" a regular feature of the magazine. Ten years later, on the eve of the 60th anniversary of the Normandy landings, reader support is still strong and *Legion Magazine* decided to expand the feature to include essays on naval and air history.

It is now time to respond to readers who have urged us to publish the articles in a book format available to the general public as well as *Legion* members. *A Nation at War* includes a number of essays from the original series as well as all those published since September 1995. We have added new maps to help orient readers, I edited out some minor errors and updated references but otherwise left the text as it was written.

The book is published by the Laurier Centre for Military Strategic and Disarmament Studies at Wilfrid Laurier University. All proceeds from the sale of the book, including author's royalties will be donated to the Royal Canadian Legion and the Canadian Battlefields Foundation; two organizations determined to keep the memory alive.

Terry Copp

The Decision To Enter WW II

Originally published, September 1995

John Keegan, the famous British military historian, has written a new book based on his Barbara Frum Lectures presented in Toronto last spring. Entitled *The Battle For History: ReFighting World War Two*, it introduces readers to some of the historical controversies that enliven university classrooms. The book is very thin, both in length and substance, and it ignores Canada, but the idea behind it is excellent. In this new series of articles for *Legion Magazine* I will offer some insight into the battle for WW II history, emphasizing issues of concern to Canadians without ignoring the larger picture.

We need to begin with an understanding of why historians, journalists and ordinary citizens often disagree about the past. A moment's reflection will remind us that the past cannot be studied directly. There is no laboratory where we can recreate events to verify our ideas. We are stuck with interpreting the available evidence. Only some evidence survives and in the case of WW II history, the experiences and knowledge of millions of participants is lost to us forever. Much written evidence is available but there are large gaps in the record. Bernard Montgomery, probably for security reasons, destroyed his files on Dieppe. Guy Simonds left few significant personal papers and his divisional commanders were equally circumspect. Admiral L.M. Murray's papers in the National Archives reveal little about the only Canadian to command a theatre of operations.

In contrast, former prime minister Mackenzie King left far too much, including a lot about his fantasies. The Eisenhower and Churchill papers also fill libraries and you could argue that the vast collections of routine records of military units support the view that the war was fought with reports and memos, as much as bombs and bullets. In other words, while we know that a lot of evidence is missing, the amount available is so enormous that no one can claim to have considered all of it unless he or she studies a very limited topic.

Understanding the challenge facing historians may provoke some sympathy, but the reality is most controversies are created by people who disagree about the present and seek to use the past as ammunition in political or ideological battles. Historians claim to agree the past should be studied for its own sake and on its own terms, but few are able to resist imposing their own agenda. Readers need to be aware of this and historians and journalists could help by making their ideas more explicit.

My own agenda is easily identified. Having just returned from our sixth trip to Normandy and Northwest Europe, my wife and I remain in awe of the achievements of the Canadian and Allied forces. This time we introduced a group of students from across Canada to the battlefields. The study tour, sponsored by the Canadian Battlefields Foundation, began on the night of June 5 at the memorial to 1st Canadian Parachute Battalion. The following day we walked Juno beach at low tide and joined in a simple ceremony organized by local villagers. The next night we stood together in the memorial garden at the Abbaye d'Ardenne and listened as Hamilton Southam, a veteran of the Italian campaign, read out the names of the young Canadians murdered there by the 12th SS Panzer Division 51 years ago. We placed flowers on the memorial and spoke the words of the Lord's Prayer.

We were all deeply moved by these and similar events. The students who were seeing these places for the first time were profoundly touched by the vast war cemeteries. They walked the rows, identifying names of relatives and family friends, and pausing before inscriptions that described the sense of loss. These were the graves of young men of their own age and emotions ran high.

All across France and Belgium we see plaques offering thanks to the Canadian liberators. The word "liberation" is used over and over again in

NAC 38723

Joining up, saying goodbye.

speeches and on memorials and our discussions got better as we understood the significance of the battles for those who were freed from Nazi tyranny. In the fields north of Falaise we came to the cross marking the place where the British Columbia and Algonquin regiments suffered grievous losses in August 1944. The Canadian flag, which had flown so bravely on previous visits, had disappeared, but the memorial with its simple inscription –To Those Who Fell – provoked a renewed discussion of the strategy and tactics employed in the battle to close the gap. No one offered easy judgments or proposed simplistic solutions to the problems of overcoming a desperate enemy.

Two days later we were in Dieppe to examine the failed raid of 1942 and celebrate the liberation of 1944. Beaumont-Hamel, where the Newfoundland Regiment fought on July 1, 1916, and Vimy were next. Both memorials are among the most visited places in northern France and both tell a story that is a vital part of our heritage.

In Adagem, Belgium, we were met by two men who have dedicated time and a great deal of money to building a new liberation museum. Gilbert van Landschoot told us his father, a member of the Belgian resistance, had escaped arrest and certain death because of the swift arrival of 4th Canadian Armoured Division. His Canadian Memorial Museum is a personal tribute to the liberators. We had expected a modest collection of artifacts in a village shop, but we found a large, new building of stone with enormous oak beams. Curator Alex Martens has set the Canadian contribution firmly in the context of the origins of the war, the defeat of 1940 and the occupation and resistance. The last rooms are devoted to the Canadian battles for the liberation of the region. Most of the visitors will be Belgian and Dutch schoolchildren, but surely many Canadians will want to see this extraordinary offering of thanks.

At the site of the Breskens Pocket we were joined by a young Dutch historian who described the horrors of the occupation and the relief of liberation. We began our study of the struggle to clear the Scheldt estuary while standing on the large German pillbox that anchored their defence of the Leopold Canal. It was not difficult to think our way back into the minds of those who planned the battle or those who fought it. But how could we imagine what it was like to storm across a canal under heavy fire. How did they do it, we asked? Where does such courage come from? Discipline and training play a part, but in the end the basic motivation was not to let your comrades down.

On our way to the site of 9th Brigade's amphibious landing on the northeast coast of the Breskens Pocket we paused at Milestone One of the Liberation March that takes place here every November 1. Thousands of Dutch and Belgian citizens including many schoolchildren, set out from Hoofdplaat to trace 3rd Canadian Division's route to Knocke-Heist on the Belgian coast. The walk is 32 kilometres and not everyone goes the whole way but Canadians who doubt the value of our contribution to the Allied cause would not have to travel far before they began to understand that liberation is more than just a word.

Seeing the battlefields with these young men and women reinforced pride in being a Canadian and humility in the face of such courage and sacrifice. As an historian my bias is the desire to understand and celebrate the achievements of our veterans. This means emphasizing the profound moral purpose that motivated participation in the war and documenting the significance of the Canadian contribution to victory. This does not mean avoiding controversial issues or ignoring mistakes, but it does require writing about the past without constantly judging events with the benefit of hindsight.

In the summer of 1918 the Allied coalition launched a series of attacks upon the German army that culminated in its defeat and surrender. The Canadian Corps played a major role in these battles beginning with the Amiens offensive on August 8. At the Paris Peace Conference the victorious powers imposed terms on the vanquished foe forcing Germany to acknowledge war guilt, pay reparations, limit its armed forces and sur-

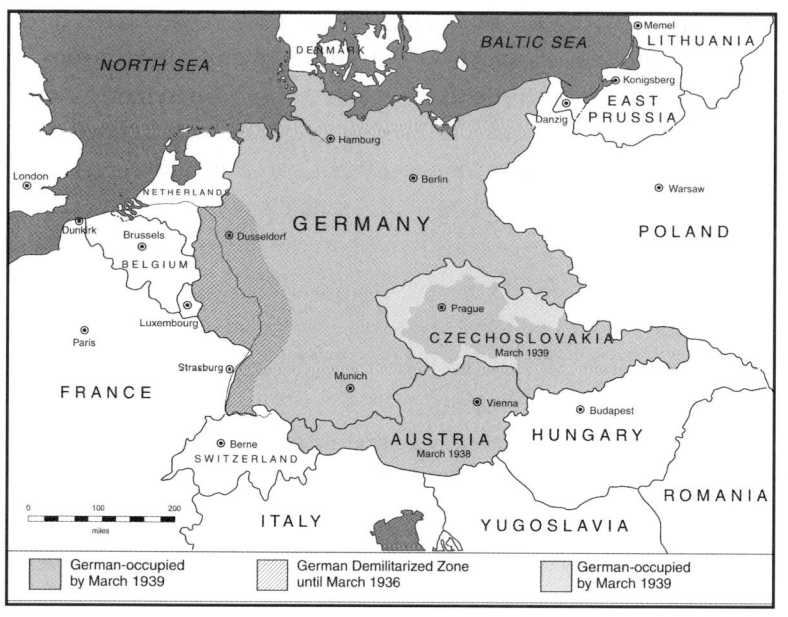

German expansion 1938-39

were beginning to understand this. The majority still wished to avoid confrontation, hoping Hitler did not really believe in the paranoid racial fantasies described in his autobiography *Mein Kampf*.

It is ironic that the best contemporary historians view these events very differently. In the 1960s, Fritz Fischer, a German historian, began to challenge WW I revisionism. He argued–convincingly–that Germany had sought war in 1914 and pursued war aims designed to bring most of Europe under German control. France and Britain fought a defensive war to prevent German domination. So the Great War had not been a meaningless blood bath. The fighting had continued for four years because the alternative was a German victory with peace terms that would have made Versailles seem mild. This was exactly what Canadian veterans thought the war was about and it is why there was broad support for restraining Germany at Versailles.

render some territory. There was nothing unusual or new in the Versailles Treaty. It was much less severe than the one the Germans had imposed on the Soviets the previous year and very much in the tradition of previous European treaties. Throughout the 1920s the terms of the settlement were constantly modified, always in favour of Germany.

Unfortunately, the postwar generation quickly lost sight of the purpose of Versailles which was to restrain Germany's military power. American and British historians developed a revisionist interpretation of the causes of the war that minimized Germany's responsibility. They criticized Versailles as an unjust treaty and helped to reinforce the view that Germany, not the countries its armies had destroyed, was the primary victim of the war.

This revisionist view provided a rationale for the policy of appeasement that came to dominate British diplomacy in the 1930s. France, with its conscript army, was seen as the main obstacle to permanent peace and when Germany began to arm itself again the majority view in the West was sympathetic. Indeed, if Germany had been controlled by a normal nationalist leader committed to restoring Germany's pride and power there would have been little opposition in the West. Hitler and his National Socialists were far from normal and by the mid-1930s many people

Historians are much less divided over the issues of the late 1930s after Hitler was firmly in power. Few serious scholars question Hitler's determination to conquer Europe. He may not have had the precise timetable that Winston Churchill warned about, but he was determined to annex Austria, crush Czechoslovakia and destroy the French army before turning to his main goal of gaining "living space" for his Thousand-Year Reich in the heartland of Russia and the Ukraine.

Canadian élites, like those in other democratic countries, were blinded by the prevailing view of the causes of WW I and the injustice of the peace. When Hitler sent his troops into the demilitarized Rhineland, violating both Versailles and the postwar Treaty of Locarno, the West went along with the notion that Hitler was only entering his own backyard. Belgium's subsequent declaration of neutrality was shrugged off even though it jeopardized the survival of France. When Hitler engineered the annexation of Austria, outflanking the defences of democratic Czechoslovakia, the West remained inert.

Everyone knew Hitler's Germany was a pretty nasty place. There was plenty of prejudice and some very real restrictions on civil liberties of Jews, blacks and orientals in Canada and other countries, but the vicious and systematic anti-Semitism of the Nuremberg Laws was another matter entirely. So was the glorification of power and the militarization of German society. But as long as Hitler focused on Germany no one considered intervention and few thought that any increase in expenditure to prepare our armed forces was necessary.

Most Canadian historians believe this attitude persisted right up to the declaration of war. Relying on the views of French Canadian nationalists, a few left wing politicians and anti-British intellectuals, our history books insist we went to war "because Britain went to war. Not for democracy, not to stop Hitler, not to save Poland."

This view was attractive to a postwar generation trying to promote decolonization of Canada by attacking the British connection, but it tells us little about English-Canadian opinion in the 1930s. The evidence from newspapers, church conferences, volunteer organizations and ordinary citizens presents a very different picture. In English-speaking Canada, where almost 75 per cent of the population was of British ancestry (523,000 of Toronto's 667,000 people were of British background in 1941) close links with the mother country were natural and inevitable. But this closeness did not mean blind loyalty to the policies of British politicians.

Most Canadians came to understand that Hitler threatened France, Britain and the security of the entire Western world in the context of his threats to Czechoslovakia. The Munich Agreement, which sacrificed that country's fortified zone when the Sudetanland was transferred to the Nazis, was welcomed by Canadians as a reprieve from a war they were reluctantly ready to fight.

One month later Nazi terror in the *Kristalnacht*–the night of broken glass–against Germany's Jews prompted protests across the country. In Toronto tens of thousands filled Maple Leaf Gardens to overflowing as civic and religious leaders' condemned Nazi racism and urged the federal government to admit Jewish refugees.

The final straw was Hitler's occupation of Prague and the rest of Czechoslovakia in March 1939. English-speaking Canadians were part of that "underground explosion of public opinion" that forced governments in Britain, France and Canada to abandon appeasement and begin preparations for a war that Hitler was determined to start. Many French-speaking Canadians were less ready to go to war, but opposition was muted in the face of the intense reaction in the rest of the country.

One week after the British declared war, in fulfillment of the promise to Poland, Canada's Parliament assembled to decide on Canada's role. The debate began with a speech by H.S. Hamilton, a veteran of WW I, who expressed the views of the overwhelming majority of Canadians. Hitler, he reminded the members, threatened everything Canadians believed in. "This war," he insisted, "is Canada's war. The effective defence of Canada consists in the utilization of the organized and united power and strength of this Dominion however, wherever and whenever it can best be used to defeat Germany's armed forces and to destroy the philosophy on which they are based."

Hamilton sat down to thunderous applause. Canada was at war and for all the right reasons.

Dunkirk 1940

The Fall Of France

Originally published, October 1995

Historians now explain the collapse of French military resistance in June 1940 in ways that make defeat seem inevitable. But at the time, the fall of France was, in the words of the British foreign secretary, "so unbelievable as to be almost surely unreal". Thoughtful people everywhere recognized that the world had suddenly changed; this was either the beginning of Hitler's Thousand-Year Reich, or–if Germany was defeated–the end of the European age.

The fate of France was probably determined in 1936 when Belgium, France's vital ally in the west, stuck its head in the sand and declared neutrality. Thereafter, the French army confronted a strategic problem that no one then or since has been able to resolve. Put in its simplest terms the French were required to defend a perimeter that stretched from the English Channel to the Mediterranean. If they extended the Maginot Line to fortify their border with Belgium, there would be little choice except to stand by and watch Hitler destroy the Belgian army and advance towards them. France could not violate Belgium's neutrality before a German attack, so plans were drawn up to move into the Low Countries

after a Nazi offensive had begun. This required the French to deploy their most mobile armies in the north to make the rapid moves required.

French General Maurice Gamelin could afford to thin out his forces along the Maginot Line but the hostility of Italy and the possibility of a German attack through Switzerland required heavy commitments in the south. This meant that the 94 French divisions available in 1940 could not possibly develop defences in depth or assemble a large strategic reserve.

The Belgian problem also made it difficult for France to take advantage of German weakness during the invasion of Poland. Hitler was confident there would be no French violation of neutrality and so he concentrated the 35 divisions left in the west along a 100-mile sector in the Rhineland. No French general could agree to attacking such a narrow, and, well defended front so pleas from Poland for action went unanswered.

Some historians attribute the defeat of France to a lack of will, low morale and defeatism among politicians and the military. No matter what form the German attack took, it is argued, France would have been crushed. Other analysts focus on German strategic planning for the breakthrough at Sedan and the rapid advance to the Channel coast while military historians emphasize the operational and tactical skill of the German army whose troops overwhelmed French, Belgian and British units in a war of manoeuvre that the press called Blitzkrieg.

All of these explanations add to our knowledge of what happened but it is not clear they help explain what alternative strategies should have been pursued in 1940. It is worth reminding ourselves that a year later the Soviet Union, forced to defend an even longer frontier, almost collapsed under the impact of surprise attacks delivered at a time and place of Hitler's choosing. And in 1944, faced with the need to defend the Atlantic Wall from Holland to the south of France, Hitler and his generals spread out their forces with the smallest of mobile reserves. They too misjudged the location of the main attack and lost all of France in a little over two months. Eisenhower's dispositions at the time of the second Ardennes offensive, the Battle of the Bulge, were strangely similar to those of Gamelin in 1940, though this time the Germans lacked the strength to take advantage of it.

The armies of NATO, during the long years of the Cold War, found themselves forced to develop a strategy based on the forward defence of the entire frontier between east and west. The planners were well aware of the supposed lessons of the Battle of France but just as in 1940 there seemed no choice. If you are not prepared to attack first, your enemy can choose his time and place. If you decline to defend part of your territory you sacrifice land and people without resolving your dilemma. NATO would not deliberately abandon large sections of Germany any more than France could give up its industrial zone or allow the 18 divisions of the Belgian army to be isolated. France's only hope in 1940, or NATO's if a Soviet attack had ever come, was to absorb the blows, fall back and reform a new perimeter defence. The French lost because they had not adjusted, mentally or physically, to the new age of mobile and mechanized warfare. Fortunately, we will never know if NATO planners succeeded where the French, Soviets and Germans failed.

Canadian involvement in the battle of France is a largely forgotten chapter in our history, but it is worth recalling for a number of reasons. Historians have been very critical of the performance of the Canadian armed forces in WW II and have questioned the competence of virtually every senior officer. No one has suffered more criticism than General Andy McNaughton, the man the wartime generation knew as "the father of the Canadian Army".

A.G.L. McNaughton won recognition as an outstanding gunner in WW I and rose to the highest rank in the Canadian Army before becoming President of the National Research Council. In 1939 he was recalled to active service and given command of the First Canadian Infantry Division. McNaughton and the Red Patch Division reached England in December 1939 carrying with them the exalted reputation of the Canadian Corps. The arrival lifted the spirits of everyone in Britain and although the division lacked equipment and needed training it was made up of Canadians, cut from the same cloth as the victors of Vimy Ridge and the Amiens offensive.

It settled into the old permanent barracks at Aldershot and began preparations to join the small British Expeditionary Force that made up eight of the 28 Anglo-French divisions slated to advance into Belgium. Given priority in equipment and training facilities, they were to be ready to go to France by May 1940.

One of Canada's most brilliant professional soldiers, retired Lieutenant-Colonel John A. English, has argued that McNaughton must bear a large share of the responsibility for what he sees as the inadequate performance of the Canadian Army and its senior officers. We will examine this issue in other parts of the series but for the moment we should look closely at McNaughton and his men during the crisis of May-June 1940.

The first call on the Canadians came with the sudden onslaught on Norway. A force of some 800 men were requested for combined operations against the Norwegian port of Trondheim. McNaughton agreed immediately and the Loyal Edmonton Regiment, with the Princess Patricia's Canadian Light Infantry, were on their way to Scotland in 36 hours. The assault was called off but everyone was impressed with the rapid reaction capacity demonstrated by the Canadians.

General Sir Edmund Ironside, the Chief of the Imperial General staff, turned to McNaughton again when the British Expeditionary Force began its retreat to Dunkirk. On May 22, as a German Panzer

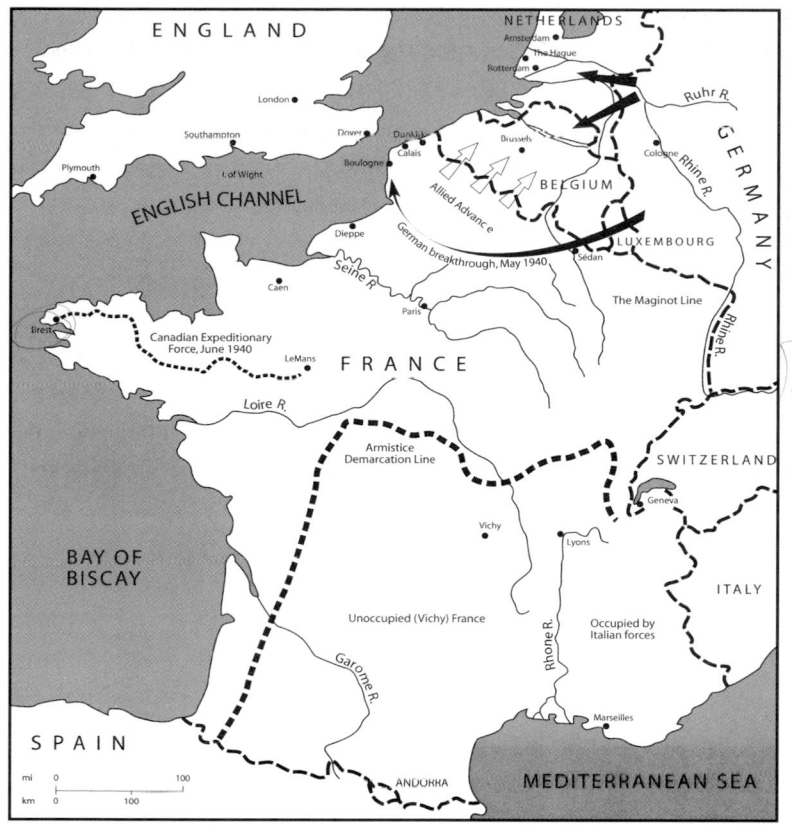

around 52nd Lowland and 1st Canadian Division. They were to move to Brittany to support the French in holding the new Weygand Line, or failing that, to join in the defence of Brittany as a last fortified foothold on the continent.

First Brigade sailed for Brest on June 13, the day before the Germans entered an undefended Paris. The level of confusion in France was such that the Canadians, who were supposed to concentrate near the port before linking up with the Lowland division, were sent inland to Le Mans well past the proposed Brittany defence line.

The next day orders were issued reversing the movement; the Canadians were to return to England. Some elements of the

The Defeat of France

division reached Boulogne, McNaughton was asked to prepare a battle group to go to France and restore communications between the expeditionary force and the remaining Channel ports. He quickly crossed to Calais and Dunkirk to survey the situation, concluding that the Canadians could be best used at Calais to delay the enemy armour from reaching Dunkirk.

While McNaughton tried to make sense of the situation in Calais and Dunkirk, First Brigade–the Royal Canadian Regiment, the Hastings and Prince Edward Regiment and the 48th Highlanders of Canada, with field and anti-tank artillery regiments–was ready and waiting to embark from Dover and Southampton. However, German pressure on Calais and the arrival of French troops to defend Dunkirk led McNaughton to insist that Operation "Angel Move" be cancelled. It was his belief that the Dunkirk area was already quite congested and what the Allies needed there was not reinforcement, but re-organization.

McNaughton, was now convinced that the "coast of the United Kingdom is the citadel which must be held", everything else was of secondary importance. Churchill thought otherwise and insisted on the formation of a Second British Expeditionary Force built

division were 250 miles inland while much of First Brigade was en route to Le Mans by road. There was much cursing, frustration, disappointment and some reports of drunkenness, but the entire force was re-embarked in good order. Most of the brigade's vehicles were lost though Lieutenant-Colonel J.H. Roberts, commanding The 1st Field Regiment, Royal Canadian Horse Artillery, insisted his precious 25-pounder guns had to be saved. He was given less than two hours to accomplish this but it was more than enough time. The RCHA war diary noted bitterly: "Although there was evidently no enemy for 200 miles the withdrawal was conducted as a rout." This was no doubt unfair but the Canadians had little reason to be impressed with the strategic or operational skill of the British army.

The Canadian role in the last days of the Battle of France did not involve any actual combat and is quite properly ignored in most accounts. But for Canadians, the actions of McNaughton and the performance of Canadian troops are of continuing interest. By any reasonable standard both McNaughton and his men came off well. It was as if the famous Canadian Corps had been reborn.

The Battle Over Britain

Originally published, November/December 1995

When Winston Churchill rose to speak in the British House of Commons on June 4, 1940, the rescue of British and French troops from Dunkirk was complete.

The attempts to create a second British Expeditionary Force for France could not disguise the scale of the disaster that had overcome the Allies, and Churchill made no attempt to do so. "Wars," he insisted, "are not won by evacuations." There was, however, "a victory inside the deliverance ... gained by the air force" that had protected the hundreds of ships and prevented the enemy from gaining air superiority over the beaches. The air force, he reminded the Commons, would have a greater advantage defending Britain and thus "the cause of civilization itself will be defended by the skill and devotion of a few thousand airmen." Churchill's speech ended with the famous phrases heard and remembered around the world: "We shall fight on the beaches, we shall fight on the landing grounds ... we shall never surrender." However, he knew that what he called The Battle of Britain would be decided in the air.

Churchill could speak with considerable confidence about the defence of Great Britain because the Royal Air Force had devoted time, energy, resources and the best brains available to the challenge of defending the island from air attack. The Battle of Britain is often remembered as a victory won against great odds, an example of what individual bravery and fortitude can accomplish. Churchill himself popularized this view when he immortalized the pilots of Fighter Command with the words: "Never in the field of human conflict was so much owed by so many to so few." It in no way diminishes the skill or achievement of the 'few' to recognize that this was a battle won by a military organization, Fighter Command, which–unlike the army or navy–was well equipped, well trained, and well prepared for precisely the kind of battle seen on 'Eagle Day'—August 15, 1940.

The story begins in December 1934, when the RAF established a committee for the Scientific Survey of Air Defence, to consider "how recent advances in scientific and technical knowledge" could improve methods of destroying hostile aircraft. Sir Henry Tizard, who chaired the committee, was a scientist of exceptional ability. Though he was skeptical of proposals to find the kind of death ray that science fiction writers so admired, he asked the country's leading radio wave expert to comment on the matter. No such ray could be created, Robert Watson-Watt reported, but even if it could how would the aircraft you wished to destroy be located? Watson-Watt thought he could help with that problem, so Air Marshal Hugh Dowding acted promptly to establish a research and testing centre in Suffolk. Dowding's decision to give priority to the development of what was then called RDF, Radio Direction Finding was as decisive for his country as any event recorded in British history. The next year, Fighter Command was established with a mandate to defend the home islands. Orders were given for two new single-engined, short range fighter interceptors, the Hurricane and the Spitfire, and work on radar was further accelerated.

The first major trial of what we know as radar began in the summer of 1937, and it was quickly apparent that while a single station could give advance warning of a raid nothing could be learned about the destination. Four new radar stations were built, in the belief that simple tracking would solve this problem. But the massive air defence exercises of 1938 demonstrated that there was now too much information, most of it conflicting. The RAF was bitterly disappointed for, even with the new Hurricane, Fighter Command could not position its aircraft in time to intercept the enemy. Neville Chamberlain used this information to justify his decision to sacrifice Czechoslovakia, even though the feared knock-out blow against England by air attack was impossible without German airfields in France and Belgium.

Fortunately, science again came to the aid of Fighter Command in the form of research into the operational–as distinct from technical–aspects of radar. One of the key figures in the new field of

Hurricane fighters in the skies over Britain 1940.

operational research was a graduate of Dalhousie University, Harold Lardner, a radio engineer who specialized in long-distance transmission. Lardner and his colleagues worked out methods for dealing with information received from the main 'Chain Home' stations. They encouraged the development of 'Chain Home Low' radars, which tracked low-flying aircraft and worked out methods of integrating information from the Royal Observer Corps. The filter room system, which permitted Dowding and Air Marshal Keith Park to focus on the changing battle, was just one result of this work.

Lardner was selected to head the Stanmore Research Section, which reported directly to Dowding. One of his first major contributions was to provide the information and supporting graphs that Dowding used to persuade Churchill to limit the number of fighters sent to reinforce the RAF in the Battle of France. After the war Lardner, who worked quietly in Ottawa for the Defence Research Board, insisted that Dowding had a shrewd knowledge of the problem and that he had only helped by presenting the data in graphical form. Dowding, in turn, insisted that Lardner's

graphs "did the trick" with Churchill.

The Stanmore Research Section carefully analysed the early air raids on Britain and worked out the best methods of deploying and controlling fighter aircraft before the main attack began. The key to success was to ensure that Fighter Command pilots attained the tactical advantages of altitude and the use of the sun at their backs. Operational research helped Fighter Command achieve this often enough to prevent the Luftwaffe from winning the air battle. When the battle was won, and Dowding unceremoniously replaced, he wrote a note to Lardner that said: "Thanks. This war will be won by science thoughtfully applied to operational methods. H.D."

Science could shorten the odds, but the Battle of Britain still had to be fought in the skies over southern England. Canadian airmen played a major role in the events of August and September 1940. Only one Royal Canadian Air Force unit, No. 1–later 401–Squadron was in the order of battle, but RAF 242 Squadron was all-Canadian. Its first squadron leader, F.M. Gobeil, was the first RCAF pilot to shoot down an enemy aircraft.

Gobeil was replaced by the famous Douglas Bader, Britain's legless war ace, but the rest of 242 Squadron remained "all-Canadian." Arthur Bishop's book *The Splendid Hundred* tells the individual stories of fully 100 Canadian pilots who fought in the battle.

The Germans would later insist there had never been a Battle of Britain, but the record of their intentions in 1940 is clear enough. Hitler still hoped for a British surrender but plans for "Sea Lion", the invasion of the south coast of England, called for absolute air superiority over the Channel and the other German options for forcing a capitulation required the destruction of British air power, including Bomber Command and the aircraft plants.

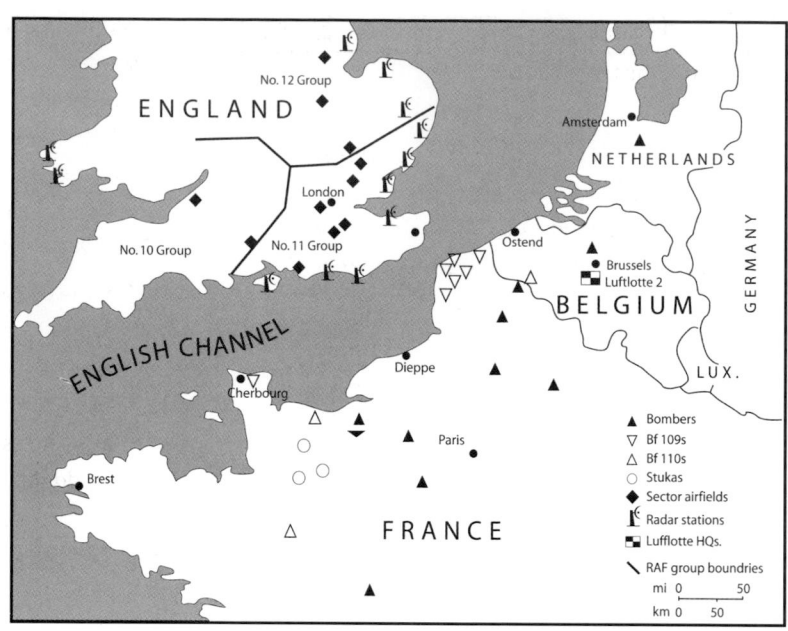

Dowding had good intelligence on German air strength thanks to Ultra, the system of decoding German radio messages enciphered on Enigma machines. The Air Ministry had overestimated German bomber and fighter strength by a factor of four, though the actual number–3,000 aircraft–was bad enough. Fighter Command began the battle with 257 Spitfires and 373 Hurricanes to the Luftwaffe's 809 Messerschmitt 109s, enough to guarantee a warm reception to the German air force.

In the first phase of the action, up until August 14, the Luftwaffe lost almost twice as many aircraft as the RAF. From Eagle Day to the end of August, the delivery of new and repaired planes kept Fighter Command up to strength despite the loss of 301 aircraft. The real problem was pilot losses, 126 Hurricane and Spitfire pilots in the last 10 days of August alone. But Dowding and his Stanmore Research Section had analysed the pattern of losses; new orders were soon issued forbidding pilots to pursue German fighters out over the Channel, and instructing them to concentrate on German bombers, not the ME 109s. The results were immediately apparent. In the ferocious bat-

tles of mid-September, just 67 pilots were lost.

"Dowding understood better than anyone that his task was to maintain air superiority over the south coast of England. More aggressive tactics such as the 'Big Wing' concept promoted by Douglas Bader made a good deal of sense if you wished to gamble on trying to crush the Luftwaffe, but Dowding knew that Fighter Command was all that stood between Britain and a German invasion. If he is to be criticized, it is for failing to abandon some of the forward air fields and transferring more squadrons north of the Thames–beyond the range of German fighter escorts. The battle for air superiority could easily have been fought from such bases.

However, Dowding was saved from having to make a decision when Hitler ordered the first bombing of London on September 7. Eight days later, the climax of the battle came with a massive daylight assault on London. Commemorated now as Battle of Britain Day, September 15 was the moment when all the years of preparation paid off. Fighter Command dealt a devastating blow, destroying some 60 German aircraft for losses of 26 Hurricanes and Spitfires. The Luftwaffe had lost the battle for air superiority and Sea Lion was indefinitely postponed. Hitler had suffered his first defeat.

The Battle
of Britain

Standing Up To The Blitz

Originally published, January 1996

The Blitz started without any warning. Churchill and the defence chiefs met for an emergency meeting the day before it began but their concerns were intelligence reports indicating that the invasion of England–Operation "Sea Lion"–was about to start. Nerves were stretched to the breaking point and the code-word Cromwell, which meant "invasion imminent", was announced without Churchill's knowledge.

In Sussex, even the recently arrived 2nd Canadian Infantry Division was ordered to "standby at immediate notice". Everyone would be needed no matter how incomplete their training or equipment. However, Hitler had decided on another form of assault; the whole strength of Germany's air force was to be used against British cities and civilians.

Hitler had not hesitated to bomb Warsaw or Rotterdam and civilian refugees had been deliberately targeted throughout the Battle of France, but attacks on British cities would bring retaliation so Hitler held off until some bombs fell on Berlin. Frustrated with the Luftwaffe's failure to overcome Fighter Command he agreed to a change in air strategy that led to the first systematic area-bombing campaign in history.

The Blitz began on the night of September 7, 1940, and lasted until May 16, 1941. At first the Luftwaffe concentrated on London and for 68 consecutive nights hundreds of bombs and incendiaries rained down on the city. Initially morale was shaky and thousands fled the bombed areas. Charles Ritchie, a Canadian diplomat in London, described the mood in his diary:

September 14, 1940

The attacks on London have only been going on for 10 days. So far people are steady, there has been no panic. But they are depressed. Everyone is suffering from lack of sleep and nervous tension. There is some feeling that the poor are taking it the hardest and many complaints about lack of

shelters. The ideal thing from Hitler's point of view would be to continue this all winter and then to attack in the spring. Is he strong enough to wait? That is the question hanging over us. His raids certainly have not been a spectacular success, but they are making a dent all right.

As the bombing continued the casualty lists grew. During one night in mid-October more than 900 fires were reported in the London region and 400 civilians were killed, many of them in shelters that collapsed. Damage to public utilities, docks and railway stations caused great hardship and the problem of unexploded bombs kept everyone on edge.

Contrary to all expectations morale improved in October and November. One factor was the decision to fire continuous anti-aircraft barrages during raids, even though ack-ack was known to be wildly inaccurate.

Searchlights were not effective at altitudes greater than 12,000 feet and the chance of actually hitting an enemy aircraft without radar-controlled guns was just about nil. The first gun-laying radar consisted of an antenna on top of a small hut that was rotated, hut and all, by bicycle pedals. Anti-aircraft radar was steadily improved and it played an important role against the V-1 or "buzz" bomb in 1944 but it was of little use during the Blitz. Nevertheless people wanted to believe they were hitting back and noisy gunfire, was proof that the army was trying.

The opinions of ordinary Britons were carefully surveyed throughout the Blitz period in an attempt to identify and head off any sign of defeatism or panic. Home intelligence reports developed by the Ministry of Information as well as Mass Observation surveys prepared by volunteers noted isolated cases of despair and apprehension about the lack of air cover or ack-ack support. Overall, however, people recovered quickly from even the heaviest raids.

Before the war psychiatrists had warned that air raids would lead to thousands of nervous breakdowns as fragile individuals cracked under the strain of continuous bombing. Mental hospitals in the south of England transferred their patients in preparation for a new influx but it never came. Under the pressure of the Blitz neurotic symptoms disappeared as even the most isolated individual became caught up in the collective struggle to survive and help the less fortunate. A Gallup Poll taken in November 1940 reported that more than 80 per cent of the population was optimistic and confident Britain would win the war.

By November 13 the German air force had dropped more than 13,000 tons of bombs and 12,500 incendiary canisters on London. On an average night 163 aircraft attacked the city but there was no sign of a British surrender. The Luftwaffe decided to begin a new series of raids on industrial towns employing radio beams to guide pathfinder aircraft that would mark the targets with incendiaries.

The most successful of these raids occurred on November 14 when 449 bombers struck a devastating blow at Coventry. More than 500 tons of high explosive and 900 incendiaries destroyed the famous cathedral and much of the city killing 507 men, women and children and seriously injuring 420 more. In the 1940s the government believed that two more raids of similar intensity would cripple the city's war production for months to come but the Luftwaffe turned its attention elsewhere boasting that it would "Coventrate" other British towns.

The Luftwaffe staged a series of major assaults on Birmingham, Liverpool and Manchester. Southampton, Plymouth, Portsmouth and Bristol were also frequent targets while Cardiff, Sheffield, Belfast and Glasgow were hit in carefully organized large-scale raids. Plymouth may have been the most blitzed city in Britain. The central area was completely destroyed and more than 1,100 civilians were killed in 59 separate raids. Glasgow and the Clydebank were the primary targets on five separate occasions. The

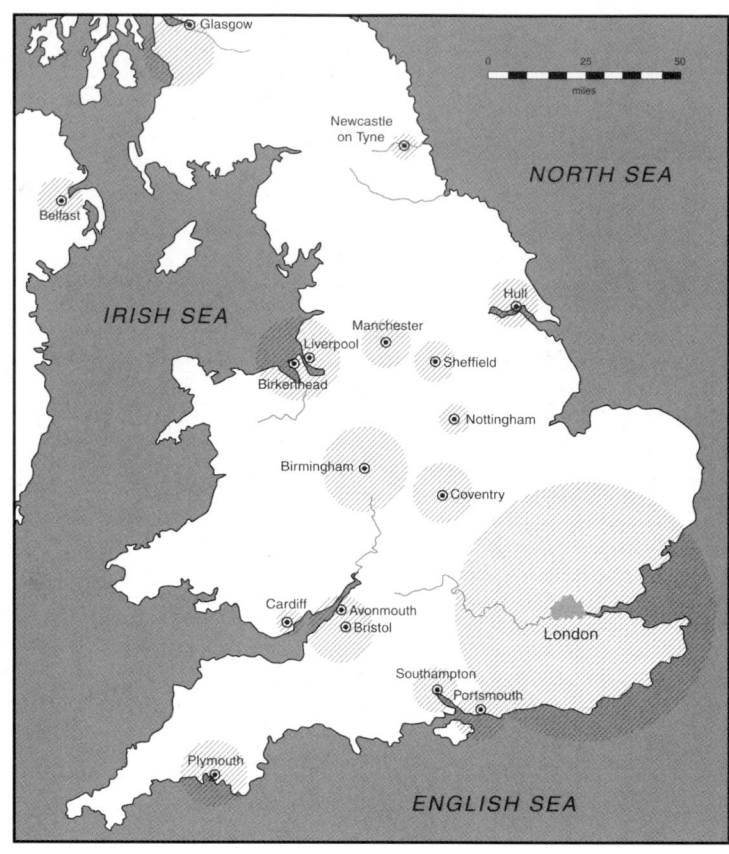

worst attack on May 5 involved 386 bombers using a high proportion of incendiaries. More than 200 bombers returned the next night again attempting to set fire to the city. Belfast was attacked only twice but more than 2,600 incendiaries were dropped in one night and the fires quickly got out of control forcing thousands to flee their homes. Overall more than 51,000 British civilians died from wartime bombing and 61,000 were seriously injured.

By the spring of 1941 British scientists had learned to "bend" or block the German radio beams and Royal Air Force night fighter defences were slowly improving. Whereas in December 1940 just 14 aircraft were shot down, 10 by ack-ack, four by night fighters, German losses in April totaled 75 bombers.

Canadians serving with the RAF played an important role in the night battle and three Royal Canadian Air Force night-fighter squadrons, 406, 409, and 410, were formed and equipped by the spring of 1941. The improved night-fighter defences were rarely tested for Hitler ordered the transfer of most of the Luftwaffe to Poland to

The Blitz, September 1940-May 1941. The shaded circles represent the weight of bombing on each city. London was the most frequently attacked of British cities with 18,000 tons of bombs dropped in eight months. Liverpool and Birmingham were next, but Coventry and Plymouth were the most heavily attacked in relation to their size.

LCMSDS

The meaning of the Blitz

prepare for the invasion of Russia. London's last big raid came on May 10, 1941, when 507 bombers struck the city. Night fighters destroyed seven German aircraft and Air Marshal Sir William Sholto Douglas was quite serious when he claimed: "If the enemy had not chosen that moment to pull out we should soon have been inflicting such casualties in his night bombers that the continuation of his night offensive on a similar scale would have been impossible."

Our memory of the horrors of the Blitz has been overshadowed by the much more devastating bombing of German and Japanese cities. More people were killed in Hamburg and Tokyo in one night than were killed in the entire war in Britain so the importance of the bombing of London and other British cities is said to be diminished. This is a curious view of the past that ignores cause and effect. In 1941 the British believed, correctly, that they had survived one of the most terrible experiments in the history of war. Hitler had threatened to exterminate the population of their cities and he had tried his best to achieve that goal. Was it any wonder that popular and parlia-

mentary opinion supported retaliation?

Churchill was by no means certain that Britain should place a priority on strategic bombing. After the German invasion of Russia he wanted to explore a number of other options designed to take the offensive against Germany. His military advisers rejected schemes for the invasion of Norway and tried to resist pressure to attack prematurely in North Africa. Churchill continued to press for a Turkish declaration of war against Germany and suggested British troops be used to assist the Russians in Persia. Something had to be done to help the Soviet Union survive and in the end the only force available to accomplish that goal was Bomber Command.

When the newly appointed Air Marshal Sir Arthur Harris prepared his first report on the actions of Bomber Command in June 1942 he reinforced Churchill's decision to give priority to strategic bombing. Harris wrote:

Bomber Command provides our only offensive action yet pressed home directly against Germany. All our other efforts are defensive in their nature, and are not intended to do more, and can never do more, than enable us to exist in the face of the enemy. Bomber Command provides the only means of bringing assistance to Russia at this time. The only means of physically weakening Germany to an extent which will make subsequent invasion a possible proposition, and is therefore the only force which can, in fact, hurt our enemy in the present or in the future secure our victory.

Hitler and the Luftwaffe had sown the seeds, German civilians would reap the harvest.

Historians have not hesitated to challenge this straightforward interpretation of the Blitz. The raid on Coventry became one of the most hotly debated issues when allegations were made that the British government had identified the target through special intelligence but failed to take action for fear of compromising the Ultra Secret. This controversy led to the publication of Professor F.H. Hinsley's multi-volume *British Intelligence in the Second World War* which carefully examined such issues. He concluded that the Government Code and Cypher School had decrypted Luftwaffe signals, radioed via their Enigma machines, which referred to a large-scale raid called Moonlight Sonata. Unfortunately nothing in the messages confirmed the target or date and it was not until 1500 hours on November 14—when the German radio beams were intersected over Coventry—that the target was identified and defensive preparations, including an RAF Bomber Command attack on German airfields, begun.

A more fundamental challenge to the traditional interpretation was launched by a historian previously known for his sympathetic study Originally published, 1969 with the title *The People's War, Britain 1939—1945*. By the 1980s Angus Calder had become a Scottish nationalist and trenchant critic of Margaret Thatcher's Britain. He set out to revise his own work which he saw as having confirmed a myth about the unity of the British people and their cheerful courage in the face of adversity. Other historians were attacking the "myth" of Dunkirk and writing sensational attacks on Churchill's leadership so Calder tried "to undermine the credibility of the mythical narrative" by questioning everything, including evidence about the morale of the British people.

Fortunately, Calder is an excellent historian with a good analytical mind. His new book, *The Myth of the Blitz*, begins with the statement that "myth" does not mean "untruth" and goes on to demonstrate that traditional narratives including his own are strongly supported by the available evidence. Calder's real grievance is with postwar politicians whom he believes have exploited wartime ideals but he cannot bring himself to distort evidence in support of his political views.

When Churchill issued the call to his countrymen "to ride out the storm of war and to outlive the menace of tyranny, if necessary for years, if necessary alone" he was expressing views which the vast majority embraced. When he spoke of the threat posed by the large German bombing forces that were deployed against Britain, the words were simple and direct: "I do not underrate the severity of the ordeal which lies before us but I believe our countrymen ... will be able to stand up to it, and carry on in spite of it, as well as any other people in the world. Much will depend on this; every man and every woman will have the chance to show the finest qualities of their race, and render the highest service to their cause. For all of us, at this time, whatever our sphere or our duties, it will help to remember the famous lines:

He nothing common did or mean

Upon that memorable scene.

Calder recognizes that Churchill was the embodiment of a spirit which animated the people of Great Britain. There were of course incidents that were common and mean. People were not always heroic, self-sacrificing or united in 1940 but no one can deny the bravery and resolution of those who endured the Blitz and emerged ready to carry on a war intended to liberate Europe. As Tom Harrison, the founder of Mass Observation, put it: "The final achievement of so many Britons was enormous.... Maybe monumental is not putting it too high. They did not let their soldiers or leaders down."

NAC 112993

Merchant ships in Bedford Basin, Halifax, Nova Scotia waiting for a RCN Convoy Escort Group.

Achievement On The Atlantic

Originally published, February 1996

The full story of the Royal Canadian Navy's contribution to Allied victory in WW II has not been told. In Ottawa, the much-reduced Directorate of History at the Department of National Defence is preparing a multi-volume official history, but this will take some years to complete.*

Until these books are published we must rely on Joseph Schull's *Far Distant Ships* and on a number of detailed accounts of specific parts of the story. Marc Milner's two books *North Atlantic Run* and *The U-boat Hunters* are first-rate studies of the Canadian role in the Battle of the Atlantic and David Zimmerman has introduced us to the politics of the naval war effort in *The Great Naval Battle of Ottawa*. However, we lack an overview that would allow us to place such specialized studies in perspective.

Looking at the pieces of the story leads to a typically Canadian tendency to see failure where others might claim success.

Milner offers an analysis of the events that led to the withdrawal of Canadian Escort Groups from the mid-Atlantic in January 1943. He describes the decision to give the sorely tried navy an opportunity to re-equip its ships and obtain long overdue training as evidence that the RCN had failed.

Failure is a difficult judgment to apply unless you have a realistic idea of what constitutes success. A brief look at the challenges faced by the RCN and its achievements in the first three years of the war may help us to decide how we wish to evaluate the navy's contribution.

The RCN was created amidst great political controversy in 1910 and emerged from WW I with a handful of small coastal defence ships. In the 1920s the navy with just two destroyers and two minesweepers–divided between the two coasts–almost disappeared. Fortunately two new

*W.A.B. Douglas, Roger Sarty, Michael Whitby, *No Higher Purpose*, Volume II, Part 1, was published in 2002.

destroyers, *Saguenay* and *Skeena*, were ordered in 1929 and their delivery helped to ward off depression-era threats to disband the entire navy. With the return of Mackenzie King to power in 1935 the Liberals, still sympathetic to plans for a Canadian navy, found the money to purchase four more destroyers before the outbreak of war.

Given the Canadian government's reluctance to permit general rearmament and King's whole-hearted support for appeasement the navy had done very well, but what role could six destroyers and a few minesweepers play? The only likely tasks were to assist the Royal Navy as part of a destroyer screen for battle-ships or local defence against German commerce raiders. Perhaps someone should have argued the case for anti-submarine warfare training but no one did because the German navy possessed few U-boats and the Royal Navy was confident that air patrols, sonar and convoys would quickly crush a submarine offensive.

This conventional wisdom on the U-boat threat is often used as evidence to attack the leadership of the RN, but in the late 1930s it was based on the best information available. The real threats to the freedom of the seas were the Japanese and Italian fleets plus the new German pocket battleships. No one could have foreseen that the fall of France would provide Admiral Karl Donitz with bases on the French coast avoiding the bottleneck of the North Sea passages and providing easy access to the Atlantic. Hitler had no idea that the U-boat would become his principle weapon in a war of attrition against Britain. He thought the British would accept the inevitable and sue for peace when the Luftwaffe had demolished London. After a year of war German industry only succeeded in replacing the 28 U-boats lost

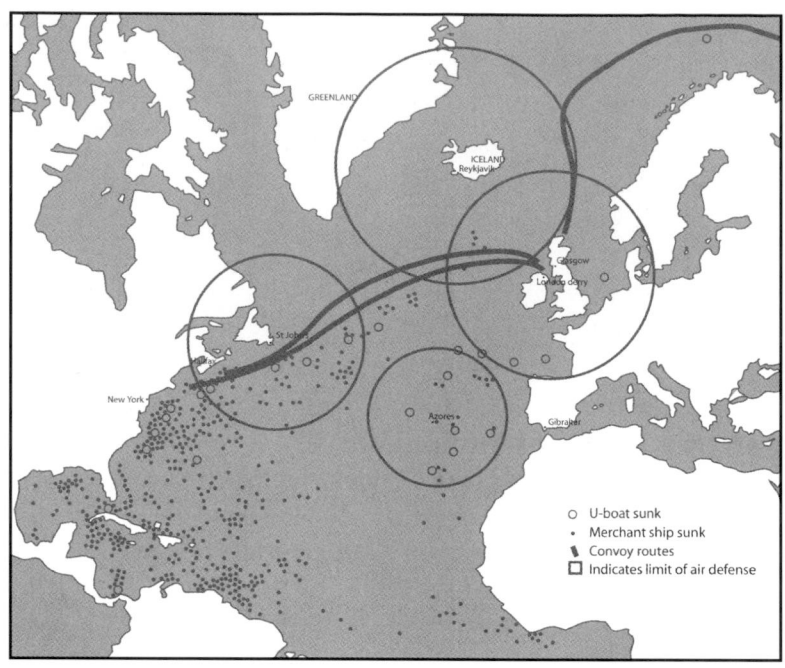

at sea and it was not until mid-1941 that enough subs were available to challenge convoys in the mid-Atlantic.

The RCN, which relied on the RN for technical advice as well as operational guidance, did not pay much attention to anti-submarine warfare. Trying to cope with a tenfold increase in ships and an eightfold increase in ratings while teaching the rudiments of navigation and gunnery kept everyone busy. Much was accomplished when the entire fleet of Canadian destroyers sailed for British waters in the summer of 1940 the RCN was well prepared to join in the vital task of defending the British Isles from German invasion.

The sinking of the unarmed passenger liner *Athenia* in September 1939 reminded Canadians of the U-boat menace from WW I. The first contracts for a new escort, to be called a corvette, were issued. Corvettes, "cheap and nasties" in Churchill's phrase, were to be used in coastal waters. No one imagined they would be needed in the mid-Atlantic.

The first Canadian-built corvettes, intended for the RN and manned with scratch RCN crews for the passage to Britain, were caught up in the U-boat crisis of the winter of 1940-41. They joined the RCN destroyers, now assigned to the

The Battle of the Atlantic, 1942. Germany's declaration of war against the United States led to a highly successful U-boat campaign off the east coast of North America. U-boats operated in the St. Lawrence River, sinking merchant ships without the loss of a single U-boat.

Clyde Escort Force, in the crucial struggle to defeat the U-boat wolf-packs that were concentrated in the western approaches to Britain.

From a purely Canadian point of view the emergency employment of the corvettes before they could be properly manned or equipped was a serious problem. It was on a par with the request that the RCN accept six of the 50 WW I destroyers obtained from the United States in the destroyers-for-bases deal. Finding crews with enough trained officers and ratings for six destroyers that you didn't need or want was no easy task. However, it was impossible to argue with the strategic value of an agreement that involved the still-neutral U.S. in the defence of the western Atlantic.

Despite these demands, which placed the core of the RCN in the United Kingdom under British command, the navy found the resources to commission 23 corvettes for use in North American waters. Unfortunately, plans for Halifax-based convoy escort were thrown overboard when the U-boats, seeking easier targets, moved west of Iceland. On May 20, 1941, the British admiralty asked the RCN to establish a new base in St. John's, Newfoundland, and to use its own resources to escort convoys from St. John's to the mid-ocean meeting point south of Iceland.

The new Canadian corvettes were far from ready for mid-ocean escort duty, but there was little choice except to improvise and learn on the job. The first group, *Agassiz, Alberni, Chambly, Cobalt, Collingwood, Orillia* and *Wetaskiwin* sailed for "Newfyjohn" on May 23, 1941. Beyond a small number of professionals and a sprinkling of veteran petty officers, the ships were manned by volunteers of the Wavy Navy, the Royal Canadian Naval Volunteer Reserve.

The ships were as ill-prepared as their crews, lacking even a breakwater to prevent the sea from cascading into the open well-deck. The RCN was also short of gyro compasses and modern sonar so the new corvettes got magnetic compasses and obsolete asdic sets. There was no radar to install and no clear sense that it was needed. The senior officer, Commander J.D. "Chummy" Prentice, was an innovative leader who worked steadily to improve efficiency but with new ships arriving each month there was a limit to what could be done.

There were bright moments amidst the gloom. In September 1941 Prentice took his HMCS *Chambly* with HMCS *Moose Jaw* to sea on a training exercise. When reports of a wolf-pack attack on an eastbound convoy arrived, his small task force raced to assist the outnumbered escort group. *Chambly's* asdic operator got a firm contact and depth charges brought U-501 to the surface where it was rammed by *Moose Jaw.*

This was the RCN's first kill of a German submarine and there was good reason for satisfaction though none for complacency. The convoy had lost 16 ships because an escort of one destroyer and three corvettes could not possibly hold off a determined attack by a dozen U-boats. The solution was simple; more and better escorts, improved training and air cover in the "Black Hole" south of Greenland.

In time all of this would happen, but not in 1942. The RCN was constantly overwhelmed by new demands and there was neither the time nor resources to provide the training, refits or new equipment required. The RCN was required to join in the task of escorting convoys all the way across the Atlantic, but it was also needed to help the Americans overcome the U-boat campaign off the east coast of the U.S.

The decision to withdraw the RCN from mid-ocean escort in January 1943 was long overdue. If circumstances had permitted this respite in the first half of the year the Canadians would have played an active part in the climactic battle of May 1943 and historians would write about the RCN's extraordinary achievement. Someday, upon reflection, they will.

Hong Kong:
There Was A Reason

Originally published, March 1996

Last year Canadian veterans who fought in the defence of Hong Kong were awarded a bar to be worn on the ribbon of the Canadian Volunteer Service Medal. This recognition reminded us of the debt we owe to the men and women who endured so much pain on our behalf. Unfortunately media coverage of the events provided little beyond the most superficial references to it being a "sacrifice" and "a hopeless cause."

To understand the decision to reinforce the colony we must try to place ourselves within the swirling events of 1941 and remember that none of the decision makers, including the Japanese, knew that war in the Pacific would begin before the year was out. The United States took the lead in shaping policy in the Pacific. Throughout 1941 American President Franklin Delano Roosevelt tried to find the right mixture of policies that would limit Japanese expansion.

He first committed money and resources to strengthening Chiang Kai-shek, hoping the Chinese nationalist army would play a major role in restraining Japan. When the Japanese seized southern Indo China in July 1941, Roosevelt responded with an embargo and began to plan for war. The Americans reversed their long-standing policy against further military commitments in the western Pacific and General Douglas MacArthur was brought back into the American army. The defence of the Philippines was given a new priority and thousands of U.S. soldiers joined MacArthur's forces. In addition, a force of B-17 bombers was sent to the islands as a high profile deterrent to Japanese aggression. More troops and additional B-17s were on their way when war began.

These decisions were made without consulting the British government, but in August 1941 Roosevelt and Churchill met at Placentia Bay, Newfoundland. Here, at the conference that produced the Atlantic Charter, the main topic of discussion was Japan. Churchill sought an American commitment to go to war if British or Dutch territory was attacked and suggested that the American Pacific fleet move its base to Singapore. Roosevelt would not accept either proposal but the two men did agree on a co-coordinated effort to deter Japan. Churchill ordered the Royal Navy to find the resources to send a fleet to Singapore and he stepped up the reinforcement of Malaya. The British chiefs of staff added Hong Kong to the list when it was suggested Canada might provide reinforcements for the colony.

On September 15, 1941, Churchill approved a letter to Prime Minister Mackenzie King requesting "one or two Canadian battalions for Hong Kong." The message noted: "The situation in the Orient has now altered. There have been signs of a certain weakening in attitude of Japan towards the United States and ourselves." Even a small reinforcement "would reassure Chiang Kai-shek…and have a great moral affect throughout the Far East." Canada was being asked to participate, as an allied nation, in a high-stakes gamble to prevent war in the Pacific.

King had deeply resented his exclusion from the Newfoundland meeting and had invited himself to England where he learned of the changes in Anglo-American strategy. His diary indicates he believed war with Japan was inevitable and he expected it would begin by December. Yet when the request for Canadian troops for Hong Kong arrived, King and his colleagues offered no objections. As the minister of defence, J.L. Ralston, put it: "Anything which would either defer or deter Japan from coming in would be highly desirable from our point of view."

The cabinet sought the advice of the army before giving final approval and Major-General Harry Crerar–the chief of the general staff–did not hesitate. Dr. Paul Dickson, who is writing a biography on Canada's senior army commander, discovered Crerar had carefully studied the problems of defending Hong Kong as a student at the British Staff College and the Imperial Defence College. But Dickson concludes Crerar saw the issue in political and strategic terms. "Whatever the military risks," Crerar wrote, "the enterprise needed

US Battleship *Arizona* sunk in the surprise attack on Pearl Harbor. The Canadians in Hong Kong were part of a high stakes gamble to prevent war in the Pacific.

as mortars or artillery. The Grenadiers were also under strength and had to absorb a large number of men and 15 new officers in the two weeks before sailing from Vancouver. There has been much controversy over the selection of these units, but in 1941 none of the other battalions still in Canada was much better prepared for combat. Brigadier J.K. Lawson, who commanded C Force, was impressed by what he saw. He reported: "Both units contain excellent material and a number of good instructors."

to be examined from the broad view…" Crerar recommended Canada send a force of two battalions, the Royal Rifles of Canada and the Winnipeg Grenadiers.

The Royal Rifles of Canada was one of the oldest regiments in the Canadian reserves, then known as the Non-Permanent Active Militia. Based in Quebec City, it was organized as an English-speaking unit, although its ranks eventually contained a significant number of French-speaking Canadians fluent in English. The regiment was ordered to mobilize an active service force as the 1st Battalion of the Royal Rifles of Canada in July 1940. It was quickly brought up to strength, recruiting men from eastern Quebec and northern New Brunswick. After basic training in New Brunswick the battalion was sent to garrison Newfoundland where some further training was carried out. In October 1941 it moved to Valcartier, Quebec, to prepare for service in a tropical region. Few guessed their destination was Hong Kong.

The Winnipeg Grenadiers was one of the first battalions mobilized at the outbreak of the war. Organized initially as a machine-gun battalion, it was converted to a regular rifle battalion while located in the West Indies in 1940. Garrison duty in Jamaica provided some opportunity for individual and company training but the Grenadiers had no experience with infantry support weapons such

The battalions were well equipped with the weapons available in 1941. The men were equipped with rifles, Bren guns and two- and three-inch mortars. C Force was supposed to have 212 vehicles, including motorcycles, trucks and universal carriers, but these never reached the colony. This failure increased the burden borne by the troops in combat but was not as serious as the shortage of mortar ammunition the British had promised but failed to supply.

The Canadians who arrived at Hong Kong on November 16, 1941, can best be compared to a peacekeeping force deployed into an especially dangerous situation. The British garrison commander, Major-General C.M. Maltby, assigned them to the defence of Hong Kong Island against amphibious attack. He stationed three of his four British and Indian battalions on the mainland with the task of defending a hastily constructed position known as the Gin Drinker's Line.

These professional soldiers had been fully trained to prewar standards and knew the territory they were to defend. Unfortunately the British War Office failed to provide ammunition for the basic infantry support weapon, the three-inch mortar, until the eve of the battle and then each battalion received just 70 rounds.

The Japanese deployed a reinforced division against this thin red line and had little difficulty in achieving a breakthrough that forced a hasty retreat to Hong Kong Island. A company of the Winnipeg Grenadiers assisted the British withdrawal.

Maltby reorganized the garrison, removing the Royal Rifles from Lawson's control and placing them under Brigadier C. Wallis, an Indian army officer. On December 18, after a week of shelling and bombing, the Japanese landed on the island overwhelming the Rajput battalion and seizing the high ground. C Company of the Royal Rifles was called on to counter-attack and it inflicted heavy losses on the enemy before withdrawing to avoid encirclement.

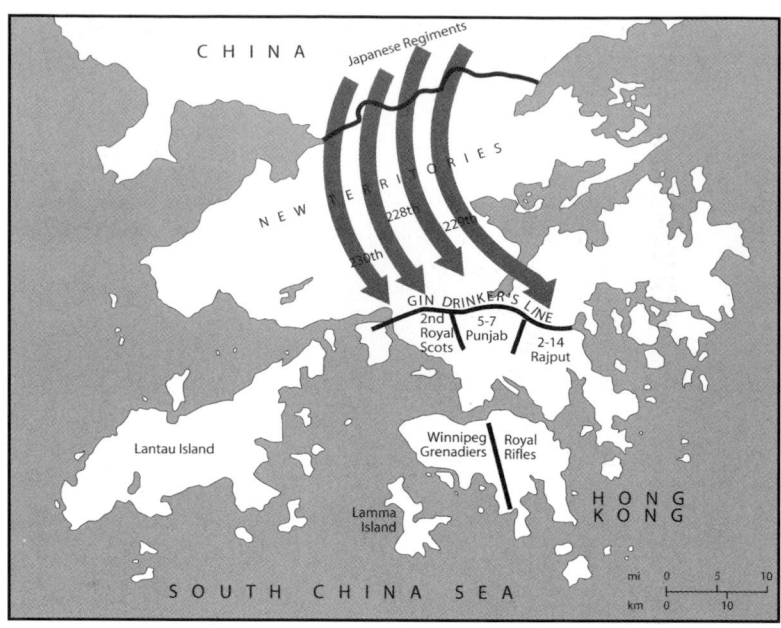

Urged on by promises of relief from a Chinese nationalist force and by a message from Churchill that insisted "there must be no thought of surrender," Maltby ordered repeated counter-attacks that, given the odds, were doomed to costly failure. Lawson was killed on December 19 after his headquarters was surrounded. His last message reported that he was going outside "to fight it out."

Lieutenant-Colonel W.J. Home, the commanding officer of the Royal Rifles, became the senior Canadian officer. His men, who had been fighting continuously, were exhausted and demoralized. As his second-in-command, Major John Price, noted: "It required no great military genius to predict the outcome of the battle once the Japanese had landed on the island..." Home, who had lost all confidence in British direction of the battle, believed further resistance was pointless and would simply waste lives. When his request to end hostilities was rejected he insisted on a period of rest for his regiment. Price recalled these events in 1948: "The enemy controlled the sea and the air. Three-inch mortar ammunition had run out. Only one battery of 18-pounder guns was available for artillery support. Only light machine-guns and rifles left to fight with. The men had been fighting without much food and practically no sleep and were dead tired. They were obviously in no condi-

tion to put up a spirited defence without some rest. A request that they be given 24 hours rest was a reasonable one particularly as it was judged there were ample troops available who had participated up to date only to a comparatively small degree in the battle and also as the plan then was to contract the front held by a retirement to the Stanley Peninsula itself."

The Royal Rifles were allowed to withdraw from contact but Maltby still refused to face reality and the battalion returned to action for two more grueling days. Maltby finally agreed to surrender on December 25.

The fighting cost the Canadians 290 men killed with almost 500 wounded. During the long years of forced labor in prisoner of war camps another 264 died, including four men executed for trying to escape. After the war the 1,418 veterans who returned waged a second struggle for pension rights, compensation and public recognition.

The Canadian government had sent these young men into harm's way for the best of reasons: The attempt to "defer or deter war." Later generations, with little understanding of the circumstances of 1941, were quick to condemn this decision. It is now time to move beyond the obvious judgment that sending any reinforcements to the Pacific was a mistake and recognize the purpose as well as the sacrifice involved in the defence of Hong Kong.

The Japanese attack on Hong Kong.

The Early Days Of WW II

Originally published, April 1996

For most Canadians WW II began on September 1, 1939, when Hitler's armies invaded Poland. That event, coupled with the sinking of the passenger liner *Athenia* on September 3, provided ordinary Canadians with all the incentive they needed and thousands rushed to enlist. The Canadian government was much more cautious. Prime Minister Mackenzie King had promised Parliament would decide Canada's foreign policy so it was not until September 10, after a brief debate, that Canada was officially, and very tentatively, at war.

The government hoped it could avoid sending an expeditionary force overseas and had done as little as possible to prepare one. Last minute additions to defence estimates in 1939 provided $7.5 million for the Royal Canadian Air Force to buy aircraft, but less than one million dollars for the Canadian Army, none of it for equipment. The crisis atmosphere of late August led to a call-out of the militia, but the purpose was not to train or go into combat, but to guard canal locks, railway bridges and airports. On September 1, the cabinet met to invoke the War Measures Act and authorize the expansion of the Army. The prime minister insisted that the name "field force" be changed to "active service force" and enlistment limited to service in Canada.

The Army ignored the implications of this decision and began recruiting an expeditionary force of two divisions plus all the ancillary troops necessary to re-create a Canadian Corps, thus beginning the prolonged debate over the size and purpose of the Canadian Army.

In cabinet, King, and the majority of his colleagues, opposed every stage of the expansion of what they termed "The Big Army"; but they dared not express their opposition in public. The Army and its commander, Lieutenant-General A.G.L. McNaughton, were the primary symbols of the "nation-in-arms" and the prime minister knew that English-speaking Canadians would turn on any government that threatened their national army. After J.L. Ralston became minister of national defence in June 1940 the Army had a champion no one could easily challenge.

Success in forcing a reluctant government to authorize a two-division expeditionary force did not lead to any dramatic change in the military budget. There were not enough uniforms or boots, never mind weapons. When 1st Division left for the United Kingdom in December 1939, it was untrained and ill-equipped for war. The Bren light machine-guns of Canadian manufacture were not available, so apart from rifles, some obsolete artillery was all that Canada could provide its young men.

Once overseas, 1st Division was equipped from British sources and realistic training began. At home 2nd Division units spent the winter in overcrowded armouries, empty factories or office buildings. The Canadian National Exhibition grounds in Toronto were requisitioned and those assigned to the Horse Palace were billeted four to a stall. As late as the summer of 1940, infantry battalions had only received enough mortars, anti-tank rifles, Bren guns, grenades, mines and radios to permit demonstrations. Artillery and armoured units were in even worse shape. The best training done in 1940 was accomplished on the skating rinks, playing fields and gymnasiums. Team sports were not just a way of keeping men busy; organized on a platoon, company and battalion basis they provided the foundation for the teamwork essential in successful military organizations.

The Canadian government had done little to help its young men prepare for the challenges of modern war. Fortunately there was time to make up for years of neglect, and the raw material–the men who volunteered–was excellent. Canada's servicemen were drawn from a generation that came of age during the Great Depression. This obvious fact has led to stories about an army drawn from the margins of society. The evidence suggests the contrary, more than 80 per cent left jobs to enlist. There was intense competition for places in most battalions and thousands of men were turned down because of age or ill health.

Saying goodbye,
1940

Many more were returned to civilian life when X-rays and a new physical examination were instituted. There was no personal failing involved in being young and unemployed in the late 1930's any more than there is today and it is time to put the old stereotype to rest.

1st Division drew half its total strength from the regular army or militia, providing a head start that the other divisions might envy. Once in England 2nd Division quickly caught up. In early 1942, General Bernard Montgomery, who was suspicious of all WW I veterans except himself, offered scathing criticism of Major-General George Pearkes VC, while praising Major-General "Ham" Roberts and 2nd Division. Montgomery's views resulted in selection of 2nd Division for the Dieppe raid so this was one competition 1st Division was lucky to lose!

Montgomery's survey of the Canadian Army in the first months of 1942 provides an important measure of what had been accomplished in the two years since mobilization. Dr. John A. English, a distinguished historian and former infantry officer, has used Montgomery's reports to support his argument that the Canadian Army was badly led and poorly trained when it entered combat. His 1991 book, *The Canadian Army and the Normandy Campaign: A Study of Failure In High Command* should be read by all those with a serious interest in our military history, but it should be read critically. English never explains why the army that he thinks "failed" in Normandy did so well in Italy, nor does he explain the reasons for the Canadian victories in Northwest Europe.

Monty's inspection offered comment on the strengths and weaknesses of British and Canadian units in light of the large training exercises that began in the summer of 1941. Before then Canadians had been committed to a coastal defence role with little opportunity to develop skills in large-scale manoeuvres. Reports on exercises "Waterloo" and "Bumper" criticized the mistakes made by British and Canadian formations. However, such exercises are supposed to be learning experiences. Indeed, "Bumper" was one of the turning points in the

Commonwealth war effort because it led to the development of centralized control of artillery and the famous "Uncle" target where all guns in the division fired on a single target in response to a single command.

Such exercises were of vital importance to generals and staff officers but combat soldiers learned very little except that snafus–situation normal all fouled up–had to be accepted. Fortunately, battalion officers did not wait until the general staff got around to their needs. In the fall of 1941 the Canadian Army was introduced to battle drill. Veterans who recall battle drill training, with its emphasis on physical conditioning, field craft and elaborate obstacle courses, may find it hard to believe that it was initially rejected by British and Canadian senior officers. The first divisional battle school and a training manual were produced by 47th (London) Division in the summer of 1941. Major-General J.E. Utterson-Kelso, who some described sarcastically as the "best platoon commander in the British army," used an extensive training area to teach drills for fire and movement at the section, platoon and company level. He invited Lieutenant-Colonel Fred Scott, commanding officer of the Calgary Highlanders, to a demonstration in the fall of 1941. Scott was convinced this revolutionary system of training could refocus the energy and enthusiasm of his men. Calgary officers and non-commissioned officers were put through the 47th Division course while a battle drill school was created. On October 23, Captain John Campbell led a platoon through the new course at Burnt Wood, Bexhill, before an audience that included Colonel J.L. Ralston, the minister of national defence, as well as McNaughton, corps commander Harry Crerar and Major-General Victor Odlum. In the weeks that followed, battle drill fever spread "like wildfire" through the Calgaries and the whole battalion passed through a two-week course. Visitors from other units came to see what was going on and left clasping a copy of the "Battle Drill Bible" that the Calgaries had copied from 47th Division.

Crerar was uncertain about how to react to this grassroots revolt. After a visit to Bexhill he thanked Scott for providing a "satisfactory number" of officers and NCOs in the "tactical and psychological advantages" of battle drill training but noted that, "with the invasion season not many weeks off", schools and courses would have to be closed. Students were to return to their sub-units to "apply their knowledge." Crerar did not, however, order the Calgaries to close their school immediately or to cease training other battalions. Roberts, who assumed command of 2nd Division in early November, had authorized two other demonstration days to which all Canadian units were invited. The British army then announced that Utterson-Kelso was to command the infantry-training directorate while his chief battle drill instructor took charge of a new headquarters battle school at Barnard Castle in Yorkshire. The British also authorized the formation of battle schools in each division.

The Canadians soon followed the British lead. Scott was ordered to return to Canada to run a course for "senior officers" at the Royal Military College in Kingston, Ontario, but in May he was placed in charge of The Canadian Battle Drill School in Vernon, B.C. In England a Battle Drill Wing was added to the Canadian Training School with Campbell of the Calgaries in command.

Utterson-Kelso and Scott had transformed the training procedures of the British and Canadian armies at the platoon and company level, but what was to be done about preparing for a return to the continent?

Practice in small unit tactics would help men to survive and win in certain phases of a battle but the Anglo-Canadian armies would also need new dimensions of fire support and a well thought-out battle doctrine for divisions and corps if they were to take on the German army. Both requirements were utterly lacking in 1942.

This was the gist of Montgomery's criticism of both British and Canadian divisions in 1942. After watching the Canadian formations in Exercise "Beaver", April 1942, he wrote:

1st Division has very fine material and should be a first-class division. But it was very badly handled on this exercise and, in consequence, failed badly.

Pearkes is unable to appreciate the essentials of a military problem and to formulate a sound plan. His mind works in a groove and he gets the bit between his teeth, puts on blinkers, and drives ahead blindly. He is a gallant soldier without doubt; but he has no brains. There is good material to hand. Salmon would command a division well. Mann and Snow would make good brigadiers.

I would put Roberts down as the best divisional commander in the corps. He is very sound, but he is not any way brilliant... I watched 2nd Division carefully and there is no doubt that Church (C.C.) Mann is a very big influence in that division.

As a result of this exercise, 2nd Division has gained a high morale, and we want the show to crack along now, to make progress, and not to become unsettled."

Montgomery's evaluation of brigade and battalion officers helped McNaughton and Crerar decide necessary changes though in many cases it was simply a matter of replacing officers considered too old for active service. Montgomery also identified a number of outstanding Canadian officers who were promoted in the course of 1942 and 1943. A great deal remained to be done before the citizen army was ready to confront the Germans but much had been accomplished by the summer of 1942.

Selective Reasoning In WW II

Originally published, May 1996

During the summer of 1941 Hitler was somewhat preoccupied with the invasion of the Soviet Union and apparently missed reports that Canada planned to employ psychologists to screen and classify its armed forces. The decision was big news in Ottawa, however. Professor Edward Alexander Bott, a well known child psychologist, was commissioned as a group captain in the Royal Canadian Air Force and sent to England to consult with British experts, while Dr. Brock Chisholm established a Directorate of Personnel Selection in Canada.

Churchill and Mackenzie King

Have struggled on for years;

What good without psychologists,

Are blood, sweat and tears?

But now the Bott Battalion's
on its way,

So give three cheers

The war will soon be won!

Who will break the news to Hitler

That Bott and his brainy boys

Are hurrying off to war

    – C.R. Myers

Once in England Bott became involved in programs for children evacuated during the Blitz and had little to do with testing air force personnel. However, Chisholm became a major force within the Canadian services. He was one of the most famous and controversial Canadians of his generation. Now remembered for his campaign to abolish Santa Claus as harmful to children, his international reputation as an advocate of health reforms was recog-

nized in the late 1940s when he became the first director general of the World Health Organization.

In 1941, Chisholm, a decorated WW I veteran, was serving as commander of the Northern Ontario Military District. Trained as a medical doctor, Freudian-psychiatrist and professional soldier, he produced a pamphlet entitled *A Platoon Leader's Responsibility for the Morale of his Men*. This was widely distributed throughout the three services and he was brought to Ottawa to take charge of training. However, he was soon transferred to personnel selection. Chisholm brought a number of university professors, "Bott's brainy boys," into the directorate before being appointed to the senior medical position in the Army. As director general, Chisholm could overcome the wide spread resistance to psychologists and personnel selection that existed in the Army and especially among medical officers.

It would be easy to dismiss this opposition to scientific manpower management as typical military conservatism, but there were in fact good reasons to challenge the new program. Young Canadians who volunteered for military service in the first years of the war quickly learned that a high school education or some special skill was needed to join the air force. The navy had no firm rules, but with far more recruits than could be absorbed, high physical and educational standards were applied. The Army had always accepted men with little formal education and knew from experience that a man could be an effective soldier even if he was illiterate or a little slow.

The first recruits were accepted with few formalities. Those with militia experience were automatically enrolled and other volunteers were judged by their appearance and motivation. The 58,000 men who signed up in September, 1939, were enlisted with only a brief physical exam. When X-rays and urinalysis were required in November several thousand failed the new medical and were sent back to civvy street. The Army ignored Major-General McNaughton's attempt to introduce intelligence and aptitude tests, simply requiring medical boards to establish that "the recruit is sufficiently intelligent by questioning him." The Army was confident it could train all manner of men to perform useful roles.

The psychologists were equally convinced their tests could help the services to scientifically allocate available manpower. Their science largely consisted of an instrument known as the M Test. The M Test–no one knows if the M stood for mental or McGill University–was made up of eight short subtests. The first three were non-language, picture association tests designed to be understood whatever the soldier's degree of literacy. Parts four and five related to common tools and were said to measure mechanical aptitude. The last three offered conventional arithmetic, vocabulary and word relationship questions.

The M Test was closely modeled on the U.S. Army's infamous Alpha and Beta tests developed during WW I. American psychologists claimed their tests measured inborn intelligence–the draftee's "native intellectual capacity"–and this was expressed by assigning a mental age to each soldier. The average, according to army psychologists, was a mental age of 13. Men who scored below it were classified as "morons" incapable of learning. More than 30 per cent of white males were said to be morons while fully 79 per cent of blacks subject to the draft were given this classification.

Canadian psychologists were careful to avoid loaded terms like moron. They did not assign mental ages to recruits but the raw score of the M Test became the basis for determining the assignment for each soldier. Those with high scores within the Army went to armoured units, the engineers, artillery or signals. The rest joined the service corps or the infantry. Once attached to a unit the test result helped determine the soldier's career for the rest of the war.

The tests, however, were of limited value in measuring how much a man or woman knew because they were administered under widely varying conditions. They had absolutely no validity as a measure of how much a person could learn. Psychologists were reluctant to admit this, but they did recognize that individuals who were unstable, neurotic or psychopathic could not be identified by the M Test. To remedy this the Directorate of Personnel Selection introduced a brief "psychiatric" interview into the recruiting and classification process. After 1942 hundreds of thousands of young Canadians were interviewed by "Assistant Army Examiners," usually school teachers or recent college graduates, who were supposed to refer suspect cases to a psychiatrist. The interview, which often took place immediately after the physical exam–while the recruit was still stark naked–consisted of questions about personal behavior and family background.

The examiners took to their work with enthusiasm, referring thousands of volunteers and conscripts to the psychiatrists. The new Director of Personnel Selection, another University of Toronto professor, Colonel Bill Line, was shocked by the results. After the first month of interviews he wrote a "secret" memorandum ordering examiners to stop using terms like "moron", "imbecile", "sexual pervert" or "insane" in their reports. These comments and slang expressions like "ignorant hobo" or "needs a good thrashing" were he said, unacceptable, especially in a document the soldier had the right to see. Colonel Line concluded that the phrases no doubt expressed the examiner's feelings but were of no other value.

All of this might be seen as one of the funnier examples of the Army bureaucracy's growing pains. Certainly the poet and novelist Earle Birney made good use of his own experience as a personnel selection officer in writing his 1949 comic novel Turvey. But in 1942, the first year under the new system, the rate of rejections for psychiatric reasons skyrocketed depriving the Army of thousands of recruits. The U.S. Army, which adopted a similar system in late 1942, found that psychiatric rejections and discharges in 1943 exceeded the number of new men enlisted. Orders were issued to change the procedure and the rate dropped as sharply as it had risen. No one reported any difference in the quality of the recruits.

The situation in Canada was less serious. However, more than 200,000 of the 1.8 million registered under the National Resources Mobilization Act were classified as unfit for service for psychiatric reasons. One follow-up study of 22,000 men released from the Army in 1943 as psychoneurotic showed almost all had found civilian employment with 43 per cent reporting they now had a "better job" than before enlisting. The large number of rejections for medical reasons became a public scandal in 1943 particularly when athletes and others engaged in strenuous activity were pronounced "unfit" for service.

Chisholm responded by introducing new guidelines, including a category "accept for re-check" that allowed many allegedly doubtful cases to complete basic training. More than 75 per cent of these turned out to be effective soldiers who completed training "without difficulty". The Army also introduced a new system of physical and mental classification known as PULHEMS. The letters stood for Physique, Upper body, Lower body and locomotion, Hearing, Eyes, Mental capacity and Stability. The M Test still provided the score for mental capacity, and the psychiatric interviews the grade for stability, but there were only five possible grades and in practice the vast majority were given enough points to be "fit for service anywhere."

The PULHEMS classification system allowed the Army to transform personnel selection from a liability into a constructive asset. Selection officers now had the choice of classifying men and women in four categories of fitness for service, namely combat, anywhere but front line combat, line of communications or service in Canada only. Almost everyone could be assigned to one of those classifications. The rate of psychiatric rejections dropped dramati-

cally for volunteers, though almost one third of conscripts continued to be rejected on psychiatric grounds, largely because examiners hesitated to force men determined to avoid military service into the Army.

All those who served in the Canadian Armed Forces have the right to obtain copies of their personnel records from the National Archives. Those who do read their dossiers should remember that the words in the report often tell us more about the person who wrote it than the person being evaluated.

At the time of the Korean War, when personnel selection was again an important issue, Major F.C.R. Chalke wrote a careful review of the wartime experience. He concluded that existing methods of screening recruits could at best detect 50 per cent of those who would fail and would reject an equal number of those who would become satisfactory soldiers. The Army's traditional method of selecting recruits, on the basis of character and motivation, was at least as effective as the "scientific" methods introduced by psychologists.

The Air Over Dieppe

Originally published, June/July 1996

A visit to Dieppe, France, can be a very emotional experience for Canadians. Others may walk the beaches and enjoy the sunshine and chalk cliffs where Monet and other painters found inspiration, but for Canadians the memorials at Puys, Pourville and Dieppe raise questions that crowd out these simple seaside pleasures. How, we ask ourselves, could the tragedy of August 19, 1942, have happened?

This mood is evident when students participating in the Canadian Battlefields Foundation study tour reach Dieppe. All of them have just completed two weeks of study of the Normandy battlefields where they walked the invasion beaches, studied the struggle in the bridgehead and examined the operations that led to the defeat of the German army.

They are aware that victory depended on absolute air superiority which allowed Allied commanders the freedom to assault the coast, build up resources and manoeuvre within the bridgehead without significant interference from the Luftwaffe. They also know success in combat was only possible when operations were based on extensive and flexible artillery fire.

To turn from the superbly organized Allied campaign of 1944 to the disaster at Dieppe requires all of us to make a profound adjustment. We have to remind ourselves that in 1942 the Royal Air Force had not yet created a tactical air force and that its Spitfires were fighting a costly and uncertain battle for air superiority over the French coast. We also have to recognize that the artillery-based battle doctrine, which emerged in the desert campaign and provided the key to success against the Germans for the rest of the war, had yet to win acceptance. Army planners were still mesmerized by the vision of tanks as the decisive weapon of war, and surprise as a substitute for overwhelming fire-power.

Obtaining perspective on air power is especially difficult because our collective memory of the air war is focused on the triumphs of Fighter Command in the Battle of Britain and the overwhelming power of 2nd Tactical Air Force in Normandy. The in-between years are largely ignored but if we are to understand what happened at Dieppe we must begin with an analysis of Fighter Command and its place in Allied strategy in 1942.

After the Battle of Britain, Fighter Command was the most famous military formation in the English-speaking world. The Hurricane and Spitfire pilots, their ground crew, ground controllers and commanders had saved England from invasion and given the world a precious opportunity to make up for lost time. But the command itself was placed in a strange position. Once the Luftwaffe switched to night bombing there was no significant role for day fighters to perform and Fighter Command was a force without an immediate mission.

The Canadian official history suggests the intruder raids that began over occupied Europe in 1941 were authorized "to provide a whiff of danger" for aspiring young fighter pilots. It also suggests the raids, which were known as "Rhubarbs", "Rodeos" and "Circuses", were continued after heavy losses were incurred "under the guise of maintaining morale." The authors of *The Crucible of War 1939—1945* seem quite unaware of the larger issues involved in the Allied air offensive. Their approach overlooks the challenges confronting Churchill, the chiefs of staff and the RAF in the early years of the war.

As bombs came down from the night skies over Britain both formal intelligence appreciations and common sense indicated that Operation "Sea Lion"–the invasion of Britain–might be revived in the spring of 1941. At a minimum this threat required Fighter Command to maintain a high state of readiness through constant training, operational analysis and when possible combat against the enemy.

Attempts to locate and attack German aircraft, or other targets of opportunity, by two or three aircraft were known as "Rhubarbs". "Rodeos" were larger fighter sweeps across Northern France

Dieppe Harbour
from the air.

or Belgium intended to provoke a response from the Luftwaffe. "Circuses" involved bombers accompanied by fighter escorts. These operations gave the enemy the same advantages the RAF had enjoyed in the Battle of Britain, including early warning radar and the certainty that pilots forced to bail out over Europe would end up in German hands.

The RAF might well have limited these operations but in June 1941 the invasion of the Soviet Union transformed every aspect of the war. The navy was required to begin the dangerous convoys to Murmansk and the air force, the only offensive weapon the Commonwealth possessed, had to be employed to divert German resources from the Eastern Front. Bomber Command was ordered to resume its offensive and Fighter Command told to intensify operations that might force the Germans to transfer fighter aircraft from the Russian front.

Thus in the second half of 1941 RAF and Royal Canadian Air Force fighter squadrons, which had lost 51 pilots in the first half of the year, suffered 411 further losses in attempts to help the

Russians. Fighter Command thought it was winning a battle of attrition with the German air force because it believed pilot claims that 731 enemy aircraft had been shot down over France in the same period.

This figure was accepted because there were no sources available to check the reliability of pilot reports. Neither Ultra, the information from decrypting coded messages sent via the German Enigma machines, nor any of the other methods of intelligence gathering provided accurate data on German air losses until the summer of 1943. After the war it was learned total Luftwaffe losses in these actions were 103 aircraft, less than one-seventh of Fighter Command's estimate.

Some historians use this postwar data to criticize Allied strategists in the manner of sports commentators who tell you what the coach should have done after the final score is known. But if you seek to understand the past and not just show how clever you are it is evident that decisions had to be made on the best evidence available at the time.

By the end of 1941, even though Fighter Command believed it held the upper hand, the rate of pilot losses was too high to continue and the offensive was called off. The success of the Russian counter-attacks in front of Moscow also influenced the decision to allow both fighter and bomber commands time to regroup. This situation changed dramatically in the spring of 1942 when it became clear the Germans had stemmed the Russian attacks and were preparing to resume the offensive in the East. The shifting of fighter aircraft from France to Russia, and an Ultra report that 30 of the latest ME109s had left France for Norway in March, forced Air Marshal Sir Peter Portal to order a resumption of Fighter Command's offensive.

The German response was immediate and overwhelming. Luftwaffe reinforcements began arriving in France in late March and most of the squadrons were equipped with the new Focke Wulf 190 that greatly outclassed the Spitfires then available. The air offensive succeeded in drawing resources away from the Eastern Front but at great cost to Fighter Command. By the time Hitler's armies launched the campaign that would bring them to Stalingrad, 259 Spitfires had been lost over France. The RAF believed that 197 German aircraft had been destroyed in the same period and on July 6, 1942, Allied intelligence confidently reported that "further intensive operations" would have a serious impact on Hitler's plans to reach the Soviet oilfields.

The reality was somewhat different. German losses in the West were just 59 aircraft compared to hundreds shot down in the Mediterranean and Russia. Also, Fighter Command pilots frequently found themselves overwhelmed by superior enemy fighters. The RCAF, which contributed five squadrons to the battle, suffered proportionate losses. For example, a "Rodeo" by RCAF 403 Squadron in early June cost six pilots, five of whom spent the rest of the war in prisoner of war camps. The Spitfire V was simply no match for the FW190. Individual pilots knew this, but the operational reality could not be fully understood at command level as long as German losses continued to be overestimated.

This problem became even more serious when the United States 8th Air Force joined the battle. In one large raid over France American crews claimed 102 kills and probables. RAF air intelligence decided that 60 was a more likely number but German records show only one fighter aircraft was lost in the days action!

By the spring of 1942 the RAF was confident it was winning air superiority over large parts of the French coast. The problem was that the Luftwaffe usually avoided combat in these areas preferring to draw the Spitfires deeply inland and engage them when they were low on fuel. Analysis of this situation led the RAF to take a strong interest in the proposed raid on Dieppe because it would force the Luftwaffe into battle under conditions thought to be favorable to Fighter Command. When the original raid was cancelled the RAF became one of the main lobbyists for reviving it. Once the decision was made to launch Operation "Jubilee" on August 19 all available squadrons were quickly concentrated in the south of England for what would become the largest single-day air battle of the war.

The RAF provided two Hurricane squadrons equipped for bombing and six squadrons armed with 20-mm cannon to support the landing. Four Mustang squadrons from Army Co-operation Command, including 400 and 414 RCAF squadrons, provided continuous reconnaissance, reporting on the movement of German reinforcements. An additional five squadrons of medium bombers, Bostons and Blenheims, were used to lay smoke and bomb gun batteries. The RAF also employed three squadrons equipped with Typhoons, but they were assigned to diversionary tasks because these new aircraft were still experiencing technical problems. None of the Tiffes were yet equipped with the rocket projectiles that would make them the most famous ground support aircraft of the war. In accordance with RAF doctrine no attempt was made to provide direct communication between pilots and ground troops so these squadrons operated according to an elaborate plan of prearranged support.

To protect these aircraft and destroy German planes that tried to interfere with the landings,

Fighter Command deployed 48 Spitfire squadrons, including eight from the RCAF. Four squadrons, two British and two Canadian, were equipped with the new Spitfire IX, the one aircraft that could meet the FW190 on equal terms.

The Luftwaffe was thought to have less than 200 fighter aircraft within range of Dieppe so in theory the RAF would outnumber the enemy by more than 3-1, but the actual operation proved such numbers meant very little. All four Spitfire IX squadrons were initially reserved to escort B17 bombers of the USAAF for a raid on the Luftwaffe base at Abbeville. The Americans had attempted their first mission in the European theatre two days before and it seemed wise to offer them maximum protection. On the way home from Abbeville Ken Hodson's 401 RCAF squadron approached Dieppe descending to 10,000 feet where a flight of Dornier 217s, escorted by FW190s, was starting a bombing run. 401 Squadron quickly broke up this attack damaging several bombers and destroying at least one FW190. Pilot Officer Dan Morrison closed to 25 yards before firing a two-second burst and his own aircraft was damaged by flying debris. He was picked up in the water after bailing out at 250 feet.

Fortunately the Luftwaffe was surprised by the Dieppe raid and its response was slow. The ground-support squadrons carried out their first missions without any significant interference but also without much effect. Neither the large gun emplacements nor the machine-gun positions in the cliffs were neutralized by air power. However, temporary blinding of some positions was achieved by smoke.

The air umbrella was in place from first light and if success is to be measured by the achievement of air superiority over the beaches Fighter Command won a narrow victory. During the raid more than 2,500 sorties were flown and the Luftwaffe prevented from interfering in the landings or evacuation. More than 200 ships and landing craft operated throughout the day with only minor losses from air attack.

In the air battle with the Luftwaffe the results were also seen favorably. Fighter Command's losses were 91 aircraft and 64 pilots, 17 of whom were taken prisoner. RCAF losses totalled 14 planes and nine pilots. In addition six bombers and 10 aircrew were lost in action. Air intelligence estimated German losses at 96 destroyed with 27 probables and 76 aircraft damaged. This allowed Fighter Command to believe it had struck a major blow to the German air force in the West. Unfortunately the real figures were 48 aircraft destroyed and 24 damaged with just 13 pilots killed or missing and seven wounded. The Luftwaffe in France was back at full strength within several days.

Eventually the RAF would have to rethink the roles it could play in the projected invasion of the continent but in 1942 this was not an urgent matter and Fighter Command remained committed to "Circuses", escorting USAAF B17s to targets in France. Losses continued to exceed the kills by a factor of almost 2-1 but the Germans could not afford the steady drain of skilled pilots and gradually abandoned the daylight skies over Western Europe. The battle for air superiority was won on many fronts by continuous effort and August 19, 1942, was part of that achievement.

The students on the study tour want to know what more could have been done? We agree that heavy bombers would not have helped, but maybe some system of air support in which the troops could communicate directly with the Hurricanes would have made some difference. Perhaps it would have, but the RAF was never willing to accept any system that would allow army control of its aircraft. By June 1944 a compromise involving Air Support Signal Units was in place, but this still meant delays of at least an hour before close support missions arrived. The RAF insisted the most effective contribution it could make to the land battle was to achieve air superiority and provide direct support by attacking prearranged targets. The Dieppe raid helped to convince the air force that its doctrine was sound just as it helped to persuade the army that a new strategy and new methods of providing overwhelming fire support were needed before the invasion of France began.

The Dieppe Raid

Originally published, December 1996

The Dieppe raid on August 19, 1942, continues to exercise a strong grip on the imaginations of Canadians. No other event in our military history has attracted so much attention from historians, journalists and film-makers.

The debate over the origins of the raid has obscured the actual events of August 1942 that can best be understood by studying the development of Allied military doctrine. It is also useful to remind ourselves that no one knew what the outcome of the raid would be before it happened.

Allied victories in 1944 depended upon air superiority and the application of over-whelming fire-power to the battlefield. The D-Day landings would never have been attempted if air or naval superiority had been in doubt. At Dieppe in 1942 the Allied air force was able to achieve temporary control of the skies at enormous cost, but the navy was quite unable to provide the kind of support that would contribute so much to success in Normandy.

During the Normandy landings each assault division was supported by battleships, cruisers and destroyers as well as rocket-firing landing craft and regimental field guns that fired as their landing craft approached shore. Operational research teams reported that while this enormous weight of shells destroyed only a few German gun positions, fire from the sea neutralized the enemy during the run-in and suppressed the larger German gun batteries throughout the day. Since weather conditions prevented the heavy bombers from striking at the beach defence, for fear of short bombing, the navy was absolutely essential to success on June 6, 1944.

The contrast with Dieppe is striking. In the summer of 1942 the Royal Navy was stretched well beyond its capacity. The sinking of the *Prince of Wales* and the *Repulse* by land-based Japanese aircraft was fresh in everyone's mind and the demands of the Battle of the Atlantic and the

"Blue Beach" Puys France, 1944.

Mediterranean were absorbing energy and resources. When the Dieppe raid was planned the navy offered full co-operation, but no responsible officer could recommend employing battleships, cruisers or precious fleet destroyers at Dieppe. Mountbatten, who ought to have known better, asked for a battleship but Admiral Sir Dudley Pound is said to have replied "Battleships by daylight off the French coast? You must be mad Dickie!"

The fleet the navy did assemble for the raid included eight destroyers, a fleet minesweeper and a river gunboat. The small destroyers had four four-inch guns available for use against shore batteries and gun positions in the cliffs. Other steam and motor gunboats added fire-power, but the total weight of high explosive that could be directed at the defenders could not neutralize the enemy either during the run-in or the fight on the beaches. Naval support was to be supplemented by medium bombers and Hurricane fighter-bombers, but the number of aircraft committed to a ground-support role was too limited to make up the difference.

If the navy could not be counted on to provide much fire support and the air force had to concentrate on its battle with the Luftwaffe, how did the planners imagine that Canadian troops could overcome the enemy's fixed defence at Dieppe? The outline plan for the original raid—code-named Operation "Rutter"—seems to have been devised by men who believed that battles could be won by surprise, speed and the shock effect of landing tanks alongside the infantry. This doctrine was also evident in the planning of Operation "Sledgehammer", the projected emergency invasion of France in 1942.

The Canadian Army's brightest staff officer, Lieutenant-Colonel C.C. "Church" Mann—a soldier who had won the highest praise from General Bernard Montgomery—focused his attention on these factors in his initial response to the outline plan. Mann rejected the idea of using the available armour to support the flank attack at Pourville. He wrote that while the idea of landing tanks directly on the main beach "is almost a fantastic conception" the advantages of

"surprise" and the "terrific moral effects on the Germans and the French" convinced him that the appearance of tanks on the main beach could be decisive.

Lieutenant-Colonel Mann was not alone in his belief that tanks were the key to success in military operations. While the Canadians were rehearsing for Dieppe the battle in the Western Desert of North Africa was being fought and lost by British commanders who tried to employ armoured units as if they were fleets of ships. The desert campaign dominated the military imagination in 1942 and of course the use of the tank in North Africa seemed to follow logically from the successes of the German Blitzkrieg in Poland, France and Russia.

The importance of armoured warfare was also very much evident in training exercises in England. Exercise "Tiger", which lasted from May 19-30, 1942, pitted 1st Canadian Corps against the 12th British Corps in a complicated encounter designed to test the latest theories

about the use of armour. The War Office had approved a new divisional organization that provided each infantry division with an army tank brigade in place of one of its infantry brigades. Armoured divisions were to consist of one armoured brigade and one fully motorized infantry brigade.

For the exercise, 12th British Corps was organized in the new style while 1st Canadian Corps retained the older order of battle. The results offered little evidence that the new system made any sense, and the 1942 "reforms" were abandoned, but the proposals tell us a great deal about the Commonwealth idea of war in 1942.

The focus on armoured warfare did not mean that another characteristically British concept—the use of commandos—was abandoned. Churchill was a firm supporter of the idea believing that such raids, however costly, helped to convince the citizens of occupied Europe that the Allies were committed to their liberation.

In retrospect we can see that both ideas were unrealistic. In the desert, Commonwealth generals gradually learned that Rommel employed his tanks against soft targets relying on anti-tank

The main beach at Dieppe, after the battle.

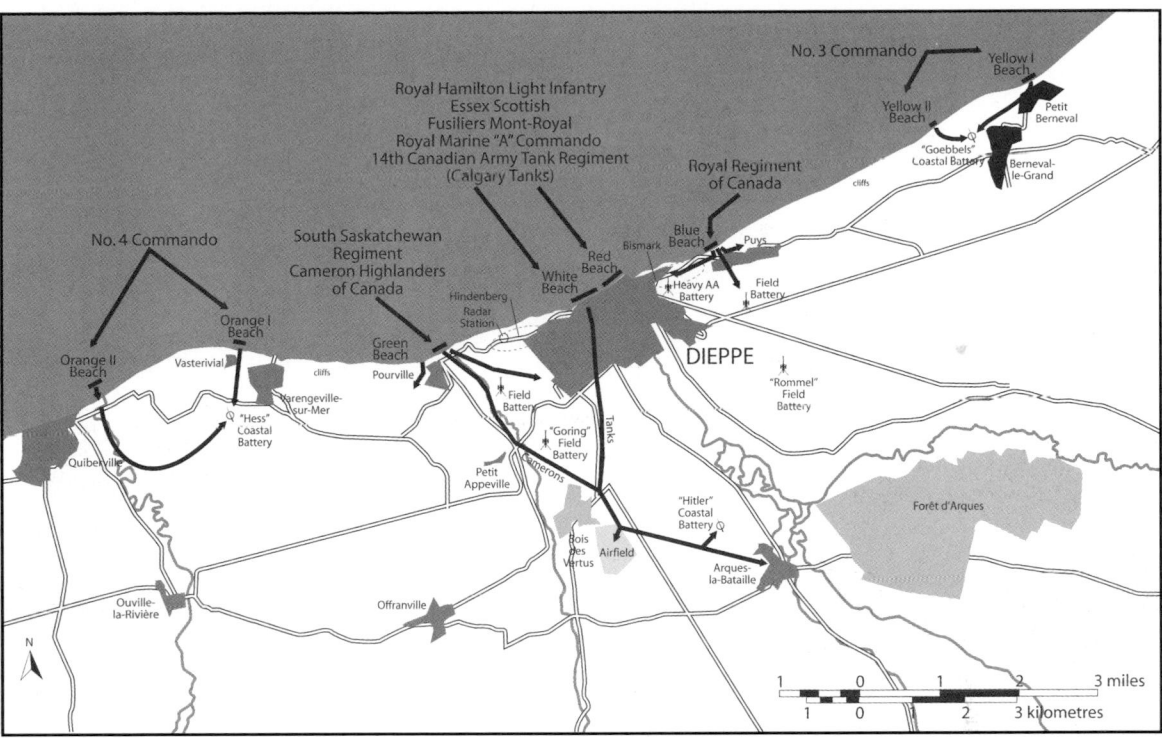

The map shows coastal area with the following labels:

No. 3 Commando — Yellow I Beach, Yellow II Beach, Petit Berneval, "Goebbels" Coastal Battery, Berneval-le-Grand

Royal Hamilton Light Infantry
Essex Scottish
Fusiliers Mont-Royal
Royal Marine "A" Commando
14th Canadian Army Tank Regiment
(Calgary Tanks)

Royal Regiment of Canada — Blue Beach, Puys, Bismark, Heavy AA Battery, Field Battery

No. 4 Commando

South Saskatchewan Regiment
Cameron Highlanders of Canada

Red Beach, White Beach, Hindenberg Radar Station, cliffs

Orange I Beach, Orange II Beach, Vasterival, Varengeville-sur-Mer, "Hess" Coastal Battery, Quiberville, Green Beach, Pourville, Field Battery, Petit Appeville, Camerons, "Goring" Field Battery, Tanks

DIEPPE, "Rommel" Field Battery, "Hitler" Coastal Battery, Bois des Vertus, Airfield, Arques-la-Bataille, Forêt d'Arques

Ouville-la-Rivière, Offranville

N

1 0 1 2 3 miles
1 0 2 3 kilometres

Operation "Jubilee", August 19, 1942.

guns, especially the dreaded 88, to deal with British armour. With the arrival of the six- and 17-pounder anti-tank guns and the Sherman tank, Commonwealth forces quickly developed a doctrine for armoured warfare that served them well.

During the Dieppe raid, the performance of the Calgary Tanks exceeded reasonable expectations. The first wave landed 10 minutes late but this was much earlier than on many of the D-Day beaches. Of the 29 tanks that tried to land, 27 made it to shore and 15 got off the beach, climbed the seawall and drove along the promenade. The tank guns were used in a largely fruitless attempt to destroy concrete road blocks and other fortified positions. The available German anti-tank guns could not penetrate the armour of the Churchill tanks. However, the engineers and infantry who were needed to carry out demolitions and assist the tanks did not survive the streams of machine-gun and mortar fire directed from the cliffs.

Commando raids also lost priority after Dieppe despite Churchill's opposition to any restrictions. The troops who landed on D-Day, including the commandos, were part of an integrated operation that employed armour, artillery, naval gunnery and air power. The Allies had learned a great deal about war since 1942.

Experience obtained through the Dieppe raid made an important contribution to improving Allied doctrine. Historians have frequently dismissed this obvious reality by insisting that the lessons of the raid could have been learned at far less cost through a combination of common sense, forethought and hard work. Perhaps this would have been true if armchair generals instead of real ones were in charge but only if they were able to make decisions after the battle was over.

The Bomber Command Offensive

Originally published, September 1996

The May 1996 issue of *Legion Magazine* offers another in the series of reflective articles addressed to his fellow veterans by Douglas Fisher, in which he tries to explain why Canadians take "such little pride in the mighty achievements of WW II," comparatively less than their American or British counterparts. He offers a number of reasons, including the tendency of post-war writers and producers to focus on "what had gone wrong, not on what had gone well."

Fisher continues, "In this litany of agony and injustice were the capture of Hong Kong, the removal of the Japanese and Japanese Canadians from the British Columbia coast, the Dieppe raid, the western Atlantic convoy troubles, and the brutal bombing of German cities and civilians by the Royal Air Force and Royal Canadian Air Force…a catalogue of Canadian disasters and brutalities."

When The Valour And The Horror was shown on television, most veterans knew that–whatever else was right or wrong about the series–what was missing was any understanding of the context of events.

"It wasn't like that," RCAF veterans insisted. "We were not dupes or victims, we knew what we were bombing. We understood the odds of surviving a tour, and we knew what we were fighting for."

The absence of any appreciation of what the war was about could be understood, if not forgiven, in a television series. But the publication in 1994 of the third volume of the RCAF's official history, *The Crucible Of War 1939-1945*, presented the public–and especially serious students of the war years–with a version of events remarkably similar to the one portrayed on television.

Written by Brereton Greenhous, Stephen Harris, William Johnston and William Rawling, the book is well-researched and free of the factual errors. It contains some highly original, well-argued sections on the technical development of Bomber Command's navigation aids and the German countermeasures. The authors also provide examples of RCAF operational failures and achievements in a reasonably balanced manner, but the book removes the bomber offensive from the context of war and presents it as a brutal, costly and largely ineffective campaign lacking purpose or justification. It is not surprising that many Canadians view it in this light.

The authors of *The Crucible Of War* would no doubt argue that their task was to write an opera-

A Lancaster at work.

tional history of the RCAF, not to study the larger issues of the war. This approach to military history is all too common, and is largely responsible for the discipline's poor reputation in Canadian universities. Military historians are far too ready to focus on operational detail, weapons systems and the exploits of individuals without attempting to attach broader meaning to what they are studying. War becomes a closed system within such a historiography, and only those with specialized interests find satisfaction in such a pursuit.

The historian's primary task is to try to determine what happened in the past as thoroughly as possible. To do this he or she must, in the words of R.G. Collingwood, "rethink the thoughts behind past actions." This is a long, complex process, but when applied to Bomber Command it requires a clear understanding of the ideas, values and state of knowledge of those who made the crucial decisions and those who carried them out.

As the British official history makes clear, historians must not fall into the error of "expecting commanders and their staffs to know facts which the historian has found out but which could not be known or inferred from information available when the war was in progress." For example, it is clearly impossible to understand the first night offensive against German cities in the winter of 1940-41 without assessing the impact of the Blitz on public and parliamentary opinion in Britain and Canada. By the spring of 1941, 44,000 British civilians had died and more than 86,000 more were seriously injured. Almost a quarter of a million homes had been destroyed.

The Canadian official history barely mentions the Blitz. The authors argue "there was also an emotional element to policy-making, tied to public demands and fed by the media, that the RAF must respond in kind to the bombing of British cities." They suggest the attack on Coventry provided the "excuse" for an RAF offensive against German civilians.

Whether Coventry was an excuse or a significant influence on British strategy is, of course, a matter of opinion. What is not in dispute is the failure of the RAF-RCAF night bombing offensive in 1940-41. Doubts about the accuracy and effectiveness of bombing were expressed by many observers before the Butt Report of August 1941 offered irrefutable evidence that of all aircraft recorded as having attacked their targets, only one-third got within five miles of them and, over the Ruhr, only one in 10 got within five miles with moonlight, or one in 15 without.

The cabinet's response to the devastating news was immediate, and probably inevitable. The situation on the Russian front, where the Germans were encircling Kiev and threatening Moscow and Leningrad, filled the newspapers and dominated discussion at all levels. With the Royal Navy and its Canadian partner stretched to breaking point in the North Atlantic and the Commonwealth armies struggling to acquire modern weapons and an appropriate battle doctrine, the air force–especially Bomber Command–was the only force available to carry the war to the enemy, providing assistance to Russia and beginning the process of wearing down Germany.

Nations make war as they can, not as they might wish to–and in the fall of 1941 there was broad consensus on the need to improve night bombing through increased training, technical development of navigation aids, a program to construct thousands of the new four-engined bombers and a further expansion of the British Commonwealth Air Training Plan (BCATP).

No other decision was possible at that time. Churchill's oft-quoted reply to Bomber Command's request for 4,000 heavy bombers "which could break Germany in six months" must not be confused with the government's decision. Churchill told Sir Charles Portal that he doubted whether bombing by itself would be a "decisive" factor in the war, but his government authorized a construction program that came to absorb 15 percent of the British war effort and, through the BCATP, a large part of Canada's contribution.

Thus began a new phase of "the never-ending struggle to circumvent the law that we cannot see in the dark." The struggle took the form of intensive efforts to develop electronic navigation aids while a targeting policy, known to the world as area bombing, was implemented in the hope of maximizing the destruction inflicted on Germany.

In March 1942, high loss rates and further evidence of navigation and bombing errors led the chiefs of staff to order a review of air strategy. The Joint Intelligence Committee reported it was unable to estimate the impact of bombing on Germany and suggested a study of the effects of Luftwaffe bombing of British cities. This sparked the famous debate between Churchill's scientific adviser, 'The Prof' Lord Cherwell, and Sir Henry Tizard over the weight of bombs required to destroy the homes of German workers. The controversy led the cabinet to ask Mr. Justice Singleton to estimate "what results we are likely to achieve from continuing our air attacks on Germany at the greatest possible strength for periods of six, 12 and 18 months."

The Singleton Report, the political and strategic basis of the offensive carried out under the leadership of Sir Arthur Harris, is of vital importance to understanding the broad political and public support for the bombing offensive. Throughout 1942 demands for a 'Second Front' dominated much of the debate over grand strategy. A second front in France was quite impossible, but Singleton believed a stepped-up bombing offensive might not only affect German industry but would force the Germans to divert fighter aircraft to defensive activities and "keep large numbers of men and guns on anti-aircraft work and searchlights and a very large number on air raid precautions."

In his conclusion, Singleton wrote:

I do not think it (the bombing offensive) ought to be regarded as of itself sufficient to win the war or to produce decisive results; the area is too vast for the effort we can put forth: on the other hand, if Germany does not achieve great success on land before the winter it may well turn out to have a decisive effect, and in the meantime, if carried out on the lines suggested, it must impede Germany and help Russia. If Germany succeeds in her attack on Russia there will be little apparent gain from our bombing policy in six months' time, but the drain on Germany will be present all the time: and if Russia stands it will remain a powerful weapon on our hands. It is impossible to say what its effect will be in 12 or 18 months without considering the position of Russia. If Russia can hold Germany on land I doubt whether Germany will stand 12 or 18 months' continuous, intensified and increased bombing, affecting, as it must, her war production, her power of resistance, her industries and her will to resist (by which I mean morale).

The Commonwealth aircrew who risked their lives to attack the Third Reich in 1942-43 opened the true 'Second Front,' engaging German forces desperately needed on the Eastern Front. It is crucial that this contribution to victory be recognized. The Crucible Of War authors recognize this, noting the Germans "used 500,000 to 800,000 workers to repair bomb damage and organize the dispersal of vital industries...while the Flak arm required some 900,000 men in 1943...." Thanks to the Commonwealth airmen, German aircraft and 88-mm guns were also kept away from Russia to defend the Reich.

These men who brought the war directly to the heart of Germany may not have won the war by themselves, as the bomber enthusiasts promised, but it is difficult to imagine how we could have won the war without them.

The Role Of Jill Canuck

Originally published, October 1996

History, according to one definition, is a word with three distinct meanings. First it refers to the actual events that took place in the past, then the memory of those events and finally the historian's attempt to understand and interpret the surviving evidence. The third kind of history is always written from the perspective of the present—even when the historian makes a conscious effort to avoid imposing contemporary values on the past.

I was sharply reminded of this while reading a variety of books and articles on the 50,000 women who served in the Canadian Armed Forces in WW II. Memoirs like Phyllis Bowman's *We Skirted The War* or Rosamond Greer's *The Girls Of The King's Navy* convey the sense of excitement, adventure and achievement that so many women who served recall. As "Fiddy" Greer writes: "Of course nobody was liberated in the navy, but during the time we spent as members of the (Women's Royal Canadian Naval Service) we did consider ourselves to be a very important part of a very important mission."

When the war ended, Greer, like most of the other women who served or worked in industry, "returned home, married, bore children and according to the mores of the time remained at home to care for them." This experience, which seemed so natural to women in the 1940s, was viewed very differently by academic writers who took their cue from Betty Friedan's 1963 book, *The Feminine Mystique*. Friedan argued that the progress women made towards greater equality during the war was quickly reversed by deliberate policy and elaborate propaganda. Women were denied 'men jobs' and forced to return to their traditional role.

The view of the wartime years as a time of responsibility—and then lost opportunity—for Canadian women was challenged in the mid-1970s by Ruth Pierson, who was then teaching a course on the history of women at Memorial University in Newfoundland. Pierson questioned the view that women had made significant strides towards equality during the war, and argued that the "sexual division of labour re-emerged stronger than ever" in 1945. She was particularly critical of the record of the Canadian Women's Army Corps. Despite publicity photos and head-lines claiming that "Jill Canuck Has Become CWAC of All Trades," the overwhelming majority of CWACs were employed in traditional women's occupations as stenographers, clerks and kitchen workers.

Of the 11,706 CWACs serving in Canada at the end of the war, just 111 had been trained as driver mechanics, 69 as wireless operators and 22 in the highly publicized role of kinetheodolite operators testing the accuracy of anti-aircraft gun equipment. At the peak period, in the spring of 1944, half of the 853 other ranks serving in England were clerks. The next-largest occupation was laundry worker. There were just 24 CWAC drivers in the United Kingdom, two of whom had been trained as driver mechanics. Overall, more than 21,000 women served in the CWAC in WW II.

The subordinate position of women in the army was further emphasized by the legal position of the corps, and its decision to set women's basic pay at two-thirds of that paid to men of the same rank. The army was initially reluctant to increase pay rates, but it did agree to change the status of the CWACs, who had been recruited as a separate organization "broadly similar" to the army. In March 1942, women were incorporated within the army and placed on active service. A "volunteer" became a private, a "junior commander" a captain, and the "honorary controller" a colonel. Standard rank badges replaced beaver and maple leaf insignia.

These changes helped to remove one of the most obvious barriers, but the army was still not attracting enough women volunteers. An official inquiry conducted in the spring of 1943 surveyed both women serving in the army and public opinion across the country to try to determine why women joined up and "why more young eligible women are not offering themselves for enlistment." The survey results help us to gain considerable insight into Canadian society in 1943. According to the

1941 census there were 800,000 women in the country eligible to enlist. Seventy thousand of these had made enquiries, 37,000 had been medically examined and 28,000 enlisted in one of the three services. Three-quarters of them were under 25 years of age and only seven per cent were over age 34. They were from Canadian cities and towns, not rural areas, and more than 80 per cent had left paid employment to join up.

When asked why they joined, most women spoke of wanting to contribute to winning the war. More than half had brothers in uniform and many had fathers, sisters or boyfriends in the services. The biggest single obstacle to recruitment was the lack of any sense of urgency. The CWACs did not seem to be doing much of vital importance to the war effort, so many women felt they were of more use in war industry and should be left there. But the issue of wages and wage rates were also important. By the end of 1942, public opinion polls showed that the majority of Canadians supported the principle of equal pay for equal work. Systematic discrimination against women in the services–where the pay was already low–seemed especially unfair, and in July 1943 pay for servicewomen was raised from two-thirds to 80 per cent of the men's rate. Trades pay was made the same for everyone.

Whether it was these improvements or a new sense of purpose related to the commitment of Canadian troops to action in Italy, many more women joined the services in late 1943 and 1944 and no further changes in their status occurred. When the war ended some women wanted to make a career in the army, but the CWAC–along with the Wrens and Women's Division of the Royal Canadian Air Force–were disbanded. A few years later, a hot war in Korea and a Cold War in Europe brought women back into uniform, this time for good.

What do we make of this experience with the perspective of 50 years available to us? Pierson, now a professor at the University of Toronto, remains unconvinced that the wartime experience brought any "increase in power to women as a group." In her book *They're Still Women After All* she argues that because women were denied combat roles,

NAC 128260

CWAC's preparing Ram tanks for shipment overseas.

and could not rise to the highest positions in the army, their military service did little to advance the overall status of women. She maintains it may even have reinforced their subordination. Pierson also emphasizes the negative impact of government publicity designed to reassure an apparently nervous public that servicewomen were both respectable and feminine. Press releases emphasized that servicewomen were still attractive to men and could get married while serving. Photo stories pictured beautiful, ladylike women with carefully coiffured hair and full makeup. A great deal of effort was required to counter the whispering campaign about "loose women" in uniform, all of it directed at proving that the army was protecting traditional feminine values. When the war ended such women would return home, making way for men to reclaim all that was their due as the "superior sex."

Is Pierson right? Was the wartime experience of service so much different than the official memory? Certainly public opinion shifted dramatically once the war was over, with 60 per cent reporting that they favored preferential treatment for men and just 25 per cent opting for equal opportunities. Among women alone, 62 per cent favored preference for men. But this kind of evidence does not allow us to understand how the wartime experience affected the way women saw themselves or their place in society. Nor does it tell us anything about the attitudes and values they passed on to their children. For example, the 1943 survey asked CWACs what they liked about the army. One in three women placed companionship and fellowship first. Most enjoyed their jobs, the discipline, meeting new people, travel opportunities and the healthy life. They did not like restrictions on their social life, deplored favoritism and complained about unequal pay.

Before we decide that the wartime experience had little impact on women we had better explore these issues. And before that can be done, we need to know something about the experience of nurses and of the women who served in the navy and the air services. Perhaps the navy and the air force did things differently.

NAC 108174

Servicewomen of WW II

Originally published, November/December 1996

Remembrance day in our community begins when small knots of people gather at the cenotaph that overlooks a quiet mill pond. The township has built a children's playground nearby so we share the space with swings and a brightly coloured slide. On this cold, crisp November morning the children are in school so they miss the skirl of pipes that announce the arrival of the men and women of the Legion colour party.

We participate in these acts of remembrance because they re-establish our connection with those who died and help us reconfirm our fragile Canadian identity. But will there be anyone left to observe such moments in the 21st century or will a new generation discard this part of our past as irrelevant to a future in which regional, ethnic and group identities dissolve the last bonds of patriotism?

My thoughts are prompted by the academic literature I have read on the role of women in WW II. For if we teach our children that women were recruited largely to do laundry and other domestic

chores then there will be less reason to remember them as role models or to honour their wartime contributions. This negative view of the experience of women in WW II still dominates Canadian historical writing, but a new generation is beginning to challenge the wisdom. In 1992 a young doctoral student, Barbara Winters, presented a paper to the Canadian Historical Association that asked: "Why did so many women view their service in the military favorably while revisionist historians continue to portray it as oppressive and non-liberating?"

Winters chose to answer her own question by suggesting that too much attention is given to the Canadian Women's Army Corps, the service in which the least progress on women's issues was made. The story of women's part in the war effort is very different, Winters argues, if the history of women who served in the Royal Canadian Air Force is considered. Although they were recruited through the slogan They Serve That Men May Fly, women were an integral part of the RCAF from the beginning and were employed in a number of non-traditional roles. This equality of status led the air force to drop the name Canadian Women's Auxiliary Air Force and adopt RCAF (Women's Division). Nicknamed the WDs,

Nursing Sisters of No. 10 Canadian General Hospital, France 1944.

women held the same rank and were subject to the same chain of command as men. Female officers and non-commissioned officers issued orders to airmen as well as airwomen. When posted overseas the RCAF insisted that WDs, known affectionately as WIDs in Britain, serve under RAF or RCAF command and not with the British Women's Auxiliary Air Force.

Women in air force blue were not permitted to serve in combat roles and were therefore excluded from aircrew trades. However, everything else was open to them and by 1944 WDs were working in 65 of the 102 RCAF trades. Men and women trained together, served together and were promoted according to merit not gender. C.G. Power, the minister of national defence for air, favored the employment of women as ferry and staff pilots, but the War Cabinet hesitated, withholding approval until there was a shortage of male pilots, a circumstance that never developed.

By allowing women's basic wages to remain at 80 per cent of the men's rate, the RCAF never resolved the issue of pay equity. This was rationalized by claiming that all men in the air force were trained for, and could be committed to, a combat role in the event of any enemy attack. But as Winters points out, one of the strongest supporters of equal pay for equal work was the man responsible for all personnel questions. Air Vice-Marshal J.A. Scully did not hesitate to campaign for equal rights for women. In a memorandum written in 1942, he noted that since "women who enlist in the air force are obliged the same as men, to fly" and are also "obligated to serve overseas" the principle of equal pay for equal work ought to be accepted. He dismissed the combat role argument by noting women who serve overseas in Britain "take more risk than male personnel in Canada".

Scully failed to carry the day on basic pay rates, but on other issues, including allowances and post-discharge benefits, women were treated as equals. Of perhaps greater importance was the actual work women performed. There were of course cooks–male as well as female–and clerks, nursing orderlies and stenographers, but many women were employed as wireless operators, code and cypher clerks, aero-engine mechanics, meteorolo-

gists, parachute riggers, air photo interpreters and in entertainment shows.

One WD described her job in the control tower of a training school to Jean Bruce for her 1985 book, *Back the Attack! Canadian Women During the Second World War–at Home and Abroad*. "I was the NCO in charge of the Orderly Room.... I never ran into the feeling that a woman shouldn't be there. I did quite a bit of flying. When the weather flight went up, they always wanted a weather observer who could report any visual flight problems to the meteorological officer aboard."

Another WD recalled "learning the basics of intelligence and air photo interpretation" before arriving at No. 6 Group Headquarters in Yorkshire.

"Intelligence officers interrogated crews when they came back from a bombing mission.... It was very high powered. You got raw answers to questions.... You had to find out where the concentrations of power were, where the searchlights and ack-ack guns were...later we examined the photographs they'd taken during a bombing raid."

More than 17,000 women served in the WDs during WW II and at peak strength there were 600 officers and 15,000 other ranks in uniform. Among the honors and awards bestowed were 50 mentioned in dispatches.

Winters has made a pretty solid case for her argument that the air force did things differently and with different results.

What then can be said about the senior service that resisted enlisting women until the summer of 1942? The Women's Royal Canadian Naval Service was based on the British model but with one important difference; women were recruited into the Royal Canadian Navy and not an auxiliary.

Recruiting literature emphasized the same themes as the air force, exhorting women to Join The Wrens And Hasten Victory. You Too Can Free A Man To Serve At Sea. Initially women were enlisted to take on jobs as cooks, stewards, clerks and stenographers. One trade category, communications and operations, promised access to jobs as plotters, coders, telegraphists and other more war-related postings, but recruits had first to train as general clerks. Wrens began their career at HMCS *Conestoga*, the stone frigate on the outskirts of Galt, Ontario, where recruits learned to call the kitchen the galley and the bathroom the head. They also learned drill, discipline and the firm navy doctrine that a Wren was first and foremost a lady. Women were up against a very traditional service ethic, but gradually it became clear to all that Wrens could contribute more than domestic service to the navy. By 1944, women were employed in a variety of operational, communications and intelligence postings in Canada and overseas. Wrens served at remote naval stations, including ones commanded by Wren officers.

The navy recruited more than 6,500 women and 1,000 of them served overseas. The purpose of the Wrens to release men for duty at sea was fulfilled, but more than that happened. Wrens proved to themselves and to men that they could succeed and excel at jobs reserved for men.

The navy also offered women a chance to enlist and perform in one very traditional occupation, that of dancer and showgirl. This was true of all services, but it is the company of Meet The Navy, an extraordinary touring show that required 15 railway coaches to move cast, props, costumes and equipment, that is best remembered. The cast included the Rockettes and the most famous Wren of all, Blanche Lund who became an international star along with her husband Alan. Meet The Navy played to half a million people in Canada before going overseas where it became the hit of 1945 in London.

The spirit that animated the Wrens and other women in uniform was particularly strong among nursing sisters of all three services. The Royal Canadian Army Medical Corps recruited 3,656 nurses, 2,625 of whom served overseas. The RCAF with 482, and the RCN with 345 nurses brought the total to more than 4,400. Nursing was, of course, a traditional women's occupation so at first sight it may appear the military offered little that was new.

The reality is very different. The prewar nursing profession in Canada suffered a serious loss of

prestige when the Depression reduced salaries and encouraged the employment of untrained practitioners. The Canadian Nurses Association hoped the war would reverse the declining status of nurses and assist their campaign for decent wages. The government did its best to oblige. Nursing sisters were enlisted into all three services as officers, as were other medical professionals.

After training, nurses were full lieutenants while matrons served as captains or majors. All received pay, allowances and officer privileges that contrasted sharply with their lot in civilian life. Author Jean Bruce interviewed one nurse who recalled: "It was hard to get into the RCAMC. The pay was fantastic, $150 a month compared to $70 I was making before and our accommodation and meals were paid."

The services provided new opportunities as well as better status and improved pay. Army nurses worked close to the front lines in Italy and Northwest Europe. They served on hospital ships that carried the wounded to Canada through U-Boat infested seas. In England and in Canada nurses took on new responsibilities as specialized medical units were created. No one could doubt that the war experience had changed the nursing profession by laying the foundation for postwar reforms.

After demobilization, servicewomen had the same opportunity as men to attend university or register for vocational training. However, they faced two barriers: one, a general climate of opinion in which fears of a postwar recession reinforced traditional beliefs that married women should stay out of the workforce; and two, their own desire to marry, raise a family and stay at home to look after husband and children. Not all women felt this way and not all adjusted to a world that denied women equal access to jobs. Many stayed in the labour force, struggling to develop new careers. Those who returned to remain at home had also been changed. Perhaps that is why they raised their children to believe a woman should expect the same rights and opportunities as a man.

LCMSDS

The Big Three Josef Stalin, Franklin Roosevelt and Winston Churchill, 1943, Tehran.

The Mediterranean Theatre

Originally published, January/February 1997

World War II was fought on many strange battlefields, but none was more unusual than North Africa. Fighting began there because Italian dictator Benito Mussolini, surprised by the rapid collapse of the French army, decided he needed a "few thousand corpses" or Italy would not have a place at an early peace conference. The Italian army first attacked France and then began operations against the British in East Africa and Egypt.

The story of the Italian advance and the Commonwealth counter-offensive is well known. British Lieutenant-General Sir Richard O'Connor employed the 7th Armoured and the 4th Indian divisions in a campaign that resulted in the destruction of 14 enemy divisions and the capture of 130,000 prisoners. This was done at a cost of 2,000 casualties, 500 of them fatal.

Lieutenant-General O'Connor's troops might well have conquered Libya and ended the war in North Africa in 1941, but Winston Churchill and his advisers decided the defence of Greece must have priority. In the spring of 1941, the Germans overran Greece, captured Crete and under General Erwin Rommel swept back into Egypt. Churchill had gambled and lost. Instead of reinforcing success he had contrived to make the Commonwealth forces weak everywhere.

Defeat in the Balkans and the western desert were serious blows to morale, but by the end of 1941 the invasion of the Soviet Union, and America's entry into the war, greatly reduced the strategic importance of the Mediterranean. The war would be decided on the plains of eastern Europe, on the waters of the North Atlantic, in the skies over Germany and on the battlefields of France. The optimum policy for the Allies required the defence of Egypt and the Mideast oil fields, but little else.

Such a strategy proved impossible to follow, Churchill and the British chiefs of staff were determined to restore British prestige and defeat General Rommel's Africa Corps. Resources were found to mount a major desert offensive in the spring of 1942, but initial success soon turned to costly defeat as the 8th Army was forced to retreat to El Alamein.

Churchill's commitment to the Mediterranean theatre was now an obsession. He persuaded Franklin Delano Roosevelt to ignore the advice of his own military advisers and agree to an Anglo-American invasion of French North Africa. This operation, code-named Operation "Torch", was to form one arm of a great Allied pincer movement designed to clear the shores of North Africa. Commonwealth forces, under General Bernard Montgomery, would attack General Rommel's forces from the east, while General Dwight Eisenhower's armies overcame French resistance and advanced into Tunisia.

This extraordinary decision meant that in the winter of 1942-43—as millions of men struggled to decide the fate of Europe in the snows of Russia—Britain and the U.S. were employing enormous resources to capture a remote area of little strategic importance.

Fortunately, Hitler had his own obsessions. Convinced that Mussolini's armies would collapse without German support, and fearful of an early Italian surrender, Hitler reinforced Tunisia with air force and army units drawn from the eastern front. If such resources had been saved for the defence of Sicily, the Allies would never have attempted to attack the island.

Canadians had escaped involvement in the desert campaigns of 1941 and '42, but Operation "Torch" led to Canada's entry into the Mediterranean. The first elements to arrive were five Royal Canadian Navy corvettes, *Louisburg*, *Prescott*, *Woodstock*, *Weyburn* and *Lunenburg*. These were employed to escort the invasion armada. The decision to use 17 RCN corvettes in support of Operation "Torch" and the follow-up convoys says a great deal about Allied priorities. In the winter of 1942—43, the Battle of the Atlantic was "still undecided, but rapidly escalating to a climax," notes naval historian Marc

Milner in his book *North Atlantic Run: The Royal Canadian Navy and the Battle for the Convoys*. "The "Torch" landings drew off much needed escort forces, and indeed the impact of "Torch" on the merchant shipping situation was very nearly catastrophic." Quite apart from additional losses in the North Atlantic, Operation "Torch" forced cancellation of the arctic convoys to Russia and the diversion of 100 merchant ships a month to North Africa.

The balance sheet was not all negative, the Germans detached an increasing number of U-boats to the Mediterranean. One of them, U-224, was operating off Algiers when it was sunk by HMCS *Ville de Québec* in January. Italian submarines were destroyed by *Port Arthur* and *Regina*. Unfortunately, there were Canadian losses to report as well; *Louisburg* was sunk by an aerial torpedo in February 1943 while escorting a convoy from Gibraltar to Bone, Algeria. *Weyburn* was lost during the same month after she struck a mine laid off Gibraltar.

A second group of Canadians arrived in North Africa in time to take part in the battle for Tunisia. General Andrew McNaughton wanted to keep the five divisions and two tank brigades of 1st Canadian Army together, but he was well aware of the value of combat experience. In 1943, 201 Canadian officers and 147 non-commissioned officers were sent to join units of the 1st British Army. They served in both combat and staff positions and suffered 25 casualties, including eight fatalities.

This experiment foreshadowed the Canloan plan of 1944 that sent hundreds of Canadian officers to serve with British units. The difference was that the North African experience was designed to improve the training of the Canadian Army. Generals Henry Crerar and Guy Simonds also travelled to North Africa to visit Montgomery's 8th Army to learn battle lessons first hand.

These minor contacts with the Mediterranean theatre might well have been the sum of Canada's participation were it not for political pressures in Ottawa. As the third year of the war drew to a close, many Canadians were questioning the direction of a war effort that left Canada's army in England "as a sort of adjunct" to the British Home Guard.

American divisions were fighting in North Africa less than one year after Pearl Harbor, while Canadians had been limited to the tragic battles of Hong Kong and Dieppe. Pressure for Canadian participation intensified when the Canadian government learned of the decision taken at the Casablanca conference to launch "further amphibious operations on a large scale" in the Mediterranean. In March 1943, Prime Minister Mackenzie King agreed to send a telegram to Churchill asking him to reconsider the decision not to employ Canadian troops in the Mediterranean. A further lobbying effort was undertaken when the British Foreign Secretary Anthony Eden visited Ottawa later in the month and this seems to have won the day. General Eisenhower, as supreme Allied commander, was informed that for both "political and military" reasons 1st Canadian Division and 1st Canadian Tank Brigade would replace 3rd British Division for Operation "Husky", the invasion of Sicily.

Once the decision to employ Canadian troops was made the selection of the Red Patch Division was inevitable. The division had been in the United Kingdom since December 1939 and it included Canada's three permanent force infantry battalions, the Royal Canadian Regiment, the Princess Patricia's Canadian Light Infantry and the Royal 22nd Regiment.

The division, along with the rest of the army, worked hard at training in the fall of 1942. However, as 1943 began the prospect of another year of inactivity led to a natural decline in enthusiasm. The sudden announcement that the division and 1st Tank Brigade were to take part in an amphibious invasion posed an immediate challenge to everyone.

The infantry and armoured battalions were put through an intensive advanced training course to fit them for action in "an opposed landing and subsequent operations in mountainous country."

Each infantry brigade was sent to Inveraray on the west coast of Scotland for an intense eight-

day course in the techniques of assault landing. The armoured brigade was equipped with Sherman tanks and had to master the arts of waterproofing so that the tanks could wade ashore in up to six feet of water.

At Inveraray it was soon evident that the Canadians were not fully ready for action. Second Brigade, the PPCLI, Seaforth Highlanders of Canada and the Loyal Edmonton Regiment did fairly well, and 1st Brigade, the Royal Canadian Regiment, the Hastings and Prince Edward Regiment and the 48th Highlanders of Canada were acceptable, but 3rd Brigade was judged to be quite unfit for action. The commandant of the school recommended that it be replaced "in view of the forthcoming operation."

Brigadier George Pangman, who was serving as the brigade major in 1943, recalled that the report described problems of "insubordination, lack of physical fitness and insufficient training.... The West Novas were the worst, Royal 22nd next and the Carleton and Yorks were pretty bad." It was quite impossible to substitute another brigade, but some changes would be made. The West Nova Scotia Regiment got a new commanding officer, the highly regarded Lieutenant-Colonel Pat Bogert, and a number of other officers and non-commissioned officers were replaced.

The problems in 1st Division were indicative of the difficulties the Canadian Army experienced during its long sojourn in England. An army with a small cadre of professional soldiers had attempted to teach itself the art of modern war while training with obsolete equipment and out-dated doctrine. The sudden transformation from "adjunct to the British Home Guard" to assault division challenged everyone to get their act together. Fortunately, much was accomplished before the division sailed, and once ashore in Sicily there was time to make further changes before heavy fighting began. First Division, including 3rd Brigade, proved itself able to learn and adapt. It quickly became one of the most effective divisions in the Allied order of battle.

The Invasion Of Sicily

Originally published, March/April 1997

One of the most enduring myths about Canadian military history is that historians and writers have concentrated their attention on the campaign in Northwest Europe ignoring the "D-Day Dodgers" and the battles in the Mediterranean. This view persists despite the popularity of Farley Mowat's books, the high quality of the official history of the campaign and the excellence of the popular history *The D-Day Dodgers: The Canadians in Italy 1943-45* by Daniel G. Dancocks.* The Canadian role in Italy is also the subject of some of our best memoirs including Sydney Frost's *Once a Patricia* and Strome Galloway's books and articles. In 1996 the superbly designed and illustrated *Canadians and the Italian Campaign 1943-45* by Bill McAndrew was published.

This new title is the latest in a series sponsored by the Directorate of History and Heritage of the Department of National Defence. Once again no expense has been spared in producing the volume, but do not let the coffee-table format confuse you. McAndrew has written an original and insightful account which will please veterans, the general reader and professional historians. Throughout the book McAndrew uses personal accounts to illuminate and humanize the analysis of a complex story. His special interest in questions of morale, combat effectiveness and battle exhaustion is evident throughout and there is much to be learned about Canada's war that goes well beyond the specifics of the Italian campaign. In the next several articles I will be exploring aspects of the war in Italy and the development of the Canadian forces in 1943. My debt to McAndrew and other specialists will be evident to all.

The decision to attack the island of Sicily was made at the Casablanca Conference in January 1943. General George C. Marshall, the U.S. Army chief of staff, and most of his countrymen, opposed the plan but were unable to offer a viable alternative. When Marshall was forced to accept the first phase of Winston Churchill's strategy of "closing the ring", he had warned President Franklin Roosevelt that the landings in North Africa in November 1942 would postpone the invasion of France until 1944, drawing the Americans into Britain's Mediterranean obsession. At Casablanca he accepted the logic of employing the Anglo-American armies against Sicily, a million men could not be kept out of action for a year, but Marshall still regarded the Mediterranean as a diversion which prolonged the war.

Historians are naturally attracted to issues involving large personalities and great debates so there are numerous studies of the Allied leaders and their interaction but surprisingly little attention has been paid to purely military considerations. By the summer of 1942, when the key decisions about the future were made, Churchill and his chiefs of staff had lost confidence in the leadership, training and morale of the British Army. The long series of defeats from Dunkirk to North Africa and the Far East seemed to raise fundamental questions about the fighting qualities of the British and Commonwealth soldier. The victory at El Alamein in the Egyptian desert had soothed some of the anxiety but British operations in Tunisia moved slowly. When the Americans suffered a tactical defeat in Tunisia at Kasserine Pass, the British concluded that the American forces were badly trained and poorly led. Could such men overcome the experienced and superbly equipped divisions of the German army on the fields of Northwest Europe? The answer for most senior British commanders was a resounding no. Far better to continue operations against Italy until Bomber Command and the Soviet armies had weakened Germany. By 1944 the Allies would have much more battle

LCMSDS

Regalbuto, Sicily, July 1943.

*Since this essay appeared Mark Zuehlke has written three well received books on the campaign; *The Gothic Line: Canada's Month of Hell in World War II Italy, Ortona: Canada's Epic World War II Battle, The Liri Valley: World War II Breakthrough to Rome.*

NAC 130249

experience and knowledge of waging war on several fronts within a coalition. The Soviet victory at Stalingrad seemed to promise that there would be time enough to learn.

The story of the transformation of the Commonwealth armies is usually seen as beginning in the desert under the leadership of General Bernard Montgomery. It is in fact far more complicated than that for much of the change took place in the United Kingdom at the Ministry of Supply. The quality of weapons and weapon systems may not determine the outcome of battles but if one side is consistently inferior the odds of defeat are very great.

When the politicians in Ottawa decided to press the British to include Canadian units in the next major operation in the Mediterranean they knew little of the actual state of their troops in Britain. The Canadians, like their British counterparts in England, had spent most of the war preparing to defend the island from invasion. This had begun to change in the summer of 1942 but as the historian John A. English has shown the army was far from ready for operations against a well trained enemy.

There is nothing sinister in the failure of the British and Canadian high command to train and equip a modern army, it was a matter of priorities. Before 1943 virtually everyone agreed

Lieutenant-General Bernard Montgomery speaking to Canadian troops, Sicily 1943.

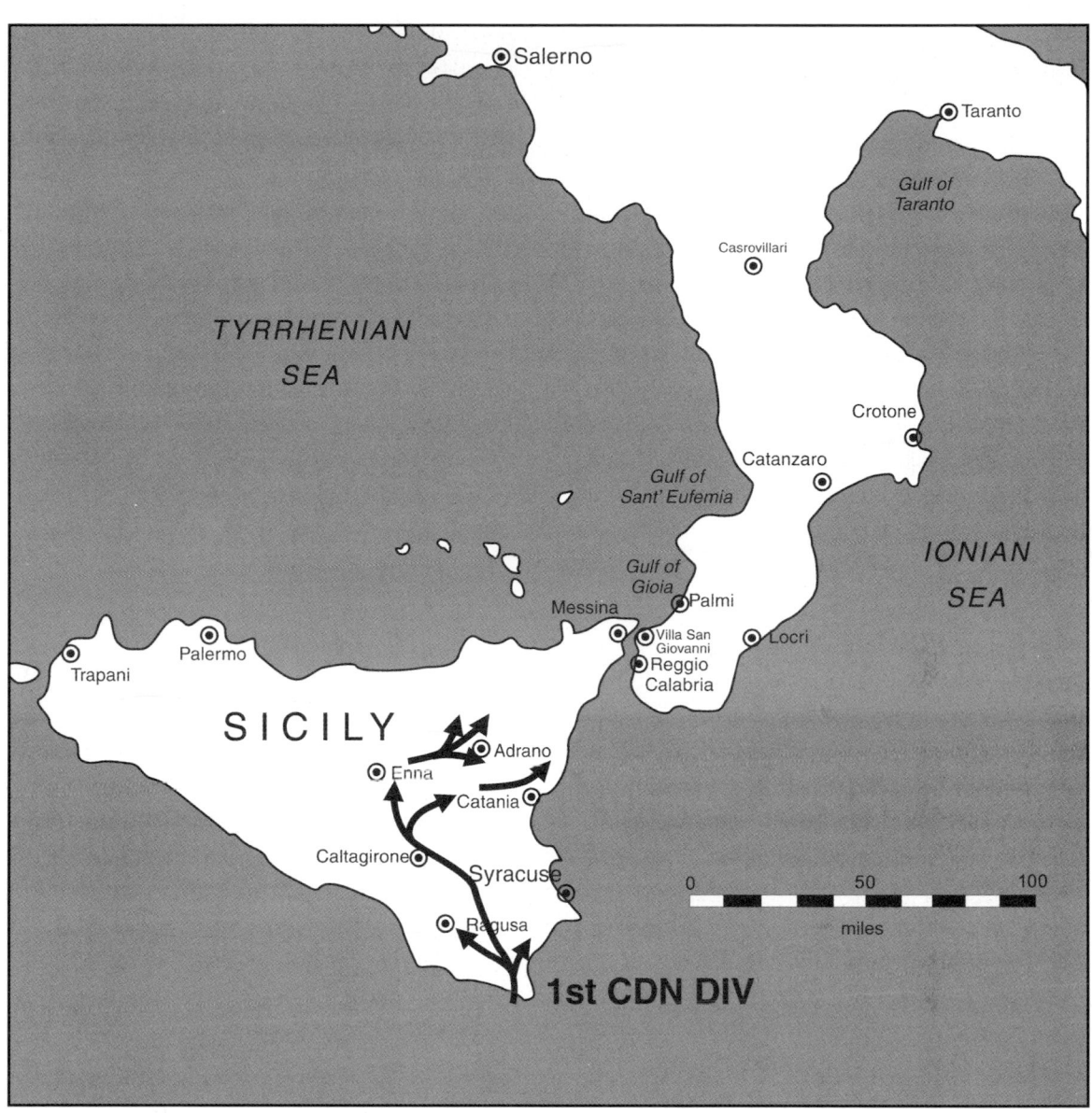

Salerno

Taranto

Gulf of
Taranto

Casrovillari

*TYRRHENIAN
SEA*

Crotone

Catanzaro

Gulf of
Sant' Eufemia

*IONIAN
SEA*

Gulf of
Gioia

Messina   Palmi

Villa San
Giovanni

Locri

Reggio
Calabria

Palermo

Trapani

S I C I L Y

Adrano

Enna

Catania

Caltagirone

Syracuse

0   50   100

miles

Ragusa

1st CDN DIV

1st Canadian
Division advance
through Sicily.

with Churchill's view that "only the navy can lose the war and only the air force can win it." The army was for home defence and sideshows like North Africa. By the end of 1942 such a view was no longer sensible and was abandoned.

Consider for example the changes made in the equipment of the Canadians after they were selected for action in Sicily. Our armoured units, the Calgary, the Three Rivers and the Ontario Regiments were equipped with the reliable, and in 1943 terms, powerful Sherman tank. The infantry battalions were introduced to the new Projector, Infantry, Anti-Tank, or PIAT, the British bazooka. The PIAT had a dangerous-

ly limited range and could not be relied upon to fire accurately but it did provide the foot soldier with a useful anti-tank weapon which an infantry section could take into battle.

Assignment to Sicily also meant that the battalion anti-tank platoons finally got their hands on the six-pounder anti-tank gun which was still a scarce commodity two years after its introduction. The gunners of the divisional anti-tank regiment were equally pleased with the 17-pounder gun which was quite accurately described as equal to the famous German 88-mm. The Saskatoon Light Infantry, the division's support battalion, was introduced to the 3-inch mortar, the infantry battalions' vital defensive weapon. By 1943 smokeless powder and improved range made the weapon a match for the German 81-mm mortar.

Other innovations helped to build confidence and improve effectiveness. The question now was whether the Canadians could find the leadership and commitment to succeed in battle. Lieutenant-General Andrew McNaughton, the commander of the First Canadian Army, first chose Harry Salmon, a decorated WW I veteran with a reputation as one of the best trainers of soldiers in any army, as divisional commander. After Salmon's death in a plane crash, McNaughton jumped a generation selecting Guy Simonds to replace him.

Simonds was to become the best known Canadian general since Arthur Currie, but in 1943 the 40-year-old Simonds was an unknown quantity. To command a division without ever having fought in a battle is unusual at any time but to begin a career with an assault landing is extraordinary. Simonds was nevertheless the obvious choice because he was simply the outstanding professional soldier in the army. He had excelled in all previous appointments and was well regarded by the British who were prone to be suspicious of Canadian officers.

Simonds inherited a divisional staff and five brigadiers who were a good cross section of Canada's officer corps. Major-General Chris Vokes who led the 2nd Brigade, and who followed Simonds in command of the division, is the best known, but the group included Bruce Matthews, an outstanding artillery officer and future divisional commander, as well as many others who proved to be capable leaders.

The Canadians had just over two months to prepare for the invasion of Sicily and they used their time well. The most serious setback in the first phase came when three merchant ships in the Slow Assault Convoy were sunk with losses of 58 men, 50 tanks and 40 guns. Divisional headquarters and the field regiments were severely hampered by equipment losses and a good deal of improvisation was needed. The landings themselves were accomplished with

few casualties and the division's first inland objective, the airfield at Pachino, was secured when the Royal Canadian Regiment overwhelmed the defenders of an artillery battery.

Contemporary historians are critical of nearly every aspect of Operation "Husky". Carlo D'Este, the leading American student of the campaign, titled his book *Bitter Victory*, emphasizing the escape of German forces to the mainland as well as the caution and confusion of Allied leadership. D'Este believes that the attritional battles fought by the 8th Army in Sicily were both poorly managed and unnecessary. D'Este cares deeply about the plight of the ordinary soldier caught up in the horror of war and imposes harsh standards on all decision makers.

The Canadian experience in Sicily produced a very different collective memory. Sicily was the army's first campaign and most thought it was a great success. When Montgomery ordered the Canadians to push hard in a left hook to outflank the German defences at Catania the division moved quickly to fulfill its tasks. The story of the next 30 days cannot be repeated too often. The extraordinary achievement of the Hastings and Prince Edward Regiment, the "Hasty Ps", in climbing a mountainside at Assoro was first told by the unit historian Farley Mowat who wrote:

Each man who made that climb performed his own private miracle. From ledge to ledge the dark figures made their way, hauling each other up, passing along their weapons and ammunition from hand to hand. A signaler made that climb with a heavy wireless set strapped to his back–a thing that in daylight was seen to be impossible. Yet no man slipped, no man dropped so much as a clip of ammunition. It was just as well, for any sound by one would have been fateful to all.

Bill McAndrew, normally a stern critic of the British-Canadian way of war, sees Assoro as just one of the extraordinary Canadian achievements in Sicily. The battle for Leonforte fought by the Princess Patricia's Canadian Light Infantry and the Loyal Edmonton Regiment, was less spectacular. However, the "speed and audacity" of the battle-group commanded by Captain Rowan Coleman which raced to the relief of the Loyal Eddies was a promising example of a combined arms operation which the division would have to master if it was to succeed in battle.

The next major battle, to seize the village of Agira, involved a more methodical and less successful set-piece attack employing five field and two medium artillery regiments. McAndrew suggests that this conventional artillery-based plan was a poor substitute for the mobile fire and movement operations which proceeded it but German resistance was stiffening all across the front as the enemy began to evacuate non-combatant troops to the mainland.

The fall of Agira came just as the Italian Dictator Benito Mussolini was deposed. His successor, Marshal Pietro Badoglio, maintained that Italy would continue to fight but few, and least of all Hitler, believed him. The invasion of Sicily had accomplished one of its major purposes.

For the next two weeks the Canadians were committed to the thankless task of attacking a German army which was conducting a well-organized withdrawal. Each piece of high ground, from low hills to mountain peaks was occupied and held by the enemy until pressure, or their timetable, forced a withdrawal. Since the senior Allied commanders were doing little to prevent the evacuation across the straits of Messina, the strategic purpose of costly assaults on prepared positions is not clear.

Where were the vaunted Allied air forces and the powerful Royal Navy while the Germans ferried men and vehicles across the narrow waters to
the toe of Italy? The Royal Air Force, with the Royal Canadian Air Force's No. 331 (Medium Bomber) Wing under command, flew just 591 sorties over the straits during the evacuation. Such bombing, from high altitudes at night, against precision targets, produced predictably minor results. If the full weight of the North

African Strategic Air Force had been diverted from the Romanian oil fields more might have been accomplished but no one had the authority to require this. The tactical air force did attempt to interfere but the heavy concentration of anti-aircraft guns and the lack of urgency at the highest levels of command meant that operations were on a modest scale. The same lack of direction and fear of shore-based gun positions kept the navy well clear of the crossing points.

The Canadians who went into reserve on August 6 were not concerned with these large questions. They had suffered 500 fatalities since landing on the island and 1,300 men had been wounded. There were ample reinforcements so the rifle companies and tank squadrons could be rebuilt but the memory of young lives lost in the Sicilian sun was sharp and poignant. It took both real courage and a strong sense of duty for men released from the threat of death in battle to begin preparation for the next phase, the invasion of the Italian mainland.

The Sicilian campaign made a significant contribution to the Allied war effort. The landings in Sicily were an important factor in Hitler's decision to end offensive operations in Russia. The reinforcements the Germans sent to Italy, especially the Luftwaffe squadrons, demonstrated Hitler's sensitivity to developments on his southern front. If the Allies maintained pressure Hitler would have no choice except to transfer German divisions from France and Russia to Italy and the Balkans. If "Husky" was an operational failure it was a strategic victory of great value.

NAC 34159

Examining A General's Dismissal

Originally published, May/June 1997

The news of General Andrew McNaughton's retirement was announced on December 26, 1943. McNaughton's brief statement offered no explanation for the decision and the men and women of what was sometimes called "Andy's army" were surprised and confused. The following week, as McNaughton and his wife left First Canadian Army headquarters to return to Canada, thousands turned out to wave and cheer in a show of affection that no other general or politician could inspire.

McNaughton, who had presided over the creation of the overseas army, had not resigned voluntarily. The official explanation of retirement due to illness made little sense to Canadian reporters who met an obviously healthy McNaughton. And so, the Ottawa rumour mill went into high gear.

The story of McNaughton's dismissal tells us a great deal about the Canadian Army and its relationship with the British high command during the war. Now that the papers of all the key figures in the dispute are in the public domain there is not much doubt about what happened, but as is often the case with history, there is little agreement on what it all means.

McNaughton and his biographer, John Swettenham, were convinced that his dismissal was arranged by Canadian Defence Minister J.L. Ralston because of a disagreement over sending 5th Armoured Division to Italy. Contemporary historians, who have read the British and Canadian documents, recognize that the initiative came from British generals who argued that McNaughton lacked the qualities required to command an army in the field.

J.L. Granatstein explored these issues in his book *The Generals* and concluded that McNaughton was replaced for good military reasons. Granatstein's view is supported by Paul Dickson's

Major-General A.G.L. (Andrew) McNaughton, the father of the Canadian Army.

exhaustive study of the events for his biography on McNaughton's successor Harry Crerar. As well, John A. English, the outstanding analyst of Canadian military leadership, insists McNaughton was an amateur who failed to develop the professional knowledge required to train or command an army.

Regular readers of this "Canadian Military History In Perspective" series will not be surprised to learn that the issues seem much less clear cut to this writer. In 1939, when McNaughton was appointed to command 1st Canadian Division, there was broad consensus that he was the logical and indeed the inevitable choice. He had developed an outstanding reputation with the Canadian Corps in WW I and had laid the foundations for the postwar army.

An engineer who devised artillery techniques during WW I, McNaughton had a breadth of vision that even his detractors recognized. He was also familiar with both the theoretical and practical side of soldiering. As the overseas army expanded he was placed in command of 1st Canadian Corps and then–in April 1942–First Canadian Army.

The first sign of difficulties arose over his insistence that Canadian forces had to serve under Canadian command. Having watched Arthur Currie resist British attempts to feed the original Canadian Corps into battle division by division, McNaughton never let his British counterparts forget that he was the commander of a national army, not a colonial force under their control.

When reviewing these political disputes with General Sir Alan Brooke, the Chief of the Imperial General Staff, it is difficult not to have considerable sympathy for the Canadian general. McNaughton had a constitutional duty and a personal commitment to the autonomy of the Canadian Army while Brooke wanted to control all Commonwealth forces as if they were British units. Australia, New Zealand and South Africa accepted British direction, why were the Canadians so difficult?

The problem was compounded by the British belief that they knew and understood modern war. Brooke believed Canadian formations ought to be commanded by British generals particularly if British units might serve with them. This was not an argument that held much appeal for Canadians, or for the Americans when their turn came. The British Army had after all failed at virtually every task it undertook from 1940 to the Battle of El Alamein and it was not obvious why anyone should believe that British generals held the key to success on the battlefield. McNaughton also insisted on expressing his own views about the best strategy for winning the war. He made no secret of his support for the direct approach to liberating Europe that was favored by generals George C. Marshall and Dwight D. Eisenhower, but strongly opposed by the British military. When McNaughton agreed, at Churchill's invitation, to re-examine the Jupiter scheme–a projected invasion of Norway which the British generals had already rejected–he created further resentment, even though his report concluded that the plan was too hazardous.

The Chief of the Imperial General Staff was not the only powerful individual to clash with McNaughton. He found himself at odds with the Minister of National Defense J.L. Ralston, a distinguished WW I veteran who had commanded an infantry battalion at Vimy Ridge. From McNaughton's perspective, Ralston was prone to interfere in matters that ought to be left to the responsible officers. Ralston, McNaughton insisted, should stick to policy and leave the details to the professional head of Canada's overseas army. Again, it is hard to disagree with McNaughton. Ralston, a man of great ability, was respected for his commitment to the army but was notorious for his inability to delegate authority.

The two men also disagreed on the role to be played by the Canadian Army. Ralston and General Kenneth Stuart, the Chief of Defence Staff, were determined to get at least part of the army into action in 1943. McNaughton, meanwhile, was anxious to keep the army together and "did not recommend pressing for employment of forces merely to satisfy desire for activity...." The irony of administrators in Ottawa arguing that the morale of the troops would suffer unless some of the men saw action was not lost on McNaughton.

When Ralston convinced a wavering Mackenzie King to press for Canadian participation in the invasion of Sicily, he emphasized opinion in Canada, not morale problems. King, ever sensitive to domestic concerns, gave in.

McNaughton accepted this decision on the understanding that 1st Canadian Division would be returned to England to participate in the invasion of France. His attention now turned to the reorganization and training of the army for its role in Operation "Overlord". McNaughton was deeply concerned about the low priority given to army weapons production and the complacent attitude of officials in the British ministry of supply. He was particularly critical of British tank and anti-tank gun design and his criticism helped to lend a new urgency to army issues, though it won him few friends.

The first major task confronting McNaughton in 1943 was the reorganization of the 4th and 5th Canadian armoured divisions to fit the latest British model. Next came the challenge of forming 2nd Canadian Corps Headquarters and finding enough staff officers to make it work. This led to the fateful decision to use the new corps headquarters to control 5th Canadian and the Guards Armoured Divisons in a major exercise scheduled for March 1943.

Code-named "Spartan", the exercise was one of the largest ever to take place in Britain. It was planned as an opportunity to practice McNaughton's recently formed army headquarters in a complex offensive operation. To add another new headquarters to the mix may appear foolhardy, but exercises were supposed to be for learning and 2nd Canadian Corps needed the experience. "Spartan" began on March 4 as a dress rehearsal for the Canadian role in the invasion of the continent. The army's task was to break out of a bridgehead, exactly the role it would perform in 1944.

McNaughton rejected the obvious strategy believing correctly that his opponent could read a map and would prepare a trap in the open country west of Oxford. He ordered 1st Canadian Corps to seize a bridgehead across the Thames drawing the

enemy into battle. British 10th Corps then crossed the river forming one arm of the pincer.

Unfortunately, 2nd Canadian Corps was unable to complete the encirclement as its tanks and trucks became snarled in a monstrous traffic jam centred in the town of Malmesbury. "Spartan" ended without the decisive victory; nevertheless 1st Canadian Army officers thought they had done very well considering the inexperience of their headquarters and that of 2nd Canadian Corps. Historians disagree on McNaughton's performance in "Spartan". John A. English insists that the Canadian commander lacked "professional knowledge" and "failed to demonstrate a capacity for higher command." He acknowledges that much of the difficulty arose in 2nd Canadian Corps which did not receive its signal equipment until a few days before the exercise. However, English sees McNaughton as a hesitant leader quite unable to manage his command.

John Swettenham, McNaughton's biographer reached very different conclusions arguing that McNaughton's bold scheme to seize the initiative and encircle his opponent was evidence of superior generalship. Problems with traffic control and signals would be dealt with as 2nd Canadian Corps gained experience.

Canada's official historian C.P. Stacey was far more cautious, but his own observation of "Spartan" and subsequent study of the documents convinced him that McNaughton had done very well and had proven himself as a field commander.

Brooke was however highly critical of McNaughton's performance. And so it seems likely that the problems encountered in "Spartan", combined with Brooke's resentment of the Canadian general's nationalism, led him to prefer the more co-operative Harry Crerar as Canadian Army commander.

McNaughton's problems deepened when he refused to fire the commander of 2nd Canadian Corps, Lieutenant-General E.W. Sansom, as requested by the British. McNaughton agreed that Sansom had not done well in "Spartan", but insisted that he deserved a chance to lead the corps in another exercise. This may have been the final straw for Brooke who now began a not-to-subtle campaign to persuade the Canadian government to replace the troublesome McNaughton.

Whatever opinions one has of McNaughton it is surely evident that Brooke should have made his views known to McNaughton instead of lobbying behind his back. Brooke began the process at the Trident Conference in Washington, D.C., in May 1943. In a "casual conversation" with Stuart and Ralston he questioned McNaughton's fitness to command. Crerar, who owed his advancement to McNaughton, shared Brooke's doubts and entered into discussions on how to replace his mentor.

While these events unfolded, McNaughton found himself involved in a bitter dispute with General Bernard Montgomery who refused to allow McNaughton to visit Canadian forces in Sicily. Montgomery later explained that he did this after consulting General Guy Simonds, because such visits were likely to interfere with 1st Canadian Infantry Division's operations. However, at the time, McNaughton was simply informed that he was denied permission to land in Sicily. On his return to England, McNaughton spoke to Brooke who denied that the Canadian commander had any right to visit Canadian troops.

Brooke was more determined than ever to be free of this difficult Canadian. His diary for July 1943 contains several references to conversations with Stuart and Crerar about replacing McNaughton and an August entry notes a two-hour conversation with Ralston "discussing how we are to get rid of McNaughton."

The question had become more urgent because Ralston and Stuart were proposing that 5th Canadian Armoured Division and 1st Canadian Corps Headquarters be sent to Italy. Ralston appears to have genuinely believed that the war might end before May 1944 and he wanted more Canadians in action. Italy, he believed, was the only place where that could happen. Ralston informed the prime minister that the British "no longer had confidence in McNaughton's capacity to command troops" and preferred Crerar. Brooke elaborated on this view when he met with Mackenzie King at the Quebec Conference in

August 1943 and McNaughton's fate was sealed. In November, Ralston and Stuart crossed the Atlantic to inform the general that he would not lead the army in the field. One week later, McNaughton resigned.

What can be made of this at a distance of 53 years? McNaughton, in the words of Stacey, "was one of the most remarkable Canadians of his generation. He was a man of vast and far-ranging abilities, he had a singularly vivid and compelling personality and he was a great Canadian patriot.

When he lost command of the army he had created he was 56 years of age…it would be absurd to say he was burned out in 1943; but it is pretty evident he was tired…." Stacey goes on to suggest McNaughton was "hardly in a mental or physical state to undertake the responsibilities of high command in a great campaign" and that the "more workaday qualities of the less brilliant but solid Crerar were what the occasion required in 1944." Stacey adds one further point: "…it seems quite impossible to conceive of McNaughton as an army commander under Montgomery."

Perhaps I should allow Stacey, whose judgment was always sensible and balanced, the last word, but instead let me imagine a Canadian Army commanded by a man with outstanding leadership qualities and the ability to inspire men to greatness. Certainly McNaughton would have clashed with Montgomery, but the British general might have greatly benefited from a second opinion. Would McNaughton have accepted the limited resources and large tasks that Monty assigned to Crerar in 1944? Would the Canadians have felt differently about themselves and their contribution if McNaughton had led them into Germany and brought them home? The answers are not certain but the questions are worth asking because they focus on the subject of leadership, a topic of considerable importance for Canadians in 1943 and today.

The Invasion of Italy

Originally published, September/October 1997

The University of Edinburgh in Scotland has recently established a centre for WW II studies that could serve as a model for Canadian universities. Its mandate is "to promote knowledge and understanding of all aspects" of WW II and to "stimulate research into major themes and problems relating to war." To accomplish this, the centre–under director Paul Addison–has established a masters degree program that focuses on home fronts and battlefronts.

Addison also persuaded renowned spy novelist and popular historian Len Deighton to join the centre, and Deighton has written the foreword to a new book containing the papers presented at the 1995 conference on The Soldier's Experience of War. The book, titled *A Time To Kill* is described by Deighton as "the most stimulating collection of military history" he has yet encountered. As one of the contributors I must be appropriately modest about my own discussion of 1st Canadian Army in the Rhineland battle, but otherwise Deighton is right: This book is full of interesting, provocative essays.

The collection includes a number of articles on the war in Italy that help to provide some important perspectives on a campaign that was central to the experience of Canadians in WW II. For example, an article by Brian Sullivan examines the Italian soldier in combat and offers information on training, or lack of it, equipment and leadership instead of stereotypes about the Italians as fighting men. Another essay–appropriately titled "Matters of Honour"–examines the role of the Indian Army in the battles for Cassino and the Gothic Line. With thousands of young Canadians of South Asian descent in our schools and universities it is important to learn and teach about the role of the Indian soldier in the defeat of Nazi Germany. The 8th Indian Infantry Division fought alongside Canadians at Moro River, Ortona and elsewhere while 1st Canadian Armoured Brigade supported the 8th in the assault on the Gothic

Line. Their war was as heroic and costly as everyone else's and their story needs to be told. The author, Gerard Douds, concludes his account with a verse from a song sung in the 8th Division that tells part of that story.

Oh bury me at Cassino
My duty to England is done
And when you get back to Blighty
And you are drinking your whiskey and rum
Remember the old Indian soldier
When the war that he fought has been won!

A history conference held in the heart of Scotland could not help but address the particular experience of the Scottish soldier and the conference organizers invited Hamish Henderson, the soldier and poet, to discuss the impact of the war on the Scottish soldier.

Henderson served as an intelligence officer with 51st Highland Division in North Africa and Sicily. He wrote his deeply moving poem, The Highland Division's Farewell to Sicily, when the division was recalled to Britain for Operation "Overlord". The haunting chorus of one of the great poems of the war reads;

Then farewell ye banks of Sicily,
Fare ye weel, ye valley and shaw.
There's nae Jock will mourn
the kyles of ye
Puir bluidy swaddies are weary.

Henderson was also the author of "three-thirds of the original words" to the song D-Day Dodgers which became the theme of all British and Canadian troops in Italy. He recalled writing the verses to fit the tune of Lili Marlene after learning that Lady Nancy Astor had used the phrase D-Day Dodgers in a speech. Hamish Henderson, then sang the song in a light, true tenor voice that took people back to 1944.

The final paper on the long bloody crawl up the Italian peninsula was presented by Richard Holmes, one of the most interesting and innovative military historians in Britain. His recent book, *Riding the Retreat*, tells the story of the British Expeditionary Force's retreat from Mons, Belgium, interweaving the events of 1914 with his own experiences at retracing the route on

NAC 114482

Street fighting Campociaro, Italy October 1943.

horseback in the 1990s.

Holmes describes some of the basic realities of the war in Italy where the battlefield reminded war veterans of conditions they experienced on the Western Front in WW I. The Italian campaign, which lasted from July 10, 1943, to May 2, 1945, cost the Allies 320,995 men killed, wounded or taken prisoner. The German and Italian total–not counting those who surrendered at the capitulation–was 658,339. Of the 92,757 Canadians who served in Italy, 5,399 were killed, 19,486 were wounded and 1,004 were taken prisoner.

Holmes does not explore all dimensions of the soldiers' experience of war in Italy and there is much to be learned from other studies. Colonel Sydney Frost's outstanding memoir of his war service, *Once A Patricia*, includes a chapter simply titled Malaria. He writes: "Shortly after joining the scouts and snipers, I started having headaches ... my muscles ached and I started to run a fever. Severe chills racked my body, alternating with a fever of 105 degrees. It was obvious to everyone except me that I would have to be evacuated." Frost was one of more than 1,200 cases of malaria that afflicted 1st Canadian Division in July and August of 1943. The soldiers had been instructed to take mepacrine to prevent infection, but battle conditions did not always encourage this and after fighting through a highly malarial area the division was rested in an equally dangerous zone.

Malaria never reached these epidemic proportions again and in 1944 it was just one of the diseases that contributed to the extraordinary health problems that wreaked havoc on the Allied armies, including the Canadians. Official medical statistics show that in 1944 there were 831 disease-related admissions to medical units for every 1,000 Canadian soldiers serving in Italy. The leading problem, 143 admissions, was diseases of the digestive system, while jaundice or infectious hepatitis struck almost one in 10–nearly double the rate for malaria. Venereal disease accounted for 73 admissions per 1,000 while respiratory problems accounted for 60 skin diseases in 1944. Accidental injuries brought

the number of non-battle admissions to 910 per 1,000. Non-fatal battle casualties, including battle exhaustion, added another 210 per 1,000, creating the remarkable statistical truth that there were 1,091 admissions for every 1,000 Canadians serving in Italy.

Disease is a dimension of war that is rarely integrated into our accounts of strategy, but the implications are obvious. The decision to conduct a major campaign in Italy imposed extraordinary burdens on everyone involved. Military historians usually compare the number of combat troops engaged and conclude that tying down 20-odd German divisions with a similar number of Allied units was a good bargain. The difficulty was that maintaining Allied divisions at the end of a 1,000-mile supply line in a country like Italy required hundreds of thousands of support troops not to mention air, naval and merchant marine forces. For the Canadian Army, with its commitment to providing separate medical and psychiatric services, this also meant the buildup of no less than six general hospitals and a number of special units to deal with combat stress casualties. The war in Italy was not fought on the cheap.

The invasion of the Italian mainland began on September 3, 1943, with assaults by British and American troops at Salerno south of Naples. General Bernard Montgomery's Eighth Army, including 1st Canadian Division, made a virtually unopposed crossing of the narrow Strait of Messina to the toe of the Italian boot. The Canadians found themselves caught up in a frustratingly slow advance along narrow roads that quickly became congested with the vehicles of a motorized army. The slowness of the British and Canadian advance became a matter of urgency and controversy. Even the most generous interpretation of Montgomery's behaviour in ordering a lengthy pause while German counter-attacks threatened the Salerno beachhead questioned Montgomery's judgment and motives. The pressure was on when a group of journalists from 8th Army headquarters reached Salerno and reported that nothing opposed Montgomery's advance. The Canadians were ordered to seize Potenza, a railway junction 50 miles east of Salerno.

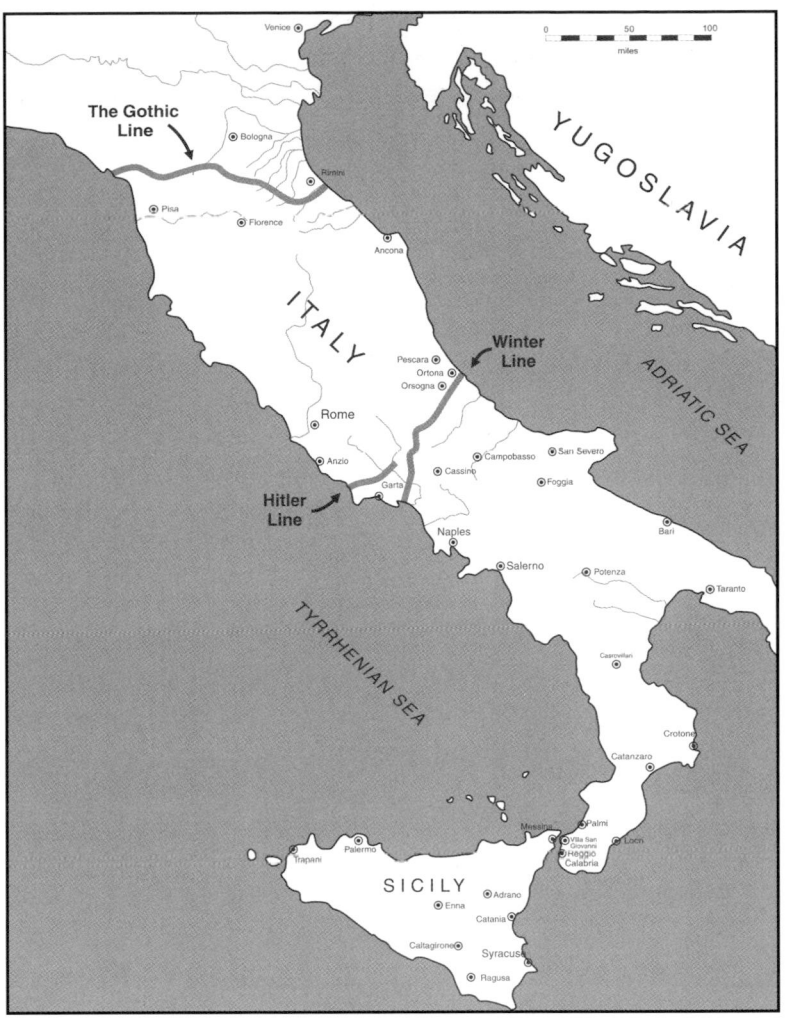

The Gothic Line

YUGOSLAVIA

ITALY

Winter Line

Hitler Line

ADRIATIC SEA

TYRRHENIAN SEA

SICILY

Venice
Bologna
Rimini
Pisa
Florence
Ancona
Pescara
Ortona
Onsogna
Rome
Anzio
Garta
Naples
Cassino
Campobasso
San Severo
Foggia
Bari
Salerno
Potenza
Taranto
Caprovillan
Crotone
Catanzaro
Messina
Palmi
Villa San Giovanni
Reggio Calabria
Loon
Palermo
Trapani
Adrano
Enna
Catania
Caltagirone
Syracuse
Ragusa

The Italian Campaign

This operation has recently been studied by Lee Windsor, a brilliant young historian who is re-examining Canada's role in the Italian campaign. His article on Boforce, which appeared in the Autumn 1995 issue of *Canadian Military History*, challenges those who question the combat effectiveness of the Canadian Army. He argues that "the thrust to take the town of Potenza is just one of the many examples of superior performance in the Italian campaign."

Boforce, named for Lieutenant-Colonel Pat Bogert, CO of the West Nova Scotia Regiment, was developed as a fully motorized flying column. It was made up of the West Novas and Calgary Tanks, artillery and anti-tank guns, plus a platoon of Saskatoon Light Infantry with their medium machine-guns. The advance moved quickly by skirting around blown bridges. By the evening of September 19, after just 36 hours on

the road, Boforce reached the high ground above Potenza. General Guy Simonds, the divisional commander, ordered Bogert to attack that night.

The Germans had already begun their withdrawal north, but they held onto Potenza with elements of 1st Parachute Division The battle for Potenza lasted until the afternoon of the 20th when the enemy withdrew to avoid being cut off. The Canadian thrust had surprised the Germans and forced them to retreat much sooner than they had planned. The success of Boforce suggests 8th Army could have moved much more quickly north if ordered to. It also demonstrates the growing professionalism of the Canadian Army and the high quality of its leadership. Guy Simonds had taken Montgomery's belated orders and created an effective all-arms battle group of the kind the German army is always being praised for employing. Unfortunately, Simonds fell victim to jaundice, an infection that has no respect for rank, and was forced to enter hospital and hand over 1st Division to Chris Vokes.

Canadian casualties at Potenza were very light by the standards of later battles: Six killed and 21 wounded. It was the civilians who suffered the greatest losses with as many as 2,000 killed in air raids directed against a town that functioned as a railway centre and route for reinforcements. The Italian people would continue to pay a high price for Mussolini's grandiose dreams.

After Salerno and the liberation of Naples, the Allied high command appeared confused and uncertain. The invasion of mainland Italy had been justified by the promise of an immediate surrender of Italian forces and the prospect of establishing airfields for the heavy bombers in the Foggia plains. As a bonus some German troops, who would otherwise be fighting on the Eastern Front or strengthening the Atlantic Wall in France, would have to remain in Italy to defend the industrial centres in the north.

Allied planning in October reflected the belief that no major operations were required. General Harold Alexander, the overall general commander, limited his objective to "the seizing of vital areas" for "all-weaker airfields, ports and centres of road communication." The retreating Germans would be harassed by light mobile forces, and the Allies planned to enter Rome before Christmas.

The Canadian role in this projected advance was to begin with the capture of Campobasso. For the first phase a Canadian battle group under Lieutenant-Colonel F.D. Adams of the Princess Louise Dragoon Guards co-operated with the famous Popski's Private Army, an irregular force that relied on jeep-mounted machine guns and bold, rapid movement. The Canadians pooled their resources with the Russo-Belgian commander Major Peniakoff. This created a combined armoured-car and jeep force that moved out ahead of the rest of the division.

The enemy was trying to delay the Allied advance, not block it. The battles on the road to Campobasso were short and sharp, but sometimes very costly. Most of them have been forgotten except by the men who were there. Take for example the capture of Motta Montecorvino and Mount Sambuco. The village was attacked by two squadrons of Calgary Tanks, part of yet another battle group, commanded by Lieutenant-Colonel C.H. Neroutsos. The infantry could not join the armour as the approaches were swept by machine-gun fire, so the tanks withdrew.

The 2nd Canadian Field Regiment, which had been stuck in traffic on the narrow east west road, dignified as Highway 17, arrived and shortly after 3 a.m. on October 2 the guns opened up on the village. The Royal Canadian Regiment, which had been repulsed earlier that night, used the artillery and a violent thunderstorm to rush the village forcing the German paratroopers to withdraw to Mount Sambuco, a mile to the west. This ridge of the Daunia Mountains dominated Highway 17 and the roads north. So, the Germans appeared determined to fight for it.

Brigadier Howard Graham directed a systematic assault. The Hastings and Prince Edward Regiment moved cross-country to the slopes of the mountain while the RCR worked its way through a series of muddy pastures to the south end of the ridge. That night the "Hasty Ps" scaled Mount Sambuco and the RCR took its objective. The official history reports that "there was bitter hand-to-hand fighting in the darkness and rain but by daylight on October 3 the whole ridge was in our hands." The two nights fighting had cost the brigade 78 casualties.

The next hill was just two miles away and so a new attack–with the 48th Highlanders of Canada in the lead–was mounted. Volturava fell quickly but just ahead was the Fortore River, sure to be defended. Fortunately 3rd Brigade was available to take over and the men of 1st Brigade could pull back to find a place to sleep.

These bald accounts of battalion level actions can not possibly convey the reality of the soldier's experience of war. Let us hope that young historians will take up the challenge and tell some of the hundreds of stories that will illuminate and give meaning to the contribution of those who sang the Canadian version of Hamish Henderson's song:

We fought in Agira, a holiday with pay;
Jerry brought his bands out to cheer us
on our way,
Showed us the sights and gave us tea
We all sang songs, the beer was free.
We are the D-Day dodgers,
in sunny Italy.

The Battle For Ortona

Originally published, November/December 1997

The actual terrain over which a battle is fought may be the most important primary source of information available to the historian, but ground must be related to weather. Canadians who visit Italy's Adriatic coast are unlikely to arrive in the grey of winter, when the rains turn rivers into racing torrents and the ground into thick, clinging mud. Yet this was the reality that confronted the men of the 1st Canadian, 8th Indian and New Zealand divisions in their struggle for Ortona, Villa Grande and Orsogna in December 1943.

It all began with General Dwight Eisenhower's telegram to Winston Churchill, October 25, 1943: "My principal commanders and I are in complete agreement that it is essential for us to retain the initiative until the time approaches for mounting "Overlord", otherwise the enemy will himself seize the initiative and may force us on the defensive prematurely, thus enabling him to withdraw divisions from our front in time to oppose "Overlord". If we can keep him on his heels until early spring, then the more divisions he uses in a counter-offensive against us the better it will be for "Overlord" and it then makes little difference what happens to us if "Overlord" is a success."

Next came General Harold Alexander's directive to General Bernard Montgomery's Eighth Army. Alexander realized that Fifth Army, facing Monte Cassino and the Liri Valley, had little chance of moving on Rome unless the enemy was outflanked. Eventually this would lead to the landings at Anzio in January 1944, but initially Alexander wanted Eighth Army to accomplish the task by seizing control of the main east-west highway (the Via Valeria) that ran from Pescara on the Adriatic to Rome. If Montgomery could gain control of the highway, the German army's lines of communication would be threatened, Cassino quickly abandoned, and Fifth Army's advance resumed.

The Via Valeria was just 22 miles north of the Sangro River, where Eighth Army was preparing for a new advance, so those who planned battles on large-scale maps had little doubt the Allies would be in Rome for Christmas. After all, 8th Army had advanced 400 miles to reach the Sangro. How difficult could it be to push on to Pescara?

Unfortunately, the Germans were constructing a series of defensive positions–collectively known as the Winter Line–and had been ordered to "fight for every house and tree." The first position, the Bernhardt Line, was just three miles north of the Sangro, where the Li Colli ridge paralleled the river valley. Montgomery gave the task of breaching this position to 8th Indian and 78th British divisions, with the attack set for November 20. On the 16th the rains began, and the river quickly lost its banks. A 150-foot-wide stream became a flood zone 1,000 yards across. The engineers worked miracles to bridge the river; the attack began just a week late.

The enemy was quickly overcome, though at a terrible cost: 2,500 men on each side. Realizing the Eighth Army was mounting a major offensive, German commander Field Marshal Albert Kesselring ordered his reserves, 90th Panzer Grenadier Division and 1st Parachute Division, to defend the coastal sector. A new line based on the Ortona-Orsogna road was to be built and held, to the bitter end.

Kesselring's subordinates employed their "unbreakable" Enigma code machines to organize these changes, unaware that British codebreakers at Bletchley Park were speedily decrypting their secrets. The result, known as Ultra intelligence, was made available to Montgomery in time to plan for the next stage. Clearly, both 78th and 8th Indian divisions needed rest and reinforcement, so the New Zealand and Canadian divisions took over the front. The New Zealanders, commanded by the feisty, self-confident Bernard Freyberg, a WW I Victoria Cross holder, were allotted Orsogna.

Ultra decrypts reported the exact location of the boundary between the two German divisions defending the forward line, but the enemy was getting suspicious. Kesselring reminded his commanders, "The enemy always comes on our boundaries...the Devil knows how he always finds out where they are," so this time the meeting point at the village of Castelfretano would be reinforced.

The battles for Orsogna were among the most difficult of the Italian campaign. The New Zealand Division, made up of two infantry and one armoured brigade, was too weak in riflemen to overcome the German defences. A stalemate developed. The New Zealand official historian suggested that "the Germans were willing to sell ground, but only at a price the New Zealanders were not willing to pay." After losing 1,200 men, including more than one-third of the division's infantry, there was little choice but to stop.

The 1st Canadian Division was well rested and up to strength. The new divisional commander Chris Vokes, who had replaced Guy Simonds in November was a loud, profane, energetic brigade commander who had received much credit for the outstanding performance of 2nd Canadian Infantry Brigade in Sicily. Vokes critics, and there are many, point out that the brigade turned in a consistently superior performance no matter who was at headquarters. In 1942 Montgomery had singled out the brigade for praise, adding that the "Seaforths (Seaforth Highlanders of Canada) have the best officers, PPCLI (Princess Patricia's Canadian Light Infantry) have the best non-commissioned officers, Edmontons (Loyal Edmonton Regiment) have the best men." Could Vokes do as well with a division?

Vokes approached his first divisional battle with enthusiasm. The rain had let up and the Moro River, the first obstacle, could be forded at any point on the two-mile front. The junction of coastal highway 16 and the Ortona-Orsogna road was just seven miles away; he hoped to be there in 72 hours. Vokes ordered 2nd Brigade, now commanded by Brigadier Bert Hoffmeister,

to make the main effort against San Leonardo and Villa Rogatti. Meanwhile, 1st Brigade would try to draw the enemy to the coastal highway. Both attacks went in on the night of December 5-6 without any artillery support, to achieve surprise. By nightfall the next day, the Seaforths and PPCLI had been forced back by a series of well organized counter-attacks. Only one battalion, from the Hastings and Prince Edward Regiment, was still across the river. The diversion now became the key to unlocking the German defences.

Corps commander Lieutenant-General Charles Allfrey sent the 21st Indian Brigade to take over the Canadians' left flank and secure Villa Rogatti, allowing Vokes to concentrate his forces. The Desert Air Force, including Royal Canadian Air Force Squadron 417 commanded by Bert Houle, joined in the preparations. On the afternoon of December 8, the Royal Canadian Regiment launched a wide right hook out of the Hastings bridgehead. The newly arrived German paratroopers had just started their own attack on the "Hasty Ps", and the two forces clashed furiously. While this battle raged, the 48th Highlanders quickly moved to the edge of San Leonardo and established a firm base for a morning attack on the village.

The next day was one of the hardest of the campaign, as the enemy put in repeated counter-attacks all across the front. The Calgary Regiment, supporting the Seaforths' main thrust, lost 27 of its 51 tanks in providing the kind of close support that can mean life or death to the infantry. In the streets of San Leonardo, Major E.A.C. Amy's squadron, reduced to just four tanks, knocked out the last German armour at ranges of less than 100 yards. Amy reported that one Seaforth soldier ran up to a tank, patted it on the side and said: "You big cast-iron son of a bitch, I could kiss you."

The Indian troops, attacking 1,000 yards to the east, ran into the same kind of demonic fury. They carved out a small bridgehead and fended off counter-attacks as engineers from the 69 Field Company Bengal Sappers built the "impossible bridge." When it proved impossible

A Sherman tank of the Three Rivers Regiment, Ortona.

to assemble a Bailey bridge from the south side, the sappers "manhandled their equipment to the enemy bank and built their bridge backwards." With San Leonardo lost, the enemy withdrew to the Ortona-Orsogna road where the defenders occupied a low ridge overlooking a ravine known to Canadians as The Gully. For the next eight days the Canadians beat their heads against this position in a series of single battalion attacks that resulted in close to 1,000 casualties. These attacks failed largely because the artillery was unable to meet the demands placed upon it.

Field artillery regiments, with their 25-pounder guns and medium regiments employing 4.5-inch guns, fired more than 3,000 tons of shells at the enemy—but much of it was in vain. Brigadier Bruce Matthews, the division's commander, Royal Artillery, had cautioned Vokes about the inaccuracy of the survey that was the basis of Italian topographical maps. If a feature was 500 metres distant from the position on the map, unobserved fire was of limited value. Even when fire could be corrected, winds from the Adriatic and drastic temperature changes played havoc with fire plans.

The stalemate was finally broken not by fire and movement but by manoeuvre. A track leading around the German right flank was used to send the Royal 22nd Regiment and a squadron of Ontario Regiment tanks to seize Casa Berardi. The achievement of the small band of Van Doos, under Captain Paul Triquet, and the four surviving tanks, commanded by Major H.A. Smith, is one of the most famous episodes in Canadian military history. Triquet's leadership, epitomized by his battle-cry "Ils ne passeront pas", earned him the Victoria Cross.

With Casa Berardi as a base the rest of the ridge could be attacked systematically. The corps commander met with Vokes and urged him to organize a major attack. The repulse of the New Zealanders and the 8th Indian Division's slow progress meant that all 8th Army hopes for a breakthrough to Pescara were invested in the Canadians. General Allfrey had a heart-to-heart

talk with Vokes and "warned him he was tiring out his division and producing nothing because of lack of co-ordination." Allfrey insisted it was the Royal Artillery commander's responsibility to develop and control the fire plan. Vokes accepted the advice and allowed Matthews to create fire plans for two large-scale attacks out of the Van Doo position. The 48th Highlanders, striking to the northeast, got accurate fire support and quickly reached their objective. The barrage leading the RCR to the main German pivot position at Cider crossroads was wildly inaccurate, however, with shells falling short and wide. Matthews ordered the guns to fire 400 metres forward, leaving the RCR to face what one officer called a "death trap." By the next morning, the gunners had made the necessary changes and two RCR reserve companies took the crossroads in a quick, decisive thrust.

The German paratroopers had lost control of the Ortona road, but their orders "to fight for every house and tree" remained in force. Montgomery was now employing two corps with elements of four divisions on a 12-mile front. He hoped the 8th Indian Division would make the main effort through Villa Grande, outflanking Ortona, but it took five December days of bitter fighting to claim the village on December 27. By then, Hoffmeister's 2nd Brigade was committed to a pitched battle in the streets of Ortona.

Historian Shaun Brown provided a most valuable study of Ortona in an article originally published, in *Canadian Military History* about the Loyal Edmonton Regiment at war. Brown's father, the late Major-General George Brown, was a company commander at Ortona, and the author's interviews with Brown, Lieutenant-Colonel Jim Stone and other veterans of the Loyal Eddies give special insight into what became one of the most famous battles of the Italian campaign.

At dawn on December 21, two under strength companies and a half-squadron of Three Rivers Regiment tanks moved cautiously up the main street towards the first of three large public squares. By mid-afternoon the advance had slowed to a halt, and Hoffmeister sent a compa-

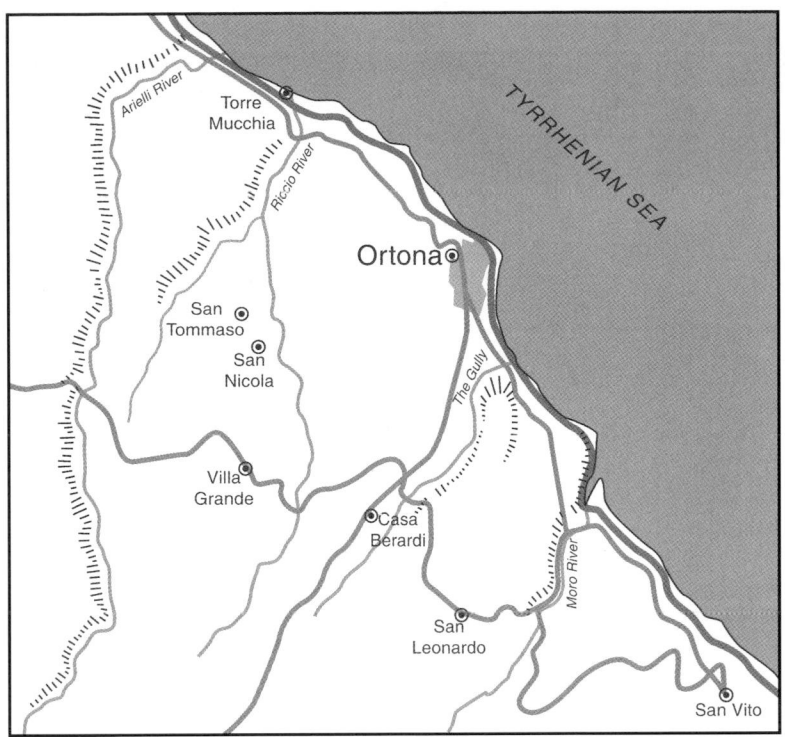

The Moro River, the "Gully" and Ortona – the famous Canadian battlefields of 1943.

...ny of Seaforths to help. The next morning it was apparent the German resistance had stiffened and Hoffmeister committed the balance of the Seaforths, assigning each battalion to half the town.

The Canadians now fought for Ortona house by house, often fighting from the top floor down. They used a "mouse-holing" technique–blasting through walls, lobbing grenades through the gaps and then using more grenades to move down the stairs. Here the Canadians wrote the book on street-fighting. After the war, former Seaforths commander Colonel S.W. Thomson recalled that the standard training film for British and Commonwealth forces, *Fighting In Built-up Areas*, was based on interviews with Seaforth and Edmonton veterans.

War correspondents anxious to cover the last phase of a month-long campaign arrived in Ortona and quickly revised their initial optimistic reports. Ortona became "little Stalingrad" as radio journalist Matthew Halton and reporter Ralph Allen wrote feature stories on the battle. Christopher Buckley, a British correspondent whose beautifully written 1945 book *The Road To Rome* should be reprinted, insisted "a painter of genius, Goya perhaps"

was needed to record the poignant images of Ortona. In one "half-darkened room," he wrote, "there were five or six Canadian soldiers, there were old women and there were innumerable children. The children clambered over the Canadian soldiers and clutched them convulsively every time one of our anti-tank guns fired down the street.... Soon each of us had a squirming, terrified child in our arms."

The rifle companies had begun the operation at little better than half-strength, so the arrival of reinforcements was particularly welcome. The Edmontons got a draft of 75 men from the Cape Breton Highlanders on Christmas Eve, "tremendously good soldiers" who fitted in right away. The end was now in sight; Kesselring insisted that "we do not want to defend Ortona decisively" and authorized a withdrawal. With 90 per cent of Ortona in Canadian hands and 1st Brigade threatening to cut off any retreat, there was little choice.

Ortona was a victory for all of the Canadian troops–and all Canadians. Ordinary men, leaving civilian life behind because they were needed, had forged regimental extended families and small cohesive sub-units that fought with skill and determination. Looking back, Major-General Brown spoke of mutual confidence between officers and men "built on the rock of accomplishment."

Battle Exhaustion In WW II

Originally published, January/February 1998

When 1st Canadian Division veterans recall the Italian campaign, memories of Ortona and the winter that followed are never far from the surface. The battles of December 1943 produced casualties on a scale that reminded men of the western front in 1916. One month of combat cost 1st Division 176 officers and 2,163 other ranks killed, wounded or missing. A further 1,617 all ranks were admitted to hospitals as sick, including more than 500 men diagnosed as suffering from battle exhaustion. These losses were concentrated in the rifle companies of the nine infantry battalions and as 1944 began most companies operated at half-strength.

There was little that Major-General Chris Vokes and his staff could do about the physically sick or wounded men in the care of the Royal Canadian Army Medical Corps. And although it accounted for more than one in four non-fatal casualties, few people understood what "battle exhaustion" was.

In 1943 most people were still using the WW I term "shell shock" to describe men who broke under the stress of combat and ceased to function as soldiers. British army psychiatrists insisted that a new label, which encouraged men to believe the condition was temporary and treatable, had to be devised. At first the term "Not yet diagnosed (nervous)" was used, but during the retreat to El Alamein, Egypt, cases were described as suffering from "exhaustion." In their medical notes doctors still distinguish between simple fear states, anxiety neuroses and campaign neuroses that hit soldiers who had served in combat for several years, but battle exhaustion became the term of choice.

The staff of General Bernard Montgomery's Eighth Army, including its medical officers, were reluctant to introduce forward psychiatry, using specially designated casualty clearing stations. They believed it would encourage men to give in to their fears. The Australians disagreed. Their experience during the siege at the Libyan port of Tobruk in 1941 convinced them that early treatment within sound of guns was highly effective. Rest, sedation and frank discussion of the need to discipline fear encouraged many soldiers to resume duty.

In 1942, 9th Australian Division used a casualty clearing station to treat men with battle exhaustion. It required that patients contribute a pint of blood as part of the treatment process "to atone for the breakdown" and "to feel that he remained a useful member of the group."

The United States Army arrived in North Africa completely unprepared for combat stress casualties. American psychiatrists had convinced themselves that personnel selection would eliminate men predisposed to "anxiety neurosis." The shock of combat at Kasserine Pass and the battles for Tunis shattered this illusion producing hundreds of psychiatric cases. Colonel Fred Hanson was brought to North Africa to organize treatment of what the U.S. Army decided to call combat exhaustion. Hanson, who was studying with the famous neurosurgeon Wilder Penfield at the Montreal Neurological Institute when war broke out, had joined the Canadian Army serving as a neuropsychiatrist at No. 1 Neurological Hospital in Basingstoke, England.

The hospital, which was also known as "No. 1 Nuts", expanded to include plastic surgery, but the bulk of its patients were admitted for mental problems. Hanson and most of the Canadian psychiatrists who worked at Basingstoke were convinced that intense combat would produce large numbers of acute psychiatric casualties.

They believed that while such casualties would occur among men who had previous histories of nervousness and instability many normal men would also suffer breakdowns. Every man had a limited store of courage to draw from and some would use up their reserves quickly. During the Dunkirk evacuation hundreds of men broke under an accumulation of physical and mental strain developing the classic symptoms of war neurosis; listless apathy, terrifying nightmares, depression and a pronounced startle reaction to the least noise. Few of those who were hospitalized would ever be fit to return to combat.

Many psychiatrists were convinced that more men could be returned to combat if treatment was provided before the symptoms became fixed. This approach came to be summed up in three words: proximity, immediacy and expectancy. Exhaustion should be dealt close to the action, as quickly as possible and in an atmosphere that encouraged the soldier to see his condition as temporary.

This was the official Canadian view when 1st Canadian Division left for the Mediterranean as the only unit to have its own divisional psychiatrist. Major Arthur Manning Doyle had trained at Basingstoke and was well prepared to practice the principles of forward psychiatry advocated there. He found little to do in Sicily where the exhaustion cases, following British practice, were quickly evacuated. Doyle did not hear about the notorious incident when General George Patton slapped a hospitalized soldier who said he "just couldn't take it". He only learned about it when a story appeared in the press and Patton was forced to apologize. But Doyle was well aware that many Canadian officers also believed that discipline, not medical treatment, was the answer to soldiers suffering from combat exhaustion.

As the Canadians began their advance to the Moro River, Doyle established his treatment unit in the ruins of the village of Rocca, north of the Sangro River. "It was surrounded by our batteries," he wrote, "and a day-long barrage was going on almost constantly." This settled the question of proximity, but events were soon to overwhelm hopes of immediacy or expectancy. The reality of intense combat over a prolonged period produced 226 psychiatric casualties in a single week and on one memorable day Doyle "examined 57 patients and still could not keep abreast of the deluge." He quickly decided to evacuate all but the most hopeful cases to a British hospital well behind the lines.

The flood of battle exhaustion cases at Ortona transformed Doyle's ideas about psychiatric casualties. Brief interviews with scores of frightened and shaky men persuaded him that "84 per cent of all cases…were suffering from some form of psychiatric disorder prior to military service." When the corps commander visited Doyle to ask about the high number of psychiatric casualties he was assured that "the division had now had a good and overdue house cleaning and the morale of the troops in general was good."

Doyle's sudden reversal of Canadian doctrine on combat stress had a significant effect on manpower policy in Italy. After Ortona, divisional medical and staff officers accepted Doyle's view that large numbers of battle exhaustion casualties were inevitable given the quality of the replacements sent to Italy. In 1944, while the division was in a defensive role north of Ortona, Doyle treated 30 to 35 psychiatric casualties a week. He assigned most of them to non-combat duties. By April 1944, 1,234 battle exhaustion cases had been evacuated and less than one third had been returned to their units. The rest were assigned to tasks in the rear areas, and Special Employment companies were created to administer them.

Vokes took a very different view of the crisis in morale that was affecting his division. He argued that his "infantry units will not be in fit condition to undertake further intensive operations until they have had a period of rest free of operational commitments, during which they can carry out intensive training." Instead of rest and retraining, the rifle companies were required to undertake aggressive patrolling and spend days in the frozen ground under mortar fire. Some men–67 were identified–decided to inflict wounds on themselves, others went absent without leave, the vast majority groused and endured, and found strength in friendships and youthful optimism.

The arrival of 5th Armoured Division and 1st Canadian Corps Headquarters did little to alter this situation. The new division's infantry battalions were needed in the line and the "spit and polish" directives sent out by corps headquarters made General Harry Crerar and his successor, Lieutenant-General E.L.M. Burns, less than popular with the veterans. Fifth Division's first operation north of Ortona–the "Arielli Show"–was a costly failure and patrols proved equally fruitless. No one seemed able to explain the purpose of such battles and morale plummeted.

The Allied attempt to end the stalemate in Italy with a "left hook" amphibious assault at Anzio failed to achieve its primary purpose because the enemy used its reserves to seal off the beachhead. In the larger scheme of things, where all aspects of the Italian campaign were judged for their impact on the forthcoming invasion of France, Anzio was a success. German units could not be withdrawn from Italy. For the men fighting in Italy the crisis at Anzio meant the 8th Army would launch a major offensive in the Liri Valley.

Operation "Diadem" began on May 11, 1944 with 4th British and 8th Indian divisions cracking through the Gustav Line. The lead Indian Army brigades were supported by Canadian armoured regiments and were on their objectives in four days . First Canadian Division took over the lead advancing rapidly to the Hitler Line. Here the fighting reached Ortona levels of intensity. The Germans had prepared their main defensive positions with care employing thousands of anti-personnel mines, especially S mines that did not explode at foot level, but were catapulted up to chest height before exploding. Sown amongst the barb wire defenses they helped to slow down all attempts to attack German positions on the higher ground. On May 23, 2nd Brigade, which thought it had seen it all at Ortona, lost 543 men. One hundred and sixty two killed, 306 wounded and 75 taken prisoner. Historian Shaun Brown has noted that this was the worst single day of the war for any Canadian brigade in Italy.

The preparations for the assault on the Hitler Line had included new policies on psychiatric matters. Burns and his medical advisers rejected Doyle's assumptions about the causes of exhaustion casualties and "banished him to corps maintenance area well away from the front." Corps believed that tighter discipline and a restoration of forward psychiatry using regimental medical officers would minimize the problem. In one sense they were right, significant numbers of mild cases were treated well forward and were able to return to their units, but as the battle continued more and more men had to be sedated and evacuated. By the end of June, 1st Division had suffered 1,601 casualties and 23 per cent were due to battle exhaustion. While fighting its first sustained action, 5th Division lost 785 men during May. Thirteen per cent of them were psychiatric casualties.

It ought to have been apparent to all that battle exhaustion ratios rose and fell with the intensity and duration of combat. Discipline, good leadership and high unit morale could help to limit the consequences of prolonged stress, but factors such as the loss of a close friend could precipitate a breakdown in the bravest of men.

Back in Britain, 1st Canadian Army was preparing for Operation "Overlord" and trying to draw lessons from the Italian experience. The senior Canadian psychiatrist, Colonel F.H. Van Nostrand, was a WW I veteran known for his blunt language and common sense. He had visited the Italian front and knew that the fighting in Normandy might produce similar levels of exhaustion casualties. He believed that men who had shown signs of instability in training should be "weeded out" but doubted that this would make much difference. Bob Gregory, the psychiatrist he assigned to 3rd Canadian Division was quite willing to weed people out, but during three months of screening units he was able to identify only 127 men in a division of 20,000 who "were apt to give trouble in action."

He reported that the morale in 3rd Division was excellent. "The troops are relaxed and in the highest spirits." They had complete confidence in their ability to breach the Atlantic Wall.

"They feel," he wrote, "they have the firepower, the naval support and air superiority." The achievements of the division on D-Day and the advance inland suggest that their confidence was justified and despite setbacks morale remained high and battle exhaustion casualties low.

The situation changed dramatically by the third week in June 1944. The Canadians and their D-Day partners, 3rd and 50th British divisions, occupied positions north of Caen that were under continuous mortar and artillery fire. At Hell's Corners and at a dozen other places, front-line battalions suffered a steady stream of casualties including men suffering from battle exhaustion. While the men waited, the Germans constructed evermore elaborate defensive positions, turning villages like Buron, St. Contest and Authie into fortified strongpoints. On July 4th at Carpiquet, 8th Brigade, reinforced by the Royal Winnipeg Rifles, advanced across open ground to seize the village and airfield. Major J.E. Anderson of the North Shore (New Brunswick) Regiment spoke for everyone when he wrote: "I am sure that at some time during the attack every man felt he could not go on. Men were being killed or wounded on all sides and the advance seemed pointless as well as hopeless. I never realized until the attack at Carpiquet how far discipline, pride of unit, and above all, pride in oneself and family, can carry a man even when each step forward meant possible death."

But not everyone could endure battles like Carpiquet and when the main attack on Caen was launched four days later, medical officers described battle exhaustion as the outstanding problem facing the division.

By the standards of Italy the exhaustion ratios were still very low, more like one in eight than one in four, but by the end of July the crisis reached Ortona proportions.

After eight weeks of combat, 3rd Division had lost the equivalent of its total strength in riflemen and 3/4 of the casualties were concentrated in the rifle companies.

Under these conditions battle exhaustion was bound to be a major problem and the senior medical officer, Colonel M.C. Watson, reported that without a rest period and time to re-organize the rifle companies, the division would face a major collapse of morale.

Gregory and Major Burdett McNeel, who commanded the corps exhaustion unit, were sensible men who understood that intense and prolonged combat could traumatize anyone. They did their best to reassure their patients and only those who were both willing and able were returned to combat. The British and U.S. armies experienced similar problems and implemented comparable treatment programs.

The German army took another route. The Nazi-inspired code of military law demanded the death sentence or long prison terms for offences that included battle exhaustion. By June 1944 more than 7,000 German soldiers had been executed for such crimes and the toll would grow throughout the last months of the war.

Attack On
The Gothic Line

Originally published, September 1994

War at the sharp end is a series of isolated moments in which a handful of men draw upon their reserves of courage to overcome the terrain, the enemy and their own fear. On September 1, 1944, 11th Platoon of Princess Patricia's Canadian Light Infantry was one of the many small units at the tip of the spear. They were part of Operation "Olive", Eighth Army's attack on the Gothic Line. Tens of thousands of men were involved but 11th Platoon was very much on its own.

The battalion had crossed the River Foglia without meeting any opposition, but between the banks of the river and the Pesaro road the enemy had constructed a barrier of wire obstacles and mines. The West Nova Scotia Regiment had already come to grief on this minefield and 1st Division's advance was in danger of stalling.

Lieutenant Egan Chambers, the PPCLI platoon commander, went forward on his hands and knees exploring a path that bypassed the obstacles. The trail was sown with *schu* mines, small wooden boxes with just enough explosive to blow off a man's foot. The Germans had developed these difficult-to-detect mines to maim rather than kill. A wounded soldier had to be helped to safety, taking extra men away from combat.

Chambers organized his platoon in single file, telling each man to follow exactly in his footsteps. The strange procession began to move as the first faint rays of light broke through the darkness. The platoon, and behind them the rest of "B" Company, advanced step by very careful step. Chambers was almost across the field when mortar and spandau fire began. The last yards were taken at a quick pace and three men were hurt by *schu* mines. Chambers was knocked down and wounded by one explosion, but he was able to form up the platoon and lead it on a quick attack across an anti-tank ditch

and into the village. The buildings were in rubble, providing cover against German artillery. The counter-attack was beaten off with the aid of 5th Division tanks.

Chambers was awarded an immediate Military Cross, for his "coolness in action" and "bold and skilful handling" of the platoon. His courage and that of the men of "B" Company surely call for a less restrained tribute! Chambers' leadership and daring were extraordinary and the men of "B" Company all endured the same nerve-racking tension. When the first mines exploded, there was no panic and everyone kept it together moving on to the objective.

The PPCLI was not the only Canadian battalion assaulting the Gothic Line, and "B" Company was not alone in penetrating the outer defences. The Perth Regiment took Point 111 with a bayonet charge. Other regiments of Bert Hoffmeister's mighty maroon machine, 5th Canadian Armoured Division, were equally successful. The 8th Princess Louise's (N.B.) Hussars and the Cape Breton Highlanders cracked one of the key German positions at Monte Marone, where concrete-emplaced anti-tank guns in steel tank turrets covered the approaches. By the afternoon of September 1 the Canadians had broken through the Gothic Line on a mile-wide front. The coastal plain, south of Rimini, was within reach.

Enemy reserves in the form of 26th Panzer Division arrived to try to reclaim Point 204 but the Perths and Lord Strathcona's Horse held off all counter-attacks. The next day the Red Patch Division was on the move. The Royal 22nd Regiment secured Point 131 while the Seaforth Highlanders of Canada, working with British tanks, circled north beyond the Gothic Line defences. The Loyal Edmonton Regiment took the next bound, racing to Monte Luro which fell as the Irish Regiment of Canada entered Tomba Di Pesaro.

The enemy had been taken by surprise throughout 8th Army's sector. Albert Kesselring, the German commander-in-chief, was convinced

LCMSDS

Major-General
B.M. 'Bert'
Hoffmeister, Italy,
May 1944.

the Allies were planning another amphibious assault and was slow to react. He was persuaded the coastal advance was the real thing only after learning that both Canadian divisions were involved. Kesselring and his subordinates believed the Allies would rely on the Canadians to lead any major offensive. When he was certain they were in action, reinforcements were rushed to the Adriatic sector and new defensive lines established.

The first days of September were proud moments for 1st Canadian Corps. Men shrugged off fatigue, ignored the heat and endured the white dust which lay "like powdered snow" three to four inches deep. It was impossible to see moving tanks, as they were enveloped in turbulent clouds of chalk; so were the men. But despite the choking dust, thirst and danger, "the same old time-worn humor and perpetual good nature" persisted.

Before the battle, the corps commander Major-General E.L.M. Burns had urged "everyone,...to press forward until the enemy is destroyed; to strike and pursue until he can fight no longer. Then and only then shall we have won what we, as Canadians, have been fighting for –security, peace and honour for our country". Front-line soldiers are rarely impressed with messages from senior officers but Burns understood the mood of confident expectation within the Canadian Corps. This was to be the battle that ended the Italian campaign.

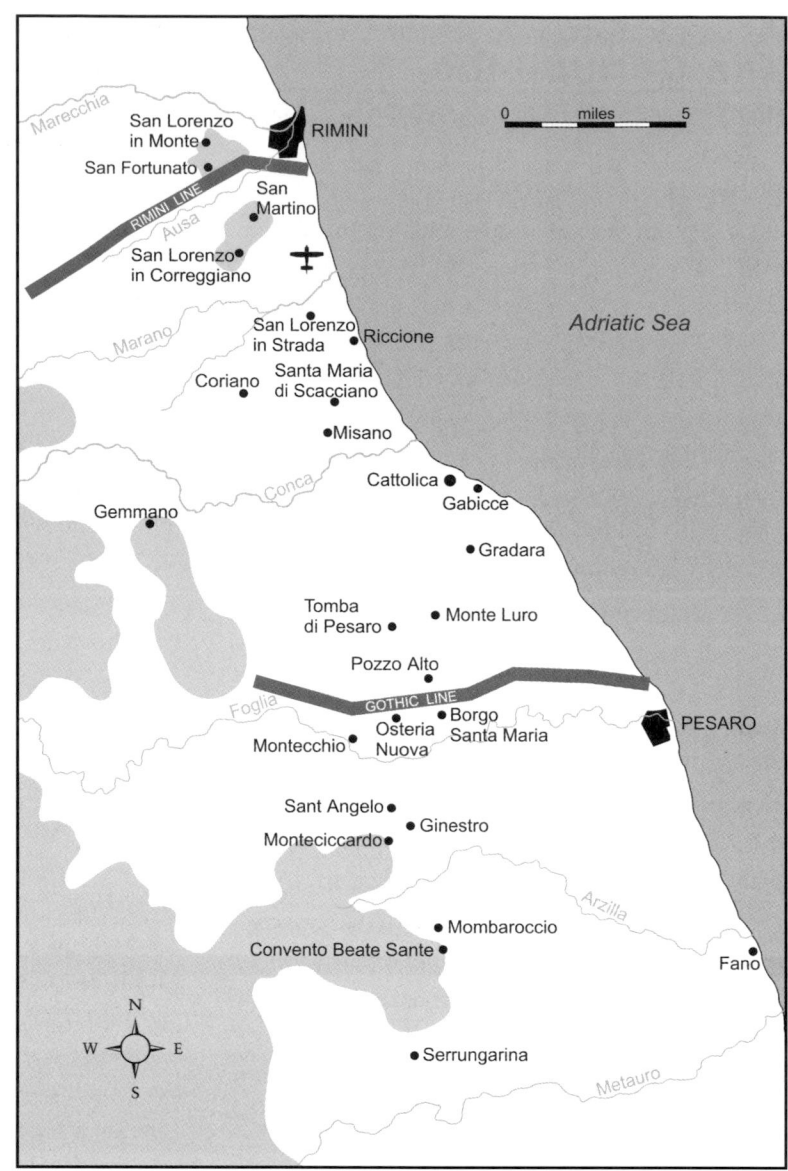

The hope of a breakthrough soon faded. The assault on the Gothic Line, which began with such promise, bogged down as enemy reinforcements arrived to man new defensive lines. Historian Bill McAndrew notes that the autumn rains intervened to immobilize tanks and limit air support, but he also insists the overall plan was flawed. The Canadians were assigned to the best sector for a break-out but were denied the necessary troops. British Fifth Corps had plenty of resources but its advance was soon stalled in the mountains. When Eighth Army commander Sir Oliver Leese recognized his error and transferred additional forces to 1st Canadian Corps, it was too late. Allied casualties were mounting

The Gothic Line, August 24 to September 22, 1944.

and new German infantry divisions had arrived.

The battlefield was controlled by artillery and mortars, and both sides had enough fire power to exact a high price for each yard gained. On September 17, Field Marshal Harold Alexander, the Allied commander, reported that" the enemy continues to put in reinforcements...he intends to fight it out where he stands." There would be another winter of misery for soldier and civilian alike.

The German forces in Italy, like their counterparts in Northwest Europe, had again avoided final defeat on the battlefield. And so the Nazi regime had been preserved for another year. Millions more would die on the battlefields, in the death camps and in the cities of Hitler's Reich.

As long as the German armed forces, and indeed the German people, were willing to support Hitler's bloody tyranny, the Allies had no choice except to persist. If German armies were not attacked and Germany not bombed, the Reich might recover and return to the offensive. The secret weapons; the V -2, the jet aircraft and the schnorkel U-boat would help to restore confidence to Germany and the war would continue to rage. We need to remind ourselves of this reality whenever we analyse the last years of the war, and especially when we think about the Italian campaign. There has always been debate and bitter controversy over the purpose of operations in the Mediterranean. American military leaders were suspicious of British motives in Italy. Was Churchill waging a campaign co-coordinated with other attacks on the Third Reich, or was it all part of a larger strategy to restore British power in the Mediterranean? It was, of course, both; but its essential feature was always to contribute to the defeat of Germany.

Supreme Allied Commander Dwight Eisenhower described this reality clearly in 1943, after Hitler ordered his armies to defend every inch of Italy. Before leaving to take command of Operation "Overlord", he outlined the purpose of the battles that would bring the Allies to Monte Cassino and Ortona: "It is essential for us to retain the initiative...If we can keep him on his heels until early spring, then the more divisions he uses against us the better it will be for "Overlord".

This was the strategy that underlay and justified the Italian campaign. Hitler reinforced Italy with troops that might have turned the tide on D-Day. In the summer of 1944 the battle for Rome prevented the transfer of German troops to Normandy. The attack on the Gothic Line served the same great purpose. In September 1944 Hitler was reeling from double defeats in France and on the Eastern Front, but he would not sacrifice Italy and new resources were found to prevent an Allied victory south of the Alps.

The soldiers in Italy called themselves the D-Day Dodgers because so little attention was paid to their efforts after June 6. The campaign in Normandy and Northwest Europe has continued to overshadow their achievement. There were no great celebrations to mark the 50th anniversary of the liberation of Rome and there will be none to commemorate the battle for the Gothic Line. The men and women who served in Italy deserve better from us. They made a vital contribution to the defeat of Hitler's Reich and they helped to bring us all "security, peace and honour for our country."

D-Day At Sea and In The Air

Originally published, March/April 1998

The long frustrating debate over the timing and location of a Second Front in Northwest Europe came to an end at the Quebec Conference of August 1943. Winston Churchill, Franklin Roosevelt and their senior military advisers were briefed on the progress of Operation "Neptune", the assault phase of Operation "Overlord". They agreed the invasion of France would take place in May 1944. The planners outlined four conditions that had to be met if the landings were to be successful. First, the enemy must remain ignorant of the actual landing area. Second, the Allies must achieve complete air and naval superiority in and over the English Channel. Third, the local defences must be largely destroyed by air and sea bombardment. Finally, the Allied air forces must prevent the enemy from bringing up reinforcements quickly, especially during the first few days after the landings.

Accomplishing these four tasks would not be easy. Fortunately, the Germans were convinced the invasion would take place at the mouth of the Somme River or in the Pas de Calais region opposite Dover. The Allied deception plan to draw attention away from Normandy worked well because the Germans wanted to believe the false intelligence they had received about possible landings north of the Seine River.

The Allied air forces promoted the deception plan while isolating Normandy from the rest of France. On the eve of the invasion, the German army reported that "constant air attacks" had destroyed bridges over the Seine and crippled rail transportation with raids on marshalling yards as far north as Brussels, Belgium. The report concluded that the "concentration of air attacks on coastal defences between Dunkirk and Dieppe...confirmed the focal point of a large-scale landing" in that area.

This deception was an extraordinary achievement, but more remarkable was the enemy's continuous belief that Normandy was a feint and a second landing would soon take place. As late as July 23,

on the eve of the destruction of the German forces in Normandy, German army commanders still thought that the "sector from north of the Somme to the Seine is in great danger." They refused to transfer infantry divisions to the Normandy battlefront.

The greatest challenge for the Allies seemed to be achieving air superiority. On D-Day the English Channel would be full of slow, vulnerable targets. The 4,126 landing ships and landing craft would be accompanied by 864 merchant ships and 736 ancillary vessels. Most of these would sail at the same time to be marshaled through the narrow shipping channels cleared of mines. The 1,213 Allied warships–the largest modern fleet ever assembled–could fight back against air or naval attack, but in the congested waters in front of the invasion beaches they too would be easy targets for the German air force.

By June 1944 the Allied air forces had more than 13,000 operational aircraft–plus 3,500 gliders–in Britain. Close to 11,590 planes were assigned to protecting the invasion. Long-range-fighter patrols covered much of France while continuous screens of low- and high-altitude fighter-bombers shielded the beaches, the Channel and the assembly areas as far back as the Isle of Wight. All told, 3,700 fighters were committed, including the Royal Canadian Air Force wings of 2nd Tactical Air Force.

The air effort on D-Day was more than sufficient. During the winter of 1943-44 and the following spring, the bomber offensive had reduced the Luftwaffe to a shadow of its former self. The American B-17 and B-24 bombers–escorted by Mustang fighters–had destroyed much of Germany's day-fighter force. British and Canadian crews of Bomber Command had forced the enemy to divert aircraft and other resources to the defence of Germany. In June 1944, the Luftwaffe had fewer than 200 available aircraft in all of France. "If it is white, it is American. If it is black, it is British. If you can't see it, it is the Luftwaffe" is how German soldiers described the situation. The German air force was completely overwhelmed and air superiority was achieved beyond the Allied planners' wildest dreams.

US AIR FORCE PHOTO

RAF "Beaufighters" in action against German destroyers. Normandy coast, 1944.

Naval superiority was never really in doubt and historians have taken the navy's role in the invasion more or less for granted. Canadians have just begun to hear about the exploits of the Canadian minesweeping flotilla at Omaha beach or the battle fought by the RCN's tribal-class destroyers *Haida* and *Huron*.

Admiral Bertram Ramsay, the overall naval commander, believed that the underwater mine was the "greatest obstacle to success" in the assault. The RCN agreed to contribute 16 Bangor minesweepers to "Neptune", but their crews had to be trained to use the serrated line or "sweep" to cut mooring cables and bring the mines to the surface for destruction. On D-Day, 10 RCN Bangor minesweepers, which formed the 31st Canadian Minesweeping Flotilla under Commander A.H.G. Storrs, led the United States 1st and 29th divisions towards Omaha beach. Our other minesweepers served with the 4th, 14th and 16th flotillas.

Haida and *Huron* were part of the 10th Destroyer Flotilla based in Plymouth. Allied air superiority meant the German navy could operate only at night. However, the German destroyer flotilla, based in the Bay of Biscay, was a serious threat. It included two destroyers armed with 5.9-inch guns and eight torpedo tubes. They were larger, faster and packed a heavier punch than the Tribals.

The German flotilla was ordered into action on D-Day, but thanks to Ultra the flotilla's moments were known and Beaufighter aircraft, including those of 404 Squadron RCAF, kept the destroyers bottled up in the harbor at Brest until June 8. Naval historian Michael Whitby says the bold tactics and persistence of *Haida* and *Huron* played a key role in sinking one of the German destroyers.

British planners, still haunted by their memories of Dieppe, insisted on an enormous air and naval bombardment designed to destroy fortified defensive positions on the coast. On the eve of June 6, Bomber Command employed more than 1,000 aircraft in attacks on 10 coastal batteries in the invasion zone. More than 5,000 tons of bombs, the most yet dropped in a single night, failed to destroy any of the batteries, but some neutralization was achieved. Just three aircraft were lost but one was a Lancaster from 6 Group RCAF.

The U.S. Eighth Air Force arrived over the coast at first light with orders to destroy enemy positions along the beach. Poor visibility meant that pathfinder bomb aimers followed instructions to avoid short bombing and the risk of hitting Allied landing craft. They delayed for up to 30 seconds after the target was identified on radar. The main American concentrations fell well inland leaving the beach defences intact.

The navy took over the counter-battery task and naval guns–assisted by spotter aircraft–were able to complete the neutralization or destruction of all large gun batteries. Unfortunately, the beach defence positions were largely untouched and when the first landing craft arrived the enemy position had to be overcome by infantry supported by tanks.

The elaborate preparations had given the army confidence that the landings could succeed; however, the war diarist of the Royal Winnipeg Rifles only exaggerated a little when he wrote that "the bombardment...failed to kill a single German or silence one weapon."

The final key to the success of "Overlord" was to prevent the enemy from counter-attacking the landings or sealing off the beach-head before it could be established in depth. The Germans had stationed just three of their 23 static coastal divisions in the invasion area. However, the powerful 352nd Division had been added to thicken the defence positions near Omaha beach and the 21st Panzer Division, provided a local reserve in the British-Canadian sector. Two other Armoured divisions, 12th SS and Panzer Lehr, were eight to 12 hours away and other units north of the Seine and Brittany could arrive in the crucial first few days unless Allied air power intervened.

The task of preventing this was the responsibility of 2nd Tactical Air Force and the U.S. 9th Tactical Air Force. Second TAF was organized in late 1943 with two composite groups of fighter-bombers, a night-fighter group and one of medium bombers. All RCAF fighter squadrons were assigned to 83 Group to support the Anglo-Canadian invasion forces.

Apart from 400 Squadron, which was part of the Photo Reconnaissance Wing, RCAF squadrons in 83 Group were assigned to one of four Canadian fighter wings, 126, 127, 143 and 144. A day- fighter wing consisted of three squadrons of 18 aircraft with a strength of 39 officers and 743 other ranks. 144 Wing was equipped with Typhoon IB fighter-bombers while the other three flew the Spitfire IXB. "Bombphoons" normally carried two 500-pound bombs and were tasked to "provide direct support to the army."

Spitfires could also carry bombs and frequently did so, but as pilot Hugh Godefroy noted "dive bombing was extremely inaccurate" because "without dive breaks, Spitfires dived so fast that the altimeter went round in a blur." The pilots could not pull out at exactly 3,000 feet if your instrument could not keep up.

Typhoons were thought to be considerably more accurate in ground attack roles but even here there were serious problems. Second TAF created its own operational research section in late 1943 when it became evident that no one knew very much about how to hit relatively small targets.

A study of operations against a viaduct in France that was 500 yards long and eight yards wide revealed that "Bombphoons" scored hits one in 82 times while Typhoons with rockets secured one hit for every 15 fired. Even rocket projectile attacks on gun positions produced discouraging results, varying from 110 strikes at a casement in Courseulles-sur-Mer with zero hits to two hits out of 127 in Fontenay.

Training courses for Spitfire and Typhoon pilots helped improve accuracy against identified targets, but average pilots still had great difficulty in navigating and locating targets. As one tactical memorandum put it: "Fighters, given a six-figure map reference, were unable to spot well camouflaged guns even when the guns were firing." All of this meant that the tactical air forces were being called upon to perform tasks for which they were not properly equipped. On D-Day the weather further hampered ground-attack operations and those German divisions ordered to the beach-head were able to take advantage of the low cloud cover.

The 12th SS Hitler Youth Division, which had been delayed by command confusion and uncertainty, began its advance in the early afternoon of June 6. To minimize losses, vehicles were camouflaged and ordered to maintain 100-metre intervals, but in the late afternoon air attacks disrupted the cohesion of the columns and slowed their advance to a crawl. By the end of that day, 12th SS had suffered 83 casualties, including 22 dead. No tanks had been hit, but none reached the battlefield.

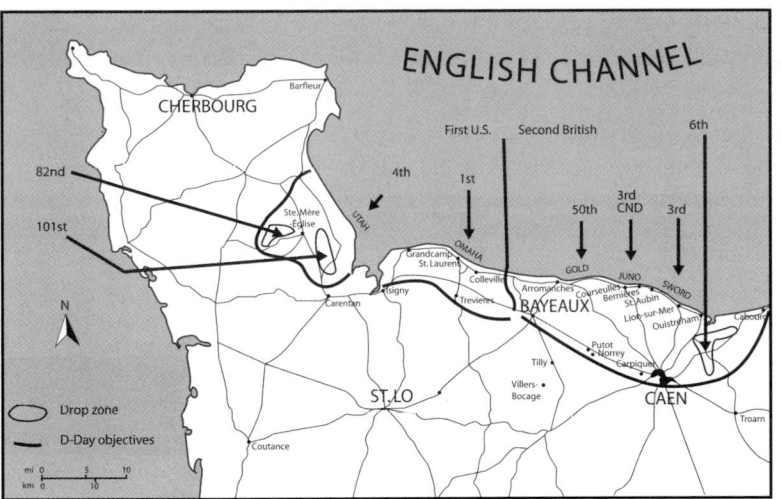

The "Overlord" Plan.

The divisions sent from Brittany to the American sector also reported only minor delays and losses due to Allied air power. The tactical air forces had helped to prevent any serious counter-attacks on D-Day, but they could not stop the enemy from sending enough additional troops to seal off the beach-head. By June 10 the Germans had established a new defensive perimeter that forced the Allies to fight a battle of attrition within sight of the Normandy coast.

Panzer Lehr, which had much further to travel, did not start its march until the evening. Darkness saved it from continuous attack but by the next morning the two approaching columns were repeatedly strafed, bombed and rocketed. Losses included a large number of soft-skinned vehicles and four tanks, but the tactical air force's most important contribution was to delay the panzers.

When the division reached the front on the morning of June 8, the 7th Canadian Infantry Brigade had secured control of the Caen-Bayeux highway and railway line, while British 50th Division had captured Bayeux. The Allies had secured their beach-heads and were moving quickly to link them together.

Canadian and British squadrons had also demonstrated the meaning of air superiority to the soldiers fighting through the Atlantic Wall. No German aircraft attacked the landings on D-Day and on June 7 when more than a dozen JU 88s tried to break through to bomb the beaches, pilots of 401 Ram Squadron destroyed six and forced the remainder to flee.

The limits of air power were evident, however, when the German army's 346 Division–the only unit transferred to the battlefield from north of the Seine–crossed the river and bicycled towards the airborne bridgehead east of the Orne River without interference.

The battle would continue to be influenced by Allied air and naval power. On June 7, the North Nova Scotia Regiment and the Sherbrooke Fusiliers ran into the 12th SS near l'Abbaye d'Ardennes. The German counter-attack was broken up by the guns of HMS *Belfast* which saturated the enemy with tons of high explosive.

On June 12 General Erwin Rommel reported that naval gunfire was so strong that "operations with infantry or panzer formations in the area commanded by this quick-firing artillery is not possible." Rommel urged Hitler to permit a withdrawal out of range of the warships but the Fuhrer would not allow ground to be given up.

Rommel was equally concerned about the long-term effect of Allied air power. "The enemy," he wrote "has complete control of the air over the battlefield and up to 100 kilometres behind the front...movements of our troops in the battle area by day are almost completely prevented, while the enemy can operate freely. Neither our flak nor the Luftwaffe seems to be in a position to check this crippling and destructive operation of the enemy air force..."

The Battle of Normandy could not be won by air or naval power, but the air force and navy helped establish the pre-conditions for victory.

The Airborne On D-Day

Originally published, May/June 1998

When historians really immerse themselves in the world inhabited by the men who planned the invasion of France in 1944, two things quickly become evident. Everyone expressed confidence that the operation would succeed and everyone feared it might fail. It was this nightmare of "the Channel running red with blood" and the possibility of another Dunkirk-like evacuation that led the generals to decide to use three of their highly trained airborne divisions, not to exploit success, but to guard against failure.

The decision to create an Allied airborne army of five divisions and commit enormous resources to gliders, special equipment and a fleet of transport aircraft was always controversial. Ever since the conquest of Crete in May 1941, when German airborne forces lost 30 per cent of their strength, with more killed and wounded than in the entire Balkan campaign, the role of lightly armed airborne units had been in question. Allied experience in the Mediterranean did little to silence the critics. In Operation "Husky", 1st British Airborne Division had suffered heavy losses and both parachute and glider troops had been too widely scattered to be effective.

A week before D-Day, Air Chief Marshal Sir Trafford L. Leigh-Mallory seriously argued that the entire airborne operation should be cancelled as the projected losses in men and aircraft were too great. The drop zone for 82nd United States Airborne Division was moved 12 miles to avert a disaster on the right flank, but 6th British Airborne Division's drop zones and landing zones for gliders could not be changed even though Ultra reported the transfer of 21th Panzer Division to the Caen sector.

The reality was that studies of the feasibility of landing on the coast of Normandy suggested that the left flank of the beach-head was the most vulnerable point in the whole operation. A counter-attack there might have rolled up the entire invasion force. To meet this threat, General Sir Frederic Morgan suggested deploying 6th British Airborne Division to seize the bridges across the Orne and hold the high ground east of the river. Almost every other detail of Morgan's plan was changed in the months that followed, but no one could come up with a better solution for securing the left flank.

The men of 1st Canadian Parachute Battalion knew nothing of these debates when they arrived in Britain in August 1943. Recruited from volunteers less than 32 years of age, "with a history of participation in rugged sports or in a civilian occupation or hobby demanding sustained exertion" the battalion had learned to jump out of airplanes at Fort Benning, Georgia, and at Camp Shilo, Manitoba. At their new home in Bulford in Salisbury Plain they measured themselves against the men of their new sister regiments, 8th and 9th parachute battalions of 3rd Parachute Brigade, 6th British Airborne Division They also met the man who would forge them into combat soldiers and lead them in battle, Brigadier James Hill.

Hill has acquired legendary status in the memories of Canadian and British veterans of the airborne division. He was 32 years old in 1943. He was a tall, rugged-looking professional soldier who had fought in the Battle of France and caught the last destroyer out of Dunkirk. Hill volunteered to join the original paratroop force and by early 1942 commanded 1st British Paratroop Battalion in its first action in North Africa. Wounded while capturing three enemy tanks, he recovered in England and was posted to command the only mixed British and Canadian brigade formed during the war.

Everyone who has the privilege of meeting Hill is strongly affected by the experience. Phrases like a soldier's soldier have been used to describe him, but there is much more to it than that. Now in his 80s, he remains a tall, erect, vital personality who dominates a room by his mere presence. As a younger man, he could do anything that he asked his men to do and still retain the focus to function as a commander conducting a wide-ranging battle. He needed these skills and all the power of his personality to succeed in Normandy.

Brian Nolan, the author of *Airborne: The Heroic Story of the 1st Canadian Parachute Battalion in the Second World War*, records one of Hill's oft-repeated stories about his new brigade. "Each battalion had a personality of its own.... The 8th were rugged, relentless in achieving an objective, very tough, and not too fussy about detail. This was the opposite of the 9th who were masters of detail, tackling an assignment only after intensive preparation and approaching all problems with precision and professionalism. The Canadian battalion displayed all the characteristics of a troop of cavalry."

The Canadians were, however, neither well disciplined nor adequately trained when they joined the brigade. Hill "kept a tight rein" on the Canadians because no matter how much he admired their spirit he did not wish to command a battalion of dead horses.

It is impossible not to be impressed by the intensity of the training for parachute battalions. Hill insisted on the highest standards of weapons training and physical fitness. Nicknamed "Speedy" because of his own rapid pace, Hill maintained that a paratrooper had to move across country twice as fast as anybody else. He insisted they had to be able to cover 10 miles in two hours with a 60-pound pack and a personal weapon. The Canadians adapted quickly. For example, there was Lieutenant-Colonel Jeff Nicklin, a football and lacrosse star, and Fraser Eadie, a noted hockey player who ate up the training and asked for more. However, others fell by the wayside. By the time the battalion was briefed for its part in the Normandy invasion, the men–whose average age was just 22–were ready for anything.

The importance of the airborne landings in the plans for D-Day was brought home to everyone when the senior officers met on D-Day minus one. Admiral Bertram Ramsay, the overall Allied naval commander, recorded the discussion in his diary: "Sunday 4 June: Commanders met at 0415 to hear latest weather report which was bad. The low cloud predicted would prohibit use of airborne troops, prohibit majority of air action, including air spotting. The sea conditions were unpromising but not prohibitive."

The supreme commander of Allied troops in Europe, Dwight Eisenhower, decided to postpone the assault for 24 hours. Then, after trusting in a weather forecast that promised minimally acceptable cloud and sea conditions, he gave the order to go. Ramsay wrote: "Monday 5 June: Held a final meeting at 0415.... Thus has been made the vital and critical decision to stage this great enterprise which will, I hope, be the immediate means of bringing about the downfall of Germany's fighting power and Nazi oppression. I am under no delusions as to the risks involved in this most difficult of all operations.... We shall require all the help that God can give us and I cannot believe that this will not be forthcoming.

"Tuesday 6 June: I was called at 0500 which meant that nothing bad had happened.... The sky was clear than God.... Surprise seemed to be achieved up to the time the paratroops had been dropped.... Only 29 transport aircraft were lost out of 1,300. H.Q. 6 Airborne Division report themselves established."

The airborne commanders had not dared to sleep. The night of June 5-6 was moonless with patchy cloud and winds gusting up to 20 miles per hour. The odds of placing the paratroop companies in the right place were not great. Major John Howard's coup de main glider assault on Pegasus Bridge was able to land on target, but high winds and flak over the coast meant the parachutists were widely scattered. Major Dick Hilborn's recollection of that night explains what happened to one "stick" or group of paratroops: "As we crossed the coast of France the red light went on for preparing to drop. We were in the process of hooking up when the plane took violent evasive action.... Five of us ended up at the back of the plane.... We got out okay and after wandering about for a bit I picked up three of my stick. It took us three hours and the assistance of a local French farmer to find out where we were.... We were one and a half miles north of the drop zone."

Despite the winds, flak and almost total failure of the radar beacons carried by the Pathfinders of 22nd Independent Parachute Company, the men of the two parachute brigades were able to capture or secure their objectives. For 1st Canadian Parachute Battalion this meant that "C" Company dropped first to secure the drop zone and eliminate the enemy at Varaville, blowing the bridge over the Divette a tributary of the river Dives. Only a fraction of "C" Company was available, but it all went like clockwork.

"A" Company was assigned to protect the flank of 9th Battalion as it advanced to capture the Merville battery where guns could hamper the landings on Sword and Juno beaches. "B" Company had to blow a bridge at Robehomme on the Dives and then join the rest of the battalion at Le Mesnil crossroads where everyone quickly dug in awaiting the inevitable German attempt to break through to the Orne bridges.

Hill warned the men that "in spite of your excellent training and orders do not be daunted if chaos reigns. It undoubtedly will." Hill was right, chaos was everywhere, but small groups of well-trained men went about their tasks knowing their comrades depended on them. Hill and his tactical headquarters landed miles away from the drop zone in a flooded area and it took four hours to make it to dry land. Leading the forced march, Hill was wounded by shrapnel that took a chunk out of his backside. More than two dozen of his men were killed in this incident that was due to "friendly fire" from fighter bombers.

Hill used a borrowed bicycle pushed by one of his men to reach his objective and for the next 48 hours issued orders while sitting on one cheek some distance from his men "because his wound smelled so bad." When asked why he refused evacuation to get medical treatment he replied, somewhat sharply, that he had not trained his brigade for 10 months to let someone else command it in action.

Most accounts of the airborne division in the Orne bridgehead concentrate on the achievements and extraordinary heroism, but June 6, 1944, was just the beginning of a long battle of attrition. The scattered detachments of the enemy's 711 Division were quickly overcome and the arrival of Brigadier Lord Lovat's commandos, 1st Special Service Brigade, on the afternoon of D-Day brought welcome support. But the enemy was also active. On the southern flank, battle groups of 21 Armoured Division launched a series of attacks and Rommel sent 346 Division across the Seine with orders to force the paratroops off the high ground and seize bridgeheads across the Orne.

The lead battalion set off on bicycles and by June 8 the entire division was in position. Naval artillery and the guns of the 51st Highland Division prevented General Erich Diestel from concentrating his power and he was forced into a series of limited attacks that the parachute battalions dealt with swiftly. Still, the situation on the heavily wooded ridge was very much in doubt. The Canadians were trying to cover a two-kilometre section of the perimeter astride the main Cabourg to Caen highway. With less than 400 men this was no easy task. Lieutenant-Colonel Bradbrooke, the battalion's

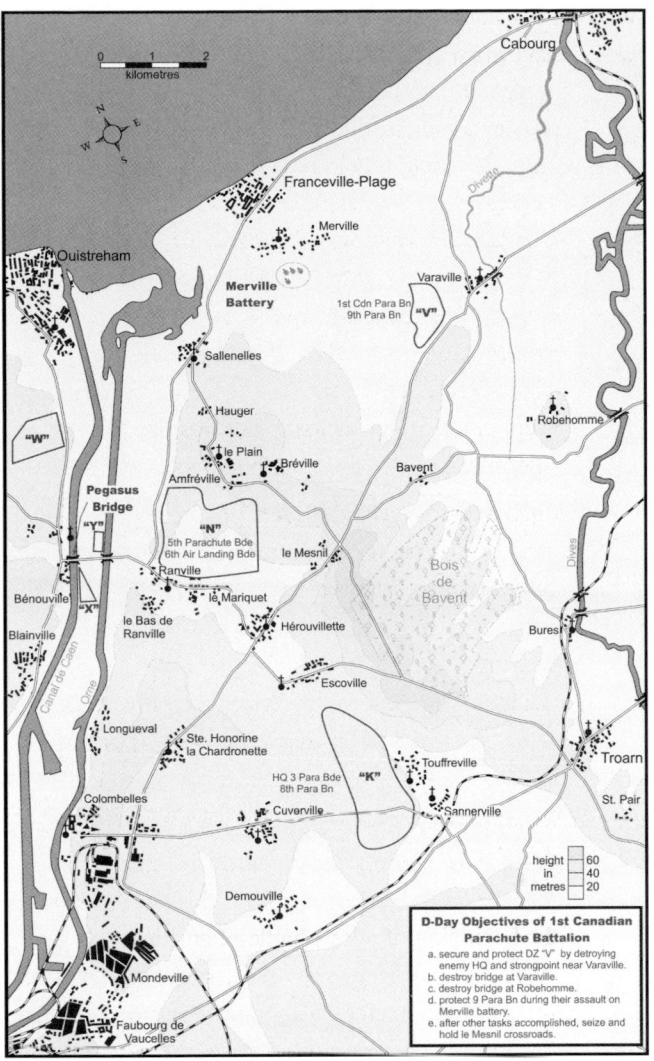

The map shows:
- Cabourg
- Franceville-Plage
- Merville
- Ouistreham
- Merville Battery
- Varaville
- 1st Cdn Para Bn / 9th Para Bn
- "V"
- Divette
- Sallenelles
- Hauger
- "Robehomme
- "W"
- le Plain
- Amfréville
- Bréville
- Bavent
- Pegasus Bridge
- "Y"
- 5th Parachute Bde / 6th Air Landing Bde
- le Mesnil
- Bois de Bavent
- Dives
- Ranville
- Bénouville
- lè Mariquet
- "N"
- "X"
- le Bas de Ranville
- Hérouvillette
- Bures
- Blainville
- Canal de Caen
- Orne
- Escoville
- Longueval
- Ste. Honorine la Chardronette
- Touffreville
- Troarn
- HQ 3 Para Bde / 8th Para Bn
- "K"
- St. Pair
- Colombelles
- Cuverville
- Sannerville
- Demouville
- height in metres: 60 40 20
- Mondeville
- Faubourg de Vaucelles

D-Day Objectives of 1st Canadian Parachute Battalion
a. secure and protect DZ "V" by detroying enemy HQ and strongpoint near Varaville.
b. destroy bridge at Varaville.
c. destroy bridge at Robehomme.
d. protect 9 Para Bn during their assault on Merville battery.
e. after other tasks accomplished, seize and hold le Mesnil crossroads.

The 6th Airborne Bridgehead.

pany's commander, led an attack on the enemy's exposed flank. Hill supported himself with a shepherd's crook and according to Nelson Macdonald, who was in the attack, he "looked like God" as he led the battle from the front.

The Canadian attack forced the Germans to retreat, but they still held Bréville. Major-General Richard Gale, who commanded 6th Airborne Division, decided to "liquidate the Bréville sore" in an immediate night attack. He arranged for fire support and employed a squadron of tanks. One of the field regiments fired short killing the battalion commander and wounding both the brigade commander and Lord Lovat. Bréville was captured in a night-long battle.

For historians of the big picture, Bréville was the last important battle in the airborne portion of the Orne bridgehead. The Germans, who had lost more than 300 men in the action, gave up their plans to drive the paratroopers off the ridge. Instead, they were content to harass and contain the paratroopers. For the men on the ground, this meant constant artillery and mortar fire, night patrols and fire fights to fend off enemy probes. After a brief break, the Canadians returned to the area around Le Mesnil crossroads to endure six more weeks or mortar fire and mosquitoes.

The airborne division ought to have been relieved and sent back to England to reorganize, but General Bernard Montgomery could not risk any reverse in the only bridgehead across the Orne that his armies held. Both 6th Airborne Division and 51st Highland were committed to a frustrating defensive battle, but when Operation "Goodwood" was launched out of the bridgehead on July 18 it was evident the strategy had paid off. One month later, 1st Canadian Parachute Battalion advanced to the Dives as part of the pursuit of a German army that had been broken in just 74 days.

commanding officer, could do little to relieve the pressure as the artillery, mortars and assault guns of 346 Division scoured the area.

The most serious problem was at Bréville. The British corps commander placed a battalion from the 51st Highland Division–the 5th Black Watch–under the command of 6th Airborne Division to capture the village. However, the desert veterans found that mastering the art of fighting in the very different terrain of Normandy was no easy matter. Disdaining advice from the paratroopers, they staged a miniature set-piece attack that was promptly thrown back.

The next day–June 12–the Germans staged their own advance and caught the Black Watch off balance. This forced a withdrawal. Hill, who was always close to the action, gathered "C" Company and together with Captain John Hanson, the com-

Merville

l'Orne

Ouistreham

Lion-sur-Mer

St. Aubin-
sur-Mer

Bernières-
sur-Mer

Courseulles-
sur-Mer

Centre
Juno
Beach

Launching The Liberation

Originally published, June/July 1994

The seaside village of Courseulles-sur-Mer gradually came into view. On the right the wireless mast and lighthouse on Gold beach were visible. To the east the high church steeple at Berni SEQ CHAPTER \h \r 1?res-sur-Mer – where the Queen's Own Rifles of Canada were to land - could be seen. The navy had brought them to the right place and was now bombarding the coastal defences.

More than one soldier and sailor asked himself why they were there that fateful morning. Most of them knew the answer. Canadians had gone to war in 1939, not out of reflex loyalty to Britain but because they realized that Hitler and his Nazi thugs threatened everything they believed in. Nothing in the tumultuous events of the early war years altered that simple truth and now in June 1944 it was time to begin the final act.

Four years before, almost to the day, the small ships of the British fleet had carried the last soldiers away from the smoke-shrouded beaches at Dunkirk. Now three navies, American, British and Canadian, loomed out of the morning mist under cover of a vast air umbrella to begin the liberation of France.

Lieutenant-Colonel Foster Matheson, commanding officer of 1st Battalion Regina Rifle Regiment, was one of the many unit commanders forced to wait that morning. First the weather delayed the launch and then there was the anxiety of waiting for news from his assault companies. Major Duncan Grosch's "A" Company had the toughest job, to clear "Block One" of Courseulles, the area close to the mouth of the river where the Germans had an elaborate concrete strongpoint.

Matheson received the first reports at 0830. The Courseulles strongpoint did not appear to have been touched by the air or naval bombardment and "A" Company was pinned down on the beach. Major Grosch had been wounded and Captain Ron Shawcross was in command. The news was much better from Major F.L. Peters and "B" Company on the left flank. The duplex-drive amphibious tanks of the 1st Hussars had been launched at 4,000 yards, despite the heavy sea. The DD tank was an ordinary Sherman equipped with flotation gear. Major J.S. Duncan's own tank sank, but 14 others made it to shore ahead of the infantry. With the 1st Hussars engaging the enemy, the "Johns" -as The Reginas called themselves - raced across the sand and began to clear the eastern part of Courseulles. They were joined by "C" Company, under Major Stuart Tubb.

The situation in front of the strongpoint was problematic until Lieutenant Bill Grayson coolly rushed a machine-gun post and captured 35 prisoners, opening a way off the beach. Matheson was anxious to go ashore and co-ordinate the battle. He landed with his advance headquarters at 0900. The commanding officer of 13th Field Regiment was with him and he directed a troop of Royal Marine artillery Centaur tanks with 95-mm howitzers against the strongpoint. The "Johns" were rapidly gaining control of Courseulles when ill-fortune struck. The incoming tide had covered a number of the mined beach obstacles and two of the assault landing craft bringing "D" Company to shore exploded. Just 49 men landed safely.

Matheson did not allow this tragedy to deflect the battalion from its purpose. "D" company began the advance inland at 0930 under Lieutenant H.L. Jones, the senior platoon commander. The struggle to subdue the last holdouts in the Courseulles strong-point continued until late afternoon but by then the Reginas, with a squadron of 1st Hussars and a troop of Centaurs, were well inland. The corps commander, Lieutenant-General John Crocker, reacting to 21st Panzer Division's counter-attack at "Sword" beach, ordered the British and Canadians to dig in on their intermediate objective, dubbed "Elm". Matheson regrouped his companies to resume the advance at first light.

The Regina battle group fought with both valour and skill throughout D-Day. The weather and the friction of war conspired to create chaos, but

M. Bechthold

Juno and Sword Beaches today.

training, good all-arms co-operation, and superb leadership overcame every obstacle. Across the River Seulles the Royal Winnipeg Rifles fought an even more difficult battle and won. Elsewhere on Juno other units of 3rd Division and 2nd Armoured Brigade met enormous challenges, but by nightfall all were well inland and ready for enemy counter-attacks.

Canadians have been strangely reluctant to recognize the extraordinary achievements of their countrymen that day. Success on D-Day did not come from the overwhelming application of brute force. Weather forced the bombers to strike inland for fear of hitting the landing flotillas. Naval fire helped to demoralize and keep heads down, but did not destroy a single gun position in the Canadian sector. The field regiments-firing from pitching landing craft-were also off target. The enemy was overwhelmed in close combat, with infantry, engineers and armour co-operating to capture well fortified positions. During D-Day the Reginas suffered 45 fatal casualties and 63 wounded. The Hussars had 22 killed and 21 wounded. Each of these losses was an individual tragedy and the loss of three of the four rifle company commanders was a serious blow, but by nightfall reinforcements had arrived and the newly prompted company COs were quickly adapting to their responsibilities.

Getting ashore was only the first stage in establishing a secure beach-head. It would take time to build up supplies and bring in additional divisions, so once through the crust of coastal defences the goal was to get inland and organize defences against major counter-attacks.

The brigade orders group for June 7 was held at 0300. Two hours later- just before dawn – the battalion began its advance. By noon the Reginas reached their objective, Bretteville-l'Orgueilleuse. To their right the Royal Winnipeg Rifles nicknamed The Little Black Devils - were in position at Putot-en-Bessin. The Canadian Scottish Regiment from Victoria - known as the Canscots-was in reserve to support either forward battalions.

Major Stuart Tubb and "C" Company led the way inland. Tubb, a tall, bespectacled warrior, took one took at the terrain and decided to cross the railway line and establish control of the village of Norrey-en-Bessin. Matheson recognized the wisdom of this decision so that when Brigadier H.W. Foster ordered "C" Company back to Bretteville, Matheson insisted that Norrey be held. This proved to be one of the best tactical decisions of the Normandy campaign.

German commanders at all levels were quite uncertain as to how to respond to the Allied invasion. Hitler and his senior generals were convinced the Normandy landings were only a feint and that the real invasion would take place at the Pas de Calais. They did not abandon this belief until mid-July.

German confusion of purpose did not end there. Every German commander had been indoctrinated in the importance of an immediate counter-attack against any enemy advance. Fritz Witt, the officer commanding 12th SS Hitler Youth Division, and his regimental commanders were also brashly over-confident. Convinced that the Tommies landing in the Caen sector were no match for their young, highly motivated Hitler Youth, they proposed to throw the "little fish" back into the sea without waiting for the full force of 12th SS to assemble.

On June 7, Kurt Meyer – commanding 25th Panzer Grenadier Regiment – succeeded in checking the advance of 9th Canadian Infantry Brigade. The battle had not been easy and the costs to 12th SS, as well as the Canadians, were high, but success on the road to Carpiquet encouraged Witt to order immediate attacks on positions held by 7th Infantry Brigade.

The first attempt came on the night of June 7 with attacks on Putot and Norrey. The Germans committed two battalions at Norrey, but a torrent of small arms and artillery fire forced the Panzer grenadiers to abandon their plan. The Regina War Diary, underestimating both German intentions and the effectiveness of Canadian artillery fire, dismissed this assault as a minor irritant. Pressure continued throughout June 8, especially at Putot

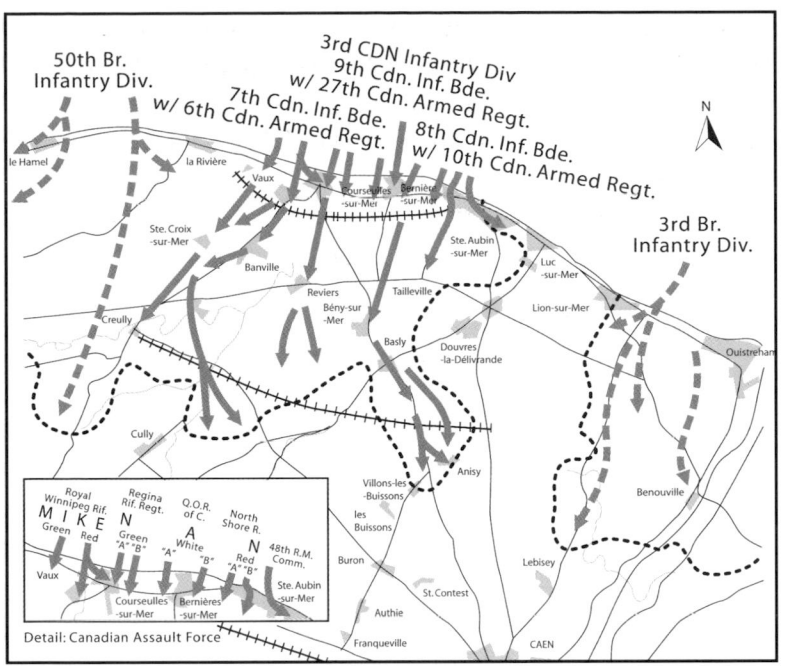

Detail: Canadian Assault Force

The Canadian Assault.

where the 12th SS was able to cross the railway and outflank The Little Black Devils. Putot was lost late in the day and then recovered through a carefully orchestrated counter-attack. The Canscots and 1st Hussars-using an artillery barrage provided by 12th and 13th field regiments-were in Putot before the enemy could recover.

Just as the Canscots were clearing the last hold-outs in Putot, Kurt Meyer's regiment launched a new attack on the Reginas. Panther tanks advanced down the highway to the edge of Bretteville before the Canadians opened fire. At dawn on June 9, Meyer withdrew his defeated forces to Rots. He did not, however, give up his belief that the "little fish" could be overwhelmed. He decided to use the one company of Panther tanks that had not been in action to overcome the Regina's key position in Norrey.

This time the attack was to be in broad daylight, timed for noon when the tactical air forces – still based in England- would be absent. The 3rd Company of the 1st Panzer Battalion crossed the railway line and advanced in three sections. They were confident that the longer ranges would protect them from the six-pounders of

the 3rd Anti-Tank Regiment in Bretteville, while the frontal armour of their Panther tanks would foil the Regina anti-tank platoon in Norrey.

Matheson, at his headquarters in Bretteville, and Tubb in Norrey watched the Panthers approach. The Germans were relying on speed and left their infantry to follow. Suddenly, one Panther was struck a jolting blow. A second hit set it on fire. In the next four minutes, five more Panthers were destroyed. This devastating attack was delivered by a 17-pounder Sherman Firefly of the 1st Hussars. The remaining Panthers withdrew in disarray. The 12th SS had been dealt a severe blow. An infantry attack ensued, but the Reginas held firm.

The battles fought by 7th Infantry Brigade in the first days of the Normandy landings are the stuff from which legends are made – in countries except ours. The Canadian victory was of vital importance in securing the Allied bridgehead. Canadian operations, and especially those of the Regina Rifles, demonstrate a level of professionalism that we have rarely mentioned in histories of our volunteer army. All Canadians should recognize the importance of what was accomplished in our name that summer 50 years ago.

The Normandy Battle Of Attrition

Originally published, September/October 1998

The American military historian Stephen Ambrose has a new bestseller in the bookstores. It is called *Citizen Soldiers* and in it he examines the role of the United States Army from the Normandy landings to the surrender of Germany. Ambrose is one of a small, but growing group of American historians who argue that the Allied armies fought with skill and determination in defeating their enemies on the battlefield. He believes that "free men fight better than slaves" and that "the sons of democracy proved to be better soldiers than the sons of Nazi Germany."

I think Ambrose overstates his case, but a re-examination of the conventional wisdom on the campaigns of WW II is badly needed.

Such a re-examination began in Canada in the early 1980s with the publication of the five-volume *Maple Leaf Route* series. In it, the late Robert Vogel and I rejected the negative view of the Canadian Army's performance and noted that Canadians had won a series of important tactical and operational victories in 1944—45. However, our argument had little impact on the country's military historians not to mention those who portrayed our history on television.

This reaction may be explained by the particular role played by historian C.P. Stacey who wrote the official history of the Canadian Army in WW II. His book, *The Victory Campaign: The Operations in North-West Europe 1944—1945*, remains the outstanding single volume account of operations in Northwest Europe. Its author was too good an historian to ignore some of the obvious achievements of the Canadians, but he attributed our success to "numerical and material superiority", "the paralysing effects of Allied air power" and the superior generalship of the Allies, especially that of Field-Marshal Bernard Montgomery. Stacey selected the delayed closing of the Falaise Gap "as his major example of failure". Running a close second, in his view, was the battle for Verrières Ridge.

Canadian troops in the ruins of Caen, July 1944.

British and American historians as well as a generation of Canadians accepted Stacey's view as definitive until John A. English wrote his penetrating study of the Canadian Army's development and its performance in Normandy. Published in 1991, his book is entitled *The Canadians in Normandy: A Study of Failure in High Command*.

English accepted Stacey's judgment that the key question was how to explain the failure of the Canadian Army, especially at Verrières Ridge and in the Falaise Gap, but he insisted that the causes were to be found in the shortcomings of the Canadian high command that "seriously impaired Canadian fighting performance" by failing to develop appropriate leadership, training or doctrine. And so English's book quickly became the new standard interpretation of the Canadian Army's experience in WW II.

However, the evidence from the battlefield demonstrates that offensive operations in Normandy, whether carried out by the Allies or their opponents, invariably failed in the sense that combat units were unable to secure the objectives called for in the operational plans. The Battle of Normandy was a battle of attrition and there are no reasonable grounds for believing it could have been otherwise. Historians must develop a reasoned case for counter-factual scenarios if they're going to suggest that there were alternate operational and tactical methods of winning the battle, more decisively, more quickly and at lesser cost. It is not enough to simply claim that the actions taken were wrong.

On June 6, 1944, the Allies launched one of the most hazardous operations in the history of war. In the planning phase of Operation "Overlord", memories of Gallipoli and Dieppe guaranteed that every conceivable precaution was taken to improve the odds of victory. However, any serious study of D-Day will echo what the Canadian artillery officer who served with 21 Army Group's Operational Research section wrote in June 1944. Major John Fairlie noted that none of the elaborate methods of bombardment of the defences destroyed any significant part of the Atlantic Wall. The defences in the Canadian sector, wrote Fairlie, were overcome by "D.D. (Duplex Drive) tank, engineer and infantry assault."

Indeed, there was little indication that the massive fire power directed at the Juno beach area had any significant neutralizing effect. "The defences," Fairlie concluded, "were substantially intact when the infantry touched down and the enemy was able to deliver lethal fire in great quantity against our troops." The evidence from the British and American beaches leads to a similar conclusion.

At the sharp end there was no "numerical and material superiority" and Allied air power had little impact on the battlefield. Apart from air superiority, which had been won long before D-Day, the contribution of the tactical air forces on D-Day was at best marginal. Interdiction produced only minor delays in the movement of German divisions to the beachhead and this allowed the enemy to stage several successful counter-attacks. The 12th SS Panzer Division caught the 9th Canadian Infantry Brigade as it advanced along a single axis on D-Day Plus One, and savaged the Canadian vanguard. The next day another Canadian battalion, the Royal Winnipeg Rifles, was overwhelmed on the right flank. In both cases the Canadian units were placed in a precarious position because the British brigades that were tasked to advance on their flanks were unable to overcome stronger resistance and keep pace.

These tactical victories on June 7-8 encouraged 12th SS to launch both its Panzer Grenadier regiments and a good deal of its armour against the positions held by the 7th Canadian Infantry Brigade astride the Caen-Bayeux railroad and highway. The terrain, natural and man-made, favoured the defenders and the Germans added to their difficulties by underestimating their opponent.

The battle that raged for the next 48 hours was one of the great neglected moments in the history of the Canadian Army. Seventh Brigade, the divisional artillery, anti-tank guns and the armour of the 1st Hussars met and defeated attack after attack. 12th SS staff officer and historian Hubert Meyers recalled that "our opponents were especially strong on the defensive and they did not allow themselves to be surprised. They fought ferociously and bravely."

The frustration and failure experienced by the 12th SS led to the murder of at least 106 Canadian prisoners of war.

The German army's failure to drive a wedge into the bridgehead meant that it had little choice except to dig in. Naturally, the officers selected high ground with good fields of fire and worked hard to ensure their men used camouflage and dug alternate machine-gun and mortar positions.

Between June and August, the Allies initiated a series of engagements designed to close with and destroy the enemy, break through his defence in depth and, if possible, obtain the ability to manoeuvre. The Canadians participated in five of these, beginning July 8 with Operation "Charnwood", the attack on Caen and its outer defensive perimeter.

It is important to note that the Allies had arrived in Normandy equipped with weapons that were distinctly inferior to those used by the enemy. Attacks on fortified villages, such as those around Caen, ought to have been carried out by battle groups built around tanks or self-propelled assault guns. Unfortunately, the Allies did not possess such armour and what's more the Allied battle doctrine reflected that reality.

When an investigation of Allied and German tank casualties in Normandy was carried out it confirmed the most pessimistic views about Allied armour. The statistics showed 60 per cent of Allied tank losses were due to a single round from a 75- or 88-mm gun. Two-thirds of all tanks brewed up when hit.

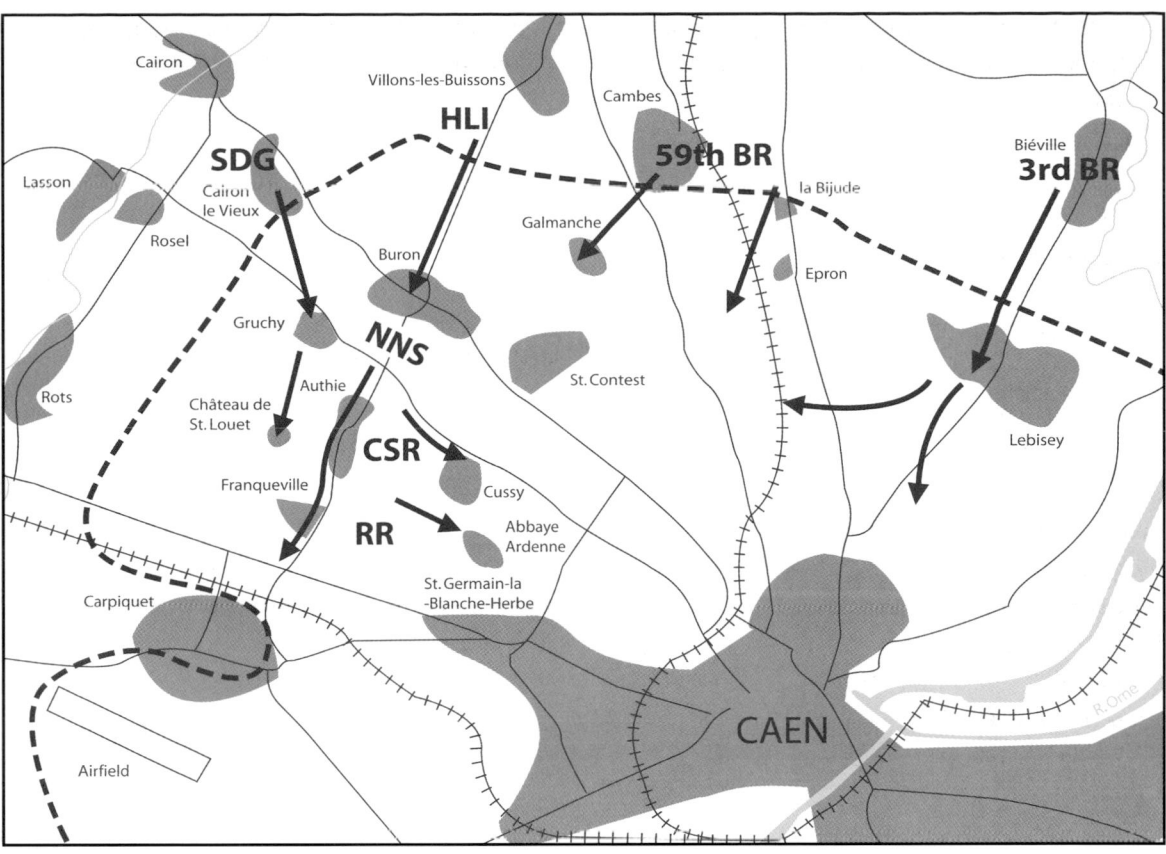

Operation "Charnwood".

German armour-piercing shells almost always penetrated and disabled a tank. In fact, the armour on our tanks offered such little protection that the only way to survive was to avoid being targeted. The contrast with German tank casualties was especially striking. Only 38 per cent of hits from the Sherman 75-mm or six-pounder-anti-tank gun penetrated German armour. What's more, German Panther and Tiger tanks often survived one or two hits. The sloping frontal armour of the Panther and the German self-propelled guns prevented penetration of 3/4 of all direct hits.

No one present on the battlefield in July 1944 would have considered using a regiment of Shermans as a manoeuvre force in attacking well-prepared defensive positions that controlled open approaches. Such a force would simply have been destroyed without effecting the battle.

Operation "Charnwood" was fought on a three-division front with, from left to right, 3rd British, 59th Staffordshire and 3rd Canadian divisions. Heavy bombers were to open the operation but given the problems of both target identification and the wide dispersal of bombs around the point of impact, the area designated for the bombers was well behind the enemy positions. The operation was based in part on an elaborate fire plan that maximized the Allies' artillery advantage. Many people thought "Charnwood" would break the defenders without too much difficulty. Instead, the operation cost Canada more casualties than on D-Day.

To understand what happened on July 8, 1944, it is necessary to examine the events closely and to make an effort to understand exactly what it was that artillery could and could not do.

The fire plan called for the navy and the medium guns to concentrate on counter-battery work and the destruction of targets well beyond the defensive perimeter. A great deal of attention was paid to rear areas to prevent reinforcements from arriving. The field artillery's self-propelled 105-mm guns, were to help the infantry get to its objectives by firing a timed barrage. The gunners would then respond to requests from forward observation officers (FOOs).

The capacity to neutralize hostile gun batteries, anti-tank positions, mortar and other sites depended on intelligence that was based almost entirely on photo reconnaissance, and the accuracy of artillery fire. Good photo reconnaissance could locate most of the larger enemy installations though it was seldom possible to distinguish between dummy positions and ones that were unoccupied. The small mortar pits and machine-gun posts, the low-profile anti-tank guns camouflaged in hedges and other infantry positions were another matter, although in the case of "Charnwood", patrolling and observation of fire helped.

Once the known positions were plotted, a fire plan was drawn up. Unfortunately, accuracy depended on a host of variables that meant that unobserved and therefore uncorrected fire was frequently plus or minus 100 to 300 yards for both range and line. Therefore, the only way to ensure success under such conditions was to fire many shells from a large number of guns.

Operation "Charnwood" was the first set-piece battle of the campaign and it is clear the gunners had a great deal to learn as they went along. The attack by the Highland Light Infantry on the village of Buron was the single most costly engagement on July 8. It is well documented and it is possible to learn a good deal about what took place.

The Germans had dug a long V-shaped anti-tank ditch in front of Buron and were intent on channeling the Allied armour into a carefully constructed killing zone. The barrage got the infantry to the obstacle easily enough but it quickly became evident that few of the German positions had been destroyed. Neutralization depended on continuous fire on the edge of the village and this depended on the forward observation officer.

The HLI got into Buron and began to clean out the defensive positions. The armour, which had circled west to try to provide support from the flank, suffered losses after it ran into a minefield. It was then out of action during the advance on the village.

As enemy shelling and mortar fire took its toll, the 12th SS attempted to recapture the village by employing a battle group of infantry and tanks. This counter-attack was quickly dealt with by the 17-pounders of a British self-propelled battery from the Corps Anti-tank Regiment. With the Stormont, Dundas and Glengarry Highlanders in firm control of Gruchy and the British in St. Contest, the fighting for the outer defences was over by late afternoon.

The North Nova Scotia Regiment captured the next objective and set the stage for 7th Brigade's assault on Cussy and the Abbaye d'Ardennes.

Operation "Charnwood" ended when the German order to withdraw across the Orne River was issued at 3:30 a.m. on July 9. That same day, British and Canadian patrols entered the city of Caen.

What might military historians learn from "Charnwood"? The operation was a battle fought and won by British and Canadian infantry battalions that used their personal and close-support weapons in accordance with their training. The heavy casualties reflected the difficulty of the task they were asked to carry out and the profound limitations of the weapon systems available to them. The German decision to retreat across the Orne rather than mount counter-attacks was a product of Field-Marshal Erwin Rommel's growing pessimism and the difficulty of movement in the area north of Caen that had been bombed and was subject to continuous shelling by naval guns. The British and Canadian troops had won an important operational victory.

The results of a bombing raid, Mezidon, Normandy.

Allied Bombing In Normandy

Originally published, November/December 1998

The ongoing debate over the role of Bomber Command in WW II generally ignores the contribution made to the direct defeat of the German army. If the role of heavy bombers in Normandy is discussed the emphasis is usually on the bombing of Caen or the casualties inflicted on our own troops by short bombing. The reality is that Bomber Command and the United States 8th Air Force played a major role in the Allied victory in Normandy, a role long overdue for recognition.

The idea of using heavy bombers in close support of the land battle developed in mid-June 1944 when the stalemate in front of Caen and the shortage of artillery ammunition led Chief Air Marshal Sir Trafford Leigh-Mallory to pro-pose an "air bombardment behind which the army might advance." Genuine differences of opinion as well as the personality clashes that plagued the British High Command aborted this proposal, but when General Bernard Montgomery planned Operation "Charnwood"–the assault on Caen–he requested and quickly received the assistance of Bomber Command.

Air Marshal Arthur Harris was willing to co-operate, but on his own terms. As he had repeatedly explained, his men had been trained to fly at night and each aircraft operated "individually, navigating by prescribed routes to the neighborhood of their objective under conditions in which no details of the ground can generally be seen." Each aircraft bombed on pyrotechnical markers placed on or near the objectives by Pathfinder aircraft and if necessary corrections were made by the master bomber. It involved grave risks to ask aircrew trained for such missions to locate and identify ground targets in close proximity to our own troops.

Harris wanted the army to understand that the pilot in a Lancaster or Halifax bomber had a very limited view of the ground as did the navigator, "a machine minder and plotter who spends most of his time in a cabin." The navigator's job was to determine the position of the aircraft using electronic aids as well as dead reckoning. The only crew member who could actually see the ground was the air bomber who had limited training and little experience in the difficult art of map reading with reference to the ground rushing beneath him. If the heavy bomber groups were to provide close support the chances of short bombings and totally misplaced concentrations would have to be expected.

With "Charnwood", Bomber Command agreed to a plan that involved 467 bombers, including most of RCAF 6 Group. The target, "four map squares", including the northwest quarter of the city of Caen was known to be well inside the ring of fortified villages and farms that encircled the city. However, Bomber Command had insisted on a bomb line 6,000 yards from the nearest Allied troops. Much attention has been focused on the decision to bomb Caen as part of the battle, but it should be remembered that the city was bombed and shelled repeatedly throughout June and July for less immediate reasons than on July 7.

The other oft repeated comment is that the bombers did little to help the capture of the city and may have hindered the advance of British and Canadian troops by blocking streets with rubble. Of course it also helped persuade Field Marshal Erwin Rommel that there was no possibility of reinforcing the 12th SS Panzer Division that was being ground into little pieces by the Allied assault. What mattered most to Montgomery and Harris is that for over an hour bombers had identified and hit a 1,000-yard-wide rectangle with virtually no spill over. They concluded that bomber crews who were well briefed could provide accurate close support.

Montgomery's scientific adviser, Brigadier Basil Schonland, asked his operational research section to study the results of the bombing and make recommendations. Their report, which was ready in time to influence the planning of the next offensive, noted that the major impact of the bombing was to raise the spirits of our troops while lowering the enemy's morale. It was therefore essential to take risks with the bomb line and avoid the use of delayed fuses that created larger craters, unless massive destruction was more important than rapid advance.

An elaborate bombing program was devised for Operation "Goodwood", the British armoured blitzkrieg of July 18, 1944, and "Atlantic"–the code-name for the Canadian portion of the operation. Christopher Evans, a young air historian who has written a detailed account of Bomber Command's role in "Goodwood", argues the bombing achieved almost all of its objectives. The weakness of the plan was the absence of a second, equally powerful onslaught the following day.

The targets were arranged in a complex U-shaped pattern. The industrial zone of Caen on the south bank of the Orne and the stone villages on the left flank of the tank corridor were to be destroyed with 1,000-pound, delayed fuse bombs. Mosquitoes of 8 Pathfinder Force employing Oboe, the navigation system based on radio beams, marked the targets with red smoke markers dropped from 22,000 feet. Behind them, flying into morning sun, the master and deputy master bombers corrected for wind drift dropping yellow target indicators. Finally, the Halifaxes and Lancasters approached the targets at heights of between 6,500 and 9,500 feet. The weather was clear and in slightly over 30 minutes the bombs were gone, leaving unbelievable destruction behind. Six of the 1,014 aircraft that took part in the operation were shot down.

For the 3rd Canadian Division, entering its sixth week of exhausting combat, the task of clearing the factories, railway yards and steel mills of Colombelles and Vaucelles had seemed a daunting prospect. For 8th Brigade, which was to lead off, memories of German resistance at Carpiquet were all too fresh, but the sight of the bombers and the evidence of their power inspired men to believe that this apparently impossible task could be carried out.

The Queen's Own Rifles of Canada on the left flank reached Giberville and took more than 200 prisoners from a totally demoralized German Luftwaffe division. Le Régiment de la Chaudière faced much tougher opposition centred on a chateau that had not been bombed. And so a new artillery fire plan was required to help overcome resistance. The North Shore (N.B.) Regiment could not move against the steelworks until early evening and it was close to midnight before 9th Brigade entered Vaucelles to link up with the Regina Rifles Regiment which had crossed the canal from Caen. The Germans had intended to defend the industrial suburbs to the last man, hoping to draw the Canadians into the kind of street fighting that cost attackers so dearly. Instead, the southern part of Caen was captured in less than a day.

The bombing was equally successful in the British sector where German formations were so thoroughly shaken that many units surrendered en masse. The companies of 22nd Panzer Regiment were destroyed along with 20 of their tanks, including some Tigers that were flipped on their backs by the force of the explosions.

All contemporary accounts of "Goodwood" agree that the Royal Air Force allowed the army to stage its initial breakthrough, but by the next day the Germans recovered and blunted the armoured advance with their superior tanks and anti-tank weaponry. When "Goodwood" ended on July 21, Allied generals were convinced the heavy bombers were the key to overcoming German defensive superiority in Normandy. The enemy was equally impressed. Field Marshal Gunther von Kluge recorded his reaction shortly before the operation was over. "The psychological effect on the fighting forces, especially the infantry, of such a mass of bombs, raining down upon them with all the force of elemental nature, is a factor which must be given serious consideration.... I am able to report that the front has been held intact until now.... However...the

moment is fast approaching when this overtaxed front line is bound to break up. And when the enemy once reaches the open country a properly co-ordinated command will be almost impossible, because of the insufficient mobility of our troops."

The operational research section confirmed this view, noting the accuracy of the concentrations and the evidence of enemy demoralization that lasted for several hours after the bombing had ended. For the U.S. Eighth Air Force preparing to attack in close support of the American army at Saint Lô, the RAF achievement was a real confidence booster. If a bomber force trained for night operations could strike with precise accuracy, surely the daylight "precision bombers" of the U.S. Army Air Force could do no less.

Unfortunately, the bombing in support of Operation "Cobra", General Omar Bradley's carefully planned breakout battle, was far less accurate. The American soldiers who had withdrawn 1,000 yards north of the main east-west highway as a safety measure, frantically dug in as bombs crashed onto their positions on July 24, when the operation was postponed, and July 25 when it went ahead. Despite the serious and demoralizing losses to "friendly fire", 90 per cent of the aircraft bombed accurately and this was the key to the early success of "Cobra".

For Operation "Bluecoat" on July 31, Montgomery asked Bomber Command and the U.S. Eighth Air Force to support his plan to hurl Second British Army into the fight on the American flank. Both air forces agreed to attack "likely points of resistance" in the later phases of the attack, leaving the artillery to shoot the troops onto their initial objectives. The operational research team reported that the "Bluecoat" bombing was generally accurate and effective.

The decision makers at 21st Army Group were now convinced that heavy bombers could be used consistently in close support of the army. Harris was not particularly happy with this conclusion. He noted it had taken a 1,000 tons of bombs to get the army forward one mile. "At this rate it will take 600,000 tons to get them to Berlin." Harris took great delight in making such provocative statements, but in fact Bomber Command co-operated with the army throughout the balance of the campaign.

For Operation "Totalize"–the Canadian offensive towards Falaise–both air forces were available. The RAF agreed to a night attack after Harris saw the results of a target-marking experiment that utilized red smoke shells. Unfortunately, only one of the villages targeted for destruction was squarely hit. The U.S. Eighth Air Force attack, designed to assist the armour in the open country north of Falaise was marred by the bombing of Canadian and Polish units well short of the bomb line. Just 24 of the 492 American bombers made targeting errors, but 65 men were killed and 250 wounded.

First Canadian Army was fighting with many of its infantry battalions at half strength and crews were desperately welding extra tank tracks to all their Shermans, so despite these errors Eisenhower was asked to provide heavy bomber support on a very large scale for Operation "Tractable", the final push to Falaise. Bomber Command carried out this operation without American involvement, but a large number of bombers, many ironically from 6 Group Royal Canadian Air Force, bombed short. This tragedy, which was similar in scale to the errors in "Totalize", might have put an end to the use of heavy bombers on the battlefield were it not for the intervention of General Harry Crerar. He got on well with Harris, and resisted the temptation of telling the air force how it should conduct its operations. He also did his best to ensure that the press recognized the contribution the air forces were making. After "Tractable", Crerar wrote to Harris thanking him for his willing co-operation and noting: "I remain a very strong advocate of the use of heavy bombers in closely integrated support of the army...by day as well as night." Crerar had good reasons for his optimism. In "Tractable", 90 per cent of the aircraft had bombed accurately and a number of enemy strongpoints were obliterated. In the wide open rolling country north of Falaise the neutraliza-

tion of a dozen key anti-tank positions would spell the difference between success and failure.

During September 1944, Bomber Command continued to co-operate closely with First Canadian Army. For Operation "Wellhit", the battle for Boulogne, the heavies were allotted a major role. There were only two brigades available to capture a city defended by an equal number of men protected by concrete. The keystone of the enemy position was Mont- Lambert which overlooked the entire battlefield. Ninth Brigade, which was assigned to take the hill, was mounted in Kangaroo personnel carriers. The brigade crossed the start line as the last bombs fell and it was on its objective within an hour. The last bunkers on Mont-Lambert were captured with flame-throwers 36 hours after the bombing, but there could be no doubt that Bomber Command had made the initial break-in possible.

For the remainder of the war, First Canadian Army continued to call upon the heavy bombers for "closely integrated support of the army." The planners drew upon the lessons of Normandy for Walcheren, the Rhineland and the Rhine crossing. A new method of substituting munitions for men's lives had been developed

CFPU RE20421-1

A Spitfire MkIX with invasion recognition stripes.

TAF Over Normandy

Originally published, January/February 1999

The 75th anniversary year for the Royal Canadian Air Force is also the 55th anniversary year for the Battle of Normandy. Without a doubt, the story of the RCAF's part in the struggle to liberate France has captured the imaginations of air historians. However, few Canadians have more than the vaguest idea of the scale of the RCAF's contribution.

The major reason for this is spelled out in Jack Granatstein's book *Who Killed Canadian History?* But it is also evident that the postwar pre-occupation with building a national air force meant that wartime experiences under Royal Air Force command were seen as less Canadian.

The history of 2nd Tactical Air Force ought to be an important chapter in our collective memory of the war because Canadians played a large role in the air battles that made victory in Europe possible. Second TAF was formed in 1943 to support

the army by establishing and maintaining air superiority, providing air reconnaissance and attacking enemy ground targets. RCAF squadrons were assigned to 83 Composite Group and formed the majority of the group's squadrons. As the most experienced formation, 83 Group was assigned to support Second British Army which, for the Normandy invasion, was to include 3rd Canadian Division and 2nd Canadian Armoured Brigade.

The new army-support role presented the air force with an incredible challenge because the RAF had failed to develop a good ground-attack aircraft and it was forced to modify its fighters to perform a dual role. The Typhoon had proved to be a poor performer in aerial combat, but it could be modified to carry bombs or rockets.

It was one thing to declare that Spitfires and Typhoons were now fighter-bombers, but it was quite another job to make this a reality. Air Marshal Arthur Coningham, who assumed command of 2nd TAF after his experience in North Africa, recognized there was not much time for training. He decided that Typhoon squadrons should specialize in either rocket-projectile attacks or dive bombing. When 438, 439 and 440 squadrons arrived from Canada in February 1944, they traded in their Hurricanes for the Typhoon IB and were assigned to a dive-bomber role. Pilots who flew the Typhoon never forgot their introduction to the "monster".

After the elegance and superb flight characteristics of the Spitfire and Hurricane, the Typhoon was a nightmare. Seven tons of aircraft with an enormous 24-cylinder Napier engine greeted the first-timer. The engine, which was five times as noisy as the Spitfire, started when a cartridge was fired and the explosion turned the motor. Fires in the engine's air intake were common and that meant ground crews had to stand by with fire extinguishers. Once the engine was roaring, exhaust gases seeped into the cockpit and so an oxygen mask was a necessity even on the ground.

To taxi, pilots employed a crab-like progress; they would weave into position while trying not to overuse the brakes that overheated quickly. Pierre Closterman, an experienced Spitfire pilot, recalled his first Typhoon flight: "I checked the plugs as per instruction by opening up to 3,000 revs and a film of oil immediately spread up to my windshield.... I tightened my straps, released the brakes...and slowly opened the throttle.... I had been warned the Typhoon swung but surely not as much as this! And the brute gathered speed like a rocket.... To hell with it. I tore her off the ground.

This plane just had no lateral stability at all.... Luckily, they hauled F hangar down after too many accidents, but even then I passed uncomfortably close to E hangar.... Half an hour quickly passed and I began to summon the courage to land.... I had just begun to ease the stick back when the whole contraption stalled and dropped like a stone.... After bucking two or three times, my Typhoon finally calmed down and rolled drunkenly down the runway.... I managed to stop before ramming the scenery in a cloud of smoke and oil.... My poor landing did not seem to have attracted much attention.... As long as the kite arrived in one piece it was considered a good landing."

Good pilots learned to cope with the worst characteristics of the Typhoon, but each takeoff and landing was a challenge.

RCAF Typhoon squadrons formed 143 Wing and began operations March 28, 1944, against railway yards and the V-1 flying bomb or "buzz bomb" launching sites. 143 Wing had undergone a short period of training in the technique of dive bombing, but practice appeared to make little difference. Average pilots could seldom hit the kinds of targets they were tasked to destroy. In one carefully measured operation, "Bombphoons"– as they were called–achieved hits once in every 41 attacks. Rocket-equipped Typhoons scored better, one hit for every 15 sorties. However, rocket-equipped Typhoons each fired six rockets so only one in 90 rockets actually struck the target. Since the objective had not been defended by anti-aircraft guns, 2nd TAF was deeply disappointed by the results.

Average pilots were unlikely to do better than this in combat, although exceptional pilots could greatly improve on the squadron's average. The limitations of dive bombing, which applied equally to Spitfires, did not mean Typhoons were ineffective in a ground-support role. Each Typhoon was armed with four 20-mm cannons that could devastate "soft" targets such as trucks and bring trains to a halt by punching the boilers on steam locomotives. "Train busting" was a specialty for many Typhoon squadrons in the run-up to D-Day.

The nine RCAF Spitfire squadrons assigned to 83 Group had a much easier time preparing for the invasion. While the Spitfire IX could be employed as a dive bomber, its major roles were to destroy enemy aircraft and strafe targets of opportunity with its cannon and machine-guns. Bill Olmstead flew with 442 Squadron in Normandy and he recalled that "strafing was a very dangerous, though thrilling assignment, and in the case of the Spitfire a difficult one as the Spit was a very unstable gun platform.... The attacking aircraft would dive at a very steep angle until about 700 yards from the target, and clocking possibly 400-miles-per-hour, when the pilot would decrease the dive angle to about 20 degrees. He would open fire at about 400 yards, closing to 100 unless his bullets blew up the target. The guns fired for only a second or two, and yet their effect could be devastating."

The RCAF also supplied three reconnaissance squadrons. Equipped with high performance Spitfire XIVs, which were able to operate at high altitudes, photo reconnaissance aircraft were–to the disgust of many pilots–too valuable to arm. Their job was to produce the thousands of vertical and oblique air photos that both the army and air force used in planning operations. Two of the reconnaissance squadrons–413 and 430–flew Mustangs in a variety of roles. On D-Day, the squadrons spotted for the Royal Navy, correcting their fire against coastal gun batteries. From then on their main task was tactical reconnaissance conducted at low levels above the battlefield.

The job of spotting enemy road and rail movement, as well as front-line targets, was necessary but costly. The Germans had been forced to concede air superiority in France, but they equipped their forces with enormous quantities of anti-aircraft guns, including the dual-purpose 88- and rapid-firing 20-and 40-mm guns.

Flak was a particularly dangerous threat to ground-support aircraft that were committed to low-level reconnaissance or tasked to attack ground targets. In the book *Blue Skies*, Olmstead writes: "Flak is the one thing that pilots, be they fighter or bomber, fear above everything else. Flying along in formation a mile or two above the earth, it is possible to avoid flak by taking evasive action through frequent alterations of course and altitude, but once committed to a dive on a target, the pilot must press home his attack while shells and bullets of all calibres flash by. We were quite philosophical about flak, as much as we hated it, because surviving flak was strictly a matter of luck, and it claimed the best pilots as well as the poorer ones in time. The 88-mm shells and heavier calibre guns burst with a bright red flash surrounded by a large ball of black, wicked-looking smoke that hung lazily in the sky. At dawn or dusk, pink tracer shells were visible, a sight that flyers will remember for years. It was a horrible feeling to climb away from a target and watch the

rosy balls of red-hot death streaming by, missing you and your aircraft by a very few feet. Then there was the reverse effect when you attacked a target, and the shells seemed to come up so slowly that you felt you were watching them for ages. Not until they were close did you get the full impression of their tremendous speed. It took steady nerves to carry on facing so many deadly messengers."

The German anti-aircraft regiments, manned by the Luftwaffe, had years of practice. They inflicted terrible losses on 2nd TAF pilots. Between April 1 and June 5, 1944, 133 fighter bombers were shot down, and the toll increased after D-Day.

As soon as the Allied beachhead on the continent was secure, the construction of airfields for 2nd TAF and United States Army Air Force fighter bombers became a top priority. The narrowness of the beachhead presented the airfield construction crews with limited choices and the first landing strips were crowded into a very small area with takeoffs and landings only possible in one direction away from the nearby enemy lines.

To move a fighter wing from the United Kingdom to France was a major undertaking. More than 300 men staffed the headquarters, providing signals, transport, medical and other services as well as mechanics for major repairs. In addition, each squadron had 18 aircraft, 26 pilots and 115 ground crew. Olmstead explains that each pilot was assigned a specific aircraft and in some cases two pilots shared the same aircraft. "Each kite had its own rigger, fitter and armourer, with assistance from squadron photographers, wireless experts, electricians, and chaps who ensured that the oxygen bottles were always full. This system promoted a good deal of co-operation between the pilots and the ground crew to ensure that each aircraft was maintained at full serviceability. As I had been with the RAF, I had always been proud of the dedication and expertise of the Canadian ground crews. I knew that every time I flew an aircraft that it had been examined and cared for to the best of human ability, and I never flew a machine in Europe that malfunctioned because of sloppy maintenance. Words are inadequate to express my admiration for the hard working, dedicated ground crew mechanics."

Once established in Normandy, 2nd TAF sought to refine the methods it had employed in the assault phase. The Luftwaffe was rarely seen in the daylight skies over Normandy because Coningham insisted that total control of the skies remained top priority even against a greatly diminished threat. Historians, secure in the knowledge that the Luftwaffe failed to recover its strength in 1944, have criticized Coningham for the way he allocated resources. However, the air marshal was determined to provide absolute security to the navy and the crowded beaches where supplies were gathered. This ongoing screen of fighter aircraft also allowed the navy to aid the land battle with its heavy guns. During June, only five of 5,000 vessels operating off the coast of Normandy were sunk by enemy aircraft, the largest being a destroyer.

After ensuring air superiority, 2nd TAF turned its attention to armed reconnaissance. One pilot recalled that armed reconnaissance was the preferable assignment, providing more opportunity for action, since pilots could shoot up anything and everything. Pilots got real delight from seeing a convoy become "flamers" under attack, or even only "smokers". The ultimate achievement was to shoot up an ammunition convoy that resulted in 15 or 20 trucks looking like a May 24th celebration.

The success of this enterprise is best measured by the response of the German army which issued elaborate orders designed to limit the effects of air attacks. Daylight movement was banned in clear weather, major roads were avoided whenever possible and vehicles on side roads moved carefully at intervals of 100 and 200 yards. Lookouts, posted at the head and rear of columns, were to provide warning that fighters were near so that vehicles could be driven under cover and personnel given the chance to scatter. Such measures permitted the Germans to manoeuvre and maintain a flow of supplies to the front. However, all movement was slow and subject to interruption. The contrast to the Allied side of the front–where everyone in the densely packed beachhead moved freely–was dramatic.

The third task of the tactical air forces was to provide more direct support to the army as it waged war on the ground. The air force, aware of the difficulties of locating and hitting small targets in close proximity to the front line, preferred what it described as pre-arranged, direct support missions against targets outside the range of Allied artillery. This allowed for careful briefing of pilots and minimized the dangers of casualties due to "friendly fire". The army, however, wanted much more because Normandy had turned into a battle of attrition and as casualties mounted there was constant pressure to employ fighter bombers in close support roles to Allied troops. To accomplish this difficult task, 2nd TAF developed a system that became widely known as "Cabrank". This was based on the use of contact vehicles in direct communication with aircraft circling over the battlefield at 5,000 feet.

The contact car passed on information about the target and provided a detailed description of landmarks, such as roads, villages and woods. After carrying out the attack, the aircraft returned to "Cabrank" or to base if their ammunition was gone or if their fuel was low. If they had to return to base, a new aircraft would take their place. "Cabrank" worked reasonably well on static fronts, but once the breakout began in August, a more direct system of communication between leading troops and aircraft was required.

The USAAF invented the armoured-column cover in time to assist General George Patton in his race into the heart of France. However, no similar system was developed by 2nd TAF and incidents of "friendly fire" multiplied throughout August as the struggle to close the Falaise Gap unfolded.

The Toronto
Scottish Regiment
Memorial at the
Canadian Battle-
fields Foundation
bellevedere, PT 67,
Verrières Ridge,
Normandy.

Operation "Atlantic"

Originally published, March/April 1999

As Canada's chief army historian between 1945-59, Colonel C.P. Stacey rarely employed emotional language in his writing about WW II, but when it came to describing the July 1944 battles for Verrières Ridge, he included the following: "Three miles or so south of Caen the present-day tourist, driving down the arrow-straight road that leads to Falaise, sees immediately to his right a rounded hill crowned by farm buildings. If the traveller be Canadian, he would do well to stay the wheels at this point and cast his mind back to the events of 1944; for this apparently insignificant eminence is Verrières Ridge. Well may the wheat and sugar beet grow green and lush upon its gentle slopes, for in that now half-forgotten summer the best blood of Canada was freely poured out upon them.".

In the first of two articles on the battles for Verrières Ridge, I want to focus on the battle experience of the newly arrived 2nd Canadian Infantry Division. Second Division arrived in France during the worst days of the battle of Normandy.

The Allies had expected heavy losses on the D-Day beaches and then, once through Hitler's Atlantic Wall, lighter casualties in a war of rapid movement. The opposite had happened. The coastal defences had been quickly breached, but then there was only slow movement and horrendous casualties. In June, more than 37,000 American troops were killed, wounded or missing, while almost 25,000 British and Canadian troops shared the same fate. The Allied air forces enjoyed total air superiority over the battlefield, but in June alone the cost was 6,200 aircrew. Soldiers on both sides were beginning to say that it was WW I all over again–a static battle of attrition–gains measured in yards and thousands of dead.

Generals in their memoirs and historians in their books on Normandy have usually focused their attention on the controversies over Allied strategy, especially the debate between General Bernard Montgomery and Supreme Allied Commander Dwight Eisenhower. However, the real problem was at the operational, not at the strategic level. It is an axiom of military science that the attacker needs a 3:1 margin over the defender to have a reasonable chance of success. If the defence is well dug in, even better odds are required. The Allies had landed in Normandy prepared for a war of mobility in which the tactical air forces and the armoured regiments would dominate the battlefield. Instead, they were confronted with a German army that was capable of maintaining a continuous defence in-depth.

Neither British nor Canadian infantry divisions had been able to break through these defences. So, in mid-July, Montgomery agreed to employ the three British armoured divisions in a blitzkrieg-like attack from the Orne River bridgehead. The plan was very ambitious and experienced armoured commanders—conscious of the vulnerability of their Sherman tanks—argued for a stage-by-stage approach. Montgomery rejected this advice. His operational method was "to concentrate great strength at some selected place and hit the Germans a colossal crack."

The difficulty was that the enemy commanders would do anything necessary to prevent a breakout in the open country south of Caen, even if it meant committing their armoured divisions to an attritional battle. Since the Germans had massed more than 380 tanks and self-propelled assault guns as well as scores of 88-mm guns in the area, the odds were against a British breakthrough. Operation "Goodwood" began with a "colossal crack" supplied by heavy bombers. On the first day, the advance stunned the enemy. 12th SS Panzer Division, which had been pulled out of the line after its heavy losses in the battle for Caen, was rushed forward to thicken the defences.

The British armoured divisions made little progress on the second day, but over on the right flank along the Orne, 2nd Canadian Infantry Division began its first battle since Dieppe with some promising local victories.

The division had been held in reserve during the first phase of Operation "Goodwood", but it had orders to be ready to exploit southwards after 3rd Canadian Infantry Division had captured the Caen suburbs south of the Orne.

Lieutenant-General Guy Simonds, directing his first battle as a corps commander, decided not to wait. He ordered 4th Brigade to capture the village of Louvigny and cross the Orne in the hope of bypassing the German defences. Brigadier Sherwood Lett, who was wounded before the day was done, assigned the Royal Regiment of Canada and a squadron of Fort Garry Horse tanks to the first phase of this attack. The enemy—elements of 271st Infantry Division—held Louvigny as an outpost of Hill 112, the key to their defences west of the Orne. The Royals and Garries overcame them, but only after a costly hand-to-hand struggle to gain control of the chateau on the edge of the village.

Simonds was unwilling to wait. He ordered 5th Brigade to cross the Orne at Caen, striking south along the east side of the river. The Black Watch took the lead, crossing the river in assault boats in the face of intense machine-gun and mortar fire. The attack on Fleury-sur-Orne got off to a bad start when Le Régiment de Maisonneuve's two lead companies formed up on the opening line for their support barrage instead of on their assigned start-line. Both companies were hit by friendly fire.

Historians have frequently drawn attention to this incident, but at the time it seemed to be just another example of the chaos that enveloped all battlefields. War, when described by generals and historians, takes on an organized, coherent pattern that is not at all evident to the men who are asked to carry out the grand design. Lines marked hastily on a map at an orders group may be difficult to relate to on ground that has been bombed and is still under shelling. What was significant on July 19 was the speed with which the Maisonneuves recovered and pressed on to their objectives. The battalion's command structure remained intact. Morale was shaken, but it was not destroyed.

While the Maisonneuves were consolidating, the Calgary Highlanders were preparing to move over the northern spur of Verrières Ridge. This was not an inviting prospect. If you stand at the southern edge of Fleury-sur-Orne today you can see Hill 112 on the west side of the Orne.

This position was still occupied by the Germans on July 19. The route south is overlooked by this high ground all the way to May-sur-Orne. The low ridge marked Point 67 on the battlefield map seems to be of little consequence, unless you are a foot soldier who has to walk up and capture it in broad daylight. At 5:15 p.m. on July 19, the pipes began to play and the Calgary Highlanders moved carefully forward, two companies up. They were slowed by terrific mortar fire that was so accurate that the headquarters group turned off its radio set fearing that the enemy was honing in on it.

The Sherbrooke Fusiliers, in support of the brigade, sent a troop of tanks forward on each side of the road. They were able to deal with several machine-gun posts and a number of snipers. One enemy strongpoint was not so readily overcome and a quick plan was made to fire on the position from the flank in support of a platoon frontal attack. As the tanks manoeuvred into position two were hit by long-range guns, although the crews escaped. The others provided enough suppressing fire to get the Calgary Highlanders onto the strongpoint without casualties. By 6:30 p.m., the Calgaries were digging in at Point 67 under a hail of mortar bombs.

The German defences south of Caen were manned by elements of the 272th Infantry Division, a low-category unit formed in 1943. The division included large numbers of Russians who had chosen service with the Wehrmacht over near-certain death in PoW camps. On D-Day it was located in the south of France at Port Vendes. Ordered north on July 3, the division reached the front eight days later. By July 16, it had relieved units of 1st SS Panzer Corps in the section west of the Caen-Falaise road. A battle group of tanks from 1st SS Panzer Division was provided to stiffen the division's resolve. It was this battle group that staged a classic German counterattack on the evening of July 19.

The Panthers and Panzer grenadiers surged forward and, just as Simonds had predicted, they attacked individual infantry positions with close-in, aimed fire from armoured vehicles. Fortunately, the Calgaries had been warned by a fighting patrol that had probed further south. As a result of that warning, they had dug themselves in.

For the next hour, the Calgaries held on. The SS, meanwhile, was unable to commit enough infantry to take the battalion position. When darkness fell, the mortaring did not stop. However, it was possible to evacuate the wounded. There were surprisingly few fatal casualties, but 92 men were evacuated with wounds, and a number of others were sent to the rear areas as battle exhaustion casualties.

The Calgaries were not left on their own. At 7 p.m. the Royal Highland Regiment of Canada–better known as the Black Watch–moved forward to secure the left flank occupying the village of Ifs. It was supported by two troops of tanks. Probing attacks by small groups of enemy troops looking for a way around the Calgary position were beaten off and Ifs quickly became a target for German artillery and mortars. During the night, mortaring set the regimental aid post on fire. Sergeant W.F. Clements, the senior non-commissioned officer at the regimental aid post, organized the evacuation of the wounded in a demonstration of tireless resolve under fire. He was awarded the Military Medal for his action that night.

2nd Division's first day in battle had been relatively successful. There had been plenty of mistakes, as is inevitable when "green" troops, commanded by equally inexperienced officers, are committed to action for the first time. The errors had not led to undue confusion or collapse of unit morale. Infantry/tank co-operation had worked well and the field regiments had demonstrated their professionalism both with pre-arranged attacks and in rapid and accurate response to requests from the forward observation officers.

Simonds' plan for the next day called for 6 Canadian Infantry Brigade to pass through 5th Brigade and establish itself on the "Verrières feature". This order conflicted with the ones issued to 7th Armoured Division to advance along the ridge from its position at Hubert

Folie. The Desert Rats began to attack during the morning. It used a company of motorized infantry and a squadron of tanks. Troteval Farm, located north of Verrières, was the initial objective. However, "opposition was too strong" and 7th Armoured was only too happy to agree to leave the battlefield to the Canadians. Simonds believed that a fresh, reinforced infantry brigade could accomplish the task, and the evidence of growing German resistance did not dissuade him.

The attack by 6th Brigade turned into a bloody nightmare. Torrential rain that ended air sorties and artillery observation was coupled with a major German counterattack. On the right flank the Queen's Own Cameron Highlanders were able to secure a hold on part of the village of Saint-André, but in the open grain fields along the ridge German tanks roamed at will, machine-gunning the South Saskatchewans and knocking out the handful of Shermans that had ventured forward. The reserve battalion, the Essex Scottish, was also hit hard and parts of the battalion broke under pressure.

By the evening of July 20, some degree of order had been restored. However, during the next day, while the rain continued, the finger-hold on the ridge began to slip.

The Black Watch was ordered to try to restore the situation. The barrage began at 6 p.m. and the Black Watch leaned into it, moving up the hill in a "text-book operation." Tanks remained at the crossroads until the battalions' anti-tank guns were in position. The Canadians held a line that stretched along the road from Saint-André-sur-Orne to the Caen-Falaise highway, but they were still on the lower slope and Verrières Ridge loomed ahead.

Casualties had been very heavy. Second Division lost 1,349 men, including 249 killed and 200 evacuated for battle exhaustion. The scale of the losses was not fully understood at the time and many men who fought fierce engagements and bested the enemy believed that the division had done very well in its first battle.

We who are so used to employing hindsight find it hard to enter into the minds of the men who had to endure combat, absorb replacements and get ready for the next battle. However, it is clear that 2nd Division recovered quickly from its ordeal. After the war, General Charles Foulkes, who commanded the division in Normandy, claimed that "when we bumped into battle-experienced German troops we were no match for them." Foulkes, however, did not explain why some battalions were highly effective in their first battles. The evidence suggests that with the exception of a brief period on July 20, when weather and a well-timed counterattack devastated the South Saskatchewans and Essex Scottish, the battalions and armoured regiments at the sharp end of the battle held their own in the face of a determined and powerful enemy.

The performance of the Black Watch certainly requires special comment. This proud regiment experienced two of the worst single-day disasters of WW II on July 25 and October 13, 1944. These events have been allowed to overshadow its history, but it should be noted that on July 19 both the brigade and divisional commander regarded the Black Watch as a well-trained, well-led unit that could be counted on in a vanguard role. The regiment's reputation was confirmed in its success in the assault crossing of the Orne and in the two attacks during Operation "Atlantic". Success on the battlefield requires good leadership and high morale, but there are circumstances where these ingredients are not enough. The timing of events, not to mention plain old good luck, also has a great deal to do with success.

Operation "Spring"

Originally published, May/June 1999

General Bernard Montgomery's armoured blitzkrieg–Operation "Goodwood"–ended July 20, 1944, in a storm of rain and recriminations. Before the battle, Montgomery had talked confidently of a "real showdown on the eastern flank" with his armour reaching as far as Falaise. When the operation ended the industrial suburbs of Caen had been cleared and some 40 square miles added to the Orne bridgehead. Falaise, however, was a distant dream.

Montgomery's critics at Allied headquarters were scathing in their comments, arguing that Montgomery had again failed to press home his attack. Others, especially front-line soldiers, thought the operation had been far too costly. The 493 tanks that were lost could easily be replaced, but the scores of experienced tank, troop and squadron commanders and hundreds of infantry junior leaders killed and wounded were another matter. It was felt that if the British and Canadian armies continued to take casualties at such a rate, the long anticipated reinforcement crisis would occur while the Normandy battle was still in the "dogfight" stage.

Montgomery ignored both sets of critics and got on with the job of destroying the German armies in France. News of the plot to assassinate Hitler on July 20, rumours that Rommel had been killed or severely wounded, and information that the Germans had ordered 116th Panzer Division–their last uncommitted armoured division–to move to the battlefront, convinced Monty that if the Allies stayed the course the Germans would soon collapse.

Montgomery did not intend to rely on Operation "Cobra"–the American offensive–to end the Normandy stalemate. He planned a new series of battles on the Caen front. In a letter to Supreme Allied Commander Dwight D. Eisenhower, Monty wrote that he would continue "to try to bring about a major enemy withdrawal in front of General Omar Bradley...by a series of left-right-left blows east and west of the Orne to keep the enemy guessing, followed by a heavy blow towards Falaise." The letter concluded with the words: "It may well be that we shall achieve our object on the western flank by a victory on the eastern flank."

The first of Monty's left-right-left blows was Operation "Spring". It was scheduled for July 25. Both 7th Armoured Division and the Guards Armoured Division were to join in the attack once the Canadian infantry had broken through the German defences on Verrières Ridge. Operation "Spring" is one of the most controversial military operations in all of Canadian history. It was the principal topic of the Normandy episode in the television mini-series The Valour And The Horror. The operation has continued to attract armchair generals determined to prove that Lieutenant-General Guy Simonds and his commanders were careless of Canadian lives, incompetent or both. Operation "Spring", therefore, is worth careful study.

As the historian David O'Keefe has pointed out, intelligence reports, including information from Ultra, provided fairly complete evidence of the enemy order of battle. The 272nd Infantry Division, reduced by casualties in Operation "Goodwood", held Verrières Ridge with four battalions estimated at 600 men each. Battle groups of 2nd and 9th SS Panzer Division were known to be in support. East of the Caen-Falaise highway, 1st SS Panzer Division held Tilly-la-Campagne. 10th SS Panzer Division was in reserve and 116th Panzer Division on its way to the battlefront from north of the Seine.

Attacking this formidable array of guns, tanks and dug-in infantry with the limited forces available to Simonds does not seem to make a good deal of sense and the first question to ask about Operation "Spring" is why did it take place? The answer is surely quite simple. Montgomery could not permit the British and Canadian armies to ease the pressure at the precise moment the Americans were launching their major offensive. We do not need to resolve the debate about whether "Spring" was a holding attack to keep the Panzer division in the Caen sector while the Americans broke out, or an attempted break-

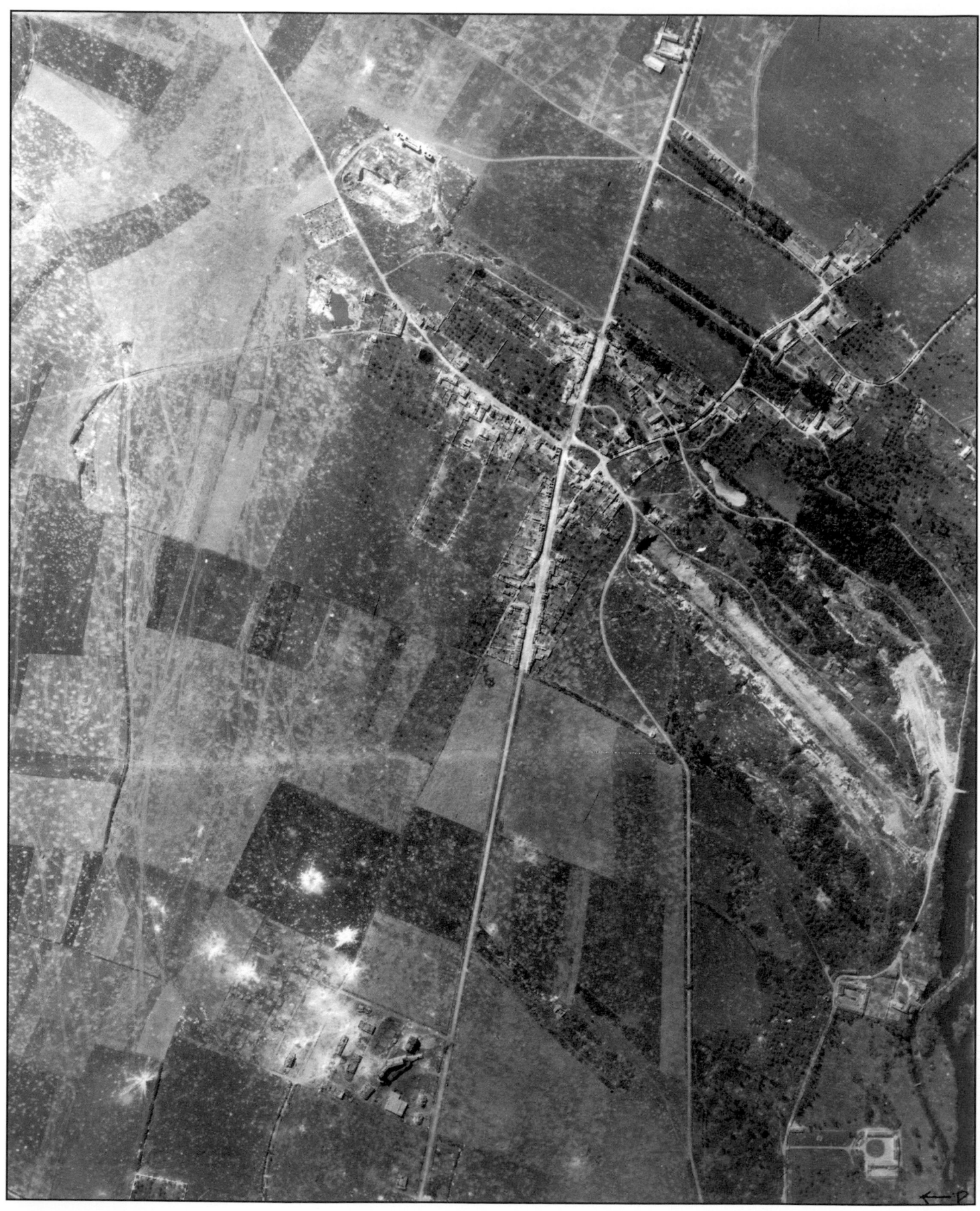

through that failed, because from Simonds' perspective none of this mattered anyway. He was ordered to attack on a specific date with the forces allotted to him. How did he respond to the challenge?

Simonds first heard of Operation "Spring" on July 21 and immediately began to draw up plans. Before D-Day he had issued a directive outlining his version of the artillery-based battle doctrine the Allied armies had been developing. "When the Germans decided to stand and fight", he wrote, "only a carefully organized attack with full artillery support on a narrow frontage will succeed." But Simonds was no longer confident that artillery, even when supplemented by massive air power, could dominate the battlefield. Throughout June and July 1944, the Allies had employed enormous quantities of shells and bombs and had apparently failed to shake German morale, never mind achieve a breakthrough.

Simonds was determined to stage Operation "Spring" as the first major night attack of the campaign. He believed that if the infantry could get onto their objectives in the darkness, clear out the enemy's forward positions and then dig in, casualties would be minimized and counter-attacks dealt with from prepared positions. Follow-up battalions attacking at first light with armoured, artillery and air support including 7th Armoured Division would occupy a second line of villages. If all went well the Guards Armoured Division would then advance to the highground and Point 122.

Simonds has been criticized for employing just three battalions in the initial attack, but it is evident that he believed the three villages were the only practical objectives in a night advance and that command and control could best be exercised within a battalion. Was he wrong? A more serious criticism was made by Brigadier W.J. Megill who commanded 5th Brigade. He thought the plan for Operation "Spring" was drawn up from maps by someone who had never seen the ground. To attack uphill into a strong enemy position was bad enough, but it seemed suicidal when every step forward exposed your flank to enemy mortar and artillery from the west bank of the Orne.

Simonds had seen the ground and that is why he proposed to attack at night. The problem was timing. H-hour was set for 0330 hours on July 25 with just two hours allotted for capturing the villages. The second phase battalions were to move into position to advance at first light at 0530. Limited visibility in the early morning mist of the Orne Valley would offer some protection from observation. Was there a better plan?

The first phase of Operation "Spring" appeared to go very well. On the left flank the North Nova Scotia Highlanders advanced steadily to the outskirts of Tilly-la-Campagne. Their lead companies fired a flare at 0430 hours, signaling success in reaching their objective. At 0525 hours, Lieutenant-Colonel Charles Petch ordered his reserve companies into the village to mop up and reported "Hamlet"—the code word for "on the objective"—to division and corps.

In the centre, the Royal Hamilton Light Infantry overcame initial opposition and seized Verrières village by 0530 hours. At 0750, Lieutenant-Colonel John Rockingham reported that his battalion was firm on the objective. Phase Two could begin. On the right, the Calgary Highlanders discovered that their start line was still under enemy fire with the enemy dug in at the factory area south of the village. Elements of two companies bypassed these positions and reached the edge of May-sur-Orne. They managed to report this before radio contact was lost. Both companies suffered heavy losses and were widely scattered. They withdrew from May but could not make contact with battalion headquarters.

As dawn broke less than three hours after the battle began, divisional commander Major-General Charles Foulkes and Simonds believed that all three assault battalions were on their objectives.

What should Simonds and his subordinate commanders have done? What would you have done? Megill described the problem this way: "You never know if your decision is the right one. Where is the line between caution and cowardice? If in doubt do you order your men to dig in? Do you refuse to carry out orders if you don't agree with them? If there are easy answers to these

LCMSDS

Air photo of May-sur-Orne and Verrières Ridge. The curve of the ridge may be seen upper left. The 'factory' or Cité de la Mine is bottom centre.

questions, I haven't heard them." Neither had Simonds or the others involved, each of whom tried to respond to a confused situation as their training and common sense dictated.

On the left flank, the Black Watch was scheduled to begin the attack on Fontenay-le-Marmion shortly after 0545. It left their assembly area on time and was at the edge of Saint-Martin at 0500 hours when the commanding officer, Lieutenant-Colonel S.S.T. Cantlie was mortally wounded by machine-gun fire. The same burst of gunfire wounded Cantlie's senior company commander. Command of the battalion passed to a 26-year-old, Major Phil Griffin.

Described as a "brilliant officer" by his peers, Griffin took control quickly. Since there was no way the battalion could reach its intended start line of May-sur-Orne on time, he deployed the battalion in a more secure position and organized a new attack for 0930. Griffin knew little about the actual position of the Calgaries, but a Black Watch patrol sent into May-sur-Orne reported that it had reached the main crossroads when a single machine-gun had opened up. Griffin assigned the task of taking out the machine-gun to a fighting patrol and informed his company commanders that the Black Watch would advance directly over the ridge to Fontenay-le-Marmion. The tanks of the 1st Hussars, which were originally intended to advance on the open left flank, were switched to the right to assist the Calgaries and help subdue resistance in May-sur-Orne.

Both brigade and battalion headquarters had received a series of messages from division demanding action, but it is clear that neither Griffin nor Megill needed any urging. When Megill, who heard of Griffin's revised plans through the artillery net, came forward to talk to the young Black Watch officer, the battlefield appeared to be deserted and the enemy guns were strangely quiet. The two men stood on the verandah of a house looking towards the ridge as Griffin calmly explained his intentions. Megill recalled suggesting that it might be better to stick to the original plan and move first to May-sur-Orne, but Griffin insisted that "they had patrols into May." Once the Black Watch attack went in,

he argued, the Calgaries "would fill in behind."

Should Megill have overruled Griffin and ordered the Black Watch to first secure May-sur-Orne? The answer is surely yes and Megill regretted his failure to intervene to the day he died. But is this just hindsight? At the time, Megill admitted, it seemed better to allow Griffin to go ahead rather than force changes that would require a new fire plan and a new orders group. Order, counter-order, confusion is one of the oldest military maxims and Megill decided not to interfere. Ironically, "Charlie" Company of the Calgary Highlanders was working its way into the village as the Black Watch formed up for the attack. When the artillery barrage began, it forced the Calgaries to go to ground while their sister battalion was systematically destroyed. The enemy held May and the ridge in strength. It had simply been exercising good fire control, ignoring patrols and waiting until the main attack began. Griffin and 122 others were killed in the attack, 101 were wounded and 83 taken prisoner.

In the centre, the Royal Hamilton Light Infantry had functioned brilliantly, seizing the village and deploying their anti-tank guns to fend off counter-attacks. Verrières village is on a reverse slope, the crest is 200 yards further south. When a 9th SS Panzer battle group tried to attack the Rileys, the fire from six-inch and 17-pounder anti-tank guns was so deadly the Germans reported "whoever crosses the ridge is a dead man" and turned away. Unfortunately, the same was true for the Royal Regiment of Canada which advanced less than 300 yards beyond the crest before its lead company was annihilated. The 1st Royal Tank Regiment, from 7th Armoured Division, lost 30 tanks in not many more minutes. There would be no further advance in the centre.

The situation on the left was far more uncertain. By 0700 hours, Petch knew his battalion was in trouble and he asked Brigadier Ben Cunningham for an armoured squadron to help break enemy resistance. The Fort Garries were supposed to be in reserve for phase two but Cunningham sent them forward. The lead tanks were quickly knocked out and the rest of the squadron moved around the village seeking hull-down positions.

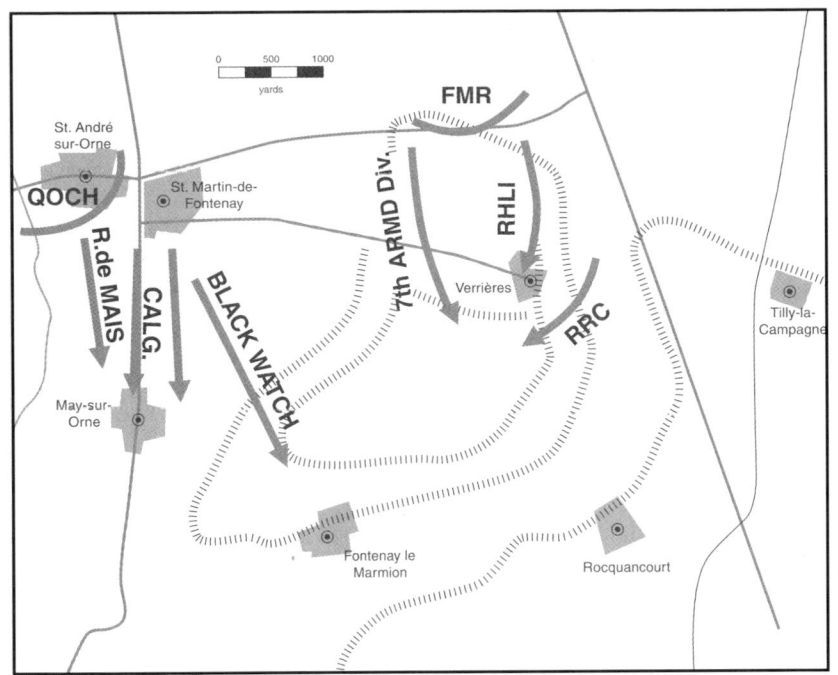

Operation "Spring"
July 25, 1944.

week, Cunningham, Christiansen and Petch were replaced.

What lessons ought we to draw from the events described in this essay? The first thing to note is that while there were lots of heroes there were no obvious villains. Any offensive in the Caen sector was bound to meet violent opposition from an enemy that would not give up the hinge of his defences. With the bulk of 2nd British Army committed east of the Orne, the Canadians were the obvious choice to attempt a break-in on Verrières Ridge. Simonds, perhaps the most innovative corps commander in the Allied armies, developed a plan that was intended to overcome the problems encountered in daylight attacks. The plan did not allow for the normal friction of war, never mind the complications of night operations, but the Canadians almost pulled it off. If the Black Watch had joined the Calgaries and cleared May-sur-Orne, the western end of the ridge might have been held.

The enemy, which suffered heavily in trying to overwhelm the Rileys, would have come under equally devastating fire approaching May-sur-Orne. There was no similar prospect of success at Tilly-la-Campagne where the 1st SS Panzer Division was dug in, but two out of three villages would have been a victory. Even one objective out of three was pretty good going against the formidable odds facing the Canadians on July 25. And the battle was not in vain! Whatever Simonds intentions, the facts are that no Panzer divisions from the Caen front were transferred in time to deal with the American breakthrough at Saint-Lô or to prevent Patton's breakout into the heart of France.

By noon, the Garries had lost 11 tanks and were withdrawn. The North Novas dug in and did what they could to survive.

Back at 9th Brigade headquarters an unusual drama was unfolding. Throughout the morning, Cunningham had listened to messages from division and corps, demanding that he begin phase two, but this was not his first battle and he trusted his own judgment. When the Garries reported their situation, Cunningham met with Lieutenant-Colonel N. Kingsmill the veteran commanding officer of the Highland Light Infantry. Kingsmill maintained that there was no point in sacrificing his battalion to a plan that had failed and made it clear he would refuse an order to try to bypass Tilly and make for the Phase Two objective. Lieutenant-Colonel G.H. Christiansen, the commanding officer of the Stormont, Dundas and Glengarry Highlanders, was equally adamant when his battalion was put on notice to assist the North Novas in Tilly. He, too, would refuse such an order.

Cunningham agreed with his subordinates and when Major-General Rod Keller arrived to relay demands to get moving, the brigadier stood firm. The highlanders would not be sacrificed in a hopeless cause. Keller insisted that this decision would cost the brigadier his job and within the

Reassessing Operation "Totalize"

Originally published, September/October 1999

On July 30, 1944, Lieutenant-General Guy Simonds summoned the senior officers of 2nd Canadian Corps to his main headquarters at the chateau in Cairon, northwest of Caen. There was complete silence as Simonds described the deeds that had won the Victoria Cross for Major J.K. Mahoney of the Westminster Regiment (Motor) in Italy just a couple of weeks before. Mahoney's company, with a troop of light recce tanks from the Lord Strathcona's Horse (Royal Canadians), had seized a bridgehead across the Melfa River and held it against repeated counterattacks.

There was an edge to Simonds' voice as he spelled out "the points in this episode" that he wanted "all officers to read and think about," and to discuss with their troops. The Westminsters, Simonds noted, were in their first major offensive action but fought like well-tried veterans. "There was no question of giving in because they had lost touch with the rest of their battalion or were cut off or under heavy fire. Under the leadership of Major Mahoney they fought, confident that if they did their part the fight would swing in their favour and the rest of the unit would get through to assist them."

The officers assembled at the chateau were unsure how they should react to this lesson. Was Simonds implying that 2 Canadian Corps units had failed to meet the standard set by the Westminsters in Italy? Did he really believe the units overwhelmed by massive German firepower in operation "Spring" had simply given in? No one dared ask, and the room remained silent as the general began a review of the progress of the Normandy Campaign to date. Simonds described "Spring" as successful despite the loss of ground and heavy casualties because the primary aim, holding German panzer divisions in the Caen sector, had been met. "It should be stressed to the troops that

their contribution made the American success possible." However, the time had come to prepare for a major operation to deliver a "knock-out blow." Simonds warned, "No division will stop until every reserve is employed."

Simonds was expressing the general belief that the American breakthrough at Avranches had transformed the Battle of Normandy, ending the stalemate and creating opportunities for mobile warfare. But much depended on the German reaction. The Allied high command, including Eisenhower and Montgomery, assumed the Germans would pivot on a series of hinge positions—Verrières Ridge, Hill 112, Mont Pinçon—and conduct a fighting retreat to the River Seine. This battle picture led Montgomery to shift most of his British divisions to the west where they could add their weight to the American offensive and drive the enemy out of Normandy. The image was of pushing against a swinging door while avoiding the hinges around Caen, which were too tough to break.

Operation "Bluecoat" began on the same day Simonds gave his pep talk in Cairon. It began well enough, but the arrival of German reinforcements and the hilly terrain of the Suisse Normande soon checked the British advance. With three panzer divisions committed against the British and four moving into position to carry out Hitler's counterattack at Mortain, only 12th SS was left in the Caen sector to support the troops defending Verrières Ridge. Montgomery therefore ordered 2nd Canadian Corps, reinforced by 51st Highland and 1st Polish Armoured divisions, to "advance in the direction of Falaise" and force a withdrawal of enemy units blocking the British advance. No one was yet planning to encircle the German armies in Normandy, though the rapid advance of Patton's 3rd Army toward Le Mans was forcing a reconsideration of the overall strategy of the campaign.

Despite the move of panzer divisions to the west, the defences in the Caen sector were still very strong. Hitler had finally concluded that there would be no second landing in the Pas de

PA 131371

Lieutenant-General HDG 'Harry' Crerar explains the plan for Operation "Totalize" to war correspondants.

Calais and ordered the transfer of all Fifteenth Army mobile divisions to Normandy. The 89th Infantry Division arrived on August 4 and took over the defences of Verrières Ridge the next night. Most accounts of the Canadian battles of August 1944 ignored the role played by the 89th, and scarcely mention the 85th which reached the battlefield on August 10. Our historians have been mesmerized by the self-serving accounts of Hitler Youth commander Kurt Meyer, who claimed that his under-strength battle groups outfought the Canadians virtually without assistance. The reality is that 89th Division was at full strength when it took over the defences south of Caen. With 12,000 men and its own artillery and anti-tank guns to add to the formidable array of 88s controlled by the

flak corps, plus scores of heavy mortars and Nebelwerfers, the division presented a serious obstacle to the Canadian advance.

Simonds understood the hard realities confronting his corps when he planned Operation "Totalize". He told his hesitant commanders that while the ground was "ideally suited to full exploitation by the enemy" because of the long range of his anti-tank guns and mortars, there were ways of overcoming these advantages. The corps would attack at night without any preliminary artillery program. Instead, Bomber Command would lead the way to the first objectives, striking villages on the flanks while the advance got under way. The artillery would begin its fire tasks after the armoured columns crossed the start line. Once begun, the barrage would reach a new level of intensity: 360 field and medium guns were to fire 60,000 shells in the first hour! Artificial moonlight and Bofors guns firing orange tracer would help the formation keep direction.

Simonds was also ready to deal with a problem that had plagued all major operations in Normandy. Without close infantry support Allied armour could not deal with German anti-tank defences, so somehow the infantry had to accompany the tanks forward "in bullet- and splinter-proof vehicles." Other commanders understood the problem; Simonds provided a solution. Artillery field regiments were turning in their self-propelled Priest 105-mm guns for the more familiar 25-pounders. Seventy-six of these vehicles were quickly converted into "unfrocked priests" or "kangaroos" by removing the gun and adding scrounged armour plating. These would carry the assault companies forward with the tanks.

Operation "Totalize" was one of the most innovative breakthrough operations of the war. The Canadian, Scottish and Polish troops advanced eight miles in the direction of Falaise, inflicting heavy losses on the enemy at a cost of 560 fatal casualties and 1,600 wounded. Canadian historians have long preferred a different version of "Totalize" that emphasizes the failure to reach Falaise, but before we consider what went wrong let us be un-Canadian and note all the things that went right.

The 51st Highland Division, harshly criticized for its alleged failures in July, captured Tilly-la-Campagne while advancing quickly to its first phase objectives. The 2nd Canadian Infantry Division, which had suffered so heavily in the attritional battles of July that it was still short 1,500 infantrymen, turned in an extraordinary performance reaching all of its objectives and capturing hundreds of prisoners. Individual battalions demonstrated remarkable resiliency. The South Saskatchewan Regiment, which had borne the brunt of the enemy counterattack on July 20 and lost 13 officers and 209 men over several hours, were able to "lean into the barrage" and seize Rocquancourt in a textbook

operation. Lieutenant-Colonel F.A. Clift maintained control throughout the day and provided two companies to assist 1st Hussars (6th Armoured Regiment) in an armoured attack on Fontenay-le-Marmion. Fontenay and May-sur-Orne held out until late August 8, but the Queen's Own Cameron Highlanders of Canada and the Fusiliers Mont-Royal gained control of the two ruined villages—which had been so crucial to the German defence of Verrières Ridge—by nightfall.

The 4th Canadian Armoured Brigade, mounted in the improvised armoured personnel carriers, reached all its objectives by early morning and the battalions dug in to meet the expected counterattacks. Meanwhile, 5th Brigade, waiting in reserve, was able to reach Bretteville-sur-Laize, penetrating the enemy's artillery and Nebelwerfer positions. The German defensive position south of Caen had been shattered. Was it possible to turn a breakthrough into a breakout?

The original plan for "Totalize" had called for a step-by-step approach, but the withdrawal of three panzer divisions from the Caen sector led Simonds to order his two armoured divisions, 4th Canadian and 1st Polish, to maintain momentum by launching the second phase at 1:45 p.m. on the 8th. To assist them, the United States Army Air Force was to employ its B-17 Flying Fortresses in a daylight precision attack. Unfortunately, two 12-plane groups bombed short, inflicting more than 300 casualties on the 1st Polish and several hundred more on other units. The North Shore (N.B.) Regiment, well behind the lines in the suburbs of Caen, lost almost 100 men and the 3rd Canadian Infantry Division commander, Major-General Rod Keller, was wounded.

This friendly fire and the continued resistance of 89th Division would have been sufficient to delay the advance without the intervention of the 12th SS, but the arrival of battlegroups that included Tigers of 101st Heavy Tank Battalion guaranteed that any advance would be sharply contested. By late afternoon, German armour and long range anti-tank guns had regained

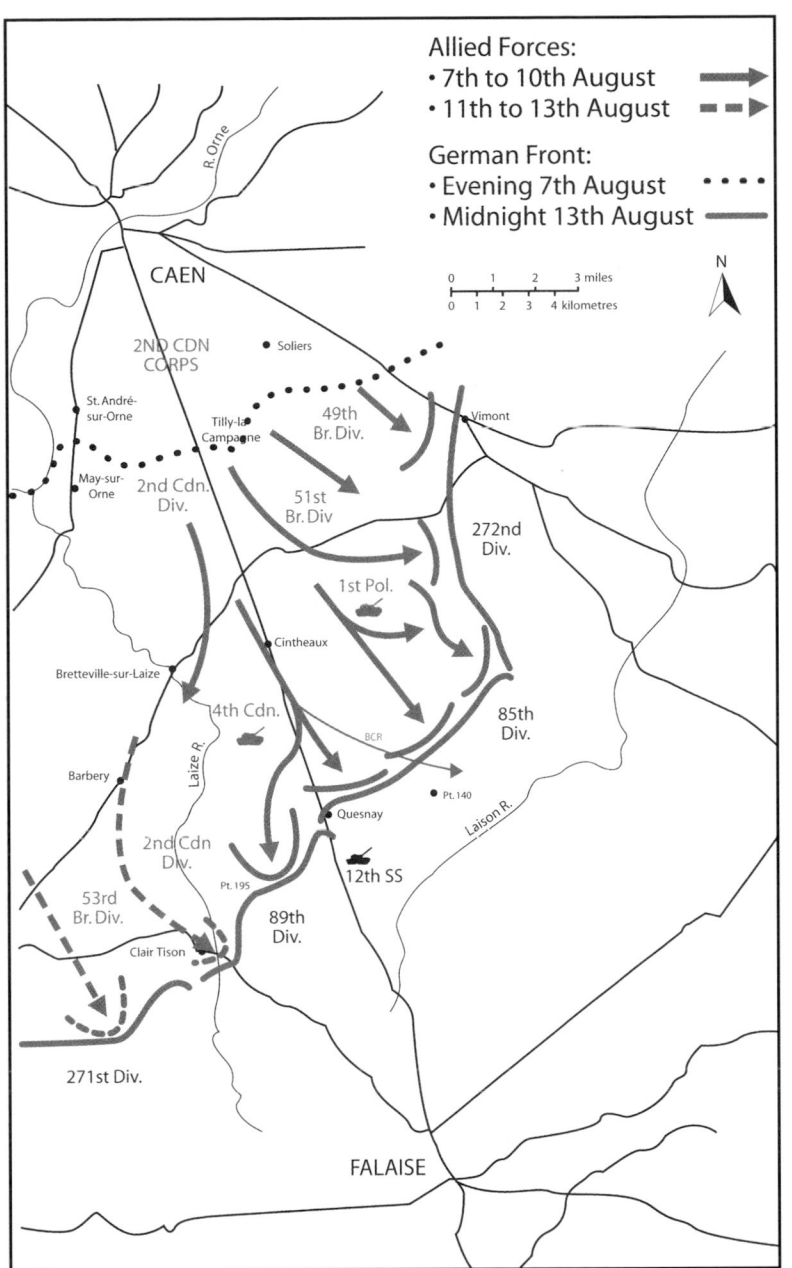

Operation "Totalize".

composed of the Canadian Grenadier Guards and the Lake Superior Regiment, was to attack Bretteville-le-Rabet; Lieutenant-Colonel Don Worthington and the British Columbia Regiment were to bypass enemy resistance and reach the Point 195 part of the ridge that guarded the Laison River valley.

The BCRs, with three companies of the Algonquin Regiment riding on the tanks, set off at 2 a.m. on August 9. Enemy fire seems to have forced them to veer to the east, and when dawn broke they headed for the high ground they hoped was Point 195. They were, in fact, some four miles east of their objective and within 1,000 yards of a 12th SS battle group equipped with Tigers and Panthers. A German lieutenant captured by the BCRs provided this graphic description of what it was like to be in the Canadian position: "Tigers and Panthers advanced in order to encircle the positions on the hill. One Canadian tank after another was knocked out and ended up in smoke and flame. Some crews...tried to reach a small woods close by. They took me along. Soon after the wood came under sustained attack from fighter bombers."

control of the battlefield in the wide-open country so ideally suited "to full exploitation by the enemy's weapons."

At this point Simonds ought to have paused and regrouped for another set-piece attack with a carefully coordinated fire plan, the kind of operation his divisions were trained for. But like all Allied commanders he desperately wanted to escape the limitations imposed by the vulnerability of his armour and his tank-mounted guns. He ordered 4th Armoured Division to form two battle groups to press the attack "while we still have surprise." Halpenny Force,

Historians have emphasized the faulty navigation of the BCRs without exploring more fundamental problems. By late July the Americans, aware of the difficulties in coordinating ground-air operations, had revised their air doctrine to create Armoured Column Cover. This provided for direct VHF radio contact between an air force officer with the armoured unit and the aircraft overhead. This system was one of the crucial methods used by the Americans in exploiting their breakthrough after July 25. If such an arrangement had existed with the Royal Air Force on August 9, Worthington would have been in constant touch with the fighterbombers, avoiding friendly fire and directing Typhoons onto the enemy. The BCR-Algonquin force had breached a position the enemy was trying desperately to hold until the newly arrived 85th Division could be deployed in depth. If reinforcements had arrived from the 1st Polish–which was less than a mile away–a very different situation would have developed. As it was, Worthington and many of his force were killed or captured.

In the spring of 1999, the two regiments rebuilt and rededicated the memorial situated above the Laison Valley. The Canadian flag, which can be seen at a great distance in this open, rolling country, flies proudly, marking an extraordinary moment in our history. Everyone who visits Normandy should go there.

The story of Worthington Force is one of great tragedy, but there are more stories of great triumph to tell. When Simonds learned that Point 195 was still in enemy hands he demanded that a new effort be made. Lieutenant-Colonel Dave Stewart's Argyll and Sutherland Highlanders of Canada were told to take the hill. Stewart was one of a number of absolutely outstanding battalion commanders with which the Canadian Army was blessed in the war. Jack Harper, then a captain, remembers the almost-instant rapport Stewart established with officers and men: "He commanded by earning respect." Stewart received his orders late on the afternoon of the 10th, and led the scout platoon to recce the route he had chosen from a map. "On the way back," he recalled, in a reminiscence originally published, in the magnificent new Argylls history Black Yesterdays, "I left members of the scout platoon at strategic points to guide the battalion." That night the Argylls, with perfect confidence in their leadership, moved single file through enemy lines towards the high ground. Stewart was up front because "you can't win battles from behind," and supervised placement. When a battery of 17-pounder anti-tank guns arrived, he sited them to control the approaches from the west and settled in to wait for the inevitable counterattack. The Lincoln and Welland Regiment had moved on a parallel course to secure the right flank, so the 12th SS was faced with a real dilemma. German doctrine required immediate counterattacks but the Argylls met each one with devastating fire.

"Totalize" ended that day in a costly attempt to capture Quesnay Wood, the focal point of German resistance north of Falaise. Simonds decided to reorganize and mount another large-scale deliberate attack. The decision to regroup came just as Montgomery was awakening to the possibility of encircling the German armies in what would soon become known as the Falaise Pocket. On August 11, he ordered both First Canadian and Second British Army to capture Falaise, "then operate with strong armoured and mobile forces to secure Argentan." The Canadians responded by ordering 2nd Division to make a wide right hook around the main German defences, approaching Falaise from the west.

The Advance To Falaise

Originally published, September/October 1999

"The opportunity that now lay before us was nothing short of fantastic. I could scarcely believe our good fortune." So spoke United States General George Patton, the commander of 3rd U.S. Army as he issued orders to turn his 15th Corps north from Le Mans, France, to Argentan on August 10, 1944. "If the enemy will only press his attack at Mortain for another 48 hours he will give us time to close at Argentan and completely destroy him."

Hitler obliged Patton by insisting on a renewed attempt to breakthrough to the coast at Avranches. This enabled the Americans-with a French armoured division-to move north without meeting any significant resistance. They were at the outskirts of Argentan on the evening of August 12. The lower jaw of the trap had formed, but where were the British and Canadians?

Montgomery's decision to shift the weight of his army group to the west in support of the American breakout made limited sense in late July when it seemed certain the Germans would stage a fighting retreat to the Seine, but after Hitler launched his Mortain offensive on August 6 the three British armoured divisions and most of the British infantry were in the wrong place at the wrong time. The hilly, hedge-rowed country around Caumont gave way to the even more difficult terrain of the Suisse Normande. There were few roads and most of them went in the wrong direction. The British were stalled and there was nothing much anyone could do about it.

Montgomery's other army-First Canadian-had also come to a halt. Operation "Totalize" ended on the night of August 10 after the Queen's Own Rifles of Canada and the North Shore (N.B.) Regiment could not overcome German resistance in Quesnay Woods. Coupled with the fierce counterattacks directed at Point 195-the ground seized by the Argyll and Sutherland Highlanders of Canada in their celebrated night march-the failure at Quesnay convinced Lieutenant-General Guy Simonds to call off offensive operations and

regroup. The armoured divisions were ordered to withdraw to reorganize their depleted squadrons while 2nd and 3rd infantry divisions took over the newly won ground.

Given these realities it is not easy to understand Montgomery's decision to issue a new directive on the morning of August 11, ordering both the British and Canadian armies to capture Falaise and instructing the Canadians to "operate with strong armoured and mobile forces to secure Argentan." Montgomery knew that Patton's 15th Corps with two armoured and three infantry divisions was moving north towards the Canadians, but he assumed it would stop well short of Argentan to meet a major enemy counterattack. Allied intelligence had concluded that the Mortain panzer divisions were still "a formidable force" and would be used against the extended American flank.

Montgomery had judged the German response correctly. Hitler's plans for a second Mortain offensive had to be put off until the American threat was dealt with. The Germans began to assemble Panzer Group Eberbach on August 11, but before a proposed "massive attack" on the American flank could be launched, the U.S. Fifth Armoured Division and the 2nd French Armoured Division moved north to the outskirts of Argentan, threatening to encircle the bulk of the German forces in Normandy.

The stage was now set for one of the great controversies of the war: Who was responsible for the "failure" to close the Falaise gap?

Here is what we know.

On the evening of August 12, Major-General Wade H. Haislip, commanding 15 Corps, reported that he expected to capture his last objective, Argentan, the next morning. What were his further orders? Patton did not hesitate. Haislip was to take Argentan and continue north. Patton phoned his superior General Omar Bradley to report the sensational news. To his surprise and anger, Bradley told Patton to stop and "build up on the shoulder…The German is beginning to pull out. You'd better button up and get ready for him."

Both Bradley and Patton were acting in character and carrying out their roles as an army group versus an army commander. Bradley was always cautious, and Patton always preferred action. However, it was Bradley's job to consider the overall picture and Patton's to pursue the goals of his army. Bradley interpreted intelligence on the build up of Panzer Group Eberbach as a threat to the extended American flank and preferred "a solid shoulder at Argentan to the possibility of a broken neck at Falaise." Patton thought this cautious approach was typical Bradley and a "monumental error."

Patton was also a proponent of the "rock soup" approach to orders. If he could persuade Bradley to give a little, a piece of rock to boil for soup, vegetables and even some meat might follow. His orders forbid an advance beyond Argentan but who knew what might happen during a battle for the city. Shortly after midnight Patton told Haislip to "push on slowly in the direction of Falaise."

Early on the morning of August 13, 5th Armoured Division began to move east of Argentan to encircle the town but the Americans now found they were facing the kind of opposition that had repeatedly stemmed the Canadian advance north of Falaise. German anti-tank guns, the U.S. official history reports, were "well sited and skillfully concealed on dominating ground."

American-crewed Sherman tanks proved as vulnerable to long range fire as Canadian ones, and losses were "surprisingly heavy." Elements of three panzer divisions had reached the Argentan sector and were immediately committed to action. There would be no massive German counterattack, but the southern side of the rapidly forming Falaise Pocket was now well defended.

With four full-strength divisions available and more on the way, Patton's 3rd Army would surely have captured Argentan and begun the advance to Falaise but only after a difficult and costly battle. Some German units would have escaped giving rise to stories about Patton's "failure" to close the gap. But 15th Corps was not sent into action. Bradley again ordered Patton to stop. That morning, Montgomery met with Bradley to review the situation and they agreed upon a new plan of action. Patton was to concentrate on operations to prevent the German army from crossing the River Seine, the so-called long envelopment. British 2nd Army was to capture Falaise and advance to meet the Americans, the Canadians were shifted to the southeast where they were to meet the Americans and close the gap at Trun.

These decisions, which were amended the next day when the Canadians were told to take Falaise as well as Trun, placed an enormous burden upon 2nd Canadian Corps.

The 51st Highland Division, which had reverted to the command of the 1st British Corps, was assigned to protect the long eastern flank, and so Simonds would have to use 2nd Canadian Division to capture Falaise. This left him with two armoured and one infantry division, all understrength, to tackle a newly arrived German infantry division, the 85th, supported by battle groups of the 12th SS and the anti-tank guns of the flak corps. These operations were to take place while the Americans on the south side of the pocket were "building a solid shoulder at Argentan." If necks were to be broken at Falaise, they would belong to Canadian and Polish soldiers.

Up to this point in the Normandy campaign, Montgomery had exercised wise control of his coalition armies. However, the fluid situation in mid-August seems to have made him hesitant and indecisive. He changed his mind on who was to capture Falaise four times and then sent the Canadians to Trun without issuing similar orders to the Americans. When he finally told Bradley to resume the attack north, 48 hours had passed and 48 more would go by before the Americans-with only one infantry division available-got under way.

The officers and men of 2nd Canadian Infantry Division knew nothing of these events, but they were the first to endure the consequences. The division had won the third battle for Verrières Ridge in a remarkable display of guts and determination. However, the price of two weeks of attritional warfare was high. On August 10, the

Troops of Les Fusiliers Mont-Royal supported by a Sherman tank of the Sherbrooke Fusiliers during a sniper hunt, Falaise, France, 17 August 1944.

NAC 115567

division reported that it needed 1,355 replacements, almost all riflemen: less than 100 were immediately available so Major-General Charles Foulkes would have to make do with rifle companies at half strength.

Foulkes ordered 4th Brigade, with the redoubtable Royal Hamilton Light Infantry in the lead, to cross the River Laize and strike southwest of Barbery. This was the first phase of a wide right hook that would bring the division to Falaise from the west. The long forgotten battle for Barbery was costly in terms of casualties, but the advance threatened the Germans holding the British at Thury-Harcourt as well as the defences of Falaise. The enemy responded to the threat by sending some of his precious Tiger tanks to block the route preventing the Royal Regiment and the Sherbrooke Fusiliers from maintaining the momentum. Foulkes now committed his other two infantry brigades. The Calgary Highlanders began 5th Brigade's move to outflank the enemy at 0145 on the morning of the 13th. The unit's war diary describes the night march: "It was a vicious dark night and we

were to travel over territory not recce'd before and over trails taken from the map through country where we had no knowledge of enemy positions…The trails were no wider than a carriage and very difficult to follow."

The Calgaries broke through into the enemy rear area and prisoners, including a complete medical unit, "poured" into the cage. "Each and every prisoner had an Allied leaflet entitled Safe Conduct assuring them of good treatment if taken prisoner."

The Calgaries carefully descended into the large valley at Clair Tizon where the main highway provided a direct route to the objective. Le Régiment de Maisonneuve, down to just two companies, moved through to continue the advance. Intense fire suggested the enemy had regrouped on the high ground, but Major Alexander Dugas brought his men forward in twos and threes and expanded the bridgehead until heavy artillery fire forced the infantry to ground.

Riflemen of
Les Fusiliers
Mont-Royal
carry a wounded
comrade to safety,
Falaise, August
1944.

Casualties, including Dugas who was mortally wounded, were 13 killed, 41 wounded. This left the Maisonneuve regiment with only one company to hold the position.

Sixth Brigade had followed a parallel route south through equally difficult country. The South Saskatchewan Regiment and Fusiliers Mont-Royal cleared Point 176, but as the Queen's Own Cameron Highlanders of Canada fought its way forward, orders came to disengage and pull back. Operation "Tractable"-the great armoured drive to Trun- had begun and the Royal Air Force was scheduled to bomb targets in the area. Ironically, the battalions that were withdrawn from action were the hardest hit when aiming errors resulted in heavy losses to the Royal Regiment of Canada and the South Sasks. The unit's war diary described the scene: "The entire battalion area was wholly unrecognizable…hardly a soul could be found and many vehicles were burning…ammunition was exploding…the bombing had the effect of so shaking moral that there was little or no fight in the troops."

Second Division's interrupted advance to Falaise was resumed early on August 15 with 4th Brigade carefully working its way to within a mile of the town. Armchair generals are invariably critical of the time it took to capture Falaise, but the rolling country with its woods and stone farmhouses offered ideal conditions for small groups of German infantry to delay the advance. The soldiers who fought these battles were not the symbolic markers used in war gaming, but real people who wished to live to see another day. They wanted firepower, as much of it as they could get, to neutralize or destroy such positions and they counted on the tanks, artillery and the mortars and machine-guns of the Toronto Scottish Regiment to help clear the way. The advance was also delayed by another major air attack, delivered on Falaise itself, by the U.S. Eighth Air Force. This time the B-24s and B-17s were on target with only a few sticks of bombs falling on Canadian positions.

By the evening of August 16, Falaise lay in ruins. The city's streets were impassable. Canadian artillery controlled the eastern exits, and two miles to the west the 53rd Welsh Division cut the main, eastwest road into Falaise. Even Hitler recognized the need for a rapid retreat and allowed Panzer Group West to pull back. Most of the 12th SS battle group defending Falaise withdrew, but a force of some 150 men was left to delay the Canadian advance.

Falaise was no longer a vital military objective. Sixth Brigade which was given the job of clearing the town, went about its task carefully. The South Sasks were held up by an anti-tank gun on the main road until Lieutenant-Colonel Freddie Clift went forward, took a rifle from one of his men, and-with the assistance of the battalion intelligence officer-knocked out three of the members of the gun crew. The remaining members then blew up the gun and withdrew.

The advance into the town was slowed by rubble that had to be cleared by armoured bulldozers. By dawn the South Sasks and the QOCHC worked their way into Falaise and the Camerons were moved south to block a secondary road.

The reserve battalion-the Fusiliers Mont-Royal with a squadron of Sherbrooke tanks-took over the final phase of the action. Its main job was to mop up the last resistance in Falaise, and this proved to be no easy task.

The FMRs-like the Maisonneuves-had proven to be a highly effective unit, but were down to two rifle companies totaling not more than 150. The remaining Hitler Youth were concentrated in the École Supérieure, a four-storey stone building. After tanks punched a hole in the outer wall, 10 FMRs broke into the school but this was only the beginning of a struggle that lasted until the early hours of August 18. There were between 50 and 60 desperate members of the Hitler Youth Division in the building. Four escaped and the rest fought to the end.

NAC 129140

Our Polish Comrades

Originally published, January/February 2000

Canadians have a particularly close relationship with the Polish Armoured Division that fought as part of the 1st Canadian Army throughout much of WW II. Many Polish veterans, unwilling to return to their country while it was under Soviet control, settled in Canada and this strengthened the connection.

The Polish Armoured Division was formed out of elements of the army that escaped from Poland and reassembled in France during the winter of 1939-40. Polish troops, serving under French command, fought in Norway and in the Battle of France.

When Paris was declared an open city and rumours of an imminent surrender reached the Polish commander, General Wladyslaw Sikorski, all units were ordered to try to escape to Britain. General Stanislas Maczek's 10th Mechanical Cavalry Brigade, which became the core of the Polish Armoured Division, lost three quarters of its tanks in battle with the Germans before disengaging and withdrawing toward the coast. Maczek donned a disguise and reached Scotland via North Africa.

Polish soldiers arriving in England in the aftermath of the Dunkirk evacuation in 1940 were quickly dispatched to Scotland where they became a colourful and welcome part of the wartime scene. A large number of officers, but relatively few other ranks, made it to Britain so plans to recruit Poles from North America were implemented. Units remained understrength until Poles released from Soviet prisoner of war camps were allowed to form a Polish corps to fight in Italy or join their comrades in Scotland.

While the Polish army regrouped and trained, veterans of the Polish air force and navy who reached Britain were plunged into the conflict. Polish squadrons played a distinguished role in the Battle of Britain and Poles made up 12 per cent of the effective strength of Fighter Command during the critical month of

Major-General Stanislas Maczek and his staff talking to war correspondents.

September 1940. Polish destroyers, sent to join the British fleet at the outbreak of the war, assisted in the Dunkirk evacuation and carried out escort work as part of the Royal Navy's 5th Destroyer Flotilla.

The Polish Armoured Division reached its authorized strength in 1944, but it was evident it would enter battle without enough reinforcements available to replace casualties.

The division was organized along standard British lines with armoured and infantry brigades, each of three battalions, together with reconnaissance, artillery and anti-tank regiments, plus a motorized infantry battalion; 14,000 men and 240 tanks.

The Polish Armoured Division arrived in France on the last day of July, which was also the first day of the 1944 Warsaw uprising. The Polish Home Army seized control of the city on the assumption that the Soviet Army, whose spearheads were just a few miles away, would maintain pressure and force a general German retreat. It quickly became evident that Stalin was quite prepared to let the Germans destroy Warsaw and the anti-commnist home army. On August 3, the guns of the Red Army fell silent. Appeals from Churchill to intervene or at least allow Allied aircraft to deliver supplies to the besieged city–using Soviet controlled airfields–were denied with Stalin insisting that "the Soviet government does not wish to associate itself either directly or indirectly with the adventure in Warsaw."

The British press and the BBC carried regular bulletins from Warsaw as well as commentary on the situation. For the men of the Polish Armoured Division the constant question was: "What news of Warsaw?"

First Canadian Army was told that the Polish Armoured Division would come under command in time for Operation "Totalize", set for August 8, 1944. The Poles had just arrived in Normandy and so there was little time to get acquainted. Lieutenant-General Guy Simonds met Maczek and his staff officers for the first time on August 4 and had one more brief discussion with them

before "Totalize" began. The Poles used British liaison officers to improve communications, but Simonds quickly learned that the Poles could not be controlled in the same way a British or Canadian division could be.

There was more than a language barrier at work. The Canadian historian and armoured theorist Roman Jaramowcyz argues that Maczek was "a modern tank officer" who found Simonds' operational plans too restrictive. On the eve of "Totalize", Maczek protested that the frontage of less than a 1,000 yards allowed no room for manoeuvre and would give German anti-tank guns concentrated fields of fire. Simonds refused to alter his plans, insisting that the armour could only function in the open country south of Caen in a set-piece battle with full air and artillery support.

Maczek's fears were realized on the afternoon of August 8 when his leading armoured regiment lost 26 tanks in a few minutes. The Germans, firing from the small woods that dotted the landscape, caught the Poles in a deadly crossfire. This bottled up elements of the division that were supposed to maintain the momentum of the attack. The Polish Armoured Division was also hampered by the disastrous "short bombing" of the United States 8th Air Force that caused scores of casualties and the loss of ammunition and equipment.

By nightfall, the Polish had made little progress and orders to continue could not be carried out. The next morning the division launched an attack on a broader front and experienced its first real success.

However, 12th SS battle groups quickly counterattacked and destroyed scores of the flimsy Sherman tanks. Elements of the Polish Armoured Division were less than a mile from Point 140 where the British Columbia and Algonquin regiments were being systematically destroyed. However, the Poles could not advance further.

It is impossible to exaggerate the inadequacy of Allied armour in such situations. The great strengths of the Sherman tank were its mechanical reliability and speed; the great weaknesses were a high profile, armour plate so thin it could easily be penetrated by any German anti-tank gun and a 75-mm main gun that was ineffective at ranges beyond 500 yards.

After Operation "Totalize", the Poles, who had lost 66 tanks, hastened to copy the experiments of the more experienced regiments that had begun to wire and weld additional tank tracks to their hulls in the hope of deflecting hits and avoiding destruction.

Simonds was either unaware of the depth of this problem or determined to ignore it. As a corps commander he could not allow his men to focus on reasons for failure. He had to plan for success and employ the resources available to him. At a commanders conference held just before launching his second armoured blitzkrieg–Operation "Tractable"–Simonds was highly critical of the performance of both armoured divisions. He accused them of every known sin under the sun, including lack of drive. He was especially disappointed in the Poles and for "Tractable", the massive daylight attack of August 14; he paired the veteran 2nd Canadian Armoured Brigade with 4th Division. This left the Polish Armoured Division to form "a firm base."

The decision gave the Poles time to recover from their first battle and from the ordeal of a second short bombing–this time by the Royal Canadian Air Force–that inflicted more than 200 casualties.

When the order to cross the River Dives and advance toward Trun was received on August 15, the Polish Armoured Division was ideally situated to launch an end run around the main enemy resistance.

Maczek embraced the new orders that were well suited to his ideas about employing an armoured division. The Polish Armoured Division was organized into battle groups and quickly formed a bridgehead across the Dives.

The Polish and Canadian advance to Trun was slowed by battle groups of the 85th, 21st and 12th SS Divisions, which were busy holding the northern edge of the Falaise Pocket. Simonds decided to leave Trun to 4th Armoured and

ordered Maczek to take Chambois and link up with the Americans in closing the gap.

The Poles, after two days of continuous combat, were to work their way across the grain of some of the most rugged terrain in Normandy. The hills in this beautiful part of France rise steeply from the river valleys and the only good roads run north-south.

Maczek decided to send one battle group to Chambois and then block the exits by seizing the high ground at Mount Ormel-Coudehard, a hill the Poles would come to call the Maczuga or mace after its appearance on the contour maps.

Unfortunately the commander of the regiment who was to lead the advance to Chambois did not communicate his intentions clearly to the guide supplied by the French resistance. The Koszutski battle group moved due east to a village called Les Champeaux astride the main Trun-Vimoutiers highway, the German escape route to the River Seine. This small force, one armoured regiment and an infantry battalion had penetrated deep into the German rear areas where it was repeatedly attacked by Royal Air Force Spitfires and Typhoons whose pilots had been briefed to bomb and strafe all movement in an area known to be occupied by the enemy. Despite casualties from friendly fire, the battle group disrupted the German retreat and helped to stem the counterattack by 9th SS Panzer Division

While Koszutski's men fought their isolated battle, the rest of the division worked its way to Chambois and the Maczuga.

On the afternoon of August 19, while Canadians were fighting for control of St-Lambert-sur-Dives, the Polish 10th Dragoons in "heavy hand-to-hand battles" fought its way into Chambois and linked up with American infantry from 90th Division. On the maps at corps and army headquarters the gap could now be marked closed, but on the ground exhausted Polish, Canadian and American soldiers had to cope with an enemy that still included thousands of men determined to break the ring and fight their way north.

During the early hours of August 20, senior German officers inside the pocket set about organizing groups of men for one last attempt at a breakout to coincide with a two-pronged attack by 2nd SS Panzer Corps from the north. The Luftwaffe made a major effort to drop supplies and ammunition and while little of it landed within German lines the operation helped morale. Lead groups crossed the Dives during the night, but the main breakout occurred shortly after dawn when thousands of shouting desperate men surged forward.

Once across the river and the Trun-Chambois highway, the Germans were faced with the Polish positions on the Maczuga.

The main road ran over the saddle of the ridge between the two Point 262s held by the Poles. Isolated bands of German soldiers moved forward under constant artillery and machine-gun fire.

On the crest of Mount Ormel, Captain Pierre Seveigny, the forward observation officer for 4th Medium Regiment, directed the fire of the 4.5-inch guns that sent 100-pound shells crashing down on the enemy. The battle that raged around Mount Ormel reminded one Pole of "medieval days, when the defence of the battlefield was organized by placing camps in a tight quadrangle. The densely wooded hills were extremely difficult for observation. As a result...German tanks could approach unnoticed, almost up to our positions. This was demonstrated by a Panther and a Sherman facing one another barrel to barrel at a distance of a few metres, both burned.... The Maczuga and Chambois were practically cut off.... All attempts to evacuate our wounded failed."

There were German prisoners everywhere. Some could be handed over to the Americans, but they, too, were cut off when the enemy recaptured the road into Chambois. Simonds ordered the Canadians to break through to the Poles and the Grenadier Guards. With their machine-guns firing almost continuously, they opened up a line of communication allowing ammunition, food and medical supplies to reach the Maczuga. The British Columbia Regiment broke through to the southern spur of Mount Ormel on the evening of August 21, while a battle group of 1st Hussars tanks and Highland Light Infantry used a full artillery barrage to help them advance toward Chambois. "Hours of bloody fighting" were required to reach the village, but by nightfall the gap was finally closed.

The Poles alone captured 6,000 prisoners and destroyed 70 tanks, 500 vehicles and more than 100 artillery pieces. Their own losses in the four days were 1,400 killed and wounded. The roads through Trun, Chambois and St-Lambert were lined with the wreckage of two German armies. Operational research teams counted 3,043 vehicles, including 187 tanks and self-propelled guns in the area they called the Shambles. Most had been destroyed by artillery and anti-tank guns or had been abandoned by their crews when forward movement became impossible.

The Allies had won a very great victory and could now pursue the broken remnants of the Wehrmacht and SS back to Germany.

If anyone had prophesied that the German army in the west would be destroyed less than three months after the Normandy invasion began on June 6, 1944, they would have been dismissed as a dreamer. With the dream fulfilled, generals, journalists and historians began to argue that the victory was incomplete. They sought to second-guess the decisions that delayed the closing of the gap, but let us leave such speculation to the armchair experts. We should, instead, celebrate the heroism, the endurance and the achievement of the Allied soldiers who won the battle.

And let us be sure and remember the Polish soldiers who fought with such courage while their countrymen and capital city were systematically destroyed. They are not forgotten in Normandy where the Polish War Cemetery is maintained by the French government and the memorial museum on the crest of the Maczuga is maintained and staffed by the citizens of nearby villages.

Victory In Normandy

Originally published, August 1994

On the morning of August 16, the Falaise pocket was approximately 35 miles deep and 12 miles wide. The survivors of two German armies - containing seven corps and elements of 21 divisions- attempted to escape through the gap between Argentan and Falaise. The American units to the south could not launch an attack for several days. The 2nd British Army was held up on the narrow roads of the Suisse Normande, an area of hills and ravines that could be defended with very few troops. The 1st Canadian Army – exhausted by a week of intense and costly combat – would have to close the gap with its limited resources.

This situation had been created by a series of decisions that were reasonable at the time, but could now be viewed as monumental errors. General Bernard Montgomery, the master of the set-piece battle, had difficulty in adapting to the fluid conditions of August. His decision to shift 2nd British Army to the west to support the late-July American break-out only made sense if the Germans were to retreat to the Seine. When Hitler's Mortain offensive began and General Omar Bradley suggested the" short envelopment" at Falaise, General Montgomery had agreed, but he failed to reinforce the Canadians. He assumed that two veteran infantry divisions and two fresh armoured divisions could close the gap from the north.

There were other serious misjudgments. On August 13, Monty had decided against allowing General Patton's 15th Corps to advance beyond Argentan. An angry General Patton sent the corps north to the Seine. When General Montgomery changed his mind on August 16 and asked Bradley to close the gap, the Americans needed two days to get organized. In desperation, Monty turned to the Canadians. The 1st Polish and 4th Canadian Armoured

divisions were ordered to close the pocket by capturing the villages of Trun and Chambois astride the main escape routes.

Initially both divisions responded with speed and skill. The Poles crossed the Dives River at Jort, while 4th Canadian Armoured Division forged a crossing at Morteaux-Couliboeuf. When Lieutenant-General Simonds issued new orders on August 17 it still seemed possible that much of the German army could be encircled. The Poles were to concentrate on Chambois, while 4th Canadian Armoured Division captured Trun.

The next morning Lieutenant-General Simonds' familiar armoured car arrived at 4th Division headquarters. He had detoured to Falaise, where Les Fusiliers Mont-Royal had overcome the last resistance in the city. The commander of 4th Canadian Armoured Division, Major-General George Kitching, reported first. His 10th Brigade had just reached the Trun cross-roads so one main route was closed, but a fierce battle was raging around the village. Waves of enemy troops - desperate to avoid encirclement - bypassed Trun, making use of secondary roads and farmers' lanes.

Major-General Maczek's report was more disappointing. The Polish units had become bogged down in a series of isolated struggles with Panzer battle groups. They had lost a large number of tanks and his troops were exhausted. Worst of all, the force sent to capture Chambois had delayed its start and then had been misdirected to the village of Les Champeaux, well to the north of its objective. It was attacked both by retreating German units and Allied pilots who had been assured no friendly forces were in the area.

Lieutenant-General Simonds issued his orders quickly. He knew – through Ultra – that the German retreat had only begun in earnest two days before and that it still might be possible to trap several hundred thousand men. With so much at stake a supreme effort had to be made. The tactical air force would do its best, flying up to 3,000 sorties a day, but only the army

NAC 131218

Major David
Currie V.C.

could seal the gap. Major-General Maczek was to use his motorized infantry battalion to seize the route to Chambois. Major-General Kitching was told to attack east from Trun, closing off the secondary escape routes. Clear, sensible orders, but not easy to carry out.

The Poles did reach the outskirts of Chambois that night, but not in sufficient strength to block the Vimoutiers highway. Polish units were scattered over 10 miles of hilly countryside, astride this escape route, but they were not in control of it. Their key positions on the twin hills they called the Maczuga or mace, would be the scene of intense combat as the Germans mounted an attack from outside the pocket to assist those fighting to escape.

The best that 4th Canadian Armoured Division could do to carry out Lieutenant-General Simonds' orders was to send a squadron of the South Alberta Regiment - under the command of Major David Currie - and a company of infantry from the Argyll and Sutherland Highlanders of Canada towards Chambois. The other armoured regiments were committed north of Trun, establishing firm control of the highways to the northeast.

The battle group assigned to close the gap consisted of 175 men, 16 tanks and four M-10 guns from the 5th Anti-Tank Regiment. Major Currie was a veteran of 10 days of combat and two years of training as an armoured corps officer. A quiet, unassuming man, he had learned to lead by example, encouragement and the appearance of calm certainty. His resolve and personal courage were quickly tested. The village of St. Lambert-sur-Dives lies halfway between Trun and Chambois. Several secondary roads converged on a small bridge that spanned the river and from there two lanes - little better than farmers' tracks - linked up with minor roads that twisted through the hills towards Vimoutiers. This small village controlled one of the few clear routes out of the pocket and the enemy would not give it up without a fight.

The lead troop from the South Alberta Regiment entered the village slowly. There were two sharp, cracking sounds, and two tanks were disabled. Under mortar fire, Major Currie organized the rescue of the tank crews and then posted his men for all-around defence. It was evident the village was full of German troops.

Major Currie asked for reinforcements, but 10th Brigade was painfully thin on the ground and the enemy had not given up the struggle to control a road through Magny, a hamlet just east of Trun. Brigadier J.C. Jefferson promised to send a second squadron from the South Alberta Regiment to Point 124, a mile north of St. Lambert. A forward observation officer of the 15th Field Regiment, Captain C. H. Clerkson, would accompany them. Two companies of infantry were also on the way. Major Currie's orders did not allow him to wait for reinforcements or artillery support. The Poles had made contact with elements of 90th U.S. Division in Chambois, but neither they nor the Americans had the strength to close the gap.

The Argylls and South Alberta regiment attacked at first light, clearing the part of the village west of the crossroads. But the resistance stiffened and as it grew in intensity, Major Currie ordered his men to consolidate and prevent the enemy from retaking ground.

Infantry reinforcements arrived that night; two half-companies, one from the Argylls and one from the Lincoln and Welland Regiment. At 0800 on August 20, the Germans mounted the first of a series of massive escapes that included counterattacks at St. Lambert and Chambois. A Polish officer describing the struggle wrote: "It reminded one of the medieval days when the defence of a battlefield was organized by placing camps in a tight quadrangle. . . the Maczuga and Chambois were practically cut off...Our wounded had to remain with our fighting soldiers. . . . "

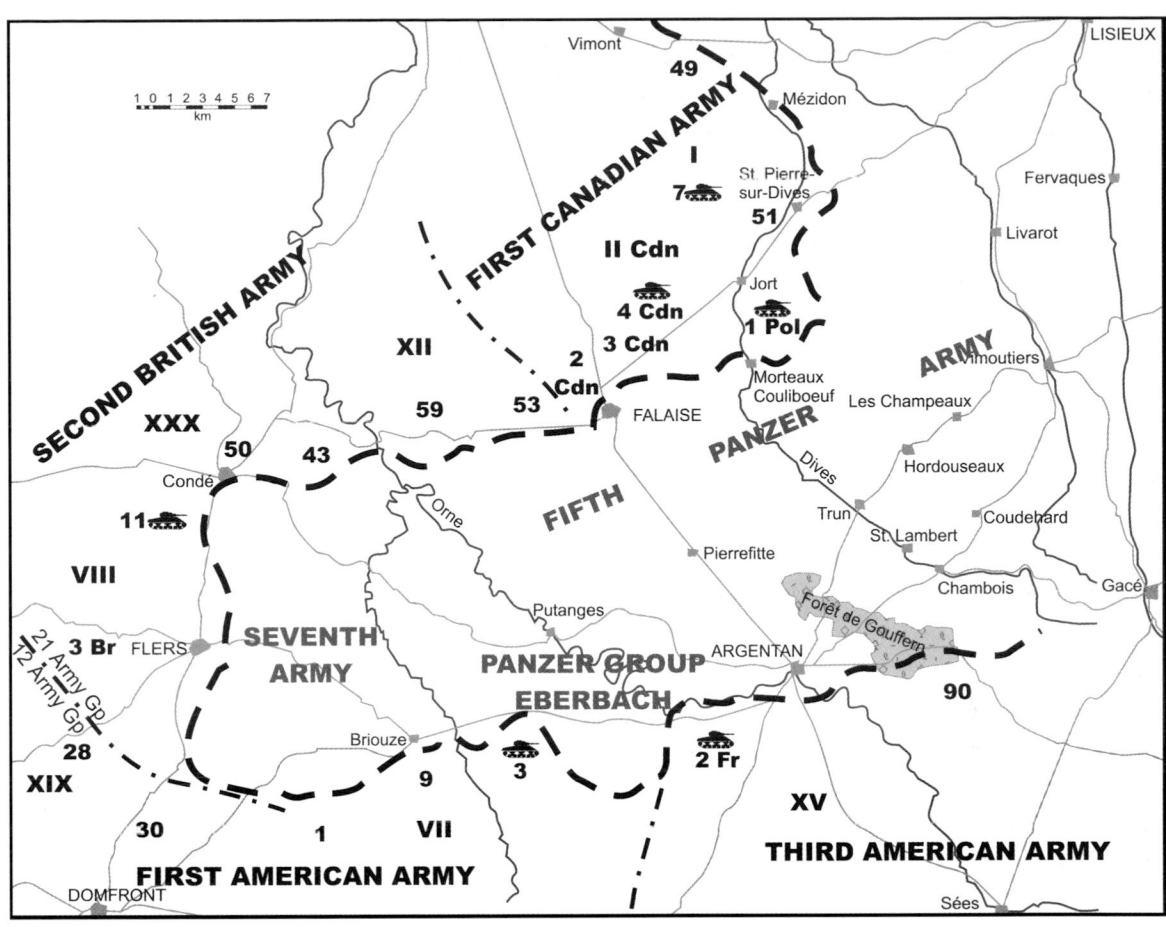

The Falaise Pocket August 16, 1944.

In St. Lambert, Major Currie's men fought on. Four Argylls stalked and destroyed a Panther. Major Currie used his command tank to knock out a Tiger and his rifle to deal with snipers who had infiltrated close to his headquarters. On the hill north of St. Lambert "B" Squadron and the 15th Field Regiment joined in the battle. Long lines of enemy trucks, tanks, wagons, carts and other vehicles could be seen approaching from the west. The tank gunners would pick off the lead and tail vehicle and then systematically shoot up the whole convoy. One artillery officer wrote: "It was as if the Americans and British were huge brooms sweeping the Germans into the dustpan, which at that moment was the Canadian Army."

Major Currie, according to one of his non-commissioned officers, remained in control. "We knew at one stage it was going to be a fight to the finish, but he was so cool about it, it was impossible for us to get excited."

The battle of the Falaise Pocket forced the enemy into a headlong retreat. Neither the Seine nor any other line in France could be defended with what was left of the German armies in the west. The Canadians had played a major role in achieving victory in Normandy. Placed at the sharpest end of the Allied order of battle in July and early August, 2nd Canadian Corps had been called upon to become the main instrument in the attempt to close the pocket. In the last stages of the battle there had been much confusion; there had also been incredible heroism, dedication and the courage to endure.

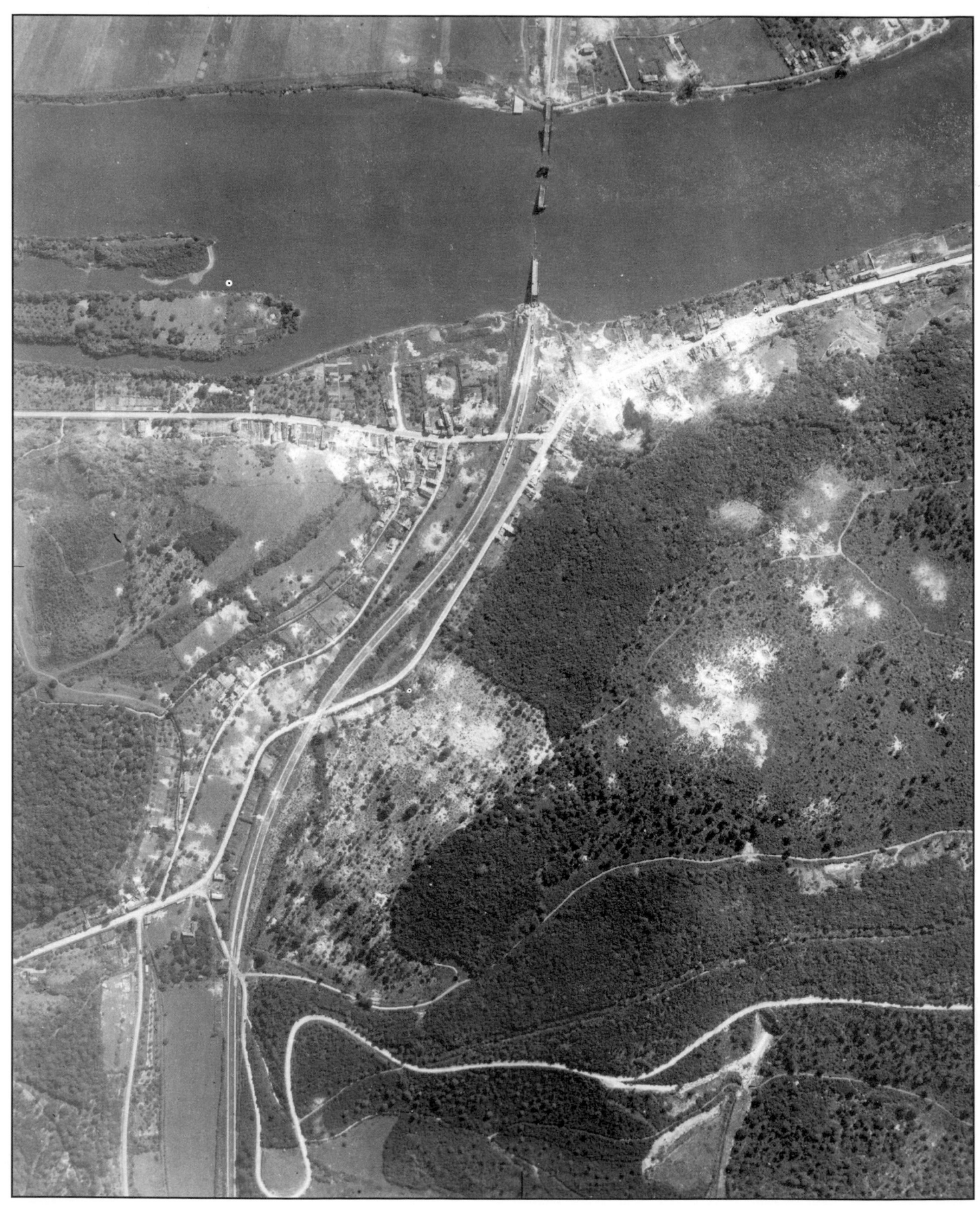

The March To The Seine

Originally published, March/April 2000

The Allied commanders planned the battle of Normandy as the first phase of a long deliberate campaign to liberate France. On D-Day plus 90–September 6, 1944–they hoped to control an area bounded by the rivers Seine and Loire and then pause long enough to build up resources for a series of operations that would bring them to the borders of Germany.

Hitler and his generals, meanwhile, poured all their resources into the defence of Normandy and so when the Allies broke through, the enemy could not muster enough troops to hold Paris or stop an Allied advance. The situation was so fluid that anything seemed possible, even a quick thrust to Berlin to end the war in 1944.

General Bernard Montgomery became obsessed with this idea. On August 17, when the battles around Falaise were still raging, he flew to General Omar Bradley's headquarters and proposed a plan for "a solid mass of 40 divisions" to advance rapidly to Belgium and the Ruhr. Neither Bradley nor General Dwight D. Eisenhower was attracted to a plan that seemed to ignore the existence of the United States 7th Army moving rapidly from the south of France, but there were more immediate problems that made Monty's "narrow front" impossible.

Much of General George Patton's Third Army was closing in on Paris, which was liberated on August 25, and moving east toward Germany, while Monty's own troops, Canadian and British, were still committed to the Falaise pocket and could not begin to move north for some time. Eisenhower would not consider stopping Patton to allow Montgomery time to bring his army forward to the Seine.

To make matters more difficult, Eisenhower was due to replace Montgomery as ground commander on September 1, an event that Monty saw as a demotion. The news of Montgomery's promotion to the rank of field marshal did little to soothe the British commander's wounded ego. This "war between the generals" would have even more serious consequences for the Canadians in October,

but for the moment it simply meant there was little rest for the weary. Second Canadian Corps was told to immediately develop a strong thrust to Rouen, cross the Seine, and capture the ports of Le Havre and Dieppe.

On August 20, 2nd Canadian Infantry Division handed over the ruins of Falaise to the British and began the pursuit. The Royal Canadian Army Service Corps provided enough trucks and drivers to lift the whole division and by August 22, 6th Brigade reached Orbec just 50 miles from Rouen. Here for the first, but not the last time in the pursuit, the 8th Reconnaissance Regiment–the 14th Canadian Hussars–proved its worth. The divisional recce regiments had been used in a variety of combat roles in Normandy, but there had been little opportunity to test their mobility and striking power in far ranging probes behind enemy lines. The corps armoured car regiment, the Manitoba Dragoons, had won praise for its exploits in August, now the 8th Recce Regiment had its chance.

The Germans were dug in at Orbec and held the northern bank of the River Touques. The Camerons of Canada, confronted with a wide valley under observed fire, were overjoyed to learn the Hussars had crossed the river to the west of the town and had circled back and taken out the enemy blocking position. That swift action broke German resistance at Orbec. However, the Fusiliers Mont-Royal discovered that St-Germain, a village a few kilometres to the north, was held by a determined battle group that had to be overcome in a difficult night action. There were many such small battles in the division's march to the Seine, but the memory of most of them is lost in the shadow of the tragedy that overwhelmed the "blue patch" division in the Forêt de la Londe.

Canadians who follow the Maple Leaf Up route to the Seine today have to look hard for evidence of these struggles, but if you drive north on the N138 and slow down in the forest near Bosqueaud de Marcouville you will find a striking memorial to the Canadians who were ambushed at dawn on August 25. Soldiers of the RCASC who joined their Black Watch comrades in beating off the attack are commemorated here with words of thanks for the liberation of the area.

LCMSDS

The Forêt de la Londe and the River Seine at Port du Gravier "The ground was immensely favourable for the defense".

After the enemy withdrew, the troop-carrying convoy continued north to Bourgtheroulde where the Germans were preparing strong defensive positions. Lieutenant-Colonel Frank Mitchell decided to push through the gauntlet of fire to the far end of the village and then attack the German position from the north. Mitchell later explained that this bold move, which left his battalion isolated and cut off by strong German forces, was justified by the surprise achieved. If he was cut off so were the enemy who could not retreat north when the Black Watch's sister battalion, le Régiment de Maisonneuve, mounted a set-piece attack on the village that evening.

Back at the Trun-Chambois battlefield, 4th Canadian Armoured Division had less than 36 hours to reorganize before starting north. The British Columbia Regiment, rebuilt to full strength after its ordeal at Point 145, led off on the Green centre line toward Bernay. A scratch force of German infantry and tanks allowed the armoured cars of the Manitoba Dragoons to pass. It then knocked out the leading tanks.

Frantic orders to press on were obeyed, but nine more tanks were hit in the attempts to bypass the position. The Lake Superior Regiment's motorized company began to clear the woods, but heavy rain and darkness impeded operations. By morning, the Germans were gone, leaving a wrecked Tiger tank and two anti-tank guns.

Major-General Harry Foster, an infantry officer who had commanded the 7th Western Brigade, had just taken over command of the division and, prompted by his new armoured brigade commander Robert Moncel, decided to reorganize the division into the kind of battle group used in the advance to Falaise. The vanguard known as Keane Force, named after the commanding officer of the Lake Supes, was composed of two armoured regiments, the motor battalion and an infantry battalion as well as engineers and self-propelled artillery. This well-balanced force moved quickly north reaching Bernay the next day.

The men of the division had never before seen an undamaged town in France. Unit war diaries recorded the emotions felt by liberators and by the liberated. "Will Bernay ever be forgotten? Bernay where the people stood from morning to night. Bernay where they never tired of waving, of throwing flowers or fruit, of giving their best wines and spirits. Bernay where the local school mistress had her children lined along the street singing in unison and in English: "Thank you for liberating us."

The cynic might say the people of Bernay were effusive because they had been spared the ravages of war. But the town had not been spared occupation, nor the presence of the Gestapo. Bernay had its share of martyrs before the Canadians arrived to restore freedom.

Keane Force moved east to allow 3rd Division room on the road network. Their progress was slowed in traffic jams created by the withdrawal of American units that had tried to trap the retreating enemy at the River Seine. Montgomery was now trying to line up his armies for the race north, leaving the task of stopping the Germans at the Seine to the tactical air force that attacked and destroyed hundreds of the vehicles that escaped encirclement at Chambois.

The traffic congestion hampered all movement and 4th Division arrived at the Seine widely dispersed in small battle groups. The Lincoln and Welland Regiment, known as the Lincs and Winks, together with troops of 8th Light Anti-Aircraft Regiment, a platoon of New Brunswick Rangers and a squadron of South Alberta tanks reached the river at Criquebeuf-sur-Seine. The villagers, who have since named their main street Rue des Canadiens, wanted to welcome their liberators properly, but Lieutenant-Colonel Bill Cromb needed to keep his men moving because he had been ordered to bounce the Seine. Boats, borrowed from the village, were used to cross the 80-metre-wide river and the Lincs' scout platoon reported that there was no opposition.

Cromb sent "D" Company across the river to establish a bridgehead which the Lincs, the Argyll and Sutherland Highlanders of Canada and the Algonquin Regiment expanded the next morning. There followed a costly struggle for two rounded hills known as Point 88 and Point 95. This two-day battle, the last fought by the division in Normandy,

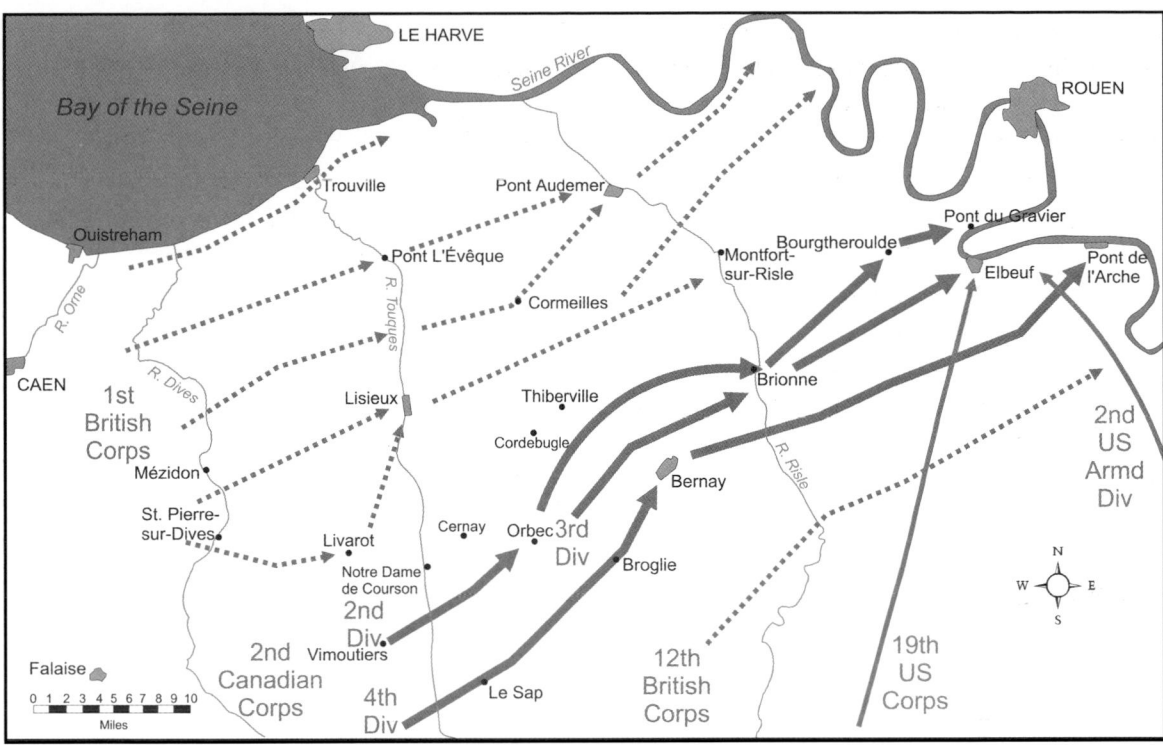

Pursuit to the Seine, August 22-30, 1944.

reminded everyone of the advance to Falaise. When the heights were occupied it was evident the enemy had enjoyed an unobstructed view of the river crossing and the bare slopes of the hillsides. There was no cover for the attackers except for smoke which was of little help against artillery and mortar concentrations. 10th Brigade suffered more than 100 casualties in this forgotten encounter.

Third Division, which reached the Seine at Elbeuf, found little resistance and 16th Field Company, Royal Canadian Engineers, immediately began construction of a Bailey Bridge. Second Division, on the left flank of the Canadian advance, left Bourgtheroulde and entered a hilly forested area known as the Forêt de la Londe which lay astride the direct route to Rouen. Thus began one of the most unfortunate and tragic events in the entire campaign.

In writing these articles, I have tried to remember that the historian should attempt to explain what happened by determining what was known or what could reasonably be inferred from what was known at the time a decision was made. In the case of the Forêt de la Londe, it is necessary to note that the planning was based on the assumption that there would be no significant resistance. In his orders of August 26, General Harry Crerar noted that "the

enemy no longer has the troops to hold any strong points–or to hold any positions for any length of time–if he is aggressively attacked. Speed of action and forcible tactics are therefore urgently required from commanders at any level."

Corps commander Lieutenant-General Guy Simonds and Major-General Charles Foulkes, the divisional commanding officer, seem to have shared this view which was avidly prompted by army, corps and divisional intelligence officers carried away with the euphoria of impending victory. The result of this optimism was that the tired understrength battalions were told that this would "probably be a non-tactical move and no or very few enemy would be encountered."

4th Brigade was rushed forward on the night of August 26 to provide flank protection for the engineers building bridges at Elbeuf. The Royal Hamilton Light Infantry was in the lead and the troops came under fire as their trucks entered Port du Gravier, a small riverside village at the narrowest point of land between the meandering loops of the Seine.

As dawn broke on August 27, the brigade had its first look at the forest. The heavily wooded neck of the meander was some 4,000 yards wide. Two railway lines, 100 yards apart, ran across the neck, one of them branching north through a tunnel built under a steep chalk hill. Close to the river, directly in front of 4th Brigade, a second hill, soon to be known by its code-name Masie, controlled two of the three roads to Rouen.

Over on the west side of the forest, 6th Brigade had come under fire from the high ground and Brigadier Fred Clift sent a company of the Fusiliers Mont-Royal on a right flanking mission. The Royals met up with the FMRs and took them under command waiting for a rendezvous with the Essex Scottish who were to support the attack on Masie. Before the two battalions could link up, they came under devastating fire from German mortar and artillery posted on the ridge the Royals called Chalk Pits Hill.

To the men on the ground, the volume of fire indicated the enemy held the ridge in considerable strength, but division and corps were impatient and the Royals were told to mount an all-out attack. Doubt about the exact position of 6th Brigade's leading units led to limits on the use of artillery and the attack failed.

At 1600 hours on August 28, Foulkes called the three battalion commanders to brigade headquarters and outlined an ambitious night attack. The Royals war diary records the reaction, though you have to read between the lines to capture the full flavour: "The COs of both the RHLI and the R Regiment C were strongly of the opinion that this task was beyond the powers of a battalion composed largely of reinforcement personnel with little training. It was suggested that the enemy was actually stronger than intelligence reports had indicated and that the ground was immensely favourable for the defence...."

This sensible analysis of the real situation fell on deaf ears. Foulkes ordered RHLI to prepare to move as soon as possible and to be in position to attack Masie at first light. The operation proved impossible to carry out though the Rileys suffered badly trying.

Foulkes had also ordered 6th Brigade to capture the high ground. The South Sasks lead company, total strength 35, crossed the railway and came under fire. The scout platoon was ambushed when it tried to outflank the enemy and the 13 remaining men, no officers were left, withdrew. A second attack employing an artillery barrage was no more successful and the Camerons were brought forward despite continuous mortar fire to join the assault. At first light on the 29th the enemy counterattacked and all semblance of control was lost. What was left of the two battalions pulled back. That night, the Germans withdrew to Rouen because 9th Brigade, with the Stormont, Dundas and Glengarry Highlanders in the lead, were closing on the city from the east. For the Germans it was now or never and they retreated to the Somme.

The Calgary Highlanders had not taken any direct part in the fighting, their task was to hold a firm base, but Calgary War diarist Lieutenant Stuart Moore described August 29 as one of the worst days in the battalion's history. "Today has been a nightmare," he wrote, "we were subjected to constant fire and had little protection." The Calgaries lost 46 men without firing a single round or seeing a German soldier.

Two brigades had been decimated during the three-day battle in the Forêt de la Londe. The South Sasks with 185 casualties and the Royals with 118 topped the list of over 600 killed and wounded. The Canadians had come up against a well-organized blocking force which was under orders to buy time for units retreating across the Seine. The soldiers of 2nd SS Panzer Division, with paratroops and infantry from the 85th Division, had fulfilled their mission.

But what of the Canadians? What was their mission? With both 3rd and 4th divisions across the river on the 27th the decision to order further costly infantry attacks in the dense forest made little military sense. Given the shortages of manpower which plagued the Canadian army the orders are even harder to understand. Canadian generals had to respond to pressure from Montgomery to speed-up the advance, but at Forêt de la Londe they seemed to forget they also had a duty to the men who served under them.

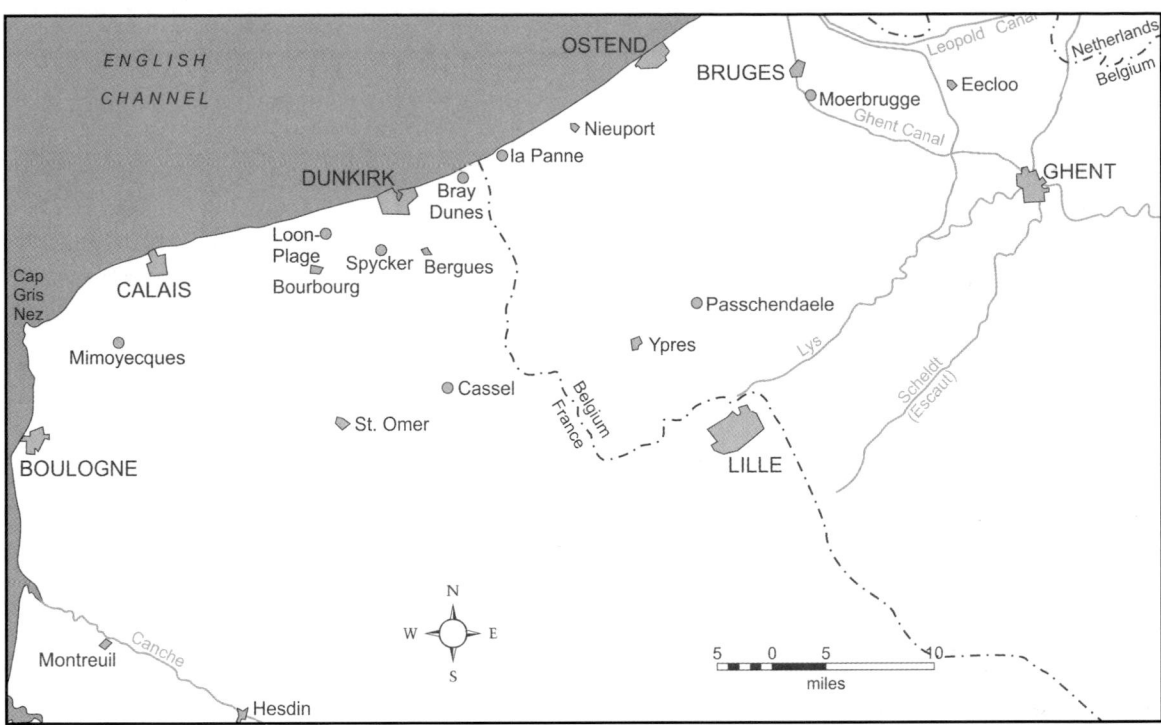

The Channel
Ports.

Opening Up
The Channel Ports

Originally published in May/June 2000

The operation was code-named "Fusilade". Its objective was a French port that had been attacked before with horrific consequences. But this time, the port would be attacked from the landward side, and not from the sea. Heavy bombers would destroy the German defences and much else in the town before the assault began. The town was Dieppe and the date was September 1, 1944.

East of the town, the armoured cars of 8 Recce Regiment–the 14th Canadian Hussars–advanced well ahead of the rest of 2nd Canadian Division. The men saw no signs of German resistance and in the early morning light two motorcyclists entered Dieppe. Suddenly, the streets were filled with people. "The crowd ran forward to meet them and was so dense that both men could advance no further," noted a Dieppe newspaper. "Women threw themselves on them and kissed them. All the citizens gathered around the Monument to Victory where both soldiers had gone to deposit the flowers that had been given to them. There ceremonies took place and the crowd sang La Marseillaise, God Save The King and Tipperary."

Fortunately, the soldiers kept their heads and reports of the German withdrawal were relayed to Bomber Command in time to divert the Lancasters to other targets. The celebrations continued as other 2nd Division units arrived and there was time for the men to visit the battlefields and the cemetery where their comrades were buried. On September 3, the whole division, in columns six abreast, paraded through the town. The ghosts of Dieppe were on everyone's mind as Lieutenant-General Harry Crerar took the salute. The liberation of the town without loss of life–civilian or military–helped to heal the wounds of August 19, 1942.

Crerar's decision to attend the ceremony in Dieppe caused him to miss a conference at Montgomery's headquarters. When Crerar arrived several hours late the Canadian general was subjected to a fit of temper that culminated in a threat to remove him from command. Crerar refused to be intimidated and replied that he had a "responsibility to Canada as well as to the C-in-C," and would therefore report the situation to the Canadian government. Montgomery cooled down instantly, the last thing he needed was another public quarrel while he was in the midst of an argument with Eisenhower. That argument heated up the next day when Eisenhower issued a directive that began with the words: "Enemy resistance on the entire front shows signs of collapse." Montgomery's armies, including 1st United States Army, were to "secure Antwerp" and "seize the Ruhr" while General George S. Patton's 3rd U.S. Army advanced to the Saar and Frankfurt.

Montgomery, convinced that there were not enough resources for an advance on a broad front, again demanded that Patton be halted and supplies reallocated to support "one really powerful thrust toward Berlin… and thus end the German war." Anxious to avoid a public airing of their differences, Eisenhower flew to Montgomery's headquarters. He had no intention of stopping Patton, but he did agree to a new plan to employ the Allied airborne army in an ambitious attempt to cross the Rhine at Arnhem–Operation "Market Garden".

Historians have pointed out the flaws in Montgomery's grand design, but on the basis of what was known in mid-September 1944, "Market Garden" was a bold and brilliant scheme to cross the Rhine and win the war. The problem was that if it failed the Allies would end up with a deep salient that would have to be defended, and they might still be dependent on Cherbourg and the Normandy beaches for supply.

Before Montgomery persuaded him to support Operation "Market Garden", Eisenhower had stressed the need to clear the approaches to Antwerp and get Europe's second largest port–captured intact on September 5–working.

The senior Allied commanders knew from Ultra that Hitler had ordered the absolute defence of both sides of the estuary so that Antwerp, 65 miles from the sea, could not be used. Hitler gave similar orders to the garrisons of Le Havre, Boulogne, Calais and Dunkirk. His hope was that he could choke off supplies to the Allies.

Montgomery wanted the Canadians to capture the Channel ports and clear the approaches to Antwerp while the British were crossing the Rhine. In early September, First Canadian Army was comprised of four infantry and two armoured divisions, plus 2nd Armoured Brigade. But during the month, Montgomery transferred the two British infantry divisions and the Polish Armoured Division to support his Arnhem offensive. He then ordered 2nd Canadian Division to Antwerp and even borrowed one of 2nd Canadian Armoured Brigade's regiments. This left the Canadians with one infantry and one armoured division to capture Boulogne, Calais and clear the south bank of the Scheldt Estuary.

Most historians have been content to echo Montgomery's complaint that throughout September, the "Canadian Army was badly handled and very slow" without troubling to examine the actual situation that confronted corps commander Lieutenant-General Guy Simonds. When 3rd Canadian Division reached the outskirts of Boulogne in early September it was quickly evident that it faced a formidable task. This was the heart of the Pas de Calais that the Germans had long believed would be the focus of the main Allied landings. The heaviest guns faced seaward, but fear of airborne landings behind the coast led to the development of all-around defences. Neither Boulogne nor Calais could be dealt with in isolation. For unless both towns and the great gun batteries of Cap Gris Nez were taken, the navy could not use either port.

Simonds had sent 4th Canadian Armoured Division racing north to Belgium where the Argyll and Sutherland Highlanders of Canada and the Lincoln and Welland Regiment fought their way across the Ghent Canal at Moerbrugge. Mortar and artillery fire of Normandy proportions struck at their bridgehead and well organized counterattacks indicated that the days of rapid pursuit of a disorganized enemy were over. After the Algonquin Regiment was forced out of a second bridgehead across the Leopold Canal, there was

NAC 137309

German prisoners of war from Boulogne.

little doubt the enemy intended to defend what Hitler named Scheldt Fortress South and the Canadians called the Breskens Pocket.

With 4th Division fully engaged in Belgium, Simonds had no choice: 3rd Division would have to take on the Channel ports by itself.

The division was now commanded by Dan Spry who had served as a brigadier in Italy before his sudden and surprising promotion to replace the wounded Rod Keller. As a new major-general, Spry had to tread carefully because his three brigadiers, Ken Blackadder, John Rockingham and Jock Spragge, were experienced commanders who doubted that the young officer was up to the task. Fortunately, Spry sought their input and when Simonds outlined the objectives for the operations at Boulogne and Calais, 3rd Division was well prepared to implement them.

The key to Boulogne was Mont Lambert, a high rounded hill overlooking the approaches to the city. The hill was heavily fortified and many of the great concrete shelters, pillboxes and gun positions survive to this day. Spry chose Rockingham's 9th Brigade for Mont Lambert with Blackadder's 8th taking on the northern

suburbs. Meanwhile, 7th Brigade would begin operations against Calais.

There were more than 10,000 German troops in Boulogne and the Canadians knew they were attacking a well dug-in enemy who actually outnumbered them. Simonds, therefore, demanded massive artillery and air support and a full range of the specialized armoured vehicles–known as Funnies–from General Percy Hobart's 79th Armoured Division.

Montgomery was unhappy with the pace of Canadian operations, but Crerar insisted he wanted Simonds to "button things up properly, taking a little more time if necessary, to assure a decisive assault." Simonds adamantly refused to attack until the specialized armour, including his own invention–the Kangaroo armoured personnel carrier–was available to clear minefields, protect troops and destroy concrete pillboxes. After the fall of Le Havre on September 12, it took four days of round-the-clock work by the Royal Canadian Army Service Corps to transport Hobart's specialized armour to the north. The assault on Boulogne began the next day.

The battle resembled the siege of a medieval fortress. Scores of visitors from rear headquarters arrived to watch it unfold. Third Division issued a special order that compelled "visiting naval, military and air force personnel as well as press correspondents" to report to a spectators stand set up on a nearby hill. Visitors were warned that the division accepted no responsibility for their safety.

At 0825 hours on September 17, waves of Lancasters and Halifaxes, including those of the Royal Canadian Air Force in 6 Group, dropped 3,000 tons of bombs on the defenders. The artillery counter-battery program began and both brigades launched their initial attack. Spry used the Fort Garry Horse to lead columns of the North Nova Scotia Regiment and the Stormont, Dundas and Glengarry Highlanders–mounted in Kangaroos–towards Mont Lambert.

The North Novas–with combat engineers–cleared the pillboxes one at a time under the protective fire of the tanks. A steady drain of casualties, most from enemy mortar and artillery fire, slowed the advance and the area was not entirely cleared until the next day. The SD&G Highlanders war diary records the results of close co-operation with 84 Group of 2nd Tactical Air Force in a verbatim report of the messages passed between the air support signals unit and Skylark, the aircraft overhead. This co-operation led to the dive-bombing of enemy positions directly in front of the infantry.

The 8th Brigade had been given a series of tasks that required each battalion to operate in isolation. Le Régiment de la Chaudière and the remaining squadrons of the Garries seized a radar station and then pressed forward into the northern suburbs. The next morning they confronted a series of blockhouses with steel turrets housing machine-guns. This grim battle fought in the shadow of Napoleon's tower was similar to the experience of the

Queen's Own Rifles of Canada who faced a large concrete strongpoint that could not be taken or bypassed without a massive artillery stonk.

Perhaps the most difficult battle was fought by the North Shore (N.B.) Regiment that tackled three heavily fortified coastal gun batteries at La Trésorerie north of the city. By dusk the infantry had worked its way into the position and cleared one of the batteries "after much grenade throwing." The remaining two were taken the next morning with the help of Projector Infantry Anti-Tank guns, PIATs and phosphorous bombs. Approximately 450 Germans were taken prisoner.

The next objective was Wimereux, the coastal town where John McCrae is buried. Lieutenant-Colonel J.G. Anderson was reluctant to use the medium artillery on a town full of civilians and so his men infiltrated, relying on the M-10s of 3rd Anti-tank Regiment to deal with the pillboxes. There ought to be a memorial to Anderson and his New Brunswickers in Wimereux, but instead the events are largely forgotten.

In Boulogne, attempts to cross the River Liane were foiled by blown bridges until 18th Field Company Royal Canadian Engineers improvised a bridge, fitting timbers together without benefit of nails. By dawn on the 19th, the Highland Light Infantry was across to begin clearing the remaining coastal gun batteries. Boulogne finally surrendered on the afternoon of September 22, 1944.

The Canadians were severely criticized for taking five days to secure the port, but a careful study by Montgomery's operational research section revealed that neither the bombing nor the artillery had neutralized more than a fraction of the enemy positions that had to be captured in close combat. The Canadians who fought in Boulogne knew this from first-hand experience. Few in the garrison had been willing to follow Hitler's orders and fight to the end. Indeed, 9,517 men surrendered, but they were perfectly willing to man their weapons and fire from concrete shelters until the Canadians attacked at close quarters.

Plans for 7th Brigade to attack Calais and Cap Gris Nez while the siege of Boulogne was under way were cancelled after probing attacks suggested the task was beyond the capacity of a single brigade. The area was defended by some 8,000 troops, including 2,500 infantry. With companies averaging 85 men, 7th Brigade could muster less than a thousand riflemen. The 1st Hussars, who were serving with 7th Brigade, reported that at least some of the coastal guns could traverse and fire inland. One veteran recalled that you had "the impression of watching a huge furnace door open and then hearing the great 'boxcars' come screaming through the air. When these 1,000-pound shells landed within a few hundred yards of the tanks, every Sherman rocked like a baby carriage."

Spry insisted on waiting until Bomber Command, the artillery and all three brigades were available so it was not until September 25 that the attack began.

The spectators had long since departed and there was nothing to see in the sand dunes along the coast or the flooded fields south of the city. There were just small groups of infantry and armour going about their work. The one prominent ridge overlooking the battlefield, Cap Blanc Nez, was occupied by the enemy. The slopes were too steep for Kangaroos or tanks so the Chauds leaned into the barrage and climbed the hill. The Canadian Scottish Regiment advanced to the coast while the Royal Winnipeg Rifles took Fort Nieulay, a classic 18th century stone fortress. The enemy agreed to surrender after feeling the heat from flame-throwing Crocodiles.

The Germans demanded a truce to evacuate the civilian population and Spry had to agree. Long columns of refugees poured out of the city and then it all began again.

The final drive to capture Calais involved the Queen's Own Rifles attacking from the north, the Regina Rifle Regiment from the south and the Canscots advancing along the coast. At 0300 hours, October 1, the last defenders were marched off to captivity.

9th Brigade had an easier time at Cap Gris Nez. The enormous concrete structures that housed the cross Channel guns were formidable, but the landward defences were not strong. Bomber Command blasted the area and the two large guns known as Winnie and Pooh fired their last rounds of the war from the coast of England before the North Novas and HLI attacked.

After the last strongpoint fell, Rockingham gathered the men to offer congratulations for their achievement in helping to open up the Channel ports. As if by magic, the first of a string of ships appeared headed for Boulogne.

The construction of the Channel tunnel and new highways has transformed the Canadian battlefields of the Pas de Calais, but the visitor can still follow what happened on the ground. The place to start is at the Canadian military cemetery that has a special exit off the A-16 near Calais. Here on a once-bare hillside–now covered with pine trees–you will find the graves of many of the 925 Canadian men who died in September 1944. Their story must not be forgotten.

2nd Division In September 1944

Originally published, May/June 2001

During September 1944, 2nd Canadian Infantry Division was involved in a series of very tough battles in northern France. On the morning of the 7th, the 8th Canadian Reconnaissance Regiment, (14th Canadian Hussars), was moving well in front of the infantry when it ran up against strong German positions in the villages of Bourbourgville and Gravelines near Dunkirk.

Field Marshal Bernard Montgomery, who had not yet made up his mind about future strategy, wanted the Canadians to secure all of the Channel ports and so operations to clear the outer ring of Dunkirk's defences got under way immediately. The 5th Canadian Infantry Brigade had missed the worst of the terrible struggle for the Forêt de la Londe, so it was in the lead. The brigade began the operation with the Royal Highland Regiment of Canada–the Black Watch–seizing a bridging site south of Bourbourgville and establishing a base for the advance.

The Germans had flooded much of the area by blowing the canal banks. Ditches were full of water and the ground–if not flooded–was soggy. The Régiment de Maisonneuve moved through the Black Watch and soon secured a canal crossing. It then advanced to the northeast edge of town. Captain Pierre Fafard described the initial stages of the attack to the divisional historical officer in 1944. "The town of Bourbourgville is remarkable for having a canal completely around it and because the church is centrally located and all the approaches across this canal can be covered from the market-square in the centre of town. The bridges were all blown by the enemy and a search had to take place for canoes and boats with which to cross...."

The approach had been difficult due to harassing fire from 75- and 88-mm guns, but the 5th Field Regiment was soon ready to deal with this and the Maisonneuves entered the town using boats supplied by the eager citizens or by swimming. Other soldiers, including Major Jacques Ostiguy's "C" Company, used an improvised plank footbridge.

The railway station was strongly defended with two 20-mm anti-aircraft guns deployed as anti-infantry weapons. No one was anxious to face this barrage until J.P. Leblanc dashed into the street and–while lying down–provided enough covering fire to silence the guns and get his men moving forward. The town was not freed until several hours before dawn, but this did not stop the population from celebrating the liberation in parts of the town that were clear.

The Calgary Highlanders moved north to the village of Loon Plage shortly after first light. Les Planches, a handful of houses halfway to their objective, was taken quickly by the lead company under Major Dalt Heyland, but when the next "bite"–a road junction–was reached, enemy artillery pounded the area. It was difficult to dig in and impossible to move forward. "D" Company moved around the flank to approach Loon Plage from the west, but it was halted at a farm 455 metres outside the village.

The Calgaries were under enormous pressure and casualties were mounting. Its war diary reports, with some emotion, that "the Régiment de Maisonneuve was then ordered to assist us moving three companies northwards along the road parallel to our axis.... They took five hours to even get to a point 1,500 metres up the road....we had to continue without help."

The Maisonneuves had started north quickly enough, but "A" Company's lead platoon had gone less than a kilometre when it ran into a carefully concealed German position. The platoon got into some farm buildings, with carefully controlled fire and movement, and an all around defensive position was created. The company commander, Major Alexander Angers,

NAC 134450

Lieutenant-General Guy Simonds and Admiral Bertram Ramsay discussing further operations, September 1944.

was wounded along with a dozen others. "A" Company's lead platoon was surrounded and unable to move without attracting artillery and direct fire. Fifth Field Regiment was contacted and it responded quickly by bringing down a barrage and allowing the Maisonneuves to withdraw from the burning buildings they had found cover in.

The Maisonneuves, like the Calgaries, tried to invest the Dunkirk perimeter against formidable odds. The enemy had ample supplies of artillery shells, enough–as it turned out–to defend Dunkirk until the war was over. The enemy also had good daylight observation points and an intimate knowledge of the terrain. The Canadian infantry battalions, meanwhile, were operating without any armour or air support, and without a clear mission. They were pressing forward without time for reconnaissance and without

making full use of intelligence from the French resistance forces in the area.

On the right flank of the brigade, the Black Watch was trying to carry out one such attack. Major Alex Pinkham's "C" Company was teamed up with a troop of armoured cars from 8th Recce Regiment. Their objective–Coppenaxfort–was some 5,000 metres east of Bourbourgville along a single, straight and elevated road on the bank of a canal. There were no trees, no shrubs–no cover of any kind. The company's soldiers could only move in single file, taking care to space themselves out considerably.

The first armoured car was roughly 100 yards behind the lead troops, but it was soon knocked out by a heavy anti-tank gun. Mortars and field guns struck at the infantry who tried to dig in.

Fifth Field Regiment was short of ammunition and fully committed to the Calgaries and Maisonneuves. So, the Black Watch had to wait until dark to withdraw and regroup. The next morning a single platoon of "C" Company, assisted by one armoured car, rushed the bridge leading into the town only to discover that the Germans had withdrawn.

These gains meant little to 5th Brigade because it was now occupying positions the Germans had carefully surveyed as artillery targets. Throughout the following weeks, the brigade used fighting patrols to harass the enemy and battalion attacks to compress the perimeter. After a furious battle, the Black Watch captured the town of Spycker on September 11. The Germans launched a strong counterattack that resulted in many casualties.

Lieutenant Joe Nixon and his scout platoon played a crucial role in stopping the counterattack. Nixon personally handled a PIAT (Projector, Infantry, Anti-Tank) gun while his sniper scouts successfully targeted enemy infantry. One sniper, Private Frank de Lutio, won the Military Medal for his efforts that day, but the cost of holding the village was too high and the Black Watch withdrew on the night of September 13.

Division was pressing brigade for information, but patrols to obtain it could be costly. Lieutenant Charles Forbes of the Maisonneuves dealt with one request by donning a priest's cassock and beret. Remarkably, he walked up to and through the German position and returned with a full report.

The Calgaries occupied Loon Plage on September 9 and used it as a base for patrols to probe the perimeter. Battalion headquarters was besieged by the resistance forces, including two rifle-toting teenage boys who arrived with three German prisoners. The war diary describes a cocktail party at Monsieur Le Mare's home with "bevies of beautiful girls and glasses of champagne, plus of all things a large, beautiful bouquet of fresh flowers."

On the other side of Dunkirk, 6th Brigade operated with the assistance of the highly organized Belgian White Brigade, the national resistance movement of the Belgian armed forces. The White Brigade was able to provide a detailed plan of the enemy's defences, including its mined areas near the Belgian-French border. But when the brigade advanced along the coast, it met strong opposition.

The South Saskatchewan Regiment was forced to deal with a major enemy strongpoint nestled in sand dunes thick with mines and carefully sited machine-gun posts that were connected to the main position by tunnels. The SSRs were virtually a brand new regiment, rebuilt with reinforcements after the nightmare at Forêt de la Londe had removed most of the men who had survived the battles of the Normandy beachhead. Its task was not made any easier by the supply crisis that led to a shortage of artillery ammunition.

An initial attack faltered under withering fire, but a second attack succeeded in breaching the outlying defences. However, an attempt to go forward on the next bound was stopped cold and the assault companies withdrew to their start-line. The guns of the 3rd Light Anti-Aircraft Regiment and the 2nd Anti-Tank Regiment were brought up and an attack by Typhoons of 84 Group was put in. Unfortunately, the additional firepower was ineffective.

Brigadier J.G. Gauvreau went forward to direct the SSR to close with its objective, but before another attack was launched a surrender demand was accepted by the Germans late on the night of September 12. The German garrison was unwilling to resist any longer because it had been told of the fall of the city of Le Havre and the capture, by the Essex Scottish Regiment, of a neighbouring strongpoint.

The SSR joined its sister regiments at Bray Dunes where the Fusiliers Mont-Royal and the Queen's Own Cameron Highlanders of Canada were engaged in a bitter, close battle against much more determined defenders.

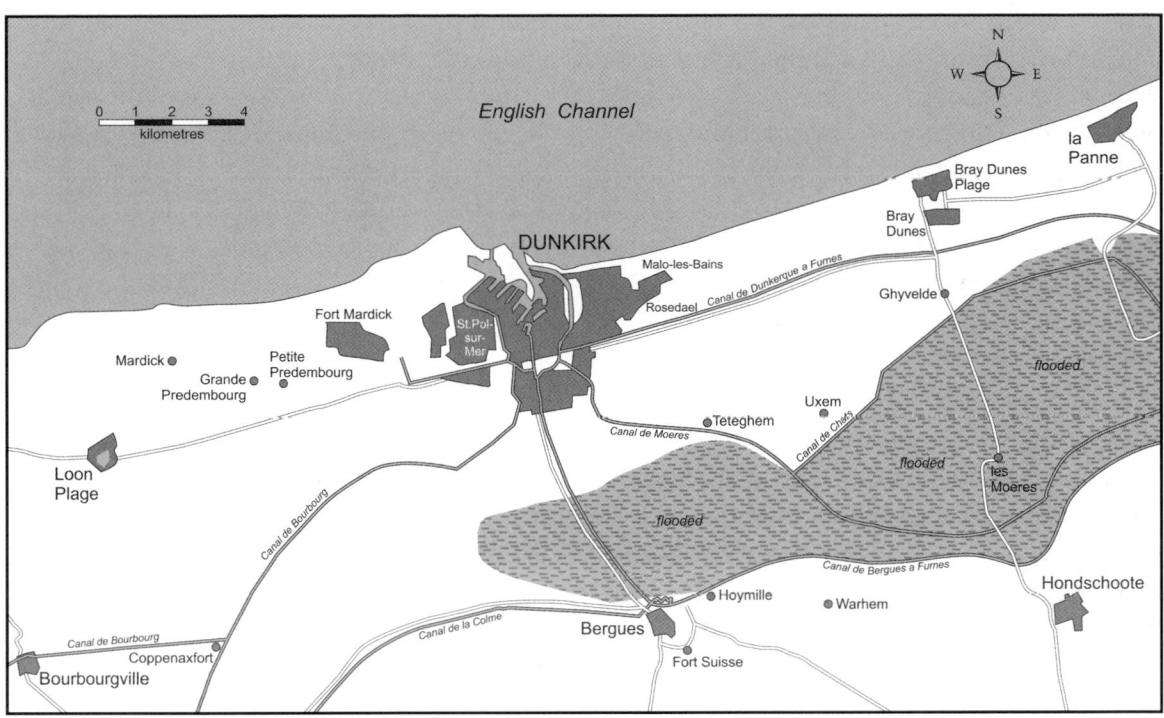

Dunkirk, 1944.

The Camerons attempted–to no avail–to out-flank the defences of Bray Dunes Plage by traversing the sand dunes along the shoreline. Further attempts on the 13th and 14th were equally unsuccessful. Typhoon aircraft hammered the defences, but coordination with the infantry was non-existent. It was not until the full brigade was committed in a series of sector attacks that the position was overcome on September 15.

Fourth Brigade had begun clearing the coast south of Ostend, but it soon ran into a well-defended strongpoint at Westende. The Essex Scottish, with platoons of the Toronto Scottish, conducted a siege operation in miniature with mortars and 17-pounder anti-tank guns from 2nd Anti-Tank Regiment It exchanged fire with four large, vintage naval guns.

To the south, the Royal Hamilton Light Infantry and the Royal Regiment began to advance on Bergues, a beautiful fortified town that appeared to be strongly defended. The steady drain of casualties was affecting all nine infantry battalions and the division had not begun to tackle the main Dunkirk defences. It was beginning to look like a very costly operation and there were no regrets when Montgomery decided to mask Dunkirk and transfer 2nd Division to Antwerp.

Fourth Brigade moved first, taking over the defences of the vital docks from 53 Welsh Division.

Antwerp was a strange place in September 1944. The civilian population was caught up in the euphoria of liberation and seemed almost oblivious to the presence of the Germans occupying the northern suburbs. Some civilians went about their affairs to the point of crossing back and forth over the Albert Canal from the German to the Allied sector. The Belgian resistance, on the other hand, was active in attempting to extend the dock area perimeter. The Essex Scottish and the RHLI took over the defences and on the night of September 20 the Essex were hit hard by a German attack that was apparently intended to seize and destroy a railway bridge. Heavy fighting raged throughout the night, but the enemy was beaten off.

The area around 4th Brigade's positions was full of water until White Brigade patrols, supported by Canadian artillery, secured the sluice gates. This allowed drainage of the tidal water. The RHLI moved its lines forward to protect the site on September 22. From that date until October 2, no major initiative was taken by either side.

The rest of the division made the trek to Antwerp on September 18 and reports from that journey show that the ride across the newly liberated Belgian countryside was an exhilarating experience. "At various points along the way, the entire convoy was showered with gifts of fruit, bread and of course at times with liqueurs. Hand clasping was just as prominent a practice as in France, and the familiar 'Cigarette for Papa' slogan greeted us.

"One very pleasant experience was hearing so many people speak English. The pubs reminded one of some of the ones in England. The sight of beautiful poppies caught the eye of many and the full meaning of Flanders fields became self-explanatory. Considerable attention was paid to the members of the fair sex. With few exceptions, the majority of women and young girls were healthy and good looking. From all early reports, it was the general opinion that a reasonably lengthy sojourn in the country would not be too great a hardship on the troops."

It was not to be.

5th Brigade was immediately committed to an advance across the Albert Canal followed by 6th Brigade's attempts to forge a bridgehead over the well-defended Turnhout Canal. With General Harry Crerar in hospital in England, General Guy Simonds had taken over command of the army. The corps was under the command of Major-General Charles Foulkes. Brigadier R.H. Keefler, the division's senior gunner, commanded 2nd Division and he decided to deal with the enemy by sending 5th Brigade on a wide flanking movement that made use of a bridgehead across the Turnhout.

This manoeuvre was a success, but the brigade soon ran into German battle groups that were determined to hold the canal line north of Antwerp. The fierce battles for the villages of St. Leonard and Brecht paved the way for the rest of the division to begin moving north and on October 2, Simonds told Keefler to "clear the area north of Antwerp and close the eastern end of the Beveland isthmus." When this was accomplished, orders would be issued to clear Beveland to the north and capture Walcheren Island. The division was thus committed to some of the most difficult battles of the war at the village of Woensdrecht and on the narrow causeway connecting Walcheren Island and the peninsula of South Beveland.

The intensity of the conflict in October has overshadowed the memory of the battles of September on the Dunkirk perimeter, the docks of Antwerp and the Turnhout Canal, but for the men who fought there, the losses and the victories were just as real and just as important as in the more famous battles. Today, visitors will find few indications of these encounters. If you seek their monument, visit the Canadian war cemeteries at Calais and Bergen Op Zoom. On the wind-swept hill overlooking the English Channel or in the deeply wooded area east of Bergen you will find places to reflect upon the events of September 1944.

Our Rescue Role At Arnhem

Originally published, September/October 2000

One of the most moving ceremonies associated with WW II takes place every September at the Arnhem-Oosterbeek war cemetery in Holland. That is when Dutch schoolchildren stand quietly next to each grave and then on a signal place bouquets of flowers. Three quarters of the 1,760 graves are for men who served with the 1st British Airborne Division, 43 Wessex Division or the Polish Parachute Brigade. These men died in the struggle to liberate Arnhem and to win control of a bridge across the lower Rhine River in September 1944.

The poignant ceremony is part of a program that includes a parachute drop and the annual Airborne Walk. More than 30,000 people participate in the 25-kilometre trek that includes a stop at a simple memorial located on the south bank of the river opposite Oosterbeek. Erected in 1989 by veterans of the airborne division, the memorial features an inscription that begins with the following words: "They Were Just Shadows and Whispers in the Night." The inscription also records the gratitude of the 2,400 airborne troops who were evacuated to safety by Canadian and British engineers while under heavy German fire.

Few people on the Airborne Walk know the full story behind the memorial and even fewer know that almost all of those who were saved owe it to the men of the 23rd Field Company, Royal Canadian Engineers.

The 20th and 23rd field companies had been attached to 43rd Wessex Division in an attempt to bolster the division's river crossing capacity. The Canadians were equipped with stormboats powered by Evinrude motors. Each boat could carry 36 men. The British made do with smaller assault boats that had to be paddled.

The original intent was to use the Canadian boats to bring reinforcements across the Rhine and expand the airborne bridgehead, but no one in the British army seems to have understood the urgency of the situation in Arnhem. The army's slow progress meant that the Wessex division arrived too late to do more than sacrifice a battalion of the Dorset Regiment which crossed the river just hours before the withdrawal order was issued.

On the morning of September 25, 1944, the confusion and uncertainty that had marked the operations of the ground forces throughout Operation "Market Garden" were still evident. When Major M.L. Tucker–the commanding officer of 23rd Field Company–arrived at an orders group he was assigned a sector and told to bring out as many survivors as he could. No one could say how many there might be and there was no information available on the enemy or the crossing sites. 20th Field Company's sector proved to be opposite an area already held by the enemy.

Tucker and Lieutenant R.J. Kennedy immediately went forward to recce an advanced marshalling area for the boats and found one a few kilometres west of Arnhem at Valburg. Kennedy, who had already scouted the south bank of the river in preparation for the proposed assault crossing, was able to report that there was a site northeast of Driel where stormboats could be launched. The convoy carrying the boats–crews and mechanics from the RCE's 10th Field Park Company– reached Valburg by mid-afternoon.

Tucker attended a second meeting at 5:15 p.m. and was told that at last light an artillery barrage would begin and that it would drown out the noise of the stormboats. Simultaneously, the Wessex division would stage a feint attack to distract the enemy. There was still no information about the airborne troops or the fate of the Dorset Regiment that had crossed the river. The Dorsets had in fact landed inside enemy lines and most of the 300 men who crossed were taken prisoner.

It is possible to argue that the Canadian engineers were better off not knowing more about their challenge. The village of Driel was the headquarters of Major-General S.F. Sobowski's Polish Independent Parachute Brigade. Sobowski and his men did not lack courage, but after landing near Driel they had been unable to get more than a handful of men across the river to join 1st Airborne Division.

Sobowski was furious over orders to stage a drop south of the river and then cross it under fire. With nothing more than six small rubber boats provided by the airborne division there was little chance of carrying out these orders. Unfortunately, the actions of the Poles and Dorsets had drawn attention to the crossing point at Driel and so it was not long before German artillery and mortar fire was ranged in on the area.

Plans for the withdrawal were left to Major-General R.E. Urquhart, the airborne commander. He decided to try and evacuate everyone that night. Urquhart's staff produced and coded a complex artillery plan that required the gunners, south of the river, to fire timed concentrations as the perimeter shrank and the troops withdrew. Medical officers and men of the field ambulance stayed with the wounded, many of whom were in serious condition. The Dutch civilians, who had done everything they could to help, were also left behind to face the wrath of the enemy. The troops were told to blacken their faces, wrap their boots in blanket strips to muffle sounds and then move off in groups, holding "the tail of the smock or the hand of the man in front."

While Urquhart and his staff relayed their orders and marked routes, Tucker organized his company by placing a bridge-building section in the lead so that boats could be brought across a drainage ditch and off-loaded just 500 yards from the river. The boats were delivered, but it was difficult to haul them to the launching site because rain had softened the ground. In his report on the operation, Tucker recalled that the "men's churning feet soon created a slippery mess which lent no footing whatsoever."

There was a lot of silent cursing, but by 9:30 p.m. the boats were in place.

On the north bank of the Rhine, the Germans had intensified their attacks by employing the newly arrived Tigers of the 106th Heavy Tank Battalion against the northern edge of the perimeter. The Tigers broke through to the airborne artillery position and their attached infantry swung south, a move that threatened the entire bridgehead. A sort of "snowball fight with grenades" ensued until the advance was stopped by close-range light artillery fire from the airborne. Continuous rain and the

coming of darkness brought an end to the attacks by German battlegroups, but there was no relief from the shelling. Martin Middlebrook's book Arnhem: 1944 is one of the best accounts of the battle. It records the words of a glider pilot making his way to freedom: "We passed several of our lads dead, laid out in open on their back, the rain pouring down on their faces.... There seemed to be quite a lot of them and having to leave them really upset me.... On top of that we were abandoning the Dutch.... I would have preferred to stay and fight it out."

Those who made it to the riverbank were organized into a queue with the walking wounded given priority. Men fell into an exhausted sleep or hunkered down to wait. The first boat to arrive was one of the small assault craft of 260th Wessex Field Company The current in the flooded river was very strong and so the British sappers had to approach diagonally while paddling furiously. On the return trip the passengers had to help out or risk being swept away. The rescue of large numbers of men depended upon the Canadians, but the first boat they launched sank after being badly holed. The second boat, captained by Lieutenant J.R. Martin, set off across the river to determine the situation and start the evacuation. Two witnesses reported that a direct mortar hit caused it to break apart in mid-river. None of the crew survived.

The third boat, commanded by a Corporal McLachlan, followed the same route. It reached the far bank without incident and wounded men were quickly loaded and rushed to safety. The fourth boat was swamped when a mortar bomb fell close by. Just four passengers survived. These setbacks might have led Tucker to question the point of the operation, but there really was no choice. Everything that could be done had to be tried. Fortunately, McLachlan and his crew seemed to lead a charmed life. They made 15 consecutive trips and evacuated nearly 500 men before they were relieved by a fresh crew. Other boats were launched at intervals of 20 minutes and by 3:30 a.m., 14 boats were at work.

It is impossible to improve upon Tucker's official report on the operation: "The night was intensely dark, but fires started by our bombers in the afternoon and the numerous flares sent up by the enemy must have revealed a great deal of our movement to him. These fires helped us greatly too, since they provided beacons by which our boat crews could direct their craft.... Heavy rain was accompanied by a bitter wind which made things most unpleasant, but the bad weather was probably less to the liking of the enemy than it was to us and most surely have resulted in our having had less casualties than we would have done had the night been clear and fine."

Tucker reported that rain caused boat motors to fail. He noted that electrical and mechanical personnel and the company's own fitters worked ceaselessly, but could not prevent a series of engine break-downs. "There was a great deal of enemy fire during the night. Machine-guns set on fixed lines swept the river and beaches on both sides.... Mortar and 88-mm fire fell everywhere. Many casualties were reported from the bridgehead, but on the river and on the south bank they were light. Three men were wounded in the off-loading area and one between there and the beach. Enemy snipers were also active and it was reported that some of the airborne troops spotted the positions of two of them in crossing the river and proceeded to liquidate them when they reached the south shore.

"It was impossible to regulate the number of passengers carried in boats at times. Men panicked and stormed onto the boats, in some cases capsizing them. In many cases they had to be beaten off or threatened with shooting to avoid having the boats swamped. With the approach of dawn this condition became worse. They were afraid that daylight would force us to cease our ferrying before they could be rescued.... A corporal operating a boat which was leaking badly decided he could make one more trip and bring off a few men before it went down. It sunk as it approached the south shore, but fortunately the water was shallow and they were able to wade ashore safely. It is estimated that approximately 150 boatloads were brought back by the stormboat crews and the average load carried was 16 passengers. Thus, approximately 2,400 to 2,500 troops were brought off."

There were very few forward facilities for the care of wounded. "Many of the rescued men were wounded and our own RAP (regimental aid post) dressed 69 stretcher cases as well as attending to over 100 walking wounded. Greatcoats and other clothing were used to improvise stretchers and were given to men who were in desperate need of cover from the elements."

Caring for the casualties proved a great drain on the company's manpower and prevented adequate relief for the boat-carrying parties and boat crews.

"The work all personnel employed in this operation was of a very high standard, but there were those who rose beyond that level. Lieutenant Kennedy, in addition to making a recce, planning the operation and supervising the off-loading and delivering the stormboats to the launching sites, took command of a boat when these tasks were completed and brought off 125 men from the bridgehead under very trying conditions which prevailed with the advent of daylight. Corporal Robinson did a tremendous night's work.... On delivering the last boat, he took command of it and completed six trips before the boat was put out of commission. All of the boat crews were magnificent, and only gave up their ferrying when their boats were no longer operable or else when they were exhausted and had to be ordered from the beach.

"Of these, Lance-Corporals Albright and Gunness and Sappers LeBouthillier and McCready were outstanding." Tucker also singled out the Roman Catholic padre—a captain by the name of Mongeon—who came under fire for the first time in his career and acquitted himself nobly. "In addition to the normal duties of attending wounded and bringing courage and cheer to the exhausted men, he helped with the carrying of stormboats, carried petrol to the beach and seemed to always be present where he was most needed. The E&M (electrical and mechanical) personnel attached from the Field Park Company rendered excellent service in keeping the Evinrude motors running."

In spring of 2001 my wife and I lead the annual Canadian Battlefields Foundation Study Tour to France, Belgium and Holland. We visited the memorial near Driel and at Groesbeek placed flowers on the graves of the Canadians who played an important role in the liberation of the Netherlands.

The Liberation Of Belgium

Originally published November/December 2000

September 1944 is remembered as the month of Arnhem, the "bridge too far", or by Canadians as the time of the battles for the Channel ports. But for the veterans of 4th Canadian Armoured Division, memories are of the rapid advance north, the liberation of western Belgium and the brief bloody struggles at the Gent and Leopold canals.

On September 6, the division was organized into two battle groups: Stewart Force and Moncel Force. The division was ordered to pursue the enemy to the area around the town of Eeklo, northwest of Ghent. The corps armoured car regiment, the 12th Manitoba Dragoons, was to feel out the situation on the coast while the Polish Armoured Division dealt with the eastern flank.

The mood at divisional and corps headquarters was optimistic, even cocky. Antwerp had fallen to the British and what was left of the vaunted Fifteenth German Army seemed to be caught with no way of escape. Army intelligence gleefully reported: "We have three divisions in the bag for sure and plus stragglers the total is now probably 50,000." The war, many thought, could not last much longer.

The apparent rout of the German armies in the aftermath of Normandy was bound to encourage this kind of optimism, but intelligence officers ought to have known better. At First Canadian Army Headquarters, the mysterious group of air force and army officers known as the Signals Liaison Unit had received the Ultra decrypt of Hitler's radio message ordering General Gustav von Zangen's Fifteenth Army to garrison the area north of the Leopold Canal, designated Scheldt Fortress South, and Walcheren Island, Scheldt Fortress North, to prevent the Allies from making use of the port of Antwerp. If the mouth of the Scheldt estuary was closed, Antwerp–60 miles inland– was of no value. Von Zangen was also ordered

to withdraw the balance of his forces across the Scheldt estuary and bring them into action north of Antwerp.

Lieutenant-Colonel Peter Wright, Canada's senior intelligence officer, and a handful of others cleared to receive material from Bletchley Park's code-breakers, discussed the situation with General Harry Crerar. They agreed to warn commanders that there was evidence of strengthened German defences, but the rapid progress of the Manitoba Dragoons, who liberated Nieuport and Ostend and probed north to Zeebrugge, seems to have convinced them that despite Ultra the enemy was too disorganized to resist effectively.

Reckless optimism was certainly the mood at Major-General Harry Foster's divisional headquarters when orders were issued to seize a crossing of the Ghent Canal at Moerbrugge. At the time, artillery was only available on call due to an ammunition shortage. It is also worth noting that there was no time for reconnaissance and that no assault boats were available. With Brigadier J.C. Jefferson in hospital, suffering from a recurrence of malaria, Lieutenant-Colonel Dave Stewart of the Argyll and Sutherland Highlanders of Canada was in command and he selected his own battalion to make the crossing.

The Argylls, one of the most consistently effective battalions in the Normandy battles, was busy enjoying Belgium where "people crowded the streets pressing bottles of champagne, cognac or best of all for the Canadians, Belgian beer upon the troops." At the canal, two heavy, leaky boats, missing their oars were scrounged and Pete Mackenzie's "D" Company went across in relays. They created a small bridgehead occupying several houses, but were held by the volume of fire and the first of what would prove to be many counterattacks. "Charlie" Company reinforced the position, but were soon cut off.

NAC 131230

Personnel of the Belgian White Brigade in a village north of Antwerp, Belgium, September 17, 1944.

The full story of this battle was finally told in Robert L. Fraser's 1996 book, *Black Yesterdays: The Argylls' War.* Major Bob Patterson of "C" Company recalled it this way: "I had 30 men and they were all there. You didn't have to give any orders. They were all going to fight.... The most important person in the whole company was Company Sergeant Major George Mitchell...he was the most wonderful man I ever served with." Mitchell's "coolness and courage under fire" earned him the Distinguished Conduct Medal at Moerbrugge. His comrades thought it should have been the Victoria Cross.

The struggle for Moerbrugge continued for three days, drawing in the Lincoln and Welland Regiment who put all four rifle companies across the canal to support the Argylls. Supplies were the real problem and the men carried double loads of ammunition into battle.

On the morning of September 10, the engineers completed a bridge. The tanks of the South Alberta Regiment joined the infantry and began flushing the enemy from houses and haystacks. The Germans quickly retreated, abandoning what they could not carry. Their task had been to delay the Canadians until the last units of the Fifteenth Army got across the Leopold Canal.

While Stewart Force fought its costly engagement at Moerbrugge, Brigadier Robert Moncel's battlegroup, made up of 4th Armoured Brigade and the Algonquin Regiment, reached the outskirts of Brugge, one of the most beautiful cities in Europe with its treasures of Flemish history. The Lake Superior Regiment probed the defences, but the roads were mined and covered by anti-tank guns. The city's mayor pleaded with both sides to avoid a battle and Moncel decided to bypass Brugge, funnelling his force through the Moerbrugge bridgehead. The Manitoba Dragoons were left as a covering force and on September 12 patrols from the RHLI and the Dragoons entered the city to find the enemy gone. The next day, Moncel was ordered to do an immediate crossing of the Leopold Canal "to keep the Germans on the move."

The battles for Moerbrugge and the resolute defence of the Channel ports ought to have warned corps and army that the situation was changing. The enemy, which had fled north in disarray in early September, was now fighting well-organized delaying actions and preparing to defend a series of "fortress" positions. No one at the sharp end could doubt this, but senior intelligence officers and commanders were still convinced that the enemy was beaten and could not survive a determined attack either at Arnhem or the Leopold Canal.

When Captain Ernie Sirluck, 4th Division's intelligence officer, reported that the enemy was holding the north bank of the canal in strength, he was ignored as was the detailed information from Ultra. Sirluck and the Argylls' intelligence officer, Claude Bissell, would both have distinguished postwar careers as scholars and university presidents, but in 1944, reports from front-line intelligence officers carried little weight with senior commanders who were convinced the war was all but won.

Moncel Force, or more exactly its infantry battalion the Algonquin Regiment, was now required to attack across a double canal line near Moerkerke, Belgium. Here, the Leopold and Lys canals run side by side separated by a 60-foot-wide dike. Today, the road beside the canals carries the name Algonquinstraat. In 1944, this quiet country lane was the start-line for a battle that was to reveal just how committed the enemy was to the defence of the approaches to Antwerp. Shortly before midnight on September 13, all four Algonquin rifle companies were ferried across the two canals despite heavy harassing fire. "Able" Company occupied the hamlet of Molentje, but increasing direct and indirect fire prevented the other companies from linking up. The Algonquins, with less than 250 men, were too thin on the ground and were forced on the defensive in three isolated pockets.

The divisional engineers, 8th and 9th field squadrons, had to stop building a bridge when they came under small arms fire. At first light, the situation looked desperate. Artillery and mortar fire, which appeared to be directed from within Moerkerke, struck the engineers, battalion headquarters and the regimental aid post. The shelling became so intense and accurate that it was impossible to get ammunition to the rifle companies across the canal. Lieutenant-Colonel R.A. Bradburn, who feared his whole battalion might be lost, requested air support and an air supply drop, but nothing was available. At 1200 hours on September 14, Moncel ordered a withdrawal. With the aid of a smoke-screen and a divisional artillery shoot, which used up the remaining ammunition, the regiment withdrew by fighting its way through enemy troops who had infiltrated as far as the dike between the two canals.

With most of the boats destroyed by shellfire, many of the men swam to the south bank. The Algonquins lost 28 killed, 40 wounded and 66 taken prisoner.

The German view of this encounter is worth recording. "The Canadians succeeded in forcing a bridgehead at Moerkerke which if it had been allowed to develop would have not only cut short our evacuation through Breskens, but would have secured the vital ground south of the Scheldt which commanded the estuary which at this stage the Germans were determined not to give up."

The German counterattack employed all available resources, but the Algonquins held. Their withdrawal took the Germans by surprise. They thought the curtain of fire brought down by the Canadian artillery was the prelude to a renewed assault. Neither side understood the position their opponent was in. Fourth Division, with three badly understrength infantry battalions, could not sustain an advance against such odds. The Germans, already geared up for a major battle, would have 16 days to get ready because no Canadian infantry division was available. Montgomery's focus was on Arnhem and so the south shore of the Scheldt would have to wait until 3rd Canadian Infantry Division had captured Boulogne and Calais.

The immediate tasks of 4th Division were to patrol the Leopold Canal and liberate the rest of western Flanders. The Canadian Grenadier Guards with the Lincoln and Welland Regiment on board led the way to Maldegem on the morning of September 15. The enemy was gone and they continued east past open fields where one day the Commonwealth War Graves Commission would establish the Canadian military cemetery at Adagem.

With bridges down, the Lincoln and Welland Regiment took over the advance, reaching the edge of Eeklo. Historian Geoff Hayes, who wrote a history of the Lincoln and Welland Regiment, notes that the battalion reached Belgium with half its authorized combat strength and after Moerbrugge, "B" Company had just 19 riflemen. When eager Belgian resistance fighters urged an immediate attack on the departing enemy, Lieutenant-Colonel Bill Cromb, who knew how tired the battalion was, replied: "That's excellent. If we stop here and have breakfast, they will all be gone by the time we get in." So the town Eeklo was liberated without a single casualty, soldier or civilian!

The Germans were not yet ready to surrender the area north of Gent since they still needed the Port of Terneuzen to evacuate men across the Scheldt. The Polish Armoured Division, with even fewer infantry than the Canadians, were closing in on the port, while 4th Division cleared the sector to the west.

The short, sharp battles for Beokhoute, Assende, Sas-van-Ghent and other villages have gone largely unrecorded, but the war diaries and casualty lists tell of brief costly engagements. What veterans remember best are the people of Flanders, especially the young women. The Argylls relate the story of three young ladies who "swam across the canal with bouquets of flowers in their hands, while the Germans up the canal were shooting at them."

The Algonquins report meeting a local resistance leader who turned out to be a "trim 21-year-old blonde, complete with tunic, Sam Brown and two pistols, one on each hip. To the Wolf Patrol at battalion headquarters it became clear she meant business and purely military business.... For once the sanctity of womanhood was most strictly upheld."

Of the many war stories that remain untold, none is more important than the work of the Belgian resistance–the White Brigade–in assisting the Allies. Denis and Shelagh Whitaker have paid tribute to Eugene Colson and his men who secured the dock area in Antwerp and helped 4th Infantry Brigade hold the city, but in September and October 1944 almost every Canadian unit worked closely with Belgian patriots. During the advance north into Holland, these volunteers fought alongside the Canadians in some of the most difficult battles of the war. It is long past time we paid tribute to them.

Indeed, Canadians who visit the Vimy Memorial would do well to turn their eyes north, not just to the World War I battlefields of Ypres and Passchendaele, but to the World War II battlefields, memorials and museums. If you were to start such a pilgrimage in Brugge, find your way to Canada Bridge where two magnificent bronze bisons, the symbol of the Manitoba Dragoons, commemorate the "memory of the Canadian forces who liberated the city." You may also want to drive to Moerbrugge where the community unveiled an abstract sculpture made out of sections of a Sherman tank on the 50th anniversary of the battle. At Molentje, the small memorial plaque is barely noticeable, but each September a small grove of wooden crosses appears in memory of the individuals who lost their lives here.

The Adegem Canadian War Cemetery is just a few miles away. It has the graves of 848 Canadian and 298 Polish and British soldiers. The town of Adegem features the superb Canada Museum, created by Gilbert van Landschoot who introduces visitors to the role Canadians had in the liberation of Belgium. He built the museum as a gift to the people of Canada because the rapid advance of the Canadians saved his father from arrest by the Gestapo. The displays relate the history of defeat, occupation and liberation of Belgium so that visitors may fully understand what men fought and died for.

Perhaps the most impressive of all the memorials is not a monument or a museum but an annual event. Every November 1, a Belgian-Dutch organizing committee plans an extraordinary Liberation March. Over the years, veterans, serving members of the Canadian Forces stationed in Europe and thousands of ordinary Dutch and Belgian citizens and schoolchildren have participated. They walk with their national flags flying proudly beside the Canadian flag and learn the story of the liberation of their region. A story we need to tell to Canadians.

NAC 131240

"Wasp" flamethowers rehearse their role in the assault across the Leopold Canal.

Crossing The Leopold

Originally published, January/February 2001

The battle to clear the Scheldt estuary and allow full use of the port of Antwerp in Belgium has long been recognized as one of the most important chapters in Canadian military history. Antwerp, the second largest port in Europe, was captured by the Allies on September 5, 1944, when 11th British Armoured Division arrived to find the city virtually abandoned by the Germans and under the control of the Belgian resistance.

Antwerp was, however, 50 miles from the North Sea and as Admiral Bertram Ramsay, the naval commander-in-chief, pointed out; occupying the port was of no value until the coastal batteries at the mouth of the estuary were captured.

Montgomery, preoccupied with plans to use the First Airborne Army to support his "single thrust" across the River Rhine, decided that the Scheldt estuary could wait. On September 6, he told Canadian General Harry Crerar: "I want Boulogne." With one good port on the English Channel and with additional transport from grounded divisions and increased airlift, Montgomery believed he could sustain his drive into Germany. Many historians, including Nigel Hamilton, Montgomery's biographer, insist this was the Field Marshal's greatest mistake for it allowed Germany's Fifteenth Army to escape across the Scheldt and join the forces defending Germany. Historians have also pointed out that this mistake allowed the enemy time to build up the Scheldt defences.

As usual, hindsight plays a large role in this analysis. Those who argued that Montgomery should have ordered his corps to advance beyond Antwerp to seal off the Beveland Peninsula—the exit route for Fifteenth Army—have failed to explain how this would have helped open the port of Antwerp. If the 82,000 men who escaped had been trapped and then used to reinforce the 20,000 German troops left behind to defend Walcheren Island and the south shore of the estuary, known to Canadians as the Breskens Pocket, the approaches to Antwerp might have remained in German hands until the end of the war.

Montgomery believed that Operation "Market Garden" might bring about victory in 1944 and so in his mind the risks were worth taking. "Market Garden", which was launched on September 17, was designed to outflank the German defensive line known as the West Wall, by establishing a bridgehead across the lower Rhine at the Dutch town of Arnhem.

Priority for Arnhem and the Channel Ports meant that the resources to begin operations to clear the Scheldt would not be available until 3rd Canadian Division completed the capture of Boulogne and Calais in France. In the meantime, Lieutenant-General Guy Simonds, who assumed command of First Canadian Army while Crerar was in hospital, did all he could to prepare the way. Simonds planned to use 3rd Canadian Division to capture the Breskens Pocket. While that operation was under way, 2nd Canadian Infantry Division would move north from Antwerp and fight its way to Walcheren Island.

The assault on the island was to be the responsibility of the 4th Special Service Brigade, made up of 41 and 47 Royal Marine commandos and a large Royal Navy task force supported by Her Majesty's Ship *Warspite* and the RN monitors *Erebus* and *Roberts*.

Much of Walcheren was below sea level and the islanders depended upon massive coastal dikes to keep out the North Sea. Simonds decided that an amphibious landing at the base of a 60-foot-high dike was not a good idea and asked Bomber Command to blast a breech in the sea-wall to flood the island, isolate the enemy and create a landing area for the commandos. Bomber Command and the Dutch government in exile were reluctant, but General Dwight D. Eisenhower accepted Simonds reasoning and decided it was a necessity.

On October 2, the civilian population was warned by radio and by leaflets dropped from aircraft. The next day, eight waves of Lancaster bombers attacked the dike at Westkapelle with great effect. A large gap was blown in the dike and the hole was quickly widened by wave action. No aircraft were lost. Four days later a second major gap was created in the dike near the town of Flushing on the south side of the island. That action spread sea water over 80 percent of the island.

Before any attack on Walcheren could be mounted, the Canadians needed to capture the Breskens Pocket. The coastal batteries on the south side of the Scheldt estuary could fire on the approaches to Walcheren and the RN adamantly refused to double the risk confronting its ships and landing craft.

Simonds knew that the German 64th Infantry Division had placed its three regiments along the Leopold Canal and had created elaborate defences in the sectors not flooded. A frontal attack was bound to yield slow results and incur high casualties and so Simonds planned to use a regiment of tracked amphibious vehicles known as Buffaloes. Each Buffalo could carry 30 men and enter and leave the water through mud flats and most dike slopes.

Operation "Switchback" called for 9th Brigade to assault the Breskens Pocket through the back door. The Buffaloes would enter the water at Terneuzen, which had been captured by the Polish, and then land the brigade on the lightly defended northeast coast near the Dutch town of Hoofdplaat. But for this to work, the enemy's

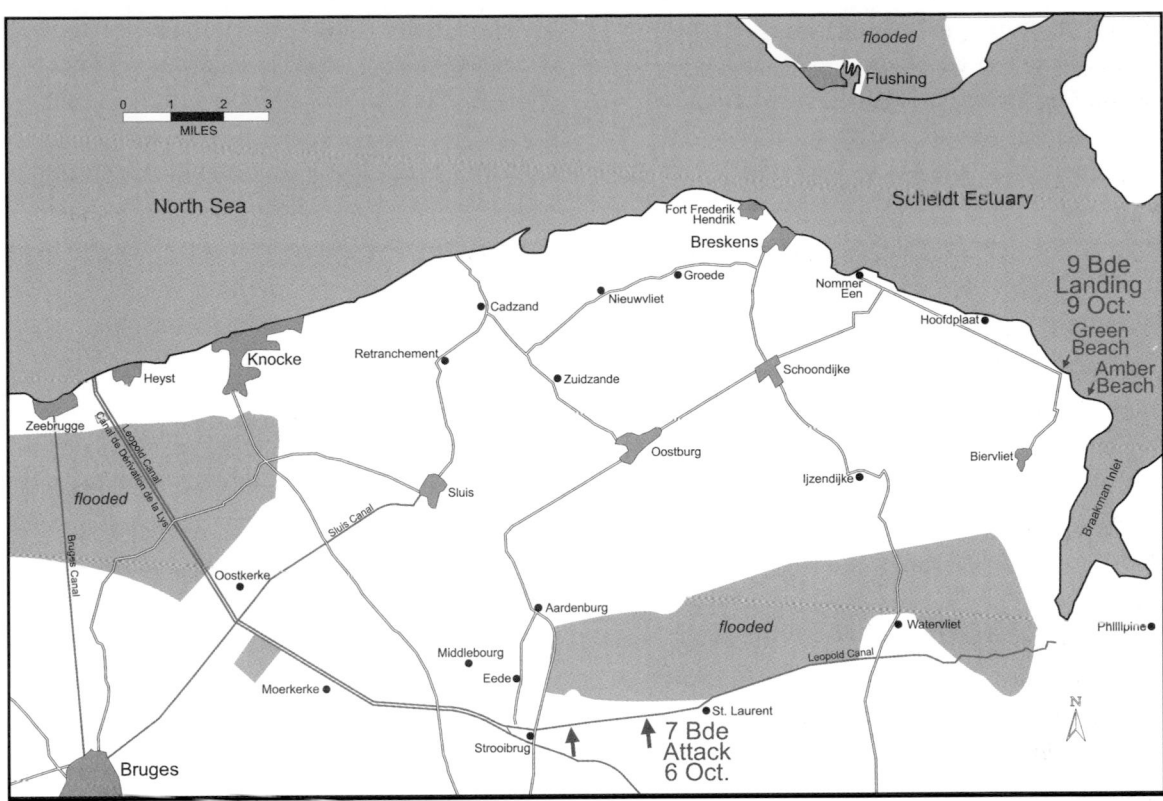

Operation "Switchback".

attention had to remain focused on the Leopold Canal. So, another brigade was ordered to carry out a frontal attack near the main Breskens road, more or less where the enemy expected it.

Simonds, acting corps commander General Charles Foulkes and the divisional commander Major-General Dan Spry knew that 7th Brigade, selected for the Leopold crossing, would have a rough 48 hours because the Germans were bound to counterattack. But, if it could hold out and draw enemy reserves, the landings on the northeast coast would meet little resistance and quickly relieve the pressure on 7th Brigade.

"Switchback" was a very risky operation. To succeed it would require surprise, extraordinary courage and maximum fire support from the artillery and air force. Overcast skies in a rainy October were bound to limit the tactical air force. This meant that the gunners had to be especially creative.

Brigadier Stanley Todd, artillery commander of the 3rd Canadian Division, devised a brilliantly conceived plan to support the infantry. Two medium artillery groups would be available. One would fire north from positions near

Bruges, Belgium, and the other would fire west from Terneuzen. The field artillery from 3rd and 4th divisions were also placed to support both brigades. All the guns were under Todd's control. The usual counter battery—defensive fire and harassing fire tasks—were laid on, but in addition Todd refined an on-call system he had used at Boulogne and Calais of linear and pinpoint concentrations known as stonks and concs. For 7th Brigade's assault over the Leopold Canal, Todd and his staff selected no less than 46 targets. The largest, code-named "Colorado", brought down eight minutes of fire on positions around a single village.

At a brigade orders group, Todd explained that the artillery tasks would be completely under the control of the infantry. "It is quite in order for example to call for "Colorado" twice which would result in the enemy positions being fired on for 16 minutes." The infantry were to have neutralizing fire when they wanted it and as often as they needed it.

The air plan for "Switchback" employed the full resources of 84 Group, 2nd Tactical Air Force. The group's story is largely untold. In contrast to 83 Group, which was made up of Royal Canadian Air Force and Royal Air Force squadrons in equal numbers, 84 Group included British, Belgian, Polish, Norwegian, French and Czech fighter wings. Canadian historians generally ignore 84 Group because there were no RCAF squadrons while British historians show little interest in an organization that supported First Canadian Army.

Canadian historian Michael Bechthold, who has studied 84 Group's operations in the Scheldt, calculates that 1,653 sorties were flown in support of Operation "Switchback" despite weather that forced cancellation of air support on 12 out of 27 days. Even when flying was possible, the low clouds restricted operations and pilots had to be especially careful to identify their targets correctly. Operational research reports on the air force role in the battle indicate that while few enemy targets were destroyed, the mere presence of aircraft caused the German artillery and infantry to stop firing and take cover. And as always, air attacks lowered the enemy's morale while raising the spirits of the Canadian foot soldier.

While conducting battlefield tours of the Scheldt, I always start analysis of the events while standing on top of a large pillbox that dominates the northern bank of the canal. It is also possible to walk the triangle of land, fringed by trees, which in 1944 was the only area not flooded. To cross a 60-foot canal under fire only to end up in a narrow confined area ringed by an enemy that outnumbers you, and has had a month to prepare his defences, is not an inviting prospect especially when air photo interpreters had identified scores of enemy positions along the canal.

Staff at 3rd Division headquarters prepared a plan that would involve Wasp flamethrowers in support of the attack. Experiments demonstrated that when the reverse slope of the dike was used to angle the Wasp, the flame could reach the other side of the canal. Spry decided to use this method instead of an artillery barrage in the hope of achieving both suppression and tactical surprise. He also approved the use of a sound effects troop that was to simulate the noise of bridge building and troop movement at a potential crossing point well to the east of the real objective. Those who witnessed the trials of the flamethrowers were impressed and there was some hope that the shock effect would stun the enemy during the early stages of the attack.

Lieutenant-Colonel Foster Matheson's Regina Rifles drew the heavily defended sector near the Breskens road. To make the crossing, Matheson selected his own "Able" Company and a company of the Royal Montreal Regiment that had joined the battalion in September. The Royal Montreal Regiment, serving as Headquarters Defence Company at First Canadian Army, had lobbied hard for a chance to serve with a front-line regiment. Matheson had supervised them closely during the fighting at Calais and was impressed with their spirit and determination. On the morning of October 6, 1944, they would need all of that determination and more.

At 5:25 a.m. the silence and darkness was broken by the roar of the flamethrowers that turned night into day. For a full five minutes the north bank was scorched and fires were still burning by the time the boats hit the water. The fires, and German flares, lit up the sky. This made it easier for enemy machine-gunners to pick out targets. One platoon of the Royal Montreal Regiment was destroyed when a "cone of fire" struck the boats. The other platoon crossed unscathed, scrambled up the bank and began to work its way westward towards the road. The commanding officer, Captain Robert Schwob and a handful of men, including the artillery forward observation officer, clung to the north bank of the canal. They fought off a heavy counterattack and tried desperately to identify targets for the gunners.

"Able" Company of the Regina Rifles was on the right flank. It had run into concentrated fire that made crossing the canal impossible. Matheson ordered "Dog" Company to take over and deal with the pillbox. Bombs from a PIAT forced the enemy to cease fire and "D" Company was able to cross and secure the area. There were only 13 Royal Montreal Regiment soldiers still in action and so they were merged with the Regina company whose own strength was now little more than 20.

The assault had gone much better for the Canadian Scottish Regiment. The enemy defences in the narrow end of the triangle that led nowhere were much less formidable and the crossing was made without initial opposition. The assault companies attacked the village of Moershoofd, while the engineers got a foot bridge built. Soon the Canadian Scottish companies were across, but attempts to move west towards Oosthoek and the Breskens road were stopped by heavy fire. The Royal Winnipeg Rifles tried to link up with the Reginas, but the volume of enemy fire made movement almost impossible.

The one positive feature of this dreadful ordeal was that the enemy behaved in accordance with its doctrine and continued to counterattack with local and divisional reserves. Todd's artillery fired repeatedly and inflicted heavy casualties on the enemy who remained blissfully unaware of the threat to their rear. The war diary of the Canadian Scottish Regiment offers the picture of life on the north bank of the Leopold: "Water and soil make mud. Mud sticks to everything. Boots weigh pounds more. Rifles and Brens operate sluggishly. Ammunition becomes wet. Slit trenches allow one to get below the ground, but also contain several inches of thick water. Matches and cigarettes are unusable. So almost everyone looks for a house. A good house is one which only has a few holes in the walls and not more than half the roof dismantled. These are hard to find after our arty (artillery) has lifted its range and after the enemy arty has found its range. So the soldier shakes his head, cleans his rifle, swears a good deal and dreams of what he'll do when he gets leave...."

The war diary of the Royal Winnipeg Rifles describes that unit's valiant struggle to reach the Reginas: "Heavy casualties were suffered by both sides and the ground was littered with both German and Royal Winnipeg dead.... Prolonged exposure to wet and cold still had to be endured in flooded slit trenches or smashed buildings as usually bold enemy snipers and machine-gunners ...succeeded in infiltrating between companies.... Few of those lived to tell their story as the Royal Winnipeg Rifles were no less aggressive. Ammunition, cold rations and casualties had to be carried for more than a mile."

The men of 7th Brigade could do little more than endure and wait for the 9th Brigade landings. Unfortunately the flotilla of Buffaloes navigating the Terneuzen canal had become stuck. Despite the best efforts of the engineers, who cut ramps in the canal bank to allow the Buffaloes to bypass the obstacle, H-hour— the hour at which an operation is scheduled to begin—had to be delayed until 2 a.m. on October 9. By then it was almost too late for 7th Brigade which came out of action October 12 after suffering 533 men killed and wounded and close to 200 cases of battle exhaustion. The value of their sacrifice in unlocking the defences of the Breskens Pocket is to be measured by the success of 9th Brigade's assault which we will consider in the next article in this series.

The Liberation: Hoofdplaat to Knocke Heist

Originally published, March/April 2001

The World War II battle for the Breskens Pocket, code named Operation "Switchback", was the crucial first stage in the struggle to open the Port of Antwerp in Belgium. It began at dawn on October 6, 1944, when 7th Canadian Infantry Brigade crossed the Leopold Canal in northern Belgium not far from the Dutch border. This frontal assault was intended to divert the enemy's attention away from the unprotected north coast of the Breskens Pocket where Brigadier John Rockingham's 9th Canadian Infantry Brigade was planning an amphibious landing. Rockingham's Highland Brigade was to mount its attack in tracked landing vehicles–known as Buffaloes–within 36 hours of crossing the Leopold Canal. However, Murphy's Law was the rule in 1944 and nearly everything started to go wrong.

The Buffaloes proved difficult to steer at the slow speeds necessary to traverse the Terneuzen Canal east of the Dutch town of Terneuzen. The canal's locks were also difficult to negotiate. A final set of locks was damaged and the engineers had to cut ramps in the canal bank to bypass the obstacle. By then it was too late to launch the operation on the night of October 7-8.

October 8 was a day of considerable tension. The delay had exposed 7th Brigade to an extra 24 hours of misery. There was also the understandable fear that the security of the amphibious assault would be compromised. Fortunately, the local Dutch resistance had rounded up known collaborators and so the enemy remained blissfully ignorant of the threat to its rear. Unfortunately, the river pilots promised by the same resistance failed to appear and a desperate search for someone to navigate the flotilla began.

The naval liaison officer at army headquarters, Lieutenant-Commander R.D. Franks, volunteered to take the soldiers to sea and shortly before midnight on October 8, the first Buffaloes "waddled down the ramp and splashed into the water." The promised artillery barrage began effectively blanketing the noise of the aircraft engines that powered the Buffaloes. Franks located the points separating the two landing beaches and then used a flickering signal lamp to guide the assault troops to their proper sector.

The Buffaloes roared towards the shore and churned through the mud flats. At Amber beach, a number of the vehicles bogged down, but at Green beach the North Novas landed on dry land. They overran a German outpost, capturing nine men who had apparently slept through the familiar sounds of artillery and aircraft engines. The North Novas quickly expanded their beachhead, but the Highland Light Infantry came under machine-gun fire while it was still sorting out the confusion of landing in a quagmire.

The HLI landing area was less than two kilometres from the Dutch village of Biervliet, headquarters of the battlegroup that had been posted by German Major-General Knut Eberding to defend the Braakman Inlet.

German battle doctrine called for an immediate counterattack, and the HLI bore the brunt of it. Major R.G. Hodgins, the battalion's second-in-command, reported that "the enemy fought tenaciously, launching one counterattack after another with great determination. These were not the garrison-type troops that were found at Boulogne and cap Gris-Nez in France, but soldiers of a highly trained field division.... The enemy dashed along the ditches, bouncing out here and there over culverts, greatcoats flapping and wearing full equipment."

The enemy was beaten back, but no advance to Biervliet or Hoofdplaat was possible until the rest of the brigade arrived.

While the assault troops carved out a beachhead, the flotilla returned to Terneuzen to lift the reserve battalion, the Stormont, Dundas and Glengarry Highlanders and the machine-gun and mortar platoons of the Camerons of Ottawa.

The second trip at 9 a.m. was skillfully screened through the efforts of 806 Royal Pioneer Smoke

LCMSDS

Despite the damage from bombs and shells the garrison & Fort Frederik Hendrik held out until October 25.

Company, a British unit under Canadian command. Major Temp Hugill of First Canadian Army's chemical warfare staff decided to use stormboats and amphibious trucks "to drop off a smoke float every 400 yards along a dogleg line running northwest from Terneuzen for 8,000 yards." Since the smoke floats lasted only 15 minutes, a complex renewal organization had to be improvised. Eventually rafts were built and anchored in the Scheldt estuary to maintain the screen.

Brigadier Rockingham reached the narrow beachhead with the second wave and immediately took control. The few precious Wasp flame-throwers were used to burn the enemy out of some well-protected gun emplacements while the Camerons employed a section of their medium machine-guns to engage the main enemy force which was concealed in an orchard. The HLI used this support to rush the orchard and capture 60-70 prisoners.

Rockingham needed to expand the bridgehead quickly because while the smokescreen curbed visibility, German gunners on nearby Walcheren Island and near the Dutch town of Breskens were beginning to find targets. The SD&G Highlanders were told to take Hoofdplaat and then advance west along the coast. The village was strongly defended. The Germans had taken advantage of the smokescreen to transfer men from Walcheren and had switched the divisional reserves to the new front.

The German situation report for the night of October 10 describes the reaction: "Today the enemy launched a decision-seeking attack on the Breskens bridgehead. While maintaining strong pressure against the southern front of 64th Division, he landed four to five battalions and some tanks on the northwestern tip establishing a new bridgehead three kilometres deep and six kilometres wide. About three and a half battalions were set against the enemy and to begin with sealed off the penetration. The situation is still tense."

The Canadians also found the situation tense. The troopers of 7th Recce Regiment were dismounted and brought forward to take over the HLI positions so the battalion could mount a co-ordinated attack on Biervliet. Here, as elsewhere in the pocket, the fields or polders were protected by dikes and drained by a network of ditches. It was impossible to advance across most of the polders saturated by the October rains or deliberately flooded by the enemy. This left the narrow dikes as the only approach routes. The HLI used two parallel dikes to reach the village at dusk on October 11. By then the enemy had withdrawn in the face of overwhelming artillery concentrations and had taken up new positions south of the village.

The inevitable counterattack began that night and one HLI platoon was overrun, but the battalion was able to restore the situation.

The North Novas were engaged in similarly ferocious combat in the centre of the bridgehead. The hamlet of Drievegan, which had been reduced to half a dozen ruined houses, was captured despite continuous heavy shelling. The North Nova war diary reported that "casualties have been fairly heavy to date, but we believe Jerry has had it worse than us."

While fighting for Hoofdplaat, the SD&G Highlanders took heavy casualties, more than 70 in two days. The Glens used six-pounder anti-tank guns to overcome a large enemy pillbox, several 20-mm gun positions and fortified houses in the village.

On battlefield tours of the Breskens Pocket it is important to put yourself in the place of the incredibly courageous young men who fought these isolated platoon and section engagements. The polders are much the same as they were and it is possible to retrace the exact routes. However, imaginations falter as we remind ourselves of the rain and mud and continuous shelling that served as a backdrop for a battle that required skill, patience and courage. How do we understand Captain B.G. Fox and his gun crew who went to the assistance of his comrades taking a six-pounder anti-tank gun forward, sighting the gun while under fire, then putting rounds into the fortified stronghold that was holding up the Glens advance? There are scores of such stories, some recorded, some lost to our collective memory.

The close combat of the first two days ended in something approaching a stalemate. The German counterattacks had in the words of their situation report "failed completely", but the price paid by 9th Brigade was sapping its ability to maintain the offensive. Lieutenant-General Guy Simonds and the divisional commander, Major-General Dan Spry, had originally intended to use their reserve brigade, the 8th, to exploit the Leopold Canal bridgehead. However, it was evident a new plan was needed. The chemical warfare team was told to maintain and extend their smokescreen while the diminished flotilla of Buffaloes was used to transport 8th Brigade into the northeast bridgehead. Once there, Brigadier K.G. Blackader's men would attack due south and link up with 4th Division to help open up a land bridge into the pocket via the Isabella Polder at the south end of the Braakman Inlet.

This manoeuvre caught the enemy by surprise. The Queen's Own Rifles took over Biervliet and launched a powerful thrust that cracked through the enemy. Joined by the North Shores and Le Régiment de la Chaudière, the QORs advanced rapidly linking up with 4th Division on October 15. The divisional engineers immediately went to work clearing minefields, exploding obstacles and improving road beds. The forces inside the pocket could now be guaranteed adequate supplies.

Spry was now in a position to conduct a carefully controlled operation designed to crush the enemy with well supported simultaneous attacks. Shells, and when possible air power, would be used to save Canadian lives. After the German commander was captured he told interrogators, with the arrogance of a typical German general, that Spry had failed to exploit opportunities for rapid advances. After two successful surprise attacks, which had cost the division almost a thousand casualties, Spry was quite certain it was better to fight the battle with overwhelming force, taking whatever time was necessary.

This attitude, which was shared by every Canadian unit, was not popular at Army Group Headquarters where Field Marshal Bernard Montgomery was under growing pressure to speed up the opening of the Port of Antwerp. Under pressure from Admiral Bertram Ramsay and the Supreme Allied Commander, General Dwight D. Eisenhower, Monty had reluctantly agreed to place 52th Lowland Division under the command of Simonds. This elite Scottish formation, which trained initially as a mountain division for employment in Norway, had just completed re-training as an air transportable division to be used in exploiting the hoped-for victory at Arnhem in the Netherlands. Now the 52nd was to join the Canadians in a battle fought over ground that was below sea level. The commitment of the Scottish Division would greatly improve the odds in the Breskens Pocket, but it would not be available until October 18 and the Canadians were not allowed to wait.

Stories of officers from Monty's staff arriving at battalion, brigade and divisional headquarters to find out why it was taking so long to open up the port are part of the history of 3rd Canadian Division. Montgomery himself met with Simonds, General Charles Foulkes and Spry to stress the need for speed, but the visits were to no avail.

After 9th Brigade broke through German defences at Sasput and 8th Brigade captured Ijzendijke, the Germans withdrew to prepared positions in the western half of the pocket. Spry ordered a pause to allow 9th Brigade a brief period of rest to prepare a deliberate assault on the port of Breskens.

Spry used 157th Lowland Brigade to take over the Leopold sector from the weary 7th Brigade and follow up the German withdrawal to the Dutch village of Sluis. This allowed 3rd Division to plan operations employing all three brigades in a coordinated offensive in the north.

The first stage, 9th Brigade's attack on Breskens, began in tragedy when a tanker carrying flame-throwing liquid exploded. The 30th Assault Brigade Royal Engineers of 79th Armoured Division lost most of its vehicles, including Flail tanks used for mine clearing and bridging tanks needed to deal with ditches. The memorial erected at the site lists the names of seven Canadians and 31 of their British comrades.

Despite this ill-omen, the Glens broke into Breskens quickly and the bomb-happy defenders of Fort Frederick Hendrik surrendered to the North Novas after token resistence. Eighth Brigade struck a much more determined or less heavily shelled enemy at Oostburg where Le Régiment de la Chaudière, attacking with characteristic elan, reported one of their companies had been cut off and all but 15 had been taken prisoner. The QORs had used a smokescreen and a "wild bayonet charge" to reach the centre of town. Riflemen call their bayonets swords so the actual order that preceded this exhibition of courage and dash was: "Fix swords!"

Oostburg was the exception. Increasingly, the enemy was surrendering rather than continuing the battle at close range. Their commander, had issued his own version of Hitler's "kith and kin" order warning that "the names of deserters will be made known to the civilian populatin at home and their next of kin will be looked on as enemies of the German people...." However, the ordinary soldier as well as his officers had had enough and white flags appeared once their lives were in danger. More than 12,700 prisoners were taken in the Breskens Pocket, 90 per cent of the enemy troops engaged.

In explaining their defeat, German prisoners, always reluctant to acknowledge the skill and courage of Allied infantry, inevitably mentioned overwhelming air power, Allied artillery and tanks. The contribution of the tactical air force and the gunners was certainly important, but there were no tanks involved in the battle. The Germans were referring to the M-10s of the 3rd Anti-Tank Regiment Royal Canadian Artillery whose contributions to victory are seldom acknowledged.

In the Scheldt, the three-inch high velocity gun mounted on a Sherman chassis was repeatedly used against concrete bunkers and other fortified positions. The M-10 was so lightly armoured that even the 20-mm anti-aircraft weapon the Germans used as super-heavy machine-guns in the Breskens Pocket could penetrate the armoured plate. On the raised roads of polder country the high profile M-10 was especially vulnerable, but its support was badly needed and the regiment rose to the occasion providing close support and giving enemy soldiers an excuse to explain their surrender.

The last phase of the battle began when 7th Brigade, reinforced from the rapidly shrinking pool of infantry replacements, began to sweep west along the coastline towards the Belgian border. The German gun positions, which were the raison d'être of the pocket, had to be taken one by one, but elsewhere the will to resist was not strong. Ninth Brigade crossed the Belgian border and entered Knocke-sur-Mer on October 31, capturing General Eberding and his staff who were packed and prepared for captivity. As of 9:50 a.m. on November 3, mopping up was complete and Operation "Switchback" was over.

3rd Division was now ordered to get ready for a new operation code-named Relax. To carry it out they were to travel to Ghent where the population was waiting to welcome the weary soldiers into their homes and hearts. More than 400 of their comrades were left behind in temporary, but well-marked graves. They lie today in the Canadian military cemetery at Adegem, Belgium, along with men from 4th Canadian and Polish Armoured divisions.

Brigadier John M. 'Rocky' Rockingham who commanded 9th Brigade in the Breskens Pocket.

Woensdrecht

Originally published, September/October 2001

On October 2, 1944, General Guy Simonds, who had temporarily replaced an ailing General Harry Crerar, issued his first directive as the acting commander of First Canadian Army. The task of clearing the approaches to the already liberated city of Antwerp in Belgium, the banks of the Scheldt Estuary, was assigned to 2nd and 3rd Canadian infantry divisions. Third Division was to attack Scheldt Fortress South which the Canadians called the Breskens Pocket. Second Division was to "clear the area north of Antwerp and close the eastern end of the Zuid-Beveland Isthmus."

Once these tasks were complete, both divisions would develop operations to clear Beveland and capture Walcheren Island to the northwest.

Simonds assumed that 2nd and 3rd divisions could complete their tasks in one or two weeks, and he focused his attention on Operation "Infatuate", the capture of Walcheren Island. He persuaded Bomber Command to flood Walcheren by bombing the dikes and he won approval for two Royal Marine Commando assaults on the island. However, the commandos would have to wait until the Canadians captured the Breskens Pocket and cleared the land approaches to the island.

Today the area north of Antwerp is criss-crossed by highways linking the city with new suburbs and towns that were small villages 57 years ago. It is still possible to follow the old road north from Antwerp to Bergen-op-Zoom in southwest Holland, but some imagination is required to see the countryside as it was in 1944. The area east of the highway was then thickly set with woods. On the left, towards the Scheldt Estuary, the Germans had flooded as many of the fields or polders as they could, confining movement to the raised roads.

As 2nd Division began to advance north through this strange landscape, the corps' intelligence summary insisted that the enemy had "given up any plan he might have had to stand on the approach to Walcheren." Unfortunately, Allied intelligence officers had failed to grasp German intentions. In fact, German General Gustav von Zangen, commanding Fifteenth Army, issued an order declaring that "the defence of the approaches to Antwerp represents a task which is decisive for the further conduct of the war." He ordered his army reserve–Battle Group Chill–which included 6 Parachute Regiment and several battalions of self-propelled guns, to bar access to Walcheren by holding positions at the village of Woensdrecht, located at the eastern end of the narrow Zuid-Beveland Isthmus connecting the mainland to South Beveland.

German Lieutenant-General Erich Diestel described the arrival of the reinforcements when he was interviewed in 1945. "On October 2, the Canadians attacked north from Merxem and in three days had driven the division's right flank back to Putte, a distance of some seven kilometres.... There was no regular line to hold at this time, but rather a series of tactical points.... About October 7, in almost melodramatic fashion, aid came in the form of the Fifteenth Army Battle School and the Von der Heydte Parachute Regiment of about 2,500 fanatical and eager young parachutists."

The Canadians did not learn of von Zangen's decision until the German reinforcements arrived, but the acting divisional commander, Brigadier R.H. Keefler, was well aware the division was running a great risk by moving north with an unprotected right flank. He decided to commit 6th Brigade and most of the one under-strength armoured regiment–the Fort Garry Horse–to that sector. This meant only two brigades–with one squadron of tanks–were available to push north to the villages Ossendrecht, Huijbergen, Hoogerheide and Woensdrecht.

The Black Watch,
Woensdrecht,
October 1944.

On the morning of October 7, the Calgary Highlanders took over the lead. The Régiment de Maisonneuve had been ordered to parallel the Calgary advance, securing the village of Huijbergen. There were few identifiable targets for the artillery and the whole attack broke down 1,500 yards short of the objective. The Maisonneuves attempted to renew their advance the next morning, but they confronted a strongly defended anti-tank ditch. Lieutenant Charles Forbes, who had a well-earned reputation for daring, led his platoon in a flanking movement, but the unit was quickly driven to ground. Forbes charged the position by himself, firing his sten gun and yelling at his men to follow. He personally "rushed two posts, killed two crew members and captured five more."

Dutch civilians and air reconnaissance had provided fairly detailed information on the arrival of German reinforcements and both divisions

and corps intelligence accepted an estimate of between 2,000 and 3,000 troops. Keefler reacted by ordering the division to go over to the defensive and prepare for a major attack that the army intelligence section, probably on the basis of Ultra decrypts, correctly predicted for the night of October 8.

The German counter-attacks failed and Von der Heydte's regiment suffered heavy casualties, estimated at 480 men, in addition to more than 50 prisoners. Much has been made over the years of the professionalism of the German officer corps and the fighting power of the German infantry, yet the battle for Hoogerheide demonstrated major deficiencies in German strategy and tactics that were not uncommon in Northwest Europe. Von der Heydte had launched a frontal attack against forces that had gone over to the defensive. He persisted in pressing forward despite heavy losses. To attack in this manner, when reconnaissance would have shown the weakness of the Canadian right flank, suggests overconfidence and doctrinal rigidity. The texture of the battle also indicates that both on their defensive positions and in tactical counter-attacks, 2nd Division was more than a match for the enemy.

In his postwar memoirs, Von der Heydte recalled: "I decided to make a counter-attack with limited aims, which brought us to the outskirts of the villages of Woensdrecht and Hoogerheide. The Canadians–I say that as a German–fought brilliantly. To the rank of brigadier, the officers stood side by side with their men on the front lines."

By the evening of October 11, the Germans came to their senses and dug-in on the Woensdrecht ridge, and the high dike that carried the railway through Beveland to Walcheren Island. For the Canadians, it was not an inviting prospect to attack these positions with six under-strength infantry battalions, a squadron of tanks and artillery regiments that had to ration ammunition. However, Field Marshal Montgomery, under pressure to open the approaches to the port of Antwerp, insisted the advance continue.

He assured Simonds that reinforcements, the 52nd Lowland Division and the 104th U.S. Infantry Division, would be available in eight to 10 days, but for the moment only 4th Canadian Division's armoured recce regiment–the South Albertas–was available to help protect the vulnerable left flank. This left Keefler with few choices and the events of the next several days were probably determined by the unexpected success of the Royal Regiment of Canada which managed to get two companies across the flooded polders where they staged an improvised and unsuccessful attack on the railway embankment. The Royals then beat off six successive counter-attacks, while maintaining a firm base from which a larger set-piece attack could be staged.

This operation, code-named "Angus", called for 5th Brigade to employ one battalion to seize the railway embankment with the other two battalions passing through to seal off the route to Walcheren Island. The first phase of the assault would have to be undertaken by the Black Watch. The Maisonneuves were still more than 200 riflemen short and the Calgaries had borne the brunt of the fighting at Hoogerheide. The Black Watch had done well since Lieutenant-Colonel Bruce Ritchie had taken charge in September and each company was led by an experienced commander. The attack was built around an elaborate scheme to shoot the battalion onto the dike, one company at a time. One medium and two field regiments, as well as the heavy mortars and machine-guns of the Toronto Scottish Regiment, would provide the basic fire support. The Fort Garry Horse supplied a troop of tanks and the Spitfires and Typhoons of 84 Royal Air Force Group would participate, weather permitting.

Ritchie examined the ground from an artillery spotter plane on the afternoon of October 12 and at 7:30 p.m. called his final Orders Group. Operation "Angus" would begin in darkness at 6:15 a.m. on Friday the 13th.

For the Black Watch, October 13 was Black Friday, the second single-day disaster in the history of the Royal Highland Regiment of Canada. It was not so much the total casualties–145–but the ratio of dead-to-wounded that marked the day's fighting. Fifty-six Black Watch soldiers were killed or died of wounds. Twenty-seven were taken prisoner. What had happened?

The plan called for "C" Company, under Captain N.G. Buch, to make the first bound to the dike junction. The fire plan attempted to neutralize the enemy by targeting positions back to the village Korteven and drenching the embankment with high explosives.

According to the divisional artillery commander, much of this was lost when "C" Company, "held up by small-arms fire from dug-in positions," was 30 minutes late on the start-line and lost much of the benefit of the initial artillery

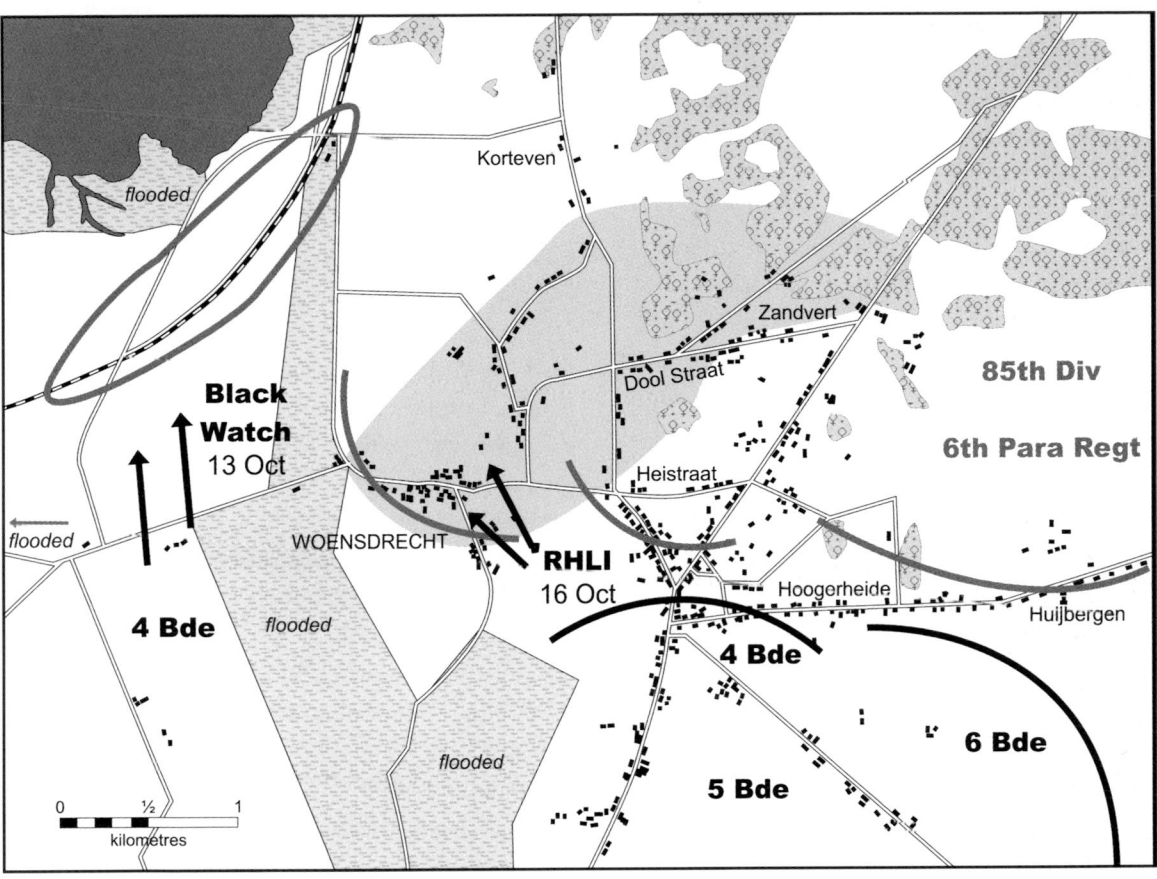

Woensdrecht.

program. At 6:45 a.m. the company passed through the Royal Regiment's positions but after less than 300 yards, perhaps halfway to the objective, the advance faltered in the face of accurate small-arms fire. "B" Company, under Major D.H. Chapman, had moved forward in preparation for the second bound and were heavily mortared while waiting to go in. By 7:30 a.m. both Buch and Chapman had been wounded and other casualties plus stragglers were filtering back. The Black Watch had tried to use the mortars and artillery to suppress the enemy fire, but owing to the nature of the country it was extremely difficult to indicate a target with any degree of precision.

It was then decided to use smoke to mask the area. At 9 a.m. the embankment was smoked and some sections of "C" Company made it to the objective, but as the men tried to dig in, grenades were lobbed over the dike at them. Most of these men were subsequently taken prisoner, many with shrapnel wounds.

Although two attacks had failed, Operation

"Angus" continued. Even before the results of the second attack were known, divisional headquarters had issued warning orders for the preparation of a third assault which would be led by Wasp flame-throwers. This attack could not take place before mid-afternoon and so all that could be done in the meantime was to request air support from 84 Group.

Ritchie called his Orders Group for 3 p.m., but the battalion was not in good shape. "C" Company consisted of 25 men, while "B" Company was down to 41, including company headquarters. Ritchie committed his remaining resources to the task of capturing and consolidating a junction in the dike code-named "Angus 1". "A" and "D" companies were to move in behind the flame-throwers that would target the embankment while a squadron of 17-pounder anti-tank guns and a troop of tanks were to engage enemy observation posts. The flame-throwers moved quickly when the artillery barrage began and were able to complete their tasks, losing just one carrier in the mud.

"D" Company lost its commanding officer in the advance, but Lieutenant Beau Lewis took command and the rest of the company "pancaked" on the objective. "A" Company, which had drawn the more exposed right flank, suffered the heaviest casualties of the day. Lieutenant Alan Mills, who led one of the platoons, described the attack in a letter to his father, written from a hospital in England: "We formed up behind a dike and advanced over open ground. When we got practically to our objective–600 yards away–the machine-guns and mortars became too hot and we began to drop right and left. Somehow a few managed to get to the objective. Those of us who were hit lay out in an open field with no cover.... The battalion seems to have horrible shows periodically and this was one of them. A couple of non-commissioned officers who lived through May-sur-Orne (in France) told me that this was just as bad as that."

Lewis and his men could be said to have captured "Angus 1", but they were quite unable to carry out the order to consolidate. As darkness fell all Jeeps and carriers in the battalion were mobilized to get the wounded out. The Black Watch diary reports that "many acts of heroism were performed in the dark which will never come to light. No words can pay sufficiently high tribute to those of our men who went out in the dark searching through flooded fields to ensure that all possible" steps had been taken to offer medical attention.

Shortly after midnight, Brigadier W.J. Megill ordered the battalion to withdraw: Operation "Angus" was over.

The Black Watch was not the only unit to suffer from Montgomery's hesitation in assigning priority to opening up the port of Antwerp. Despite a series of aggressive counter-attacks on the South Saskatchewan Regiment and evidence of further defensive preparations, the Royal Hamilton Light Infantry was ordered to assault Woensdrecht on October 16. To launch another single-battalion attack into the centre of enemy resistance did not seem like a very good idea, but if anyone could take and hold Woensdrecht it was the RHLI.

Lieutenant-Colonel Denis Whitaker, who had won a Distinguished Service Order at Dieppe and who had been wounded in Normandy, had returned to command a battalion that had established an enviable record of success. Whitaker, whose death in May 2001 was widely mourned, was an outstanding and conscientious leader. He was also blessed with seasoned company commanders and veteran non-commissioned officers. Whitaker surveyed the battlefield from the air and sent patrols forward to probe the defences. He insisted upon attacking at night with the support of three field and two medium regiments. A sandbox model of the village and the ridge were used to brief each company and ensure that the men knew exactly what was expected of them.

The attack was completely successful in the sense that the village was captured and positions established on the ridge. But with daylight the inevitable enemy counter-attacks started and a battle of attrition ensued. The fighting raged for five days and cost the RHLI 21 killed and 146 wounded. German resistance was finally broken when Montgomery's long delayed reinforcements arrived. On October 23, 1944–after two weeks of intense combat–2nd Division began the advance west to Walcheren Island.

Taking Walcheren Island

Originally published, November/December 2001

The words Luctor et Emergo, which translate into I struggle and I emerge, were emblazoned on the crest of Zeeland long before World War II began. Much of Zeeland, the southernmost province of the Netherlands, is below sea level and the land must be protected by dikes and elaborate drainage schemes. The phrase "God made the world, but the Dutch made Holland" may not be true of the whole country, but it certainly applies in Zeeland.

Walcheren, October-November 1944.

approaches to the Scheldt Estuary and Antwerp. Many of the large-calibre guns could traverse 360 degrees as 3rd Division discovered while fighting to liberate the Breskens Pocket.

Today, land reclamation has made Walcheren part of the South Beveland peninsula, but in 1944 it was joined to the mainland by a narrow causeway just wide enough for a railway line and a road. The island itself resembled a saucer with a rim of massive 60-foot dikes to hold back the sea. Walcheren appeared to be such a formidable obstacle that Lieutenant-General Guy Simonds, the acting commander of 1st Canadian Army, proposed to "break the dikes and flood all parts of the island below high water level."

This–together with constant bombing of the surviving gun batteries–would, he believed, destroy the morale of the garrison and permit limited airborne and seaborne forces "to mop up and take the surrender."

The final decision was General Dwight D. Eisenhower's and after discussions with Churchill and the Netherlands' government-in-exile, the supreme Allied commander gave the OK. Leaflets were dropped urging the population to evacuate the island and on October 3, 1944, Bomber Command blew a huge hole in the dike at Westkapelle. Two other breaches were made and salt water surged in to cover most of Walcheren.

While the flooding isolated the German garrisons, it left the gun positions on the dikes intact. Airborne commanders wanted nothing to do with operations in flooded terrain so 1st Canadian Army began to plan an amphibious assault with its own limited resources. Fortunately, Admiral Sir Bertram

When the Germans occupied Holland and began construction of the Atlantic Wall they concentrated their efforts in Zeeland and particularly on Walcheren Island. By 1943, 11 major gun batteries dotted the island controlling the

Ramsay, Eisenhower's naval chief, intervened insisting on a properly coordinated joint plan involving Royal Marine commandos, a Royal Navy amphibious landing force, plus His Majesty's Ship *Warspite* and two monitors to provide fire support.

Ramsay believed that operations to open the port of Antwerp should have top priority and he sharply criticized Montgomery for failing to "give the Canadians sufficient support." Montgomery, who still believed that his armies could reach the Ruhr area without Antwerp, refused to return the divisions he had borrowed from Simonds. Instead, he agreed to allow 52nd Lowland Division, the British Army's only remaining reserve formation, to be used for Operation "Infatuate", the capture of Walcheren. He also accepted Eisenhower's offer of an American formation, the 104th Timberwolf Division to strengthen First Canadian Army.

Neither division could arrive in time to clear the land approaches to Walcheren so 2nd Division, still engaged at Woensdrecht, was committed to operations in Beveland. The amphibious assault, dependent on tidal conditions, was scheduled for November 1. This left 2nd Division just eight days to break the German hold on South Beveland and advance to Walcheren.

On October 22, the acting corps commander arrived at 2nd Division headquarters to meet with brigade and battalion commanders. For security reasons General Charles Foulkes could not explain the reasoning behind the new orders, insisting that "a large scale appreciation had been made and all risks...were understood." The advance into the South Beveland peninsula must begin "before the last hour on 23rd October."

5th Brigade was again given the task of capturing the railway dike which controlled access to Beveland. The Calgary Highlanders, under their new commanding officer, Lieutenant-Colonel Ross Ellis, fought a difficult battle for the objectives which were not secured until the 24th when pressure from 4th Division forced an enemy withdrawal.

The results of RAF bombing of the Westkapelle Dyke.

While 5th Brigade fought its way north, the rest of the division launched Operation "Vitality I". In the early hours of a rainy, "pitch-bleak" morning, two mixed columns of armour– from the 10th Armoured Regiment and 8th Reconnaissance Regiment–and infantry from the Essex Scottish–in armoured vehicles–set out for the Beveland Canal. Progress was slow and the armoured thrust ended when three reconnaissance cars and three tanks were knocked out. The next day, a conventional infantry attack with the artillery pouring fire on two crossroads brought complete success.

That night, Operation "Vitality II", an amphibious assault across the Scheldt, carried out by a brigade of the 52nd Lowland Division, forced the enemy to abandon its new defensive line at the Beveland Canal before conducting a hasty retreat to Walcheren. The Scots, their advance slowed by mud, mines and the natural caution of green troops, were unable to prevent the exodus.

The Canadians found their new partners more than a little strange. An officer of the Royal Regiment of Canada left an account of his first meeting with the Scots which has become a classic Canadian military anecdote: "In the early hours of the 29th, I was out with a unit of carriers, maintaining a standing patrol on the left flank of the battalion. In order to complete our patrol we utilized some Dutch bicycles to patrol down a dike to the bank of the West Scheldt. All our men were desperately tired and in a filthy, wet, muddy condition. On our way we were terribly surprised to find a party of what were obviously Allied troops landing in a small boat. Then forth from the boat onto the shore stepped what seemed to me to be the finest soldier I had ever seen in my life, a fine figure of a Scottish gentleman, carrying the shepherd's crook, affected by some senior Scottish officers in place of a cane or swagger stick. He had a small pack neatly adjusted on his back. I had absolutely no idea where mine was and couldn't care less. His gas cape was neatly rolled. I had mine stuck in my breast

pocket. He was a colonel and I was a captain. His boots were neatly polished and I was wearing turned-down rubber boots. I did manage to salute, although I think it must have been haphazard. He politely enquired if we were Canadians. Although who else could have looked as we did? I assured him we were. He asked if I could direct him to battalion headquarters. I did better than that. I escorted him to battalion headquarters. I was taking no chances on losing such a beautiful specimen to the German army."

Canadian operations to clear Beveland were carried out swiftly and efficiently. However, with just 36 hours to go before the start of the hazardous commando landings at Westkappele and Flushing, the Scots, who were supposed to attack the island from Beveland, were not in position. Simonds needed immediate action. Fourth Brigade was told to seize enemy positions at the eastern end of the causeway while 5th Brigade prepared to capture a bridgehead on the island which would then be turned over to the Scots.

While the Calgaries rehearsed an assault crossing using storm boats, the Black Watch mounted a probing attack along the straight causeway. The enemy reacted with intense fire, including shells which "raised water 200 feet high when they fell short." The Black Watch withdrew and dug in. Engineers, sent to reconnoitre the crossing routes, reported there was not enough water for assault boats to operate–even at high tide. The mud flats were impassable to tracked landing vehicles. If there was to be an operation designed to divert attention away from the main attack it would have to be via the causeway.

The causeway or 'Sloedam' Walcheren Island (top).

Every November the Calgary Highlanders commemorate Walcheren day, paying tribute to men who accomplished the impossible. The first Calgary attack faltered when it became clear that the enemy had moved men out onto the causeway. The battalion withdrew until 5th Field Regiment was ready with a new fire plan that employed two regiments on a frontage of just 750 yards.

The barrage was designed to sweep the causeway, lifting 50 yards every two minutes. As dawn broke on November 1, the Calgaries advanced behind the barrage and got three companies into position on the island. The enemy's reaction was exactly what Simonds had been hoping for–intense counterattacks on the Canadian bridgehead just as the commando landings got under way.

The Calgaries now began to pay the price of their success. Heavy shelling and a series of counterattacks forced the contraction of the bridgehead until Baker Company was forced back to the edge of the causeway. Able Company lost all of its officers. Ellis, who had returned from the bridgehead, walked back across the causeway with two volunteers, the spare forward observation officer, Captain Walter Newman, and the brigade major, George Hees, who had volunteered to take over the company. Hees, who is so well remembered as a politician and minister of Veterans Affairs, was wounded in this action.

Ellis, "freshly shaved, neatly dressed and apparently calm and good humoured," checked all the forward positions and then "slowly walked back down the causeway talking to the men dug in there." At brigade headquarters he reported that the position could be held but a new major effort was required if any further advance was needed.

The commando landings, though costly in men's lives, were going well and the Scots were ready to take over operations the next morning. Fifth Brigade was told to organize a further attack designed to ensure that the bridgehead was secure before handing over. The task was given to Le Régiment de Maisonneuve which employed two of its three understrength companies. At 0400 hours on November 2, the Maisies began their advance across the causeway but were held up when the Scottish artillery barrage began 300 yards short, pummeling the Calgary positions. The acting divisional commander, Major-General Holly Keefler, had now had enough. He ordered the Maisies to dig in where they were and let the Scottish division plan and coordinate its own operation. One company of the Maisonneuve did not receive the halt order and continued onto the island.

The Maisonneuve force consisted of about 40 men, including six volunteers from the Belgium White Brigade who had been with the battalion since September. Lieutenant Charles Forbes, heading 18 Platoon, and Lieutenant D.G. Innes, a forward observation officer with 5th Field Regiment, maintained contact with the men, calling down defensive fire. Rocket-firing Typhoons were also in action, but it was the efforts of individuals, such as Private J. C. Carrière, who took out a 20-mm gun with a PIAT, that epitomized the day's brave and heroic deeds.

Carrière, a signaller, volunteered to stalk the gun. After crawling 400 yards along a shallow ditch, partly filled with water, "he reached a point from which he could bring fire to bear from his PIAT." Carrière was wounded, but he managed to knock the gun out and return to his comrades.

While the Maisonneuves fought their isolated battle, the Scottish engineers found a way onto the island through the mud flats. Infantry, moving slowly in single file, began to establish a second bridgehead and within 24 hours had outflanked the enemy. By then, 5th Brigade was on its way to Belgium for a long overdue rest. The causeway had cost the Calgaries 17 killed and 46 wounded. The Maisonneuve, with their companies of less than 60 men, had just one fatality and 10 wounded.

The battle for the causeway was not the ill-conceived disaster that it is so often portrayed as. Simonds' orders to mount an attack and maintain pressure on the enemy were a necessary part of the overall plan to capture Walcheren Island. The operation itself was carried out with considerable skill and relatively small losses. If the Scottish Brigade had been ready to take advantage of the successful Calgary assault on the morning of November 1, a large bridgehead could have been established. The 52nd Division would play a significant part in the battles of 1945, but in October 1944 there was still much to learn.

Much had been asked of the Canadians and Montgomery belatedly recognized this. He wrote to Simonds: "I think everything you are doing is excellent, and your troops are doing wonders under the most appalling conditions of ground and weather. I doubt if any other troops would do it as well and I am very glad the Canadians are on the business. Please tell your chaps how pleased I am with their good work."

With the battle for Walcheren over, the islanders and their liberators had to deal with the broken dikes and flooded farms. At first the authorities tried to evacuate the entire population. However, many refused to leave despite the danger of disease and the extensive minefields. The gaps in the dikes were temporarily closed with stone, rubble and brushwood and pumps were used to drain the island. Phoenix caissons from the Mulberry harbours in Normandy were brought north the next spring and used to seal the breaches. Walcheren once more emerged from the sea.

LCMSDS

Sherman tanks destroyed during the advance to Bergen-op-Zoom.

Advancing To The Maas

Originally published, January/February 2002

A recent battlefield tour of Belgium and the Netherlands was greatly enriched by the presence of World War II veterans, including two who served with the Algonquin Regiment in the battles to liberate the Low Countries. Georges Paquette and Ernie Hilts shared their memories with the group and encouraged us not to overlook the 4th Canadian Armoured Division and the "green centre line" marking its route.

We began at the Algonquinstraat, a narrow lane on the Moerkerke side of the double canal line that protected the once water-soddened territory in the Netherlands known as the Breskens Pocket (Taking The Breskens Pocket, March/April 2001). Our group then crossed to the north side of the canal to lay flowers at the local memorial. Fifteen miles to the east–at Isabella Polder–the commemorative plaque was a joint product of the regiment and the community and it was there where Georges Paquette explained just how determined the enemy was to safeguard the only land route into the pocket.

We also visited the city of Bergen-op-Zoom where Dr. Geoffrey Hayes of the University of Waterloo took us through the battle the Lincoln and Welland Regiment, Argyll and Sutherland Highlanders of Canada and South Alberta Regiment fought in the streets. All of this made our time at the Bergen-op-Zoom Canadian War Cemetery more meaningful, but it was evident that few in our group knew much about the battles to liberate the area.

The presence of a British military cemetery next to the Canadian graves reminded us that 49 West Riding Division had fought alongside 4th Canadian Division throughout the last two weeks of October 1944. On their right, both the Polish Armoured Division and the American 104th Timberwolf Division had joined in an advance that swept the enemy back to the Maas River to the north.

The story of the operations to trap, destroy or force the withdrawal of Hitler's Fifteenth Army is the least known part of Field Marshal Bernard Montgomery's post-Arnhem strategy. Prior to mid-October, when pressure from Supreme Allied Commander General Dwight D. Eisenhower and his naval commander,

Admiral Bertram Ramsay, forced Monty to give priority to opening the port of Antwerp, the field marshal had concentrated on advancing east to Germany.

Monty's directive of October 16 closed down those operations and ordered 12th British Corps to turn north, liberate Hertogenbosch and then move west, with its right flank on the Maas River, to seize Breda and the main escape route–the bridge at Moerdijk. At the same time, First Canadian Army would coordinate the advance of 1st Corps with its British, Polish and American divisions and the right wing of 2nd Canadian Corps, 2nd and 4th Canadian divisions. If all went well, the enemy would be caught and destroyed before they could retreat across the Maas.

The enemy was determined to avoid encirclement and planned a series of counter moves designed to save the Fifteenth Army. The vigorous defence of Hertogenbosch and a major counterattack from the east destroyed Montgomery's plans and left First Canadian Army with the task of advancing to the Maas on a wide front.

Lieutenant-General Guy Simonds, the acting army commander, ordered 4th Canadian Armoured Division to launch Operation "Suitcase" on October 20. The immediate goal was the town of Esschen, 12 kilometres east of Bergen-op-Zoom on the Dutch-Belgian border. When this was accomplished the division was to turn west towards Woensdrecht, forcing a German retreat and allowing 2nd Division to advance to Walcheren Island. Simonds would then bring the full weight of his multi-national 1st Corps into action, attacking north on a 30-mile front.

This was the first and last time an American division served under Canadian command and it is worth noting that the legendary Major-General Terry Allen, who had led the 1st United States Infantry Division in North Africa and Sicily, and who now commanded the Timberwolves, proved to be as co-operative as he was efficient. Allen had trained his men for night operations and under both Canadian

and U.S. command, the 104th U.S. Infantry Division proved to be a highly effective division.

The men of 4th Canadian Division would soon benefit from the actions of 1st Corps, but the advance to Esschen, which began October 20, 1944, involved heavy fighting and the constant threat of infiltration from the exposed right flank. Esschen was cleared by the Algonquin Regiment after a carefully executed night attack brought the lead infantry battalions to the edge of town. The enemy was relying on improvised battle groups that "fought stubbornly" until the Canadians closed in, then they "surrendered en masse." The Lincs' war diary reported the enemy soldiers were quite pleased with their future as prisoners of war.

The Canadian mood, however, was much less cheerful. The Germans had sown thousands of mines under the cobblestones of the main road and the sand of the forest tracks. Casualties in what was supposed to be the preliminary phase of Operation "Suitcase" were mounting rapidly and the soldiers' natural fear of a weapon that crippled when it did not kill was slowing the advance. The squadron leader of the mine-clearing Flail tanks that were attached to the brigade protested that his Flails would not clear the mines because the thrashing chains did not detonate mines under cobblestones and therefore the tank itself would be blown up.

Brigadier J.C. Jefferson "thought for a minute" and then crushed this mini-revolt with a curt order to get going and "if the first tank blows up push it off the road and send up another one and keep sending them up."

The advance of 4th Canadian Division provided immediate help for 2nd Canadian Division struggling to overcome German resistance on the Woensdrecht ridge. Sixth Brigade, relieved from its role guarding the right flank, took over the sector and on October 23 the Queen's Own Cameron Highlanders of Canada completed the capture of the village. Sergeant Wilf Kirk of the Camerons led the attack on the last two pillboxes in Woensdrecht while the Calgary

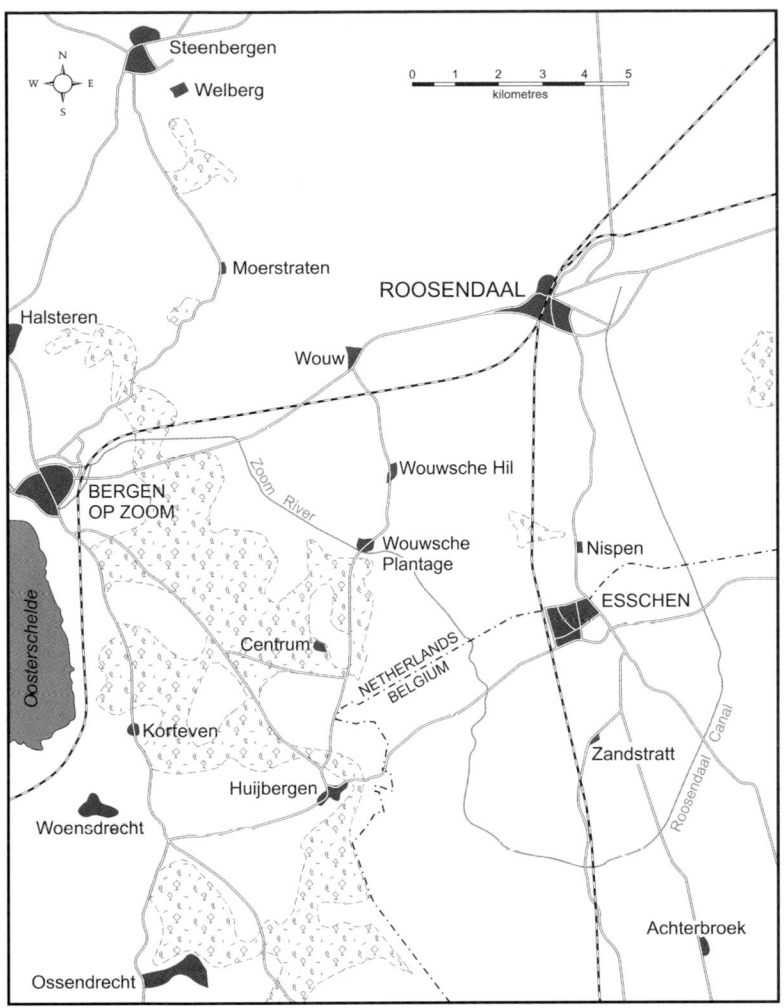

0 1 2 3 4 5
kilometres

Steenbergen

Welberg

Moerstraten

ROOSENDAAL

Halsteren

Wouw

BERGEN
OP ZOOM

Wouwsche Hil

Wouwsche
Plantage

Nispen

ESSCHEN

Oosterschelde

Centrum

NETHERLANDS
BELGIUM

Zandstratt

Roosendaal Canal

Korteven

Huijbergen

Woensdrecht

Achterbroek

Ossendrecht

**Bergen-op-Zoom
and vicinity.**

Within minutes, enemy self-propelled guns knocked out 10 of the lead squadron's tanks. When the Lake Superior Regiment moved to deal with the obstacle, the enemy withdrew to a reserve position. Infantry attacks, even with tank and artillery support were complicated by the enemy's liberal use of minefields, including ones that had been booby-trapped to counter the pioneer platoons normal methods of defusing them.

It took Moncel's force three days of bitter costly fighting to reach the railway line northeast of Bergen-op-Zoom and by then Jefferson's brigade was on the outskirts of the town.

The story of the entry into Bergen-op-Zoom is part of the lore of both the South Alberta Regiment and the Lincoln and Welland Regiment. Both Hayes and Don Graves have described the events in their superb regimental histories. Both accounts provide details which flesh out the brief sketch that follows.

Signs of an enemy withdrawal were evident even after the capture of Wouwsche Plantage and a battle group of Lincs and South Albertas moved cautiously forward. Despite the darkness of the late afternoon, civilian reports that the enemy had withdrawn to a position on the northern edge of the city tempted the two commanding officers if for no other reason than to get their men out of the pouring rain.

"Swotty" Wotherspoon of the South Albertas turned to Lieutenant-Colonel Bill Cromb and said: "Hell Bill, lets take the damn place."

Major Jim Swayze, who commanded a Lincs company, got his men moving by telling them: "They're in there and they're nice and dry.... Are we going to stay here and get soaked? No way."

Highlanders cleared the eastern end of the ridge. As 2nd Division turned towards Walcheren, Major-General Harry Foster tried to implement orders to cut off the enemy forces withdrawing to the north.

Fourth Division employed two balanced brigade groups, each with two infantry and two armoured battalions. This method, first developed in the late stages of the Normandy campaign, proved very effective in the first stages of Operation "Suitcase". The divisional plan called for Brigadier Robert Moncel's force to move in a wide circling movement to the north of Bergen-op-Zoom before Jefferson's brigade moved directly towards the city. Unfortunately, the advance to Wouwsche Plantage was contested by German armour that lay in wait guarding the narrow tracks that ran through extensive pine forest plantations.

Swayze's men, with a squadron of tanks, advanced to the Grote Market where the Hotel de Draak was commandeered. Tanks were soon stationed at the head of each of the northern facing streets with orders to keep the roads empty.

The next morning, the Dutch flag flew proudly from the town hall for the first time since 1940.

But the battle for Bergen-op-Zoom was far from over. The situation along the Zoom River, where blown bridges and a line of anti-tank obstacles assisted the German defenders, remained precarious until the morning of October 24. For the Argylls, Bergen-op-Zoom was anything but a happy adventure. The battalion was ordered to make a set-piece attack across the Zoom and the wide drainage canal that served as a tank obstacle. Short rounds from the medium artillery and well organized German resistance brought the first attempt to a grinding halt.

Casualties from friendly fire were a constant problem in WW II, but since no one wanted to attack without the largest possible amount of support, accidental losses had to be accepted. A second attack also failed and this left a small group of Lincs, who had tried to divert German attention, isolated on the enemy side of the canal. Between 3 a.m. and dawn, a third attempt brought a kind of success and the Argylls and a company of Lincs began the difficult task of clearing close-packed buildings defended by enemy machine-guns. By mid-afternoon, Jefferson committed the Algonquin Regiment and the South Alberta Regiment and both units helped complete the task. The Argylls had nine killed, 29 wounded. The Lincs had 11 killed, 27 wounded.

NAC 140429

By the time the battle at the Zoom was over, Moncel's force had broken out of the woods and reached the flat, open country north of the city. The enemy appeared to be in full retreat toward the Maas. This forecast, like so many other intelligence reports from northwest Europe, was based on the belief that the German army would behave rationally. With the British in Roosendaal and other Allied forces, including a squadron of the Manitoba Dragoons, moving up quickly on their right, the Germans had only a few days to make their escape.

The German high command, with Hitler watching over its shoulder, decided to try and hold on to some bridgeheads on the south side of the river, a policy that was to cost their army and the Allies many casualties. When operations ended November 8, the Germans held just one bridgehead at a place called Kapelsche Veer.

The South Alberta Regiment, Bergen-op-Zoom, October 1944.

The enemy's decision to contest the Canadian advance became evident when Brigadier Moncel outlined plans for a rapid strike to Steenbergen, northeast of Bergen-op-Zoom. The Canadian Grenadier Guards were teamed with the Algonquin Regiment for a night advance that was supposed to reach the edge of Steenbergen while two infantry companies dealt with opposition from the nearby villages of Bocht and Welberg. Their cross-country attack on the villages quickly turned into a nightmare when both companies were overrun by German battle groups led by self- propelled guns.

In this flat country, a slight rise–like the one at Welberg–dominated the area, and with many of the fields flooded and the roads mined, the armoured regiments would only provide indirect support. This meant a full-scale infantry attack with a divisional artillery fire plan, medium artillery and all the Typhoon aircraft 84 Group could spare. The Algonquins and the Lincs launched the second attack on Welberg on November 2. The artillery and a squadron of rocket firing Typhoons turned the village into a blazing beacon and this gave the infantry enough light to aid the advance.

Once in amongst the ruins, an intense close-quarter struggle lasted well past dawn. By then engineers had cleared the road and the self-propelled 17-pounders of the 5th Anti-Tank Regiment had moved up to deal with their enemy counterparts.

It was now the Argylls' turn to lead and this time everything went smoothly. The enemy had finally decided upon a general withdrawal and Steenbergen was left largely undefended. The next day 4th Division was squeezed out of the advance north by the arrival of 49th West Riding Infantry Division However, one task remained. The tanks of the British Columbia Regiment, working with the Lake Superior Regiment, pursued stragglers who were retreating to the islands of Tholen and Schouwen. This led to the Canadian Army's only naval battle in which British Columbia Regiment tanks sank three small German naval vessels.

The battles fought by 4th Canadian Armoured Division in October and November 1944 have been overshadowed by the more dramatic encounters at the Leopold Canal, Woensdrecht and the Walcheren causeway, but they were no less important and demanded no less courage or sacrifice. One of the most persistent themes in veterans memories of this period is the shortage of reinforcements and the limited skills of the new arrivals. It is important to note that many of the reinforcements, transferred to the infantry from other corps, were naturally hesitant and uncertain when first sent forward.

We know that many of them became fine soldiers, ready in their own turn to worry about the raw, green reinforcements who arrived in 1945. The more basic problem was sheer numbers and in the circumstances of November 1944 it could only be solved by enforcing conscription for overseas service. It was the promise of a large supply of well trained conscripts for the battles of 1945 that allowed the army to prepare for the last phase of the war, confident that the men at the sharp end would not be let down by their government.

The Conscription Crisis

Originally published, November/December 1994

On the morning of November 22, 1944, Prime Minister Mackenzie King was preparing to accept the inevitable. Soldiers from Canada's conscript army would be sent overseas. King had fought a clever delaying action, hoping that the pressure to find trained reinforcements for the Canadian Army would ease; instead public opinion in English-speaking Canada had hardened. The voluntary system was no longer working and a decision had to be made. Two weeks later the House of Commons agreed: 16,000 conscripts would join the Canadian Army in the Nijmegen bridgehead in time to participate in the battle of the Rhineland.

The conscription crisis of 1944 turned out to be a crisis only for politicians. Thirty-four French-Canadian Liberals voted against the government and editorial opinion in Quebec's nationalist press was predictably hostile, but with Louis Saint-Laurent and other French-Canadian cabinet ministers supporting the government even the political crisis was shortlived. And the conscripts? They turned out to be well-trained infantry replacements who served with distinction for the remainder of the war. What had the conscription issue been about?

In 1939 the people of the Allied nations supported the declaration of war against Nazi Germany because Hitler had repeatedly broken his pledges and was on the march again, attacking Poland. Canadians, like everyone else, went to war with few illusions about glory or adventure. Memories of the "Great War" were too recent for such foolishness. Canada would not have gone to war if Britain had failed to live up to her guarantee of Poland, but English-speaking Canadians did not act out of blind imperial loyalty. They believed that Canada had to join with Britain and France in a necessary war for the preservation of all that they valued, including the survival of Britain, their mother country. Hitler had left them no choice.

The majority of French-Canadians did not share this view. Whatever their opinions on events in Europe, few felt any emotional bond with France or involvement with the fate of Britain. Events in Europe were for Europeans to deal with.

The "two solitudes" were much further apart on the issues of war than was apparent in 1939. English-Canadians accepted plans for a very limited war effort because all the experts believed the French army, together with the Royal Navy, would block any German advance in the west. Virtually everyone supported the government's pledge not to impose conscription for overseas service in the context of a limited war that Britain and Canada would fight in the air and sea.

Then in the spring of 1940 the Scandinavian countries were conquered and unbelievably the French army collapsed. Canada, a nation of 11 million, was now the second most important military power fighting against Nazi domination of the world. A war of limited liability was no longer possible. The Canadian economy would have to be geared up for total war, vital commodities rationed, wages and prices frozen, and the men and women of Canada required to contribute to the war effort under the National Resources Mobilization Act.

NRMA also introduced compulsory military service for young Canadians who did not volunteer for one of the three services. Conscripts were required to serve only for the defence of Canada in Canada. They could not legally be sent overseas. Most Canadians accepted this compromise because there was no shortage of volunteers for the overseas army and no signs of military action.

There was also a dramatic shift in French Canada's attitude towards the war. The fall of France in June 1940 had forced all Canadians to recognize the seriousness of the Nazi threat. Throughout the summer of 1940 and well into 1941, Canadians were remarkably united in support of the war. In Quebec the radio broadcasts of Louis Francoeur brought news of the conflict and its meaning to homes across the province. Francoeur was to Quebec what Edward R. Murrow was to still-neutral Americans-a voice challenging listeners to

Campaigning for a 'yes' vote. The 1942 plebiscite on conscription for overseas service.

confront reality. His program was so popular that the texts of his broadcasts "La Situation, Ce Soir" were printed and sold at newsstands. French-Canadians enlisted in record numbers throughout 1940 and 1941 and support for Canada's war effort was widespread.

This fragile unity collapsed in the fall of 1941 with the revival of the conscription issue. The series of dramatic Allied reverses at sea, in the western desert, in Russia and then at Pearl Harbor, Hong Kong and Singapore, led many English-speaking Canadians to seek reassurance that Canada was doing all it could. Conservative newspapers began to editorialize about conscription for overseas service and the Conservative party turned to Arthur Meighen, the architect of conscription in WWI as their new leader. Meighen, never a man for compromise or conciliation, immediately raised a proclamation calling for a "National Government" and compulsion for service overseas.

King, who feared and hated Meighen, was in a state of panic. He was further stunned by the death of his Quebec lieutenant, Ernest Lapointe. The prime minister had always relied on Lapointe to guide him on matters related to French Canada.

King was now on his own, isolated, uncertain and irrational. To combat Meighen and the conscriptionist press he decided to introduce a plebiscite. In January 1942, Canadians were told that they would be asked to release the government from its pledge not to impose conscription for overseas service. Voting was to take place in late April so there was ample time for extremists on both sides to inflame public opinion. In his account of the campaign for a "no" vote in Quebec, Andre Laurendeau recalled how the nationalist cause in Quebec was dormant until the plebiscite was announced. Suddenly there was an issue that could be used to rally French-Canadians against the government and the war effort. The plebiscite split Canada along linguistic lines. In Ontario more than 80 per cent voted "yes" while in Quebec 73 per cent (85 per cent of French-Canadians) voted "no." Partisan politics had dealt a deadly blow to Canadian unity.

From the plebiscite of 1942 to the summer of 1944, conscription faded into the backgroun. At home Canadians were fully employed building the weapons and growing the food essential to an Allied victory. The navy and air force were involved in constant action, but there was never a shortage of volunteers for either service, or for the merchant marine which carried the vital supplies to England. Nor was there any shortfall of army volunteers. By 1944 almost 500,000, including 42,000 NRMA men who decided to volunteer for general service had enlisted. The casualties suffered at Dieppe and in Italy were replaced from the reinforcement pool and there seemed no reason to worry about another conscription crisis.

Unfortunately the Canadian Army had adopted British estimates of casualty rates based on experience in North Africa. In the desert, overall battle casualties had been low and were not concentrated in infantry units. British and Canadian planning for Italy and for Operation "Overlord" severely underestimated the proportion of losses that would occur in the infantry. They also ignored phenomenon of battle exhaustion that would account for one in five casualties, most of them in the infantry.

After the brilliant successes of D-Day the fighting in Normandy, like the struggle in Italy, became a battle of attrition. The Allied infantry were required to attack, occupy and hold small parcels of ground under circumstances that fully paralleled the agonies of combat in WW I. Modem memory has a firm image of suicide battalions and long casualty lists in WW I, but we are not accustomed to thinking of Italy or Normandy in these terms. For the infantry, who made up just 15 per cent of the army and suffered 70 per cent of the casualties, WW II was much like the western front in 1916.

British and Canadian planners, despite the early lessons of Italy, did not change their manpower allocations for Normandy. The British knew that if the fighting in France was heavy they would have to disband at least two infantry divisions for lack of reinforcements, but they preferred to hope the war would end quickly.

By early August 1944 the crisis was at hand and 59 (Staffordshire) Division, which had fought beside the Canadians at Caen, was cannibalized. The Canadians, for whom infantry casualties were running at 76 per cent of the total, were short 2,000 riflemen, (the equivalent of four battalions) at the beginning of August and more than 4,000

by the end of the month. Half-strength infantry companies were normal.

With only three divisions in Northwest Europe, the Canadians could not disband anything. The short-term solution was to "remuster" artillery, service corps, armoured and engineer troops to infantry. Throughout the late summer of 1944 thousands of these men were given crash courses in infantry weapons and tactics. The new riflemen and some hastily dispatched reinforcements from Canada patched up the holes for September and early October, but the struggle to clear the approaches to Antwerp and the assault on the Gothic Line in Italy quickly exhausted this supply. By mid-October men were stretched to the breaking point. Battle exhaustion casualties were again looming as a serious problem as men recognized that there was "no rest, no leave, no escape." Bitter feelings towards the government and the conscript ary at home were inevitable in this situation and when the minister of National Defence visited combat units he got an earful of straight talk.

J. L. Ralston had been a much-loved battalion commander in WW I and his commitment to the well-being of the ordinary soldier never wavered. Back in Ottawa he told the cabinet 15,000 additional trained infantry were needed overseas. The only possible source was the NRMA army. The prime minister, fearful of the country again dividing along French-English lines, looked for other solutions. He isolated Ralston from other pro-conscriptionist ministers then announced that General Andrew McNaughton would replace Ralston as minister of National Defence. McNaughton - Andy to many Canadians - tried to use his prestige as Canada's most famous soldier to persuade conscripts to volunteer. He quickly discovered that while the NRMA men would obey orders to serve overseas, no significant number would volunteer. McNaughton was strongly criticized from all sides. Public opinion in English-speaking Canada swung against him. On the morning of November 22 he telephoned the prime minister to advise him that the voluntary system would not produce enough men. There was no other solution, the conscripts would have to go overseas.

Halifax Bombers of 405 Squadron RCAF.

Bomber Command After Overlord

Originally published, March/April 2002

A new biography on Bomber Harris, written by the former head of the Royal Air Force Historical Section, Henry Probert, is re-opening debate on many aspects of the strategic bomber offensive in World War II. Interest is also heightened by the apparent success of the bombing option in the Persian Gulf War in 1990-91 and the war against terrorism in Afghanistan.

Probert's portrait of Sir Arthur Harris is based on contemporary letters and documents rather than postwar recollection and it allows us to better understand the options available to Harris at the time he made his most important decisions. For example, from April to September 1944, RAF Bomber Command was committed to the support of Operation "Overlord", the campaign to liberate France.

Initially, Harris complained bitterly about this diversion of his force from its proper strategic role–attacking German cites–and argued that his squadrons were not trained or equipped to carry out the kind of precision bombing required by the army. Nevertheless, Harris, as always, followed orders. He soon discovered that the Supreme Allied Commander, General Dwight D. Eisenhower, and his deputy, Air Marshal Sir Arthur Tedder, were much easier to work with than the staff at RAF headquarters. Indeed, in a postwar memoir, Harris recalled that the only time "when all pulled together... was during that short period when Eisenhower was the admiral and Tedder the captain on the bridge." Eisenhower expressed a similar view describing Harris as "one of the most effective and co-operative members of his team."

The months in which Bomber Command was working for Eisenhower also witnessed a renewed attempt to experiment with daylight bombing, largely abandoned since 1940 as too costly and ineffective. Many of these operations were carried out in support of First Canadian Army partly because Lieutenant-General Harry Crerar, an old friend of Harris, strongly supported the use of "heavies" on the battlefield even when a number of bombers hit Canadian troops some distance away from their proper targets.

After the worst such incident in Operation "Tractable"–the advance to Falaise–Crerar reminded everyone that most of the bombs had fallen on the enemy and "contributed greatly to success." Writing to Harris, he offered thanks and laid the groundwork for future co-operation.

For Operation "Wellhit", the attack on Boulogne, France, Crerar and Harris arranged elaborate precautions. An RAF Group Captain with a VHF radio link to the master bomber worked with Brigadier John Rockingham to ensure the target indicators were placed on the correct aiming points before bombing began. No. 6 Group, Royal Canadian Air Force, which had been responsible for much of the short bombing in "Tractable", supplied one third of the aircraft for this highly concentrated and accurate attack in which only one aircraft was lost and its crew rescued.

Even after Bomber Command ceased to answer to Eisenhower and reverted to its original role, Harris was usually willing to listen to requests to support the ground forces and did so especially in support of the battle for Walcheren Island in the Netherlands.

The skills which Bomber Command pilots honed in the summer of 1944 were soon employed in the renewed attack on German industry. By October 1944 more than 1,300 operational aircraft were available each day and it was possible to carry out raids on a wide variety of targets. Priority was to be given to oil targets in the belief that Germany's oil situation was desperate. The American daylight bombers were focused on this task and when Harris joined in, reluctantly, he too ordered daylight raids.

The first such raid was on August 27, 1944 when Halifax bombers of 4 Group attacked the synthetic oil refining plant at Meerbeck, using the same navigation aid, Oboe, as in night attacks. After further attacks in September, operational researchers estimated they had achieved a five per cent reduction in total oil output but cautioned that unless attacks continued the oil plants would soon be rebuilt

Canadian aircrew serving in RAF "mixed" squadrons participated in all of these raids and on September 11, 1944, No. 6 (RCAF) Group supplied 105 Halifax bombers for a daylight raid against oil plants at Castrop-Rauxel in western Germany. Laurence Motiuk's superb book *Thunderbirds At War: Diary Of A Bomber Squadron* notes that the operation "took place in clear weather with good visibility, against moderate to intense heavy flak." There was also excellent fighter cover provided by no less than 20 squadrons of Spitfires, Tempests and Mustangs. No enemy aircraft attempted to attack and while there was considerable flak damage no bomber was shot down.

Oil production was not the only objective of daylight raids. Two of the most successful operations of September 1944 were carried out on the German cities of Emden and Munster. The attack on the port of Emden was conducted by squadrons from 6 Group and 8 Group, escorted first by Spitfires and then by the long-range Mustangs of the United States 8th Air Force. American co-operation meant the bombers had fighter escorts throughout the flight. The attack was carried out at low altitudes, less than 2,000 feet on the approach run, to achieve surprise. Both the dock area and the submarine building yard were hit and suffered major damage. Only one Lancaster was lost.

The authors of the RCAF official history agree that "the raid was a complete success" but argue that since the crews could see what they were attacking, they "couldn't help thinking about the people down there" as "the centre of the town was the aiming point." They suggest that "at night in the dark there was greater psychological as well as physical distance between aircrew and their targets." Was this one of the reasons why Harris did not switch completely to daylight bombing, which was associated with American "precision" attacks rather than the "area" bombing of cities?

Understanding the policy adopted by Harris in the winter of 1944-45 requires careful consideration of the circumstances. First, let it be said that there is very little evidence to suggest that aircrew were upset by the sight of their bombs hitting targets in Germany, just the reverse. The second important generalization to make is that while the US 8th Air Force was supposed to deliver its bomb loads with pin-point accuracy, it rarely did so.

By the fall of 1944, Bomber Command's Halifaxes and Lancasters were at least as accurate as the Flying Fortresses and Liberators. In the cloudy weather so common in the fall and winter months both air forces were required to use navigation aids and target marking by master bombers. Bomber Command had more experience at this than the USAAF.

Throughout the war, Harris relied on the civilian-scientists of Bomber Command's Operational Research Section to provide systematic analysis of the available evidence. Each month the section produced a Report on Losses and Interceptions of Bomber Command Aircraft as well as studies on bombing accuracy and a host of other questions. In October 1944, a month in which 7,168 aircraft were dispatched in daylight and 10,394 by night, the overall loss rate was 0.8 per cent by day and 0.7 per cent by night. These low loss rates, in a force which had routinely suffered five times that number of casualties, were due to the "entire lack of fighter opposition by day" and by the success of radio countermeasures against night fighters.

The big difference between day and night operations was not accuracy or loss rates but the much higher proportion of aircraft damaged by anti-aircraft fire. Flak damage and crew casualties were several times higher in October daylight raids and this was a big improvement over September when 30 per cent of all such sorties returned with damage.

With this kind of evidence available, Harris and his staff reduced the proportion of daylight raids in November, ordering them to targets close to the edge of Germany so that flak was encountered only over the target. Of course, opportunities, such as the chance to sink the German battleship Tirpitz, called for daylight and on November 12 all of Bomber Command celebrated the achievement of No. 5 Group's Lancasters in sinking Bismarck's sister ship.

However, a great deal of training was required if large scale daylight raids were to play even a minor role in operations. The Americans flew in tight box formations with their escorts roaming the skies on the outer fringes of a relatively compact formation. RAF and RCAF crews navigated to their targets independently. With daylight raids, some kind of formation flying had to be developed and practised.

Canada's Air Vice-Marshal C.M. (Black Mike) McEwan, who commanded 6 Group in 1944 was known as a stickler for discipline and training. After numerous false starts he settled on a loose system of "gaggles", groups of 10 aircraft which were to remain reasonably close to each other. A series of gaggles made up a day bomber stream which the fighter-escorts could keep track of. Training in cross-country fighter-affiliation exercises became a regular part of the routine with all bomber squadrons.

As the daylight raids became better organized and penetrated deeper into Germany, the full extent of the decline of the enemy air force became evident. Some attempts were made to plot the course of the bombers from ground stations, but the Luftwaffe made just three brief appearances in the daytime skies in October and none in November. The last month of 1944 saw Bomber Command fly 3,776 day sorties and 11,567 at night. Loss rates remained below one per cent, but 14 per cent of all aircraft dispatched by day suffered flak damage.

December also witnessed the first serious attempt at interception of aircraft operating in daylight, but thanks to the presence of fighter-escorts only six bombers were lost to fighter attack. One of the most successful innovations of the month was the use of large groups of Mosquito bombers to carry out independent daylight attacks against oil targets.

The Operational Research Section's monthly reports focus on aircraft losses and assume that good accuracy was achieved in most raids. A very different view is put forward in the RCAF official history which quotes Air Commodore J.E. Fauquier, a former master bomber, as highly critical of the decline in bombing accuracy in the late summer and early fall of 1944. The Operational Research section's optimism was based on its detailed studies of bomb fall distribution and while Fauquier was quite right about a decline in accuracy there was no mystery about the causes. It was due to switching from carefully selected targets in France to much more difficult targets in Germany.

The key measure Bomber Command used to judge accuracy was relative density at the aiming point per 1,000 tons dropped. By this measure operations in the fall and winter of 1944-45, while less accurate than attacks on French rail yards, were five times more effectively concentrated than in 1943-44.

This improvement was due to the continuing development of electronic aids, including the increasing use of H2S, airborne radar, and the decline in enemy fighter opposition. Still, accuracy was a relative term. Neither Bomber Command nor the USAAF were ever able to achieve the kind of precision bombing that would have permitted them to avoid the destruction of cities and the death or injury of large numbers of civilians. Quite apart from problems with navigation, target identification, the visibility of markers, the limitations of bomb sights and human error, the reality was that when everything went right only five per cent of the bombs fell within 500 yards of the aiming point and only half struck within 2,000 yards of it.

When Harris and others argued for area bombing, with the aiming points in the centre of cities, they were basing their analysis on evidence which demonstrated that precision attacks were only possible under extraordinary circumstances. If the combined bomber offensive was to play a role in the defeat of Hitler it had to pose a credible threat to the survival of his empire. If this could have been accomplished by the destruction of industrial targets, with minimal collateral damage and a reasonable loss rate for the Allied air crews, that approach would have been adopted. The choice facing Harris and his political masters was how to mount a credible threat given the limitations of the available technology.

For most of the war, success for Bomber Command meant forcing the enemy to divert enormous resources in weapons and manpower away from Russia and other battlefields to counter the Second Front created over the skies of Germany. From the summer of 1944 to the end of the war in Europe, the strategic bombers also participated directly in the destruction of the Nazi war machine.

The contribution of the men and women of the RCAF to this long campaign should be recognized by all Canadians for what it was–part of a difficult, but necessary fight to win a war against what Winston Churchill called "a monstrous tyranny, never surpassed in the dark, lamentable catalogue of human crime."

The effects of bombing, Cologne, 1945.

Taking the War to Germany

Originally published, October 1994

Wing Commander D.C. Hagerman, DFC, read over the Recommendation for Honours and Awards, Immediate, dated October 23, 1944, and signed with a flourish. Flight Lieutenant John Alan (Andy) Anderson might not receive a Victoria Cross, but he certainly deserved one. Anderson had just completed 22 day and night bombing missions and at the rate he was going it would be tough to make it to 30. On no less than 10 operations his Lancaster had suffered serious damage, but he and his crew had always attacked their target and returned safely.

In July they lost an engine over the North Sea but decided to continue to Hamburg, which they bombed from 8,000 feet. On th way home German fighters attacked, but Anderson and his crew of Australians, British and Canadians shot down a FW190 and returned to base.

During August, 419 (Moose) Squadron was called upon to tackle a wide variety of targets. On three occasions Anderson's aircraft was hit but he prssed home accurate attacks against the Opel motor works in the Ruhr, a V-I rocket site in France and the Baltic port of Stettin.

On the first of these missions they were in the air for 10 1/2 hours and had to make an emergency landing. At Emden on September 6 and Dortmund on September 12, flak tore gaping holes in the fuselage. Again the target photos showed excellent results. Anderson and the rest of 419 Squadron were also part of No.6 Group's largest raid of the war when 293 Royal Canadian Air Force aircraft launched the Third Battle of the Ruhr on October 6. Operation "Hurricane" was designed to complete the destruction of the Ruhr war industries and No.6 Group's attack on Dortmund was a good start. The industrial, transportation, and residential areas of the city were severely damaged and aircraft losses were under one per cent.

Two days later, during a raid on Bochum, intense flak inflicted 27 hits on Anderson's aircraft before it turne for home. A cannon shell from a night fighter then short-circuited the electrical system, illuminating the navigation lights that could not be turned off. Once again Anderson evaded fighter attack and 11 arrived sfely home.

These were all night raids bomber crews had trained for, but in the fall of 1944 pressure to join in the offensive against oil meant Bomber Command also flew in daylight. Bottrop, an important oil production centre, was assigned to No.6 Group. When 419 Squadron arrived the area was under nine-tenths cloud. Anderson caught a glimpse of the target through a gap in the cloud cover, but it was too late to start an accurate bombing run. He decided to orbit the target and try again. On the second approach both port engines were hit and two crew members had to help control the rudder. After bombing the oil plant they set out for England on two engines. Their troubles were not over. The inner starboard engine had also been damaged and was producing half-power. Could a Lancaster 10 be flown on 11/2 engines? With the whole crew co-operating it could and was. Yorkshire never looked so good!

When the award recommendation reached Air Chief Marshal Arthur Harris it had been decided that a DSO to go with his DFC would do. Harris wrote a letter extending his "warmest congratulation" but by then Anderson was back in Canada volunteering for a second tour. Andy Anderson's story is more dramatic than most, but every veteran of Bomber Command air crew will recognize elements of their own experience in this extraordinary narrative.

But what does it all mean? Fifty years after Anderson and his comrades offered their youth, their courage and their skill to help overcome the power of Nazi Germany, the value of their contribution and sacrifice has again been called into question. Contemporary critics of Bomber Command argue - on the basis of postwar surveys - that the bombing offensive was too costly and ineffective. The destruction of German cities by area bombing, the death of large numbers of civilians, and the losses in Allied air crew were, it is said, too high a price to pay for a campaign that did not prevent German war production from steadily increasing.

This is not a new debate. Throughout the war, military and political leaders argued over the place of Bomber Command in Allied strategy and there were always questions about the accuracy of the claims made by the air forces. The arguments are well known to historians and were fully discussed in the four volume British official history, *The Strategic Air Offensive Against Germany* published in the 1960s. The secret and personal correspondence between Harris and Sir Charles Portal, Chief of the Air Staff, is also available to researchers. There can be few better examples of free and frank debate in the entire annals of military history.

The long awaited appearance of the official history of the RCAF has added more heat to the controversy for the 1990s. For all their careful scholarship and mastery of technical detail the authors fail to demonstrate any grasp of the nature of the war. The ideas, ideals and experiences of the men who directed the battles and those who fought in them are not part of the official history.

Between the Battle of Britain and the invasion of Russia, air power was the only means available to wage war against Hitler. Bomber Command was directed to hit oil and other priority targets on moonlit nights and urban centres in less favorable weather. German civilians were a legitimate target and Churchill's main complaint was that the discharge of bombs was so pitifully small" that civilian morale was unlikely to be affected. The way to correct this situation - all agreed-was to push the construction of more and bigger bombers.

The decision to give absolute priority to the production of the Halifax and Lancaster won universal approval after the invasion of Russia and apparent triumph of the Nazi armies. Bombing was the sole direct contribution Britain and the Commonwealth could make to preventing a Nazi victory. When the Butt Report of August 1941 showed just one in five aircraft bombed within five miles of the target, the only possible response was to concentrate energies on improving navigational aids. Electronic devices with code names such as Gee, Oboe and H2S were created and the British Commonwealth Air Training Plan provided the crews for the rapid expansion of the air force.

After the United States entered the war there were good grounds for optimism about the eventual defeat of Germany, but the Americans would not play a significant role in Europe before late 1943.

When the German offensive of 1942 began no one knew that German defeats at Stalingrad and Kursk-orel would transform the balance of power in Eastern Europe. Up until the fall of 1943 a German victory or a separate peace with Stalin was a real possibility. Either event would free an army of more than 200 divisions and a powerful air force to confront the western powers.

If Bomber Command could damage the German war machine by attacking "the economy which feeds it, the moral which sustains it, the supplies which nourish it, and the hopes of victory which inspire it" the war might be won. But even if bombing could not accomplish these goals the campaign was worth pursuing because increasingly the Nazis were diverting resources away from the Russian battlefields to the defence of the Fatherland. A second front was opening up in the skies above Germany.

By the summer of 1943 when the German army needed every 88-mm gun to stem the Russian tide, five of every six guns produced and 3/4 of a million men were deployed in Germany to defend its cities. The Luftwaffe was required to devote increasing resources to day and night fighter operations and their electronic war effort was focused on defeating bomber command.

The bombing offensive redirected the enemy war effort in other important ways. Simple arithmetic showed the V-I and V-2 could not deliver enough high explosive to seriously affect British war production. They were priority secret weapons for Hitler because they could be used to retaliate against London. The rocket program drew upon the best scientific manpower Germany possessed and further enormous resources were needed to build and deploy them. Allied bombing also forced the Reich to employ more than 1,000,000 men and women - military and civilian - in civil defence and damage repair. Every citizen so employed was not available to wage war or produce for it.

The combined bomber offensive may also have met many of its original objectives of reducing enemy war production. The U.S. Strategic Bombing Survey, which is the basis of most critiques of Allied bombing, has escaped scrutiny for far too long. Surprised by the resilience of German industry, the researchers assumed that they did not need to measure the impact of the effort to rebuild and disperse factories. They simply measured the number of days of production lost. A more realistic set of assumptions applied to the same data would show air power dramatically reduced production as compared to what it would have been in the absence of bombing.

The ethical issues that underlie all discussions of the bombing of cities also need to be re-examined. We know that VE-Day came in May of 1945, but as late as February of that year the Nazi war machine retained fearsome power and broad public support. Hitler and the Nazi party had told Germans that their war was a just war and the overwhelming majority of the population supported his quest for "living space" as they applauded his conquests. Germans had been taught that WW I was lost due to a "stab in the back." Germany and its armed forces, they were told, had not been defeated, but tricked into an armistice. The Allied bomber offensive demonstrated to the German people that they could not wage war against the rest of Europe with impunity. If London could be bombed to force the British to surrender and Warsaw destroyed to teach the Poles a lesson, Berlin was a necessary and legitimate target.

The Nazi war machine had built and equipped an army on a scale that the British Commonwealth and the US could not match. Young men like Andy Anderson carried the war into the heart of the Third Reich. Over four long years they fought to prepare the way for the invasion and when it came they took on new missions in support of the armies. They were not always successful and their casualties were high, but it is impossible to imagine how we could have won the war without them.

It is particularly important for Canadians to understand their accomplishments because the RCAF played such a large role in Bomber Command's war. Despite the grievous casualties and the continuous effort of will required to carry on, they persevered until victory was won. Churchill might have saved his famous tribute for these men because, indeed, so much is owed by so many to so few.

NAC 136255

The RCN in 1945

Originally published, January 1995

Escort Group 27 returned to Halifax harbour on December 29, 1944, in time to celebrate the new year and participate in the hunt for U-806 -the U-boat that sank HMCS *Clayoquot* on Christmas Eve. After a pause for refuelling, the five river-class frigates, HMC Ships *Meon, Coaticook, Lasalle, Levis* and *Ettrick*, put to sea again, but their mission was to deal with another U-boat that Allied intelligence had warned was heading to Nova Scotia.

"Ultra", the code-name for the intelligence gathered through decrypting German wireless signals, played a vital role in the defeat of the U-boat offensive in the mid-Atlantic. However, single U-boats operating in shallow coastal waters had no need to transmit or receive messages. "Ultra" could warn of sailings and destinations, but no one knew that *U-1232* had reached Canadian waters until two small merchant ships were sunk 20 miles off Halifax on January 4.

Escort Group 27 was formed in October 1944 in anticipation of a renewal of the German U-boat offensive. It was one of seven Royal Canadian Navy support groups organized to assist the close support groups that escorted convoys across the Atlantic. The senior officer, Acting Commander St. Clair Balfour, DSC, was typical of the young Royal Canadian Navy Volunteer Reserve officers so vital to RCN operations.

Commissioned in 1939, Balfour served aboard HMCS *St. Laurent* and commanded *Lethbridge*, a flower-class corvette before his appointment as Captain of HMCS *Meon*. Assigned to Escort Group 9, Meon supported the Normandy invasion and then hunted U-boats in the English Channel. By late 1944 all signs pointed to the return in the new year of German U-boats to North American coastal waters.

The defeat of the U-boat in 1943 had forced Grosadmiral Karl Donitz to abandon the wolf pack tactics that had brought such success in the first years of the war. Throughout 1944, Donitz sought to find a way of reviving the offensive, but the German navy was crushed when it tried to interfere with the Normandy landings. Of the 44 submarines used against Operation

Survivors of the sinking of HMCS *Clayoquot* on the Halifax approaches, December 24, 1944.

"Overlord", 28 were destroyed for losses of just 10 merchant ships. By August, the U-boat bases in Brittany were threatened and the withdrawal to Norway was under way.

The only option left to Donitz was to operate against merchant shipping in coastal areas where the shallow and wreck-strewn waters might prevent detection. U-boats were equipped with Schnorkel, a device that allowed batteries to be recharged under water, thus limiting the danger of discovery. U-boat captains were told to be patient. Instead of fleeing to deep waters when attacked they were to "bottom" and wait until the search moved on.

The primary target area was the coast of Great Britain, but the temptation to try the waters off Halifax proved irresistible. *U-806* made the first trip, arriving in mid-December. Her captain spent a week studying the pattern of traffic before attacking an American Liberty ship on December 21. Three days later *U-806* was in position to attack two convoys converging on Halifax. But this plan was wiped out by the appearance of three RCN escorts, the frigate HMCS *Kirkland Lake* and the bangor-class minesweepers *Clayoquot* and *Transcona*. The three ships were conducting a routine anti-submarine patrol in the harbor approaches, but the U-boat captain believed he had been discovered. A torpedo lashed out at the nearest vessel and *Clayoquot* went down in a matter of minutes. The hunt was quickly organized, but *U-806* slipped away. She returned to Germany after a four-month cruise with a damaged merchant ship and a sunken minesweeper to her credit. A trivial return for such a sustained effort.

She was barely gone when *U-1232* began operations. Kapitanleutnant Kurt Dobratz - an experienced submarine commander - missed his first two targets, but on January 4 he sank two small merchant ships moving from Sydney to Halifax. Escort Group 16, comprised of frigates *Antigonish, Charlottetown, Springhill, Stettler* and *Toronto*, was assigned to the hunt while Escort Group 27 reinforced convoy escorts.

On January 14, Convoy BX-141 arrived from Boston with a close escort of two minesweepers, *Westmount* and *Nipigon*. Escort Group 27 - now comprised of *Meon, Ettrick* and *Coaticook* - had closed with the convoy that formed single file to enter Halifax harbour. Lieutenant-Commander D.M. Maclean, who has analyzed the events in his M.A. thesis, *The Last Cruel Winter*, notes that *U-1232* had "reached a superb firing position" on the flank of the convoy. The first torpedoes struck two merchant ships, but the U-boat remained in the area and a third ship was hit. *Meon* ordered "adopt scare tactics" which meant all escorts were to fire depth-charges. *Ettrick* dropped shallow set charges along the wake of a torpedo and as the third depth-charge exploded, *Ettrick* crashed into Dobratz's conning tower, destroying the attack periscope and electronic gear. *U-1232* was out of action and fled the area to begin the long vyage home. No merchant ships were lost off Halifax again, though HMCS *Esquimalt*, a minesweeper, was sunk by *U-190* on April 16, 1945.

The professionalism demonstrated by Escort Group 27 was typical of the performance of the RCN in the last yean of the war. Escort Group 9, comprised of *Saint John, Monnow, Nene, Loch Alvie* and *Port Colborne*, was transferred from Londonderry to northern Scotland in late January 1945. It achieved outstanding results in the new area, including the sinking of *U-309* by HMCS *Saint John*. Escort Group 25 added another U-boat kill in February and Escort Group 26 got one in March. These were spectacular results at this stage of the war, but sinking U-boats was not the primary task of the navy. That task had been defined by Western Approaches Command in April of 1941 when it issued the famous instruction:

"The safe and timely arrival of the convoy at its destination is the primary object and nothing released the escort commander of his responsibility in this respect."

This primary object of naval operations in the Battle of the Atlantic is all too often neglected in accounts of a campaign that began on the first day of the war and ended in the last hours of VE-Day. Historians and naval officers in their memoirs have given us a warts-and-all picture of the RCN that is in danger obscuring what was accomplished. When the Battle of the Atlantic began the German navy had just over 50 U-boats. They were to build more than 1,000 before the war was over and Donitz's goal of 300, necessary, he said, to win the battle, was reached in late 1942. This enormous effort became the focus of German naval activity, but the Kreigsmarine suffered a crushing defeat. Over 600 U-boats were sunk and 70 per cent of all crews were lost at sea.

The RN, with its junior partner the RCN and its sometimes reluctant ally the United States navy, overcame the U-boat threat without sacrificing its traditional role. The great battle fleets, cruiser squadrons and new aircraft carriers continued to be built, manned and deployed as if the defeat of the U-boat was a matter of slight concern. Coastal Command, the poor cousin of the RAF, had to make do with the leftover aircraft while Bomber Command carried the war to the heart of Hitler's Reich.

The low priority assigned to anti-submarine warfare meant that commanders had to constantly scrounge for resources. The RCN, which began the war with a permanent force of 1,800 and 1,700 reserves, and a force of six destroyers and five minesweepers and two small training vessels, grew to a service of 100,000 men and women with 400 fighting ships, one of the largest navies in the world. This rapid expansion inevitably meant that ships went to sea with inexperienced officers and crews. There were other problems in training, ship construction, equipment, command and control. And all of these difficulties, which might readily have been overcome, became chronic problems because RCN ships were needed the moment they were available. If reasonable resources had been allocated to the U-boat war there would have been time for the RCN to train its sailors, work up its ships, and develop new skills. As it was they went to war dependent on the courage and resourcefulness of men who had to learn their trade during war.

The Battle of the Atlantic, we are told, was won in many ways. "Ultra" permitted the re-routing of convoys around the submarine wolf packs in the dangerous months of 1941 before the minimum number of escorts was available. The loss of "Ultra" intelligence in 1942 and its recovery in the spring of 1943 were also turning points in the struggle. Air power in the form of escort carriers and land based aircraft added enormous resources to the struggle. Operational research in both Coastal Command and at the Admiralty made a vital contribution to victory. Evidence that larger convoys could be organized without increasing the number of the close support escorts encouraged the formation of hunter-killer groups. Other operational research reports pointed the way to more effective air search procedures, the optimum settings for depth-charges and many other changes in doctrine. Technical developments in radar and High Frequency Direction Finding known as Huff-Duff also played a key role in the defeat of the U-boat.

The long list of innovations in equipment and tactics is a testament to the ingenuity and enterprise of scientists and training establishments. But none of this would have mattered without the little ships and iron men who struggled against the weather and the enemy to bring the convoys safely to harbour.

Nor can the contribution of the merchant marine be ignored. The men who sailed the merchant ships went through the same agonizing perils that challenged their naval comrades. In many ways their situation was more trying because they could not join in the hunt and attempt to hit back at the enemy. Victory in the Battle of the Atlantic was one of the great events of the century and there is enough glory in it for all.

The Battle For Kapelsche Veer

Originally published, May/June 2002

On November 2, 2001 a large delegation of Canadians as well as many Dutch citizens gathered at the Bergen-op-Zoom Canadian War Cemetery for the long-delayed funerals of Charles Joseph Beaudry and George Robert Barritt. Both men, privates in the Lincoln and Welland Regiment, had been reported "missing, presumed dead" in January 1945 during the battle for Kapelsche Veer. Their bodies and that of Private Victor Howey, uncovered the year before, had been found by Dutch engineers clearing mines and other explosives from a long, flat, diked island in the River Maas.

The remains of a large number of German soldiers had also been discovered, but in Canada attention was understandably focused on the young men who had volunteered to serve their country in the campaign to liberate Europe. News coverage of the event included commentary on the battle for Kapelsche Veer and fortunately journalists were able to rely on a recently published account of the action written by Donald Graves and published as part of his book, *Fighting For Canada: Seven Battles, 1758-1945*.

Canadians, long used to hearing more about defeat than victory, were now told about a successful action which may not have been worth the costs.

Canadians first heard the name Kapelsche Veer in February 1945 when newspapers carried stories describing the five-day battle to clear the enemy from its last bridgehead south of the Maas. During the previous months the news had been about Hitler's Ardennes offensive, the Battle of the Bulge, and the Allied counter-attacks that forced the enemy back to his start-line. Newspapers had also provided accounts of German offensives as well as reports on British operations, but it seemed— to ever sensitive Canadians—as if their army was on the sidelines.

The frontline soldiers saw it somewhat differently. It was true that during their "winter on the Maas" battalions were regularly rotated out of the line and action was largely limited to patrols, but in the damp cold of a Dutch winter the prospect of endless patrols was enough to challenge even the bravest.

Conflict between senior commanders and the men who have to implement their orders is common in all armies and the Canadians were no exception. Such tension was particularly evident in 4th Canadian Armoured Division where Major-General Chris Vokes, who described himself as a "great rough red hairy bastard," had taken command in December 1944. Vokes, a veteran of the Italian campaign, was determined to impress his personality and ideas on the division, telling his officers that he was "heartily sick of" hearing about their exploits at "Buggeroff-Zoom, Sphitzen-on-the-Floor and other places."

Lieutenant-Colonel Dave Stewart of the Argylls was so incensed with Vokes' attitude and the constant demands for patrols that he wrote to Lieutenant-General Guy Simonds, stating he had no confidence in his divisional commander. On January 25, the day before the battle for Kapelsche Veer began, Stewart, who had criticized the whole concept of the operation, was ordered to report to the neuropsychiatric wing of No. 10 Canadian General Hospital to be examined for battle exhaustion. Among the symptoms Stewart was alleged to have was "undue concern for his men."

The human costs of the prolonged winter war were considerable when measured in men's lives. During November 1944 the Canadians in Northwest Europe suffered 277 fatal casualties. December brought 229 more and in the first 25 days of January, before the battle for Kapelsche Veer began, 164 of our young men died while defending a static front on the western flank of the Allied armies.

The 63 fatal casualties suffered in the last week of January were a dreadful price to pay for a windswept island in the River Maas, but so was the loss of every soldier involved in the war Hitler and his Nazi supporters had inflicted upon the world.

The winter war and the battle for Kapelsche Veer were forgotten, except by those who fought there, until Geoffrey Hayes wrote a new history of the Lincoln and Welland Regiment in 1986. Hayes had first learned about the events from his uncle, Major Jim Swayze, who commanded the battalion in January 1945. Interviews with other surviving Lincs revealed that men still talked about Kapelsche Veer as a "dividing point" in the regiment's history. There was a clear perception, Hayes wrote, that something important happened there and many veterans used the words "before" or "after" Kapelsche Veer in telling their story. The Lincoln and Welland veterans believed that their worst enemy at Kapelsche Veer was not the tenacious German paratroopers or the weather but their own senior officers who committed them to a battle that could only be won at a price no combat soldier thought worth paying.

Is this a fair assessment of Kapelsche Veer and of the senior commanders? Lieutenant-General Sir John Crocker's 1st British Corps was responsible for a 60-mile front along the River Maas which he was to defend with two armoured divisions and the armoured cars of the Manitoba Dragoons. Intelligence reports suggested the need to prepare for airborne landings behind the lines as well as attacks across the Maas. The German bridgehead at Kapelsche Veer, which had been fortified in late December in preparation for a major attack, was too obvious a threat to be ignored and Crocker decided to do something about it.

The Poles tried to seize the island on the last day of 1944, but were forced to withdraw due to heavy fire from the north bank of the river. A week later a Polish infantry battalion actually captured the small harbour but could not overcome the resistance of enemy paratroops dug-in along the dike.

NAC 142421

The Corps Commander continued to insist that the bridgehead at Kapelsche Veer must be eliminated, even though the defeat of the German offensive in the Ardennes had ended any possibility of an enemy attack across the Maas. On January 13, the 47 Royal Marine Commando unit launched a third assault on the island attacking both flanks. This attempt, using lightly armed elite troops in a night attack, failed when the enemy, confident that their troops were safe underground, brought extremely heavy mortar

Soldiers of the Lincoln and Welland Regiment training for the attack on Kapelsche Veer.

fire down on their own positions causing heavy casualties among the Royal Marines.

Crocker now had two choices, he could abandon further attempts to capture the position and simply mask the island or he could order a much more elaborate attack. He chose the second option and issued new orders. "The enemy," he stated, "must be eliminated and the task will be undertaken by 4th Canadian Armd Division"

D-Day was to be "as soon as practicable" but "speed was less important" than careful preparations. Crocker also suggested that some new element be introduced into the plan "so that surprise can still be achieved." All of the resources of 1st Canadian Army, including air support and the specialized armour of 79th Armoured Division, was available to the division.

These orders left little room for debate and there is no contemporary evidence that anyone tried to argue against a new attack. The plan for Operation "Elephant" called for a smokescreen to limit the impact of observed fire from the north bank of the river and assumed that a 60-man "canoe commando" could use the smoke to cover their approach to the harbour on the north side of the island. Smokescreens were notoriously difficult to fine-tune for tactical purposes and the decision to base the operation on the success of this device was very risky. Asking men in vulnerable canoes to paddle down a river within easy reach of an enemy on both banks was simply reckless. The attack was to "be made from three directions simultaneously" with no mortar or artillery support and no smoke, other than for deception, until H-Hour. Hindsight is not required to criticize the plan.

By 1945 the Canadians along with their allies knew from experience how to fight and defeat their enemy. The method sometimes described as "bite and hold" involved carefully planned fire and movement with the artillery providing the main means of neutralizing the enemy while the infantry and, if possible, armour moved forward by bounds, consolidating at each phase. This was slow, unspectacular work and some generals, anxious to demonstrate their skill at manoeuvre warfare, preferred to short circuit the process with complex plans like the one Vokes outlined for Operation "Elephant". Such plans failed to account for the "friction of war" or for the rule that if something can go wrong it will go wrong.

The emphasis on achieving surprise prevented the Lincs from carrying out a recce of the area until the day before the attack and the companies only moved to their forming up places on the evening of January 25. Outfitted in white snowsuits, the men waited in the cold for the first faint light of morning. H-Hour was 7:25 a.m. and the four groups were on the move and ready to cross their start-lines on time. On the right flank both companies got onto the island but were delayed when their Wasp flamethrowers bogged down while trying to climb the dike. The first attempt to rush the main defenses failed because of well-positioned machine-gun and mortar fire from the north bank of the river.

Neither the smoke shells fired by the artillery nor the smoke generated by 803 Pioneer Smoke Company effectively screened the island. The failure of the smokescreen also jeopardized the "canoe commandos" who were forced into the centre of the river by ice conditions close to the bank. With two kilometres still to go and losses from enemy machine-guns mounting, Captain R.F. Dickie ordered his men to abandon their quixotic venture and join the companies on shore.

The enemy was not content with a defensive success and so shortly before 10 a.m. it launched the first of several counter-attacks. There was no choice for the Lincs except to withdraw and by 11:30 a.m. the survivors were evacuated from the eastern end of the island leaving Major Ed Brady's B Company, which was well to the west, as the only Canadians on Kapelsche Veer. It was now up to Vokes and Brigadier J.C. Jefferson to decide upon a new course of action. They chose to reinforce the bridgehead on the island with tanks from the South Alberta Regiment and order the Argyll and Sutherland Highlanders of Canada to attempt a new approach working up gradually from the east. By 10 p.m. an Argyll company, "supported by two South Alberta Regiment tanks," were dug-in on the island, relying on the rum-ration to get them through a cold, windy night.

The next day the Lincs and Argylls worked their way forward closing the arms of the pincers on the enemy strongpoint. The intricate system of underground tunnels and gun positions cut into the sides of the dikes continued to frustrate the Canadians but the lessons of the first disastrous day were not forgotten and no unnecessary risks were taken. The tanks of the South Alberta Regiment provided invaluable support in closing with the enemy. The Argylls' war diary, written by then Lieutenant Claude Bissell, later a distinguished scholar and President of the University of Toronto, records the action of one tank "which moved right onto "Raspberry"—the code name for the objective—despite the fact that the tank commander did not expect to be able to get the tank out again."

Throughout the final three days, the battle for Kapelsche Veer became a contest of wills. If Crocker's decision to attack the island is to be questioned then what of the 6th Parachute Division's determination to hold a position of little strategic or operational value? The German attempts to continuously reinforce their garrison and to mount counter-attacks simply made no sense. Allied artillery, using air bursts, inflicted enormous casualties on the enemy especially during efforts to cross the river. As late as the evening of January 30, artillery fire smashed several crossings and inflicted many casualties. This proved to be the enemy's last gasp and on the night of January 30-31 the paratroopers who were still alive abandoned the island.

Crocker ordered a "post-mortem" on the operation so that "any lessons discovered in the actions could be communicated to others faced with a similar problem." Both Jefferson and Vokes reported that a more careful approach "consolidating as one goes is a definite lesson" and advocated "attacks with limited objectives...repeated until the assault position was reached," the doctrine which had been taught at battle schools since early 1943.

There is one other lesson that those who comment on the battle might wish to consider. Historians often assume that when things go wrong some alternate course of action would naturally have worked better. There is a good case to be made for a different operational plan for Kapelsche Veer, but can we be certain the idea of seizing the island was mistaken? What if the enemy had used Kapelsche Veer to launch an attack on the understrength Polish Division? On January 18 an entire battalion of the 7th Parachute Regiment crossed the far more formidable obstacle of the Rhine near Arnhem and captured the village of Zetten. By the time 49th West Riding Division, supported by Canadian tanks, had retaken the town the Yorkshire division had suffered 220 casualties. Should we criticize Crocker for failing to mount offensive operations near Zetten? In war nothing is ever certain.

Preparing for "Veritable"

Originally published, February 1995

The year of victory 1945 did not begin auspiciously for the Allies in Northwest Europe. Today we know that total defeat of the Nazi war machine was only four months away, but matters seemed very different at the time.

The German army's Ardennes offensive - the famous Battle of the Bulge - was still raging in early January and on New Year's Eve the enemy launched yet another offensive, Operation "Norwind". Aimed at the extended southern flank of the Allied line, "Norwind" was designed to recapture Strasbourg and force Patton's 3rd U.S. army to turn away from the Bulge.

On New Year's Day, the Luftwaffe without warning -launched more than 1,000 sorties against ground targets, particularly airfields. More than 300 aircraft, including a number from Royal Canadian Air Force squadrons were destroyed. With hindsight, it is clear that German losses in all of these battles squandered reserves that were badly needed for the defence of Germany. However, as the deadline for the renewal of the Allied offensive approached, no end to the war in Europe could be foreseen.

Such a prospect - if it included the kind of casualties the Allies had sustained in the last months of 1944-was truly frightening. The manpower crisis that had forced the Canadians to draw upon 16,000 men conscripted for service in Canada was equally serious in the American and British armies. On January 12, the British war cabinet suggested for the first time that the war might not end in 1945 and a new program to find 250,000 more men for the army was set in motion.

Eisenhower was combing U.S. army service and communication units and transferring men from the air force to reinforce ground combat units. There were no more trained divisions back in the U.S. so he would continue to improvise.

One partial solution to the manpower problem was to transfer more troops from Italy to Northwest Europe. When the Joint Chiefs of Staff met at Malta in early February they agreed to send five divisions, including 1st and 5th Canadian, to strengthen Montgomery's army group. The move north began in February and by the end of the month 1st Canadian Corps was reunited with 1st Canadian Army.

Allied plans for 1945 called for the elimination of German forces west of the Rhine in a series of converging attacks. These operations were seen as a prelude to the main assault on Fortress Germany-the crossing of the Rhine. Elaborate preparations for this battle were underway and Montgomery had persuaded Eisenhower that 2nd British army should lead the attack with the support of the airborne army. The tentative date was late March.

The first major offensive of the new year- Operation "Veritable"-was to be carried out by Lieutenant-General Harry Crerar's 1st Canadian Army. Montgomery was no admirer of the quiet, nationalistic Canadian commander, but he did not question the competence of Crerar's staff officers, engineers and support troops. First Canadian Army Headquarters was well able to manage the 340,000 men and the required 10,000 tons of supplies a day.

The plan for Operation "Veritable" had originally called for rapid penetration of the Siegfried Line. It was hoped that the ground would still be frozen, allowing armoured units to be deployed in the early stages. A second assumption was that U.S. 9th Army, a powerful force of 12 divisions under General Bill Simpson, would begin its part in the Rhineland battle-Operation "Grenade" - within 48 hours of "Veritable".

When the offensive began on February 8, the ground had thawed and the Rhine dikes had been cut, flooding the northern flank. To the south the Germans had released the waters of the Roer River dams, turning the river the Americans had to cross into a raging torrent. "Grenade" was postponed for nearly two weeks.

"Veritable" began primarily as a British battle with English, Scottish and Welsh

YOU ARE ENTERING GERMANY BE ON YOUR GUARD

divisions attacking through the Reichswald Forest, while 3rd Canadian Division, now known as the Water Rats, cleared the flooded Rhine flank in Buffalo amphibious vehicles. Fifth Canadian Brigade captured Wyler to open a supply route for the British, but 2nd Canadian Corps did not take the lead for 10 days when the exhausted divisions of 30 Corps had lost momentum. The battles for Moyland Wood, Louisendorf and the Goch-Calcar road were part of a bitter, costly struggle against a well entrenched enemy assisted by enormous fire-power, including artillery firing from the east side of the Rhine. The weather was consistently awful and the tactical air force was frequently grounded. Tanks quickly bogged down in the saturated ground and everyone was cold and wet. Inevitably, combat stress became a serious problem. 53rd Welsh Division suffered 3,000 casualties in the Reichswald, more than 500 due to battle exhaustion.

The Canadian divisions soon faced a similar crisis. The corps' psychiatrists explained that many veterans were "emotionally depleted" and large numbers who had been previously wounded or treated for battle exhaustion could not, under any circumstances, be returned to their unit.

The Allied armies demanded a great deal of their combat troops. Our battle doctrine called for systematic attacks well supported by artillery and, while it was usually possible to suppress enemy fire during the advance, once on the objective the real trouble began. The enemy invariably hit back with accurate pre-registered fire, striking the Allied troops as they mopped up. Then came the first counterattacks; small groups of German infantry led by powerful tanks and self-propelled guns.

In theory, infantry battalions were to have their own six-pounder anti-tank guns in position with the heavier guns of the divisional anti-tank regiment tied in to the defence. Tanks of the supporting armoured squadron were to help out in the initial stages, but their Shermans were highly vulnerable and usually withdrew as soon as anti-tank defence was organized. From then on it was up to riflemen in slit trenches, the mortar

platoon, and above all the forward observation officer from the artillery field regiment to defend the battalion fortress.

The enemy's most lethal weapons were the mortar and the Nebelwerfer that accounted for 70 per cent of all Allied casualties. But German technical superiority in the design of light machine-guns, armoured fighting vehicles and anti-tank guns, including the fearsome 88, had a profound effect on the battlefield. Numerical superiority and dominance of the air could not compensate for marked inferiority in close-combat weaponry.

The British and Canadian armies recognized this problem in 1942 and by early 1943 operational research teams were examining all aspects of the land battle. Operational Research began as the scientific study of tactics and weaponry in Royal Air Force Fighter Command. OR also played a crucial role in improving Britain's anti-aircraft defence and in the offensive against the U-boat. The army - always at the bottom of priority lists- finally began to expand its involvement in OR to maximize the effect of new weapons such as the Projector, Infantry, Anti-Tank weapon or PIAT, the six- and 17-pounder anti-tank guns, and the new generation of tanks.

Work on armoured fighting vehicles and anti-tank guns was begun by a remarkable Canadian physiologist, Omond Solandt. Solandt, who had been at Cambridge when war broke out, initially joined the Medical Research Council's blood transfusion unit. Reports from North Africa about excessive crew fatigue in British tanks led the Royal Armoured Corps to seek scientific help and Solandt established a physiological lab to study the human factor in armoured warfare. Specifically, he was asked to investigate why tank crews were fainting in action. It was discovered that when the tank gun fired, its gases went back into the tank rather than outside.

The young Canadian scientist was able to suggest improvements in ventilation, but it was also evident that the tanks were poorly designed for combat and he began to raise

NAC 145770

Warning sign upon entering Germany, Wyler, Germany, February 10, 1945.

questions about all aspects of armoured warfare. Solandt helped to persuade the British and Canadians to adopt the Sherman tank which for all its weaknesses was vastly better than its British counterparts. He also played a key role in the development of the 17-pounder antitank gun and its use in Sherman Firefly tanks. In 1943, he became deputy director of the Army Operational Research Group and in 1944-as Colonel Solandt-he became director.

The work of army OR touched dozens of battlefield problems. These were not the men who designed weapons; their job was to get the most out of what was available. Work on improving gun accuracy had been OR's priority before Operation "Overlord", but once ashore the most urgent problem became locating and destroying enemy mortars. Army scientists had long been interested in the uses of radar and two new units, 1st Canadian and 100th British Radar batteries, were formed. For Operation "Veritable", both were used with great success to locate German mortar positions.

Experiments with radar did not end there. The operational research section attached to Montgomery's 21st Army Group had studied the problem of employing bombers close to the front lines in Normandy. The Rhineland battle would be fought in winter under cloudy skies and a new method of improving bombing accuracy was needed. OR officers supervised the use of mobile radar control posts that permitted medium bombers to fix their position in relation to fluid battle lines.

The battles of February and March were not marred by the "short bombings" of the Normandy campaign.

The OR story was not always one of triumphant success. Much of the effort to persuade the gunners that their predicted fire was far less accurate than they supposed fell on deaf ears. First Canadian Army's chief gunner, Brigadier H.O.N. Brownfield, was an exception. After the OR section demonstrated the extent of the problem in the Battle of the Scheldt, work was begun on technical questions, but improvements were modest. Radar-directed gunnery did not reach the army in 1945.

Operational research made a significant contribution to solving some battlefield problems, but German technical superiority in weaponry was never overcome. When 4th Canadian Infantry Brigade began the battle for the Goch-Calcar road, the assault companies were mounted in Kangaroo personnel carriers and a squadron of Fort Garry Horse tanks accompanied them. The attack, supported by 470 guns, went in over 2,000 yards of open ground. The rolling barrage got the troops to their objective, but tank losses were heavy and the expected counterattacks soon over-ran the Essex Scottish.

At nightfall the Fort Garry tanks withdrew to refuel. The infantry dug in and for the next seven days the Royal Hamilton Light Infantry held their position against repeated armour-led attacks. The Royal Regiment of Canada, in reserve, came forward to replace the Essex and they too held. The battle for the Goch-Calcar road was won in the sense that the RHLI was not forced to withdraw so the start-line for the next attack had been secured. To accomplish this Lieutenant-Colonel Denis Whitaker and his men had to draw upon all their skill and reserves of courage, even calling down artillery fire on their own position to ward off an attack. Scientists could help to make the soldier's job a little easier, but the essential task was still to occupy and hold ground and ultimately no one but infantry could accomplish that goal.

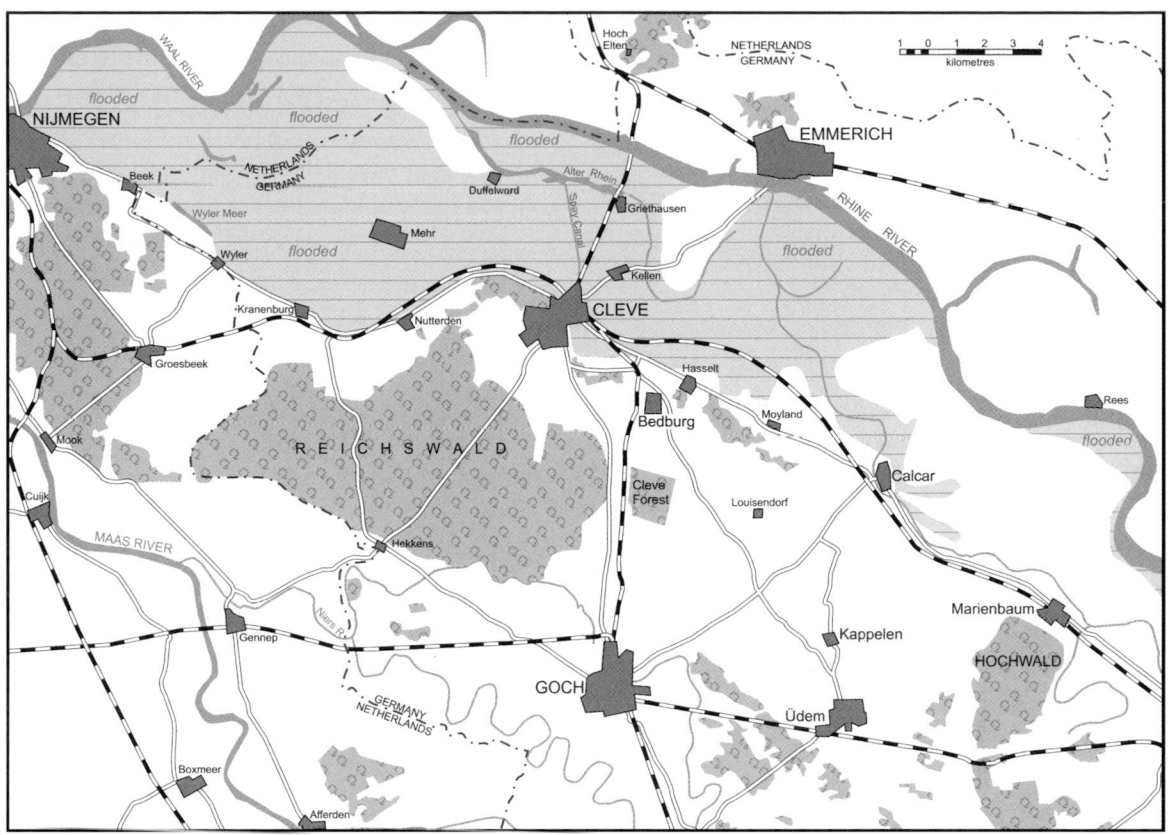

The Rhineland battlefield.

The Start Of The Rhineland Offensive

Originally published, September/October 2002

The operations carried out by First Canadian Army in the Rhineland during February and March 1945 involved as many Canadian units as fought in the last weeks of the Normandy campaign, but very little is known about their experience. This is the first of a series of essays designed to offer some insight into both command decisions and the soldiers' experience of war in the Rhineland.

The broad outline of Allied strategic plans for 1945 were agreed upon in January once it was clear that the German offensive in the Ardennes–the Battle of the Bulge–had lost momentum and would soon be crushed. The Supreme Allied Commander, Dwight D. Eisenhower, flatly refused General Bernard Montgomery's proposal that he be placed in charge of the American forces for the next offensive but Eisenhower did agree to assign the U.S. 9th Army–10 divisions strong–to Montgomery's

army group. Montgomery was to clear the west bank of the Rhine in a vast pincer movement employing General Harry Crerar's First Canadian Army in the north and Bill Simpson's Ninth U.S. Army in the south. The Canadian operation was code-named "Veritable" while the American operation was called "Grenade". Unfortunately the enemy reacted to the first signs of an offensive by opening the Roer dams and turning the river Maas, which the Americans had to cross, into a raging torrent one thousand metres wide. Operation "Grenade" had to be postponed, but "Veritable" went ahead as planned.

Crerar and the staff of First Canadian Army had been preparing for "Veritable" since November. The original plan, to launch the offensive with Lieutenant-General Brian Horrock's 30th British Corps and use 2nd Canadian Corps in a supporting role, had been modified under pressure from Lieutenant-General Guy Simonds who argued that "to leave the Canadians out of so important and decisive a battle would be a bitter disappointment to the troops." The troops were not asked if they agreed with Simonds' views, but he won his case and both 2nd and 3rd Canadian divisions were committed to the opening phase of the battle.

Three defensive belts confronted the Allies, each from 500 to 1,000 yards wide. The first, on the edge of the Reichswald Forest, covered the six-mile gap between the Maas and the town of Wyler. North of Wyler the flood plain of the Rhine, covered in several feet of water from blown dikes, provided another kind of obstacle. The extensive 'squares' of forest plantations, which made up the Reichswald, were also an obstacle, but perhaps the greatest asset the Germans possessed was the weather. When Montgomery had first outlined the operation he had expressed the hope that "dry or hard ground" would be available. "If these conditions exist," he told his commanders, "then the basis of operations will be speed and violence. The aim will be to pass armoured columns through to disrupt and disorganize enemy resistance in the rear..." However, he cautioned that if "the ground is wet and muddy, then a slower and more methodical progress may be forced upon us."

By February the ground was very wet and very muddy. Rain and grey skies covered the battle-field and this limited the air support that could be provided.

Army intelligence reported that Major-General Heinz Fieburg's 84th Infantry Division, with a strength of 10,000 men, had placed all seven of its battalions in line across the six-mile front. The division controlled 100 field guns and could call upon 36 self-propelled anti-tank guns for immediate support. Unfortunately for 30 Corps, General Alfred Schlemm, commander of First Parachute Army, sent 2nd Parachute Regiment to the Reichswald two days before the attack to take over the left flank thus allowing Fieburg to create local reserves. The 2,000 men of 2nd Parachute Regiment provided exceptionally strong resistance in the first days of "Veritable", slowing the advance of 51 Highland Division in the one open area where rapid movement might have been possible.

The Anglo-Canadian plan for "Veritable" involved the massive application of force to a narrow constricted battlefield and 1st Canadian Army was responsible for the development of an elaborate supply system to make this possible. By 1945 the Canadian army's engineers and staff officers were among the best the Allied armies possessed. Crerar paid tribute to their work in a press conference which detailed the size and scope of the buildup necessary for the operation: "1,880 tons of bridge equipment have been used in the construction of the five military bridges which have been thrown across the River Maas, and lead into the forward assembly area. The Ravenstein "high level" pontoon bridge–known as the Quebec Bridge, is the longest Bailey bridge yet constructed–1,280 ft. long.

"British and Canadian sappers in the past few weeks have constructed, widened and improved approximately 20,000 tons of stone, 20,000 logs and 30,000 pickets have been used. To move troops and their fighting equipment and supplies into position prior to D-Day (the day of the attack) will involve 35,000 vehicles travelling an average 130 miles each and using approximately 1,300,000 gallons of petrol.

"Demands have entailed the production of over 500,000 air photographs and 15,000 enlargements. Over 800,000 special maps, requiring over 30 tons of paper, have been produced. If the ammunition allotments for the operations, which consists of 350 types, were stacked side by side and five feet high, it would line a road for 30 miles. The total ammunition tonnage, provided for the supporting artillery from D-Day, to D-Day plus 3, would be the equivalent in weight to the bomb-drop of 25,000 medium bombers.

"1,100 tons of smoke materials, exclusive of artillery, will be used in the ground plan, which will produce what is believed will be the longest smoke screen in the history of this war."

Horrocks proposed to use all of this manpower and high explosives in a sudden, massive attack by three British divisions, each of which would concentrate its energies on an exceptionally narrow front. The Guards Armoured Division and

43 (Wessex) Division were in reserve, ready to pass through and exploit south in the early stages of the attack. This account of the Canadian role in "Veritable" should not obscure the fact that the overwhelming majority of men involved in the battles of February were British

Infantrymen of the Stormont, Dundas and Glengarry Highlanders Regiment in a 'Buffalo'. Mehr, Germany, February 11, 1945.

troops fighting under their own leadership in 30 Corps. Casualties to the British forces in February were four times higher than the Canadian total.

The 2nd Canadian Infantry Division had occupied the area through which 30 Corps was to attack for some weeks. There had been ample time to study the limited task assigned to the Blue Patch division–the capture of a triangle of territory south of the Nijmegen-Cleve road near the German village of Wyler. Once this fortified area had been seized, divisional engineers would open the road and hand over to 15th Scottish Division which would use the route to support its advance.

Second Division was under the command of Major-General Bruce Matthews, a peacetime militia officer who had spent the war in a series of Royal Canadian Artillery appointments, including Commander Royal Artillery of 1st Division in Italy and Commander Corps Royal Artillery for 2nd Canadian Corps, from Normandy to the Scheldt. Matthews was an aggressive, self-confident officer who had no doubts about his ability to command an infantry division. Indeed, given the kind of artillery-based operations used in the Allied armies, the appointment of a senior gunner officer appeared to be long overdue.

Matthews selected 5th Infantry Brigade to undertake the attack on Wyler and Brigadier W.G. Megill gave the main task to Lieutenant-Colonel Ross Ellis and the Calgary Highlanders. By February 1944 the Calgaries were one of the most consistently effective battalions in 21 Army Group. Their assault, supported by two companies of the Régiment de Maisonneuve, involved a quick thrust to the Cleve road before turning north to attack Wyler from the rear. The two lead companies ran into a minefield, taking heavy casualties but were astride the road and in contact with 15th Scottish Division by noon.

The attack on the village of Wyler required a long agonizing period of close fighting. Dugouts constructed in the dike banks gave the enemy near total protection from the preparatory artillery barrage. Most of the seven officers and 308 German soldiers captured during the day surrendered only when the infantry, working closely with 5th Canadian Field Regiment and

NAC 143946

The flooded Rhine flank in 'Operation Veritable'.

the Toronto Scottish Regiment's 4.5-inch mortars, fought their way into the village. The Calgaries lost 67 men, including 15 killed. The Maisonneuves, who seized the villages of Den Heuvel and Hochstrasse, thereby extending the flank of the attack, had two killed and 20 wounded. This little battle was a microcosm of the fighting on February 8. Historians, noting that Horrocks employed five divisions on a five-mile front, held by the equivalent of one and one-third German divisions, usually speak of the overwhelming strength of the Allies in "Veritable". To the Calgaries attempting to break into Wyler, or the British battalions spearheading their divisional advance, the operation appeared far less one-sided.

Dan Spry's 3rd Canadian Division, now known as "the water rats", had the task of clearing the area between the Nijmegen-Cleve road and the Rhine so as to protect the left flank of the main advance. During the week before D-Day, February 8, a thaw had softened the Rhine flood plain and breaks in two major dikes added to a flood of water that gradually submerged the battlefield the Canadians were supposed to manoeuvre over. The 79th Armoured Division was quickly called upon to supply Buffaloes and 3rd Division was reintroduced to the amphibious vehicles which had been so valuable in the Scheldt operations.

Jock Spragge's 7th Brigade had been assigned to seize the Quer Dam, a natural defensive position which dominated the front. German tunnelling efforts had weakened the dam causing its collapse and increasing the flooding, but at either end of the dam companies of 1052nd Grenadier Regiment were dug in. The Regina Rifles had little difficulty in taking the southern post and were able to advance on the village of Zyfflich with the aid of artificial moonlight supplied by searchlights reflecting off the low lying clouds. The flood waters had not yet submerged the approach to the village and the Reginas were accompanied by a troop of Shermans and a Flail tank which led the procession, clearing mines. Two companies of the Reginas, working with cool professional caution, cleared the village by midnight, taking over 100 prisoners at a cost of one officer killed and 12 men wounded.

The Canadian Scottish Regiment attacked the northern end of the dam, sending one company on foot along the face of the dam while two platoons, mounted in Buffaloes, circled around and attacked from the southwest. The Royal Winnipeg Rifles completed clearing the area.

On the left or Rhine flank of the divisional sector, 8th Brigade directed an operation which mounted the North Shore (N.B.) Regiment on Buffaloes for a quick strike to a dike barrier and the village of Zandpol. "Booby traps inflicted most of the casualties while the regiment was clearing the dike and when the enemy showed signs of life "B" Company asked for a five-minute fire plan on Zandpol to quiet it down." The 13th Field Regiment obliged and the North Shores entered the village without meeting any resistance. The Régiment de la Chaudière took the next bound to Leuth, but resistance was growing and several small counterattacks had to be beaten off first.

Brigadier J.M. "Rocky" Rockingham's 9th (Highland) Brigade waited until the afternoon of D-Day plus 2, February 10, to start the second phase of the operation. The Stormont, Dundas and Glengarry Highlanders advanced along the southern edge of the flooded area using Buffaloes to reach their objective, the Spoy Canal. Out amidst the floods the Highland Light Infantry of Canada was involved in a miserable, costly struggle for the village of Duffelward. This tiny Rhineland hamlet was the northernmost position of the Seigfried Line, with fortified houses and flood waters swirling in between. The HLI were pressed forward by a barrage of orders from division and, at midnight,

two companies were in position on the bank of Spoy Canal. The brigade's reserve battalion, the North Nova Scotia Highlanders was ordered to cross the canal and occupy Kellen. "After wading through knee to waist-deep water in various spots...they established themselves without meeting any resistance." They waited there, isolated among the floods, facing east to the Rhine. On the 14th the North Novas conducted the last operation of the first phase of "Veritable", putting in an amphibious attack across the Alter Rhine, capturing the ferry-crossing opposite Emmerich. On February 15, 3rd Division reverted to the command of 2nd Canadian Corps.

While 3rd Division struggled to complete its tasks the British divisions were experiencing some of the heaviest fighting of the war. On the Canadian flank, 15th Scottish Division had been asked to squeeze two brigade groups into the narrow zone between the Reichswald and the flood waters. The road to Cleve was the axis of their attack and their main task was the seizure of the curved ridge overlooking the ruined city. With the road flooded to depth of two feet, operations were at a standstill when Horrocks decided, on the basis of information that part of the ridge had been captured, to order the 43 (Wessex) Division, to pass through the 15th Scottish and burst out onto the plain beyond. In his memoirs, he admits that this decision was "one of the worst mistakes I made in the war" because the arrival of 43rd Division "caused one of the worst traffic jams of the war" and made the Scottish Division's task even more difficult.

"Veritable" was turning into a bloody attritional battle which the British army could ill afford. Since the Americans still could not cross the Maas the enemy was free to employ its armoured reserve, 15th Panzer Grenadier and 116th Panzer Division against the British. The German counterattacks failed but by the night of February 13 it was evident that the British-Canadian offensive had stalled. It was time for Montgomery, Crerar and the Corps commanders to think it out again.

Clearing Moyland Wood

Originally published, November/December 2002

Operation "Veritable", which began on February 8, 1945, was supposed to be the northern area of a vast pincer movement intended to destroy enemy forces west of the River Rhine. When flooding prevented the American 9th Army from carrying out Operation "Grenade", its part in the encirclement, German General Alfred Schlemm, commanding First Parachute Army, was free to use his reserve, 47 Panzer Corps, to counterattack the Anglo-Canadian forces. By February 13, "Veritable" had come to a stuttering halt. After five days of brutal combat, which veteran soldiers described as worse than Normandy, a pause to rest and re-organize was essential.

American army engineers estimated that a crossing of the River Roer, which was now a thousand-metre-wide raging torrent, would have to be postponed for at least a week. This presented some very difficult choices to the field marshal, General Bernard Montgomery. If he renewed the attack, infantry casualties, already above the 2,000 mark, were bound to increase threatening the future viability of 2nd British Army but if he waited for the Americans the enemy would have time to create new defences and bring up further reinforcements. Before making his decision, Montgomery was presented with an alternate plan of breathtaking audacity.

Lieutenant-General Guy Simonds, commanding 2nd Canadian Corps, and Major-General G.H.A. MacMillan, general officer commanding 49th (West Riding) Division, had devised a scheme to cross the Rhine at Arnhem forcing the enemy to divert resources and weaken resistance west of the Rhine.

Operation "Wallstreet" was more than a clever idea. MacMillan's Yorkshire division was comprised of the forgotten soldiers of 21 Army Group. The 49th had fought with distinction in Normandy but one of its battalions broke under extreme pressure and had to be disbanded. This event sullied the reputation of the whole division and on July 23 it was transferred to First Canadian Army where it was used to defend the coastal flank. After taking part in the capture of Le Havre in France it was deployed north of Antwerp, Belgium, joining 4th Canadian Armoured Division in the advance to the River Maas. From November 1944 to February 1945, the 49th was once again committed to a static defensive role along the Maas with no prospect of offensive action.

MacMillan and his senior officers were puzzled and annoyed by Montgomery's attitude towards their division and they developed detailed plans for Operation "Wallstreet", hoping for permission to carry it out and prove the critics wrong. MacMillan found an ally in Simonds who ordered his corps engineers to study the plan to determine if the Rhine could be bridged at Arnhem allowing supplies and 2nd Canadian Corps to cross into a bridgehead. Convinced the operation could succeed, Simonds prepared an outline plan for an immediate crossing and when this was rejected a revised plan proposed February 24 as a new D-Day.

Montgomery was not impressed, he rejected the idea and ordered Simonds to bring his corps into line on the Rhine flank of 30 British Corps to join in a renewed frontal assault beginning on February 16. This set-piece attack involved four British and two Canadian infantry divisions advancing on a 16-kilometre front. Montgomery's decision to continue a frontal assault, which was bound to turn into another attritional battle, must have been due to a belief that the Germans could be trapped or destroyed west of the Rhine once the Americans got going. A bridgehead at Arnhem, of all places, seemed far too risky.

Riflemen of the
Regina Rifles,
February 1945.

Simonds had little time to consider the new role
his corps was to carry out as the takeover of
some 2,000 metres of front was scheduled for
February 15. The next day 7th Canadian Infantry
Brigade, supported by squadrons of the Scots
Guards, attacked through positions held by 15th
Scottish Division in an attempt to reach the
Goch-Calcar road. On the right, the Royal
Winnipeg Rifles, mounted in Kangaroos of
the 1st Canadian Armoured Personnel Carrier
Regiment, rode right onto their objective at
Louisendorf, Germany, capturing 240 prisoners.
They dug in under heavy fire holding a start
line for a further advance by 4th Canadian
Infantry Brigade.

The Regina Rifles and the Canadian Scottish
Regiment drew the task of clearing the eastern
half of Moyland Wood, a mixed forest cloaking
a low, hilly escarpment. The Reginas forming up
place was marked by the yet unburied bodies of
Scottish soldiers who had fought their way
through the western end of the woods, adding to
the sombre mood of men hesitant to enter a dark
forest right out of Grimm's Fairy Tales. With elements of two enemy infantry battalions backed
up by mortars and artillery defending the woods
there was good reason to hesitate. However, the
position overlooked the corps' main axis of
advance and had to be taken.

Moyland Wood is little changed and today's visitor to the battlefield can follow the routes taken by the Reginas and Canscots in the first attempt to clear the area. It takes some imagination to picture the noise of shells crashing into the trees, the sound of concealed machine-guns and the gut-wrenching fear gripping the riflemen as they worked their way forward. The carefully camouflaged enemy soldiers allowed one Regina company to move deep into the woods before closing in behind them. One Regina platoon was overrun, the others dug-in under mortar and machine-gun fire. The Canscots, trying to clear the eastern end of the woods, were quickly pinned down by heavy fire.

A new attack was planned for February 18 with three Regina companies attacking from the south with the support of Wasps, carrier-mounted flame-throwers. The Reginas forced the enemy to withdraw beyond the crest of the western end of the ridge but could go no further. Lieutenant Warren Keating commanded the lead platoon and led his men in the defence of the crest against repeated counterattacks. He was awarded the Military Cross. The next day a Canscot attack, designed to secure the hamlet of Rosenboon at the eastern end of the woods, was beaten back by companies of a fresh parachute battalion brought in to relieve the exhausted defenders.

When Brigadier Jack Spragge reported that the enemy was too strongly entrenched to be dislodged by his two tired infantry battalions, Simonds removed the veteran commander placing the Regina commanding officer, Lieutenant-Colonel Alan Gregory, in temporary command. As often happens in such situations, Simonds allowed Gregory the time and resources Spragge had lacked. The Royal Winnipeg Rifles left their slit trenches near Louisendorf and moved into position south of Moyland Wood. Brigadier E.R. Suttie, who had replaced Brigadier Stanley Todd in command of the divisional artillery, prepared an elaborate fire plan involving medium and field artillery plus mortars, anti-tank guns, machine-guns and the tanks of the Fort Garry Horse. Gregory and Lieutenant-Colonel Lockie

Fulton, the aggressive young commander of the Royal Winnipeg Rifles or Little Black Devils, devised a plan to clear the eastern end of the wood combining Wasps with tank support and air attacks. Each of the two lead companies kept three Wasps forward with three in reserve ready to leap frog forward when fuel for the flame was exhausted. This continuous support boosted the morale of the assaulting troops while breaking the will of the enemy.

The Royal Winnipeg Rifles displayed outstanding skill as well as courage in the day-long battle that cost the battalion more than 100 casualties, 26 of them fatal. Major L.H. Denison, who led "D" Company in the final stages, received the Distinguished Service Order for his inspired leadership. Lieutenant George Aldous, temporarily blinded from grenade fragments, returned to his platoon after first aid treatment and led it in defeating repeated enemy counterattacks. He received the Military Cross.

Total casualties to the brigade, including battle exhaustion, exceeded 500 men and the westerners had to be pulled out of action. When it came time to sum up the lessons learned, emphasis was placed on the method of employing the flame-throwers, close contact between infantry and tanks and the 100 sorties flown by 84 Group of 2nd Tactical Air Force. No one mentioned the most important lesson–the enemy was fighting with a new intensity in defence of the Fatherland. German reports on the battle admitted great losses but insisted the decision to withdraw was made to straighten-out a "projecting front line" and "obtain reserves," the usual rationalization offered by German officers defeated in battle.

While 7th Brigade fought to clear Moyland Wood, 4th Canadian Infantry Brigade launched a set-piece attack to secure the Goch-Calcar road. The brigade, commanded by Brigadier F.N. Cabeldu who had landed in Normandy as commanding officer of the Canadian Scottish, was well trained, well led and fully up to strength. The plan called for an advance of some 2,000 yards behind a rolling barrage. More than 500 guns, field, medium and heavy were employed

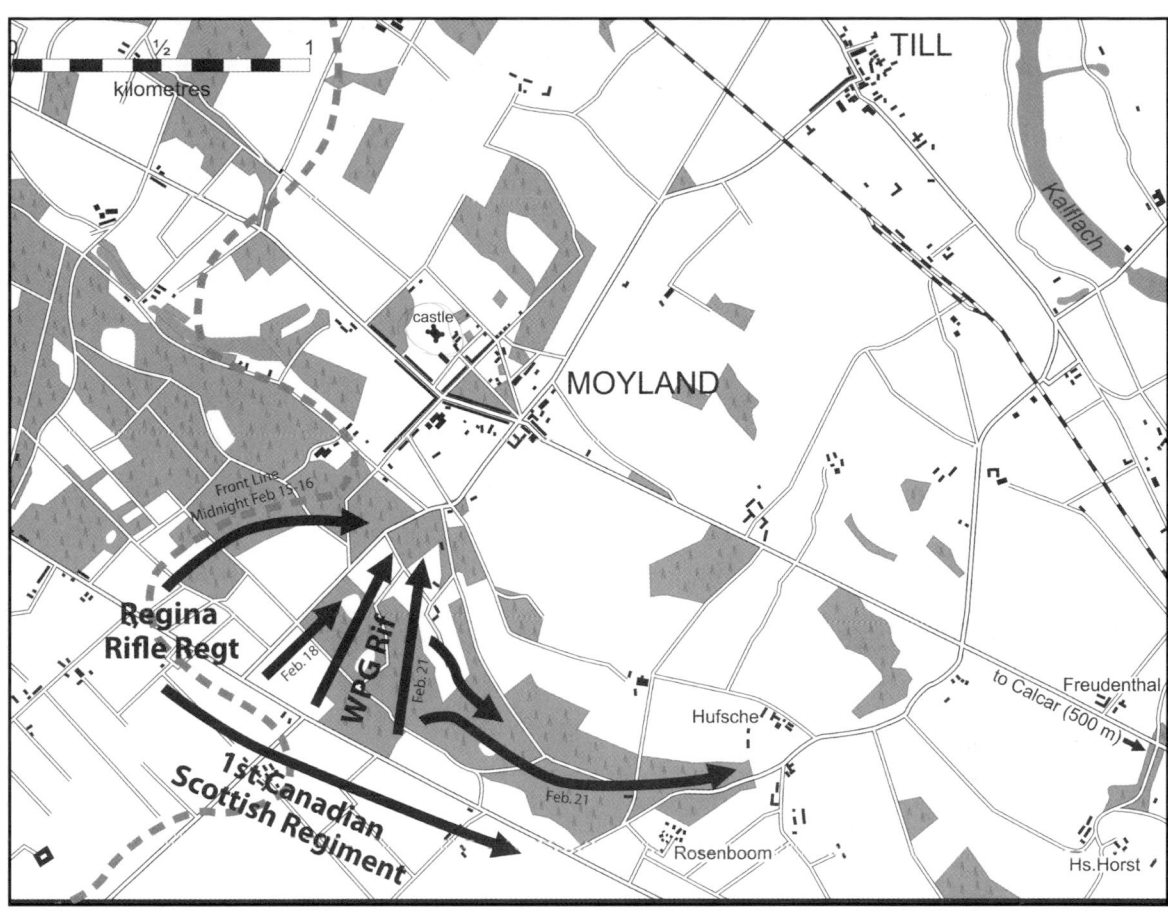

Moyland Wood.

and the lead companies were mounted in Kangaroo armoured personnel carriers that were to advance at "armoured pace" 50 yards a minute. Squadrons of the Fort Garry Horse supported the advance to ensure close support on the objective.

The attack went in much as planned. Some of the tanks and Kangaroos bogged down and at least six tanks were knocked out by anti-tank guns firing from the Calcar ridge. However, the infantry suffered few casualties before it debussed close to the planned objectives. Both the Royal Hamilton Light Infantry, RHLI, and Essex companies were able to fight their way forward to the road. Behind them the reserve companies arrived on foot and took up their designated stations. The defences in this area were, in comparison to the main positions on the high ground and in the Hochwald Forest, improvised but they were proof against the physical power of the Allied artillery. Because the Canadians got forward shortly after the barrage lifted, almost

100 German soldiers, most of them mentally dazed by the hurricane of high explosives, surrendered in the first hours. The remainder, however, fought on with considerable determination.

The German Army's doctrine of the immediate counterattack resulted in a small-scale counterthrust by elements of 116 Panzer Division, but Schlemm, the Army commander, decided more was required. Earlier that day the town of Goch had been entered by troops of 30 Corps and Schlemm must have been tempted by the common sense solution of a withdrawal to the Calcar ridge or even the Hochwald line. He knew that the flood waters of the Roer were retreating and that the Americans could not be delayed much longer. Nevertheless, he decided to commit his only real reserve, Panzer Lehr Division to an attack on 4th Brigade

Two powerful battlegroups, one from Panzer Lehr and the other from 116 Panzer Division, launched repeated attacks, "growing in fury with the passage of time." Lieutenant-Colonel

Denis Whitaker, who won his second DSO in this action, put his own counterattack force into action and restored the situation on the RHLI front, but the Essex position was overrun and not recovered until the next day by the reserve battalion, the Royal Regiment of Canada.

Canadian casualties in this two-day action were heavy, but the enemy lost even more men as well as precious tanks and self-propelled guns. The 18th Canadian Anti-Tank Battery alone accounted for seven Panthers. One German officer described the situation in his diary for February 21: "None of us believe in victory anymore. We do not talk about it anymore. We all feel indifferent we have our orders and we have to follow them.... The new front will be the Rhine."

The German army's insistence upon immediate counterattacks once again proved disastrous and the next day, February 21, the Germans abandoned Moyland Wood and the Goch-Calcar road. Panzer Lehr, considerably weakened, was rushed south to meet the long-delayed American attack, Operation "Grenade". General Bill Simpson's 9th U.S. Army had waited impatiently while the battle of the Rhineland was waged by British and Canadian troops. With 10 divisions, seven infantry and three armoured, 9th Army had over 300,000 men under command. Intelligence reports indicated that after Panzer Lehr was committed to stemming "Veritable", there were less than 30,000 German troops of widely varying quality between 9th Army and the Rhine. Simpson and his Corps commanders were understandably anxious to get such a promising operation under way.

U.S. Army engineers had been measuring the rate of flow of the Roer with great care and they estimated that the reservoirs behind the blown dams would be empty by February 24. Simpson decided to try a night attack early on the 23rd while the river was still in flood, in the hope of catching the defenders off guard. There was to be no air bombardment from "heavies" and no preliminary artillery barrage. More than 2,000 guns, the largest American artillery concentration to that point of the war—one gun per 10

yards of front—would commence firing 45 minutes before H-hour, the hour at which the operation was scheduled to begin. Engineers, protected by selected infantry patrols, crossed the Roer before H-hour and when the artillery barrage lifted, 30th U.S. Infantry Division had a footbridge in place.

This success story was not, however, typical of this very dangerous assault crossing. Most divisions had a difficult time getting their units across the fast-moving river and, as the day progressed, the footbridges were swept away. But the river crossing was described as the worst part of the first week of Operation "Grenade", and once established on the east bank of the Roer, the operation went smoothly. After 24 hours, 9th Army had 28 battalions across the river with seven bridges in operation. The cost was 93 men killed, 913 wounded and 61 missing. Most of these casualties were combat engineers involved in the river assault and bridge building.

The American hammer was well and truly aimed for the anvil of the British-Canadian forces to the north. But the anvil, as we shall see, refused to wait until the American hammer had delivered the crushing blow. Instead, a frontal attack on the main German defensive position was ordered and 2nd Canadian Corps found itself fighting Operation "Blockbuster", one of its most costly operations of the war.

LCMSDS

Canadian Infantry,
the Rhineland,
February 1945.

Operation "Blockbuster" Begins

Originally published, January/February 2003

When Operation "Veritable" began on February 8, 1945, Lieutenant-General Harry Crerar predicted that if weather conditions were poor a series of set-piece operations would be required to reach Xanten, the Army objective. The battle might, he thought, last three weeks.

Two weeks later First Canadian Army had breeched the Siegfried Line and fought its way beyond Cleve but was well short of its original objective. This partial victory had cost the Anglo-Canadian Army 490 officers and 8,023 other ranks, killed, wounded and missing. Most of the casualties–379 officers and 6,325 other ranks–were in Lieutenant-General Sir Brian Horrocks' 30th British Corps. However, the Canadian share–111 officers and 1,683 other ranks–was proportionately high considering that only three Canadian brigades had been committed to major operations.

Operation "Veritable" had imposed an enormous strain upon the morale of units and of individuals. Approximately 950 British and 350 Canadian soldiers were evacuated due to battle exhaustion during February. At least 1/3 of those had either been wounded before or had been previously treated for battle exhaustion. The next most common characteristics were short service (less than a week in action) and exceptionally long service. One Canadian psychiatrist, Dr. Travis Dancey, commenting on the "frequent appearance of the war-weary" described a typical case in these terms: "He had led a section for several months, had been blown up eight times, but had always carried on with his duties. Recently he had lost his confidence, was unable to make decisions, had become unduly cautious and felt that he was a bad influence on his section."

British Army psychiatrists, who had been returning a much greater number of exhaustion cases to duty than their Canadian counterparts, also found they were dealing with soldiers who had been "psychiatric or surgical casualties before," or "young, immature boys experiencing their first severe action." It was not possible to return significant numbers of either group to combat, adding to the problem of finding replacements for the infantry companies.

This horrendous casualty toll had occurred primarily because the flooding of the Roer River had prevented the complimentary American attack, Operation "Grenade". The enemy's First Paratroop Army had thrown its reserves against the northern front, turning the Reichswald and the Siegfried Line into a killing ground which also devastated the remaining German forces in the west. First Canadian Army processed 11,778 prisoners through its prisoner-of-war cages in the two-week period, and intelligence estimates placed the German dead at around 12,000. "Veritable" had not gone as planned, but the enemy's capacity to defend the Rhineland and the Rhine had been seriously weakened.

On the morning of February 23, when the United States 9th Army began its successful crossing of the still-flooded Roer, the fate of the German forces west of the Rhine was sealed; they could either retreat, surrender or die; they could not muster the strength to hold off the 10-division American attack, no matter how fiercely the isolated units fought. By February 26, signs of a German rout were evident to all. With the Americans 40 miles away from the Rhine, advancing three to four miles a day, it was only a matter of time. Throughout this period First Canadian Army was steadfastly ahead with plans for a new operation, code-named "Blockbuster", which called for a series of assaults on fortified positions in unfavourable terrain which the Germans would surely be forced to abandon once the American offensive pressed towards them.

Presumably Field Marshal General Bernard Montgomery and Crerar believed the American pressure from the south would require the Germans to weaken their defences in front of First Canadian Army, paving the way for a successful breakthrough in the north. So we must ask why Operation "Blockbuster" was allowed to develop into another confused battle of attrition with casualties close to 4,000 men, 2,600 of them Canadian.

Crerar told his corps commanders that if "determined enemy resistance" continued despite the American advance, "Blockbuster" would be limited to "securing the high ground east of the Calcar-Udem road." But neither Lieutenant-General Guy Simonds nor Horrocks seemed to have paid much attention to this directive. They outlined plans for a series of battles designed to break through the Schlieffen Position, the last major defensive barrier west of the River Rhine and continue south to Xanten. Once these operations were under way no one had the courage or foresight to stop them.

Simonds' plans for "Blockbuster" were typical of operations carried out by 2nd Canadian Corps: they were innovative and complex making little allowance for error or the inevitable friction of war. The initial phase called for three infantry brigades to seize the high ground while 4th Armoured Division formed up ready to advance to the Hochwald Forest. The division, commanded by Major-General Chris Vokes, was reorganized to allow Tiger Group, under Brigadier Robert Moncel, to lead off. Tiger Group was made up of three armoured and two infantry regiments subdivided into four mixed infantry-armour battle groups. Each was given specific tasks and timings which seemed unnecessarily complicated to those who had to carry them out.

During the night of February 25, the infantry, plagued by icy rain, moved into position for the assault. The barrage began at 3:45 a.m. Forty-five minutes later, 6th Brigade, mounted in armoured personnel carriers known as Kangaroos and supported by squadrons of the Fort Garry Horse and Sherbrooke Fusiliers, moved out in three straight columns. Overhead tracer fire and other navigation devices, including searchlights, horizontal and vertical, inevitably recalled Operation "Totalize", Simonds' night operation of August 8, 1944.

Brigadier R.H. Keefler's 6th Brigade had been preparing for an attack on the Calcar Ridge since February 18. This meant that there had been ample time to permit "units and supporting arms to carry out mutual planning on a most intimate basis. Sand tables were constructed and personnel down to section leaders were briefed carefully and kept in the picture from day to day." Keefler was able to hold a final run through with all commanders on February 22 and the following morning Montgomery arrived to give his blessing.

The Sherbrooke Fusiliers provided a squadron to support each of Keefler's infantry battalions and by the night of February 26–some 16 hours after the startline was crossed–the brigade had taken all of its objectives and was well dug-in. When the inevitable German counterattack developed, it came "exactly where it was expected" and the enemy was quickly crushed. This was bite and hold at its best. 5th Brigade was equally successful, though with only one squadron of tanks available Brigadier W.J. Megill found that the enemy could not be overcome without a pause for reorganization and the development of a new artillery fire plan.

Third Division was to capture the villages of Keppeln and Udem as well as the hamlets and farmhouses which dotted the countryside around them. The Queen's Own Rifles of Canada led off 8th Brigade's attack, moving forward through rising, open fields as soon as the barrage lifted. The QORs had been allotted a squadron of 1st Hussar tanks and a troop from 52 Battery (self-propelled 17- pounder guns) of the 3rd Anti-Tank Regiment, RCA, but the artillery program for their sector was severely limited. The QORs were, according to the "Blockbuster" master plan, simply securing the lower slope of the ridge, conforming to the movements of 2nd Division. This meant the barrage would move on to the crest relatively quickly.

Lieutenant-Colonel S.M. Lett did not underestimate the problems facing the regiment. He had found that "reconnoitring the final objectives, and the intermediate enemy strongpoints...was almost impossible on account of the flat open country which was completely under enemy observation." He ordered his two lead companies to make one adjustment in the divisional plan; they were not to cross the startline at the scheduled hour in the hope that they would be able to observe and avoid the inevitable counter barrage which the Germans would direct behind the moving Allied barrage. As Lett told 3rd Division's historical officer: "Enemy artillery is not very flexible. His defensive fire is brought down very accurately. However, once the

limitation of this area is determined it can be circumvented with comparative safety."

The 'late' start of the QORs allowed them to get to their first objectives without losses, but "D" Company found that the hamlet called Mooshof was difficult to secure and even harder to hold on to. It was here where Sergeant Aubrey Cosens won the Victoria Cross for actions described in the following citation:

"On the night of 25/26 February 1945, the 1st Battalion, Queen's Own Rifles of Canada, launched an attack on the hamlet of Mooshof to capture ground which was considered essential for the successful development of future operations.

"Sergeant Cosen's platoon, with two tanks in support, attacked enemy strongpoints in three farm buildings, but were twice beaten back by fanatical enemy resistance and then fiercely counterattacked, during which time the platoon suffered heavy casualties and the platoon commander was killed.

"Sergeant Cosens at once assumed command of the only other four survivors of his platoon, who he placed in a position to give him covering fire, while he himself ran across open ground under heavy mortar and shell fire to the one remaining tank, where, regardless of danger, he took up an exposed place in front of the turret and directed its fire.

"After a further enemy counterattack had been repulsed Sergeant Cosens ordered the tank to attack the farm buildings, while the four survivors of his platoon followed in close support. After the tank had rammed the first building, he entered it alone, killing several of the defenders and taking the rest prisoner.

"Single-handed he then entered the second and third buildings and personally killed or captured all the occupants, although under intense machine-gun and small arms fire. Just after the successful reduction of these important enemy strongpoints, Sergeant Cosens was shot through the head by an enemy sniper and died almost instantly.

"The outstanding gallantry, initiative and determined leadership of a brave NCO, who himself killed at least twenty of the enemy and took an equal number of prisoners, resulted in the capture of a position which was vital to the success of future operations of the brigade."

The Queen's Own captured more than 300 prisoners "practically all of them paratroopers" in a series of determined tank-infantry assaults. Lett was effusive in praise of the 1st Hussars, noting that "the excellent work of the tanks in supporting the infantry was the deciding feature in ousting the enemy from his well dug-in positions."

Tank-infantry co-operation was also the key to success for the North Shores and Chaudières. The North Shore Regiment's advance on the village of Keppeln was held back until the QORs on the left and the Régiment de la Chaudière on the right had cleared the flanks. The delay was also planned because there was not enough armour available to support three battalions and the North Shores were to depend on the timely arrival of the Hussars squadron from the QORs.

This all meant that the Chaudières with "B" Squadron, 1st Hussars, two troops of 52nd Battery, plus a company of medium machine-guns and 4.2-inch mortars from the Cameron Highlanders of Ottawa, had to strike out on their own towards the Sportzplatz to the south of Keppeln. The advance went well on the right but heavy fire from Keppeln pinned down the left flank. The Chaudières tried to exploit their initial success and pass a reserve company forward to the final objective where a white flag was seen; misunderstanding this for a sign of surrender, the company relaxed. Three Panther tanks appeared and machine-gunned the company, heavy casualties resulted.

Major F.J. L'Esperance, second in command of the regiment, told the historical officer that: "The fighting encountered by the battalion this day was as hard as any it had met to date. It accomplished much. A total of 224 prisoners were taken, in addition one company of the Paratroop Recce Regiment, believing themselves to be cut off, surrendered to 5th Guards Brigade, on the right of Le Régiment de la Chaudière. The regiment's casualties for the day were 15 ORs (other ranks) killed and three officers and 52 ORs wounded."

The North Shores' set-piece attack on Keppeln also succeeded. Initially the battalion was forced to the ground by intense mortar and machine-gun fire but the 1st Hussars rode to the rescue.

Lieutenant-Colonel F.E. White described what happened when brigade ordered his "C" Squadron to leave the QORs and come to the assistance of the North Shores: "C Squadron went directly to North Shore Regiment from QOR of Canada taking only time to refuel and load up with ammunition. The situation there was as follows. Two companies were dug in part way to Keppeln with their supporting carriers. Two reserve companies were on the startline awaiting orders to advance. About 10 enemy tanks had been seen going into Keppeln by the infantry. Between the startline and Keppeln was an open space of from 1,500 to 2,000 yards. It was decided that the tanks with PIAT (Projector, Infantry Anti-Tank) crews on their backs would make a quick dash for Keppeln. It was hoped that by speed a sufficient number of tanks and infantry would get into the town to effect its capture. A preparatory artillery concentration was put down on Keppeln; this caused six of the 10 tanks to withdraw. They did this, unknown to us, and repositioned themselves as we later discovered.

The casualties incurred in reaching Keppeln were the heaviest in the operation. Personnel casualties were about 30 per cent. Throughout the regiment, tank casualties for the day were 33; 14 were knocked out by gunfire, five on mines, and 14 were mired. On the credit side the regiment claimed to have knocked out four enemy tanks; the infantry claimed we got six in the capture of Keppeln alone. This cannot be determined as 4th Canadian Armoured Division was in the area and there had been an artillery concentration.

After the first tanks had reached the village, Lieutenant-Colonel J.H. Rowley ordered his North Shore reserve companies forward to clear the town. The battalion lost 28 killed and 62 wounded in the day's action. By late evening 8th Brigade was dug in. It had been one of the most difficult days the brigade had ever experienced and "Blockbuster" had just begun.

Wounded Canadian soldier being moved from a jeep-ambulance to regimental aid post in background. A German prisoner of war helps with the stretcher, March 8, 1945.

A Failure Of Command

Originally published, March/April 2003

"Blockbuster", one of the largest and most costly operations carried out by First Canadian Army during World War II, has always provoked bitter comments from veterans who served at the sharp end. Lieutenant-Colonel Denis Whitaker's battalion, the Royal Hamilton Light Infantry, fought a difficult battle in the heart of Germany's Hochwald Forest but as a historian he saved his hardest criticism for those who ordered 4th Canadian Armoured Division into the death trap at the Hochwald Gap.

Veterans of the regiments that fought there are unanimous in their condemnation of Major-General Chris Vokes and the "higher ups" who insisted on pressing a hopeless attack and then criticized combat soldiers for failing to overcome a determined enemy.

If we are to move beyond recriminations to an understanding of the events we need to remind ourselves that decisions were made on the basis of what was known at the time not on hindsight. For example, when the commander of 2nd Canadian Corps–Lieutenant-General Guy Simonds–made the decision to order 4th Canadian Armoured Division to move through the Hochwald Gap he did so because he believed that the first three phases of Operation "Blockbuster" had been a success. C.P. Stacey, the Canadian Army's official historian, later agreed with that assessment. He noted that as 4th Division concentrated to begin the final phase, "all across the battlefront piece after piece of the intricate puzzle fell into place as each formation, having completed its allotted task...moved on to a fresh assignment while a relieving force came up to take over the newly won ground."

Simonds and Stacey were surely right. The complex assault on the Calcar Ridge and the capture of Udem demonstrated both Simonds' skills as a general and the Canadian Army's ability to perform effectively in battle. So what went wrong in the final phase?

By 1944, the Americans, British and Canadians had developed a battle doctrine that suited their equipment, training and personnel. Objectives could always be taken and almost always held if the operation was built around an extensive, carefully prepared artillery program. The infantry, assisted if possible by tanks, would be "shot on" to the objective and protected from initial counterattacks. The position would be consolidated and new, and equally systematic bites could then be taken out of the enemy's defence until his position was untenable.

Unfortunately, many Allied generals found this method too slow, too simple, and too lacking in opportunities to demonstrate their skills as commanders. Often they were persuaded, or persuaded themselves, that German resistance was all but broken and so they ordered adventurous offensive operations. However, the nature of the war had changed drastically since the early stages and such attacks usually failed. Such failure was then attributed to the "lack of aggressiveness of the Allied infantry" or the "caution of the armoured units" instead of a failure of command.

Shortly before "Blockbuster", Vokes had lectured his division on the "tactics and thrust" he wanted them to employ and he was determined to organize a breakthrough: "This will be an all-out effort," he told them. "Strip to the absolute minimum of wheeled vehicles within units. The troops must be impressed with the vital necessity to get on and destroy the enemy. Subordinate commanders must act on their own initiative. Do not sit on the objective if you can press on. Be prepared to

go on hungry but make every effort to see adequate food is available. Tanks should try to carry extra to feed infantry. Every vehicle should contain rations and spare petrol. Tanks must be topped up in the Forming Up Place. Do not waste ammunition.

"The Boche is in a bad way as compared to ourselves and is fighting in sheer desperation. He gives up easily when cut off. This is our opportunity–we must make the best of it."

If Vokes allowed his optimism to get the better of his judgment, what about Guy Simonds, the cool, rational corps commander? What did he know on the night of February 26, 1945? For Operation "Blockbuster", 11th British Armoured Division was assigned to 2nd Canadian Corps. Its job was to provide flank support for 4th Canadian Division. However, Major-General "Pip" Roberts reported that his tanks had bogged down in the mud and were sitting ducks for enemy anti-tank guns.

On the other side of the gap, 5th Canadian Brigade was supposed to move through the Hochwald Forest and outflank enemy defences. However, it could not begin the advance until the next morning. But if 4th Division was to advance across open country, which was overlooked by higher ground in the gap, it could only be done at night. So the options were to delay everything for 24 hours or go ahead in the hope that speed and surprise would win the day. Simonds decided not to intervene and the operation went ahead.

Lion Force, made up of the Algonquins and South Albertas, began the advance at 7:20 p.m. However, blocked roads and wet muddy fields delayed everyone and the start line was not reached until 5 a.m. One South Alberta squadron, with the Algonquin carrier platoon, was sent off to carry out a "right hook" towards the railway embankment as a diversion to protect Lion Force. The balance of the small armour-infantry battlegroup moved up the slope at walking pace shielded by the darkness until the forward enemy lines were reached. By dawn, all that could be done was to dig-in and survive. The enemy, recognizing the gap was an obvious

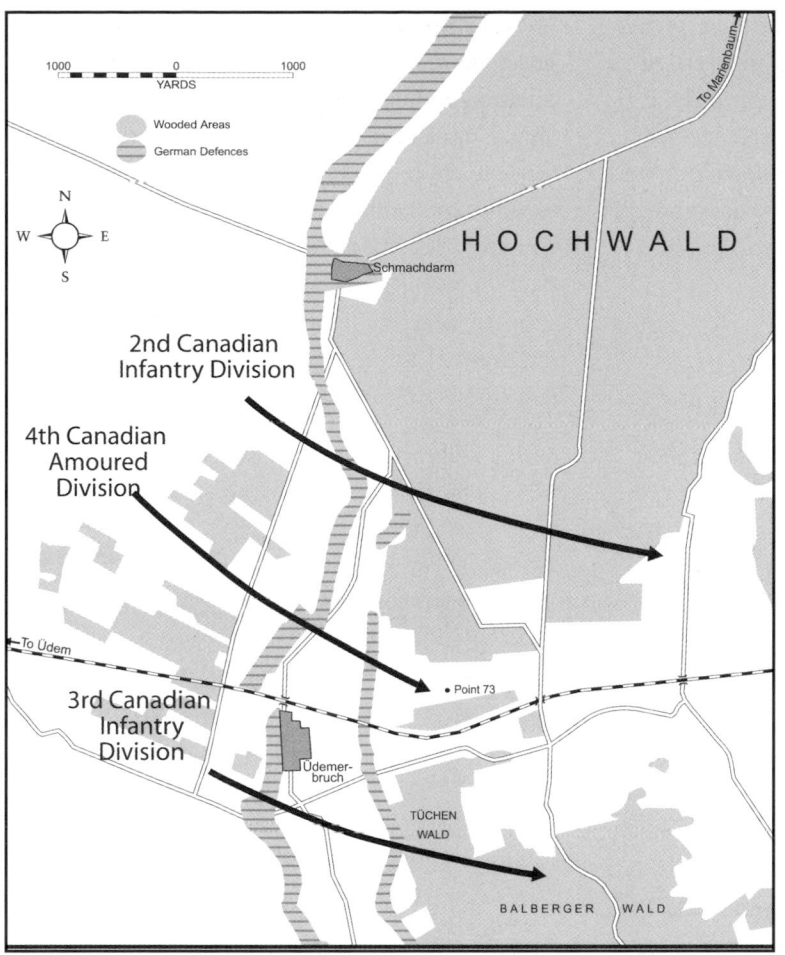

1000   0   1000
YARDS

Wooded Areas

German Defences

N
W — E
S

HOCHWALD

Schmachdarm

2nd Canadian
Infantry Division

4th Canadian
Amoured
Division

To Üdem

3rd Canadian
Infantry
Division

Üdemer-
bruch

• Point 73

TÜCHEN
WALD

BALBERGER   WALD

To Marienbaum

**The Hochwald
Gap.**

route of advance, had deployed three parachute battalions plus anti-tank guns to defend the area.

Lion Force could not possibly prevail against such odds and so what was Vokes to do? The options were clear: Withdraw what was left of Lion Force, regroup and mount a new co-ordinated attack or press on? Vokes decided to press on, ordering the Argyll and Sutherland Highlanders of Canada to push through the Algonquins into the gap.

Lieutenant-Colonel F.E. Wigle, who was appointed to replace the popular Lieutenant-Colonel Dave Stewart as the battalion's commanding officer, shared Vokes' optimism. He "did not anticipate a difficult fight" because the enemy had taken "a sound drubbing on the first day" and was surely withdrawing to the Rhine. Wigle soon learned he was wrong. The Argylls came under the heaviest fire experienced during the war and could do little except dig in behind the Algonquins. Vokes drew a different conclu-

sion sending his third infantry battalion, the Lincoln and Welland Regiment, into the inferno.

The Lincs were supposed to capture the railway crossing and clear the Tuschen Wald, but were stopped well short of their objective by a barrage of unbelievable intensity. Lieutenant-Colonel Rowan Coleman recalled that day in a 1984 interview: "I spent the whole morning there, where I could see what was happening. The Argylls had been pushed back and had withdrawn and this shell fire was coming down. I didn't move and I told the wireless operator that I was out to lunch if anybody called. I wasn't going to take any calls. This poor guy. He had a terrible time all morning answering calls and telling them that I wasn't available. They were coming from higher and higher authority.... He was only a few yards away from me. He said, 'Sir, I just have to tell you this.' He said, 'Super Colossal Sunray wants to talk to you.' So I said I guess I better answer that one.... It was Guy Simonds himself on the blower. I recognized the unmistakable English accent.... I remember being mildly amused and outraged at his breaking security. He said, 'Rowan...is there anything you can do down there?' I said, 'Well, I don't think so sir.' It was a stalemate for the time being. We were under murderous fire.... He said: 'You must do something to relieve the pressure down there.'"

Coleman, whose experience included a stint with Eighth Army in the desert and a year in Italy, was not going to allow his battalion to be destroyed. As it was, the Lincs took 49 casualties in a futile attempt to attack the enemy at its strongest point.

If 10th Brigade could not get forward it is not obvious why anyone thought the armoured brigade could, but orders were issued to send the Grenadier Guards and the British Columbia Regiment into the gap shortly before midnight. The War Diarist at 4th Armoured Brigade noted "the enemy guns took such a heavy toll that movement became impossible."

On the left or Rhine flank, Major-General Bruce Matthews was attempting to implement his orders to send 2nd Division through the forest. But 5th Brigade had run into strong resistance and he was required to send 6th Brigade to the gap to relieve the shattered infantry battalions of the armoured division so 4th Brigade was all that was available to try and break through the northern end of the Schlieffen line.

The Essex Scottish led this assault and during the course of its battle Major F.A. Tilston earned the Victoria Cross. The citation provides a detailed description of conditions on that desperate day that required so much of Tilston and his comrades: "At 0715 hours on 1st March, 1945, the attack was launched, but due to the softness of the ground it was found impossible to support that attack by tanks as had been planned.

"Across approximately 500 yards of flat open country, in face of intense enemy fire, Major Tilston personally led his company in the attack, keeping dangerously close to our own bursting shells in order to get the maximum cover from the barrage. Though wounded in the head he continued to lead his men forward, through a belt of wire 10 feet in depth, to the enemy trenches shouting orders and encouragement and using his Sten gun with great effect. When the platoon on the left came under heavy fire from an enemy machine-gun post he dashed forward personally and silenced it with a "Grenade"; he was first to reach the enemy position and took the first prisoner....

"As he approached the woods he was severely wounded in the hip and fell to the ground. Shouting to his men to carry on without him and urging them to get into the wood, he struggled to his feet and rejoined them as they reached the trenches on their objective.... Despite his wounds, Major Tilston's unyielding will to close with the enemy was a magnificent inspiration to his men as he led them in systematically clearing the trenches of the fiercely resisting enemy. In this fighting two German company headquarters were overrun and many casualties were inflicted on the fanatical defenders.

"Such had been the grimness of the fighting and so savage the enemy resistance that the company was now reduced to only 26 men, one quarter of its original strength. Before consolidation could be completed the enemy counterattacked repeatedly, supported by a hail of mortar and machine-gun fire from the open flank. Major Tilston moved in the open from platoon to platoon quickly organizing their defence and directing fire against the advancing enemy. The enemy attacks penetrated so close to the positions that grenade's were thrown into the trenches held by his troops, but this officer by personal contact, unshakeable confidence and unquenchable enthusiasm, so inspired his men that they held firm against great odds.

"When the supply of ammunition became a serious problem he repeatedly crossed the bullet-swept ground to the company on his right flank to carry grenades, rifle and Bren ammunition to his troops....

"On his last trip he was wounded for a third time, this time in the leg. He was found in a shell crater beside the road. Although very seriously wounded and barely conscious, he would not submit to medical attention until he had given complete instructions as to the defence plan, had emphasized the absolute necessity of holding the position, and had ordered his one remaining officer to take over...."

The Essex had suffered more than 100 casualties, and at the end of the day all that they could do was consolidate the position Tilston and his men had won.

South of the gap, 3rd Canadian Division entered the battle with 8th Brigade trying to clear the Balberger Wald and the high ground north of Sonsbeck. The Chaudières began this task in the evening of March 1 when they occupied the Tuschen Wald. They met only light resistance in occupying the woods, but when the heavy shelling started they were forced to withdraw and the next day a very difficult battle had to be fought to regain it. The QORs and North Shores followed through on March 2 and contact was made with 11th Armoured Division late that night. The next two days were spent in a cautious process of clearing the woods.

On March 2, 2nd Division renewed its attack when the Royal Hamilton Light Infantry pressed into the forest through the Essex Scottish position. Matthews and Brigadier F.N. Cabeldu were determined to work forward in controlled bounds, and the RHLI carefully bit off 500 yards the first day, with the Royal Regiment of Canada taking a further half mile on March 3.

Back in the gap no such caution was evident. The Lake Superior Regiment with "D" Company of the Algonquins and armoured squadrons from the Governor-General's Foot Guards and the Canadian Grenadier Guards were ordered to undertake Operation "Churchill", another night attack with Kangaroos carrying the infantry forward.

Everyone was desperately tired and when the Kangaroos were late in arriving, the commanding officer of the Lake Superiors, Lieutenant-Colonel R.A. Keane, asked brigade to postpone the operation "and give the lads a chance to rest." The Kangaroos did arrive, however, and the attack began just before first light. Major P.A. Mayer provided this description: "A terrific hail of anti-tank fire met the attacking force as it cleared the crest of the Hochwald Gap, and within a few minutes the whole area became a veritable hell."

Fortunately, the companies and squadrons had been greatly under strength for Operation "Churchill", so total casualties for March 3 were reported as "only" 19 killed, 71 wounded and 83 missing. Before another hasty operation could be mounted, the enemy withdrew to a new defensive line and Simonds ordered a pause to reorganize. The battle for the Hochwald and the infamous gap was finally over.

The battles for the Hochwald tell us much about the state of the Canadian Army in 1945. At the sharp end, battalion, company and platoon commanders possessed the skills and determination to overcome a desperate enemy, but they were not always well served by their senior commanders who sought "the bubble reputation" in their quest for a breakthrough.

The Battle For Xanten

Originally published, May/June 2003

Visitors who make the journey to the Canadian military cemetery at Groesbeek in the Netherlands seldom go on to explore the battlefields of the Rhineland. But those who do are invariably struck by the neat farmhouses, rolling fields and magnificent state forests that mark this prosperous agricultural region of Germany.

Cleve, the town that was virtually destroyed by bombing on the eve of Operation "Veritable", is a thriving modern city. Xanten, the last of the towns captured by the Canadians in March 1945, welcomes visitors to its Roman amphitheatre and archaeological sites. The war is a distant memory but in 2003 an exhibition of Canadian army photographs of the Xanten area during the war is on display thanks to the efforts of a young German historian, Ralph Trost.

Presenting the war to a new generation is always a sensitive matter. What should young German citizens or, for that matter, their Canadian counterparts learn about the events of March 1945? Photographs, personal accounts and statistics portray the horrors of war and remind us of why we work so hard to avoid conflicts. However, these are man-made events–not natural disasters–so we also need to explain why they occur.

The battle for Xanten was one small episode in a series of operations designed to bring the Allies to the banks of the Rhine River in preparation for the final assault on Hitler's Reich. We now know that the final victory was weeks rather than months away but neither the soldiers nor their commanders could imagine that the enemy forces who were fighting with such intensity were on the verge of collapse. The reality is that throughout the first months of 1945 the Allies feared the war in Europe might last until the end of the year, and they had good reason to believe that.

No one was more concerned about the direction of the war than British Prime Minister Winston Churchill. He had just returned from Greece–a country that was on the verge of civil war–and was determined to intervene and prevent a takeover by the communist resistence movement. However, he faced strong opposition from U.S. President Franklin D. Roosevelt and even protests from Canadian Prime Minister Mackenzie King.

Churchill was increasingly focusing on the state of postwar Europe and the future of the British Empire. In January he authorized the call-up of 250,000 men to add to the strength of the army. He urged Bomber Command and the 8th Air Force to plan a series of massive air raids on Berlin and other large cities in eastern Germany in the hope of breaking enemy morale and forcing an early surrender. The senior British and American air force officers agreed such raids should be carried out in addition to continuing attacks on oil and transportation targets. The cities of Chemnitz, Dresden and Leipzig were selected to share Berlin's fate.

Churchill also intervened in the strategic direction of the land war, urging Stalin to launch a winter offensive on the eastern front as soon as possible. Stalin replied that his armies would attack by mid-January "regardless of weather conditions." The first stage of that Soviet offensive began on January 12.

This was the strategic background to the events in February and March 1945 and those who are asked to learn about the war should have the opportunity to understand why the last months of the conflict brought such devastation to Germany and heavy casualties to the Allied forces.

Accounts of the attack on Dresden usually condemn the bombing and the firestorm that devoured the city partly because they believe the war was almost over. Yet the raid occurred on February 13, on the eve of the struggle for Moyland Wood, four long weeks before the capture of Xanten and the withdrawal of the last German soldiers to the east bank of the Rhine.

The continued bombing of the Ruhr and Rhineland cities was yet another price the German people paid for Hitler's decision to continue the struggle. Bombing and massive artillery barrages were a basic component of the Allied method of waging war. Shells and bombs were intended to save the lives of Allied soldiers and no responsible commander

LCMSDS

Xanten, March 1945. The Roman ampitheatre is visable in the bottom of the photograph.

would hesitate if bombing might force a surrender or reduce enemy resilience.

The set-piece attack on Xanten, which began early on the morning of March 8, was the last phase of an operation sometimes designated "Blockbuster" 2. It commenced when the enemy withdrew to hastily constructed defensive positions known as the Wesel Pocket. Field Marshal Bernard Montgomery, hoping to trap the remaining elements of the First Parachute Army on the west bank, wanted the U.S. Ninth Army to turn north along the Rhine and capture the Wesel bridges.

Montgomery made the decision because of "the hard and bitter fighting" in Germany's Hochwald area and the enemy's concentration of resources opposite the British and Canadians but he insisted new converging attacks from the north were also needed to support the American thrust.

For the Canadians this meant three separate assaults, one by each division. Third Division was ordered to clear the southern part of the state forest known as the Balberger Wald and then seize the town of Sonsbeck. They did so with their usual efficiency but at a cost of 279 additional casualties. Fourth Armoured Division formed three battle groups to fight its way forward to Veen. The last five days of the Rhineland battle cost the division 443 casualties so the order to move into reserve issued on March 10 came none too soon. "Blockbuster" was 4th Division's most costly battle of the war; by March 10 its combat elements had lost 60 per cent of their manpower.

Second Division was still bogged down in the northern part of the Hochwald, suffering close to 100 casualties a day from artillery and mortar fire bursting in trees when Major-General Bruce Matthews was told that his division was to attack Xanten as soon as it cleared the forest. Matthews, who had a lot of experience behind him, knew there was little point in protesting the order. Lieutenant-General Guy Simonds softened the blow by placing a brigade of 43rd Wessex Division under Matthews' command. The British division had been part of 2nd Canadian Corps throughout Operation "Blockbuster" but its role was limited to protecting the Rhine flank. Many Canadian soldiers believed that their division got

more than its share of tough assignments and so the decision to commit a British brigade to the battle for Xanten was good news.

Matthews made sure there was sufficient artillery available and provided each brigade with armoured support plus two squadrons of Crocodile flame-throwing tanks. Smoke was used to mask the advance from enemy observers on the east bank of the Rhine and aircraft from 84 Group began attacking prearranged targets. First Canadian Radar Battery moved its equipment into position to direct fire on enemy mortars.

All of this careful preparation was not enough to prevent the battle from deteriorating into a costly slugging match. The enemy, denied observation, saturated the approaches to Xanten with artillery fire. There was no shortage of shells for this desperate stand on German soil but the most serious obstacle confronting the British and Canadians was the continued willingness of the German generals to lead a pointless battle and the German soldiers to fight it.

The purpose of the defence of the Rhineland was to prevent the Allies from reaching the Ruhr, Germany's primary industrial zone. The Rhine and its canals were crucial to the transport of Ruhr coal, steel and heavy weaponry. Protecting the water route made sense if the war was to continue but when the U.S. Army gained the Rhine on March 4 there was no longer any point to defending a bridgehead on the west bank. To make matters worse for the Germans, U.S. First Army reached the river three days later and seized an intact railway bridge at Remagen.

Despite this, General Alfred Schlemm's orders were to hold the Wesel Pocket as long as possible and then destroy the remaining Rhine bridges in his sector. Special units were established to ensure that any dereliction of duty was punishable by death. Orders to fight to the end or face reprisals against their families had not prevented German soldiers from surrendering in other hopeless situations but the Wesel bridgehead was crawling with security troops and this may account for the determination of the defenders.

The plan called for 4th Brigade to attack through to the west side of the town while the 129th Brigade of the 43rd Wessex Division advanced down the

Marienbaum-Xanten road. The Essex Scottish and Royal Hamilton Light Infantry, RHLI, closely supported by the Sherbrooke Fusiliers and troops of flame-throwing Crocodiles, crossed the start line at 7 a.m. on March 8. The engineers provided smoke to deny the enemy observed fire, but the Germans had so much artillery available that they simply blasted away at an increased rate. The Essex Scottish, with 129th Brigade on their left, got on well but the RHLI found that their companies were cut off by enemy troops who had infiltrated from the open flank. The RHLI, with 34 casualties, accounted for almost half the division's toll at Xanten.

Brigadier F.N. Cabeldu committed his reserve battalion, the Royal Regiment, to assist the RHLI by pressing the attack into Xanten. Matthews ordered 5th Brigade forward to attack through the town to the high ground overlooking the body of water known as the Alter Rhein. Brigadier W.J. Megill persuaded Matthews to give him the South Saskatchewan Regiment so that the brigade could have "troops tight against Xanten Forest", thus protecting the flank.

The Régiment de Maisonneuve led off just before midnight. Carried forward in Kangaroos with Sherbrooke tanks and Flails in close support, the Maisonneuves were quickly on their objective. The Black Watch, on foot, passed through and were in control of Birten by 4 a.m. As daylight broke over the Rhine the shrinking Wesel Pocket still seemed to be strongly defended. Second Division's intelligence officer recorded this picture of the battle during the night March 8-9:

"The enemy's bridgehead on this side of the Rhine is steadily diminishing although no ground has been yielded willingly. Having moved their guns and heavy equipment across during the last few days, the enemy fights on stubbornly to hold the bridgehead as long as possible using infantry remnants and light weapons, and support by artillery from the East Bank. The railway bridge at Wesel is damaged but still capable of taking light single lane traffic; otherwise ferries are employed. The German reason for continued resistence is no longer logical since the need to cover the withdrawal of other troops has passed. Perhaps the stubborn resistance may be attributed to a desire to maintain prestige and to impose delay in order to prevent any further exploitation of our advance up the Rhine. However even the most desperate defence cannot postpone collapse for long, since the units in line are obviously inadequate to the task. It is estimated that the enemy has about 6,000 combat troops in the bridgehead...."

A report issued by the Supreme Headquarters, Allied Expeditionary Force echoed the same position: "By a flat refusal to admit defeat and by concentrating what remains of his resources on one front or the other Hitler may be able to prolong the struggle, but he cannot overcome the irrefutable fact that each day Germany's position deteriorates in relation to the power of the Allies....To add to the misery of the army (and the nation) the Allied air forces are crippling the ability of the Reich to move. Daily, evidence accumulates of the difficulties, almost unsurmountable, with which the enemy is faced in order to restore his vital communications. A great deal of hard fighting against an obstinate enemy still confronts us. Nevertheless, the enemy is most definitely showing signs of wear and tear which no patching can redress. Hitler and his gang are in a mess."

By the night of March 9-10, 2nd Division had taken more than 900 prisoners, including over 200 captured by the Maisonneuves. Lieutenant-Colonel J. Bibeau had learned from a prisoner that "some 300 enemy were forming up in nearby Birten Wood." Megill ordered an immediate assault with Crocodiles and regimental Wasp flame-throwers accompanying the armour and infantry. The woods were quickly captured.

The last battles of the bridgehead were fought by 52nd Lowland Division and a regiment of the U.S. 35th Division. The Germans completed their evacuation on the night of March 10-11 and blew the Wesel bridges as ordered. This minor triumph could not hide the fact that what had been saved in men and equipment was hardly enough to offer a serious defence of the river line. On March 11 Field Marshal Albert Kesselring, who had so successfully slowed the Allied advance in Italy, was placed in command of all German forces in the west. The task he faced on the Rhine would be a far different proposition.

The Rhine Crossing

Originally published, July/August 2003

The decision to destroy the German army west of the Rhine and then cross the river in a major operation north of the Ruhr River had been made in December 1944 before the Ardennes offensive. The Rhine crossing, code-named Operation "Plunder", was to be the major Allied effort to end the war by striking in a "single thrust" for Berlin. At the Malta Conference in early February 1945 the Supreme Allied Commander, General Dwight D. Eisenhower, revised this conception of the invasion of Germany with a plan that allowed for a second major Rhine crossing south of the Ruhr.

The British leaders protested that there was insufficient strength for two major operations. Since the British, especially Montgomery, were also still pressing for a single ground commander, it is possible to sympathize with the growing impatience of American battlefield commanders who could not understand why so much deference was paid to British views when they were able to supply less than one-quarter of the troops involved in the battle.

The Americans believed Montgomery had set up the northern crossing to give the glory of taking Berlin to the British Army. This skeptical view of Montgomery's motives was greatly reinforced when it was learned that he wanted to use U.S. divisions for the crossing, but under the command of British 2nd Army. Lieutenant-General Bill Simpson, the commander of 9th U.S. Army, and his corps commanders were flabbergasted by this proposal and even Montgomery realized he had gone too far. Instead, one U.S. corps of two divisions, operating under 9th U.S. Army's control, was to assault the river on D-Day. Despite this concession, 2nd Army was still to have control of the bridgehead until it was judged secure.

On March 7, while the battle for the Wesel Pocket raged, troops of the 1st U.S. Army seized the Rhine bridge at Remagen and quickly estab lished a substantial bridgehead on the east bank of the river. Since Montgomery did not plan to cross the Rhine until late March, the success of 1st U.S. Army presented the Allied command with a major dilemma. Both the army commander, General Courtney Hodges, and his superior, Omar Bradley, were reasonably confident that a breakout from Remagen could be staged whenever permission was granted. Eisenhower, perhaps fearing an even more serious row with the British, ignored intelligence estimates of German weakness and ordered Hodges to limit the bridgehead and use it as a device to draw German reserves away from the north.

First U.S. Army was certainly successful in this role because by March 23–the day of Operation "Plunder"–the Germans had moved most of their reserves opposite the Remagen bridgehead and had even attempted a counterattack. The next day, with the northern Rhine crossing safely launched, First U.S. Army was unleashed. In a matter of a few hours it had brushed aside the German defenders and was racing forward into Germany with three armoured divisions in the lead. General George S. Patton's 3rd U.S. Army also crossed the Rhine before March 24, but this was a deliberate demonstration of Patton's contempt for Montgomery's elaborate preparations. The Americans announced that the Rhine could be crossed at any point without the aid of preliminary bombardment–never mind with airborne divisions–and they released the news that they had done so "at a time calculated to take some of the lustre from the news of Montgomery's crossing." All of this, no doubt, sounds somewhat childish, but the image of feuding generals should not be allowed to obscure the fact that Hodges was right and that Eisenhower's decision to force his American armies to pause for two weeks so that Montgomery could complete preparations for a complex set-piece attack was a stiff price to pay for maintaining unity in coalition warfare. It was a price that he would not be willing to pay again in dealing with the British commanders.

NAC 145975

The 6th British Airborne Division including 1st Cdn Parachute Battalion arrives on the east bank of the Rhine.

Montgomery's plan for the Rhine called for a series of widely separated assault crossings of the river. First into battle was 51 Highland Division, which had been strengthened by the addition of the 9th Canadian Infantry Brigade. The Buffaloes once again proved their value and, with 150 available, Major-General Tom Rennie was able to lift four assault battalions and a bridgehead was quickly established. There were few casualties, but Rennie, who always worked well forward, was fatally wounded. 15 Scottish Division and 1 Commando Brigade were equally successful in the British sector and Ninth U.S. Army reported that its assault divisions, the 30th and 29th, got across with "minor casualties of 16 or 17 men killed per division."

Despite the evidence of minor German resistance, the airborne part of the crossing, Operation "Varsity", was not cancelled and the vast armada of aircraft appeared over the Rhine at 10 a.m. on the 24th. The paratroops of 6th British Airborne and 17th U.S. Airborne made their drop without undue casualties, but by 10:30 a.m., when the gliders of the air landing brigades were coming in, the German flak gunners had recovered and a terrible toll was exacted. On the ground the airborne troops were soon engulfed in the most difficult and costly part of the operation. Casualties were horrendous; the 6th Airborne lost 1,400 out of a landed strength of 7,220 and a quarter of the glider pilots were casualties. The paratroops of 17th Airborne were widely scattered and two-thirds of the gliders were hit by flak. Out of a force of 9,650 men, 1,300 were casualties. A daring re-supply mission, flown at low level by United States Army Air Force Liberators, dropped 600 tonnes of supplies to sustain the division, but at a cost of 16 bombers shot down.

The 6th British Airborne included 1st Canadian Parachute Battalion, which was dropped on the British front between Wesel and Rees. It was part of 3rd Parachute Brigade assigned to clear Diersfordt Woods. During the course of the battle, which cost the battalion 43 casualties, a medical orderly, Corporal F.G. Topham, earned the Victoria Cross. The citation reads in part: "Corporal Topham went forward through intense fire to replace the orderlies who had been killed before his eyes. As he worked on the wounded, he was himself shot through the nose. In spite of severe bleeding and intense pain, he never faltered in his task. Having completed immediate first aid he carried the wounded men steadily and slowly back through continuous fire...."

One of the fatal casualties was the commanding officer, Lieutenant-Colonel J.A. Nicklin; his brigadier, James Hill, paid this tribute to Nicklin and his men: "I thought you would not mind my writing to you directly to tell you what a very wonderful show the battalion has put up since our operations over the Rhine on March 24th last. They really put up a most tremendous performance on D-Day and as a result of their tremendous dash and enthusiasm they overcame their objectives, which were very sticky ones, with considerable ease, killing a very large number of Germans and capturing many others. Unfortunately, the price was high in that they lost their colonel, Jeff Nicklin, who was one of the best fellows that I have met, and was the ideal man to command that battalion as he fairly used to bang their heads together and they used to like it and accept it. He is and will be a tremendous loss to the battalion and of course to me. I only hope that the people back in Canada appreciate the really wonderful job of work he had done in producing his battalion at the starting line in such outstanding form."

While the airborne troops regrouped and completed their assignments, General Alfred Schlemm, who commanded Hitler's First Parachute Army, deployed his reserves. The 47th Panzer Corps, composed of 116th Panzer Division and 15th Panzer Grenadier Division had taken advantage of the two-week pause in Allied operations to move north into Holland. Here, safe from Allied air forces that were reluctant to bomb Dutch villages, they rested, re-equipped and absorbed reinforcements. Their determination to defend Germany was now stronger than ever. Schlemm waited until noon on the 24th to commit his reserves. He sent 116th Panzer south to slow the American advance and committed 15th Panzer Grenadier to the defence of the northern sector. Since 51st Highland Division was already engaged in a furious battle with two parachute divisions, expanding the bridgehead to the north and east was now bound to prove slow and costly. 9th Canadian Brigade, originally slated to lead the advance to Emmerich, joined the 154th Highland Brigade in close combat with a powerful enemy.

Historian Lee Windsor, who led our 2002 battlefield tour through the area, has closely studied the events of late March 1945 using both archival and interview sources. A PhD candidate at the University of New Brunswick and a specialist on the Italian campaign, Windsor became interested in the Rhine crossing after meeting Justice D.M. Dickson who commanded "D" Company of the North Nova Scotia Highlanders. Justice Dickson related the story of the battle for Bienen and recent efforts to erect a plaque commemorating the Canadian and German soldiers who were killed-in-action in the village on March 25, 1945.

Windsor argues that whatever the situation was elsewhere on the Rhine front, at Speldrop and Bienen the Canadians faced a well-entrenched enemy that equalled or outnumbered the Canadian and Scottish troops advancing towards them. When the Highland Light Infantry of Canada was ordered to clear Speldrop, it was warned that two platoons of a highland division Black Watch battalion were still holding out in the village resisting large-scale counterattacks.

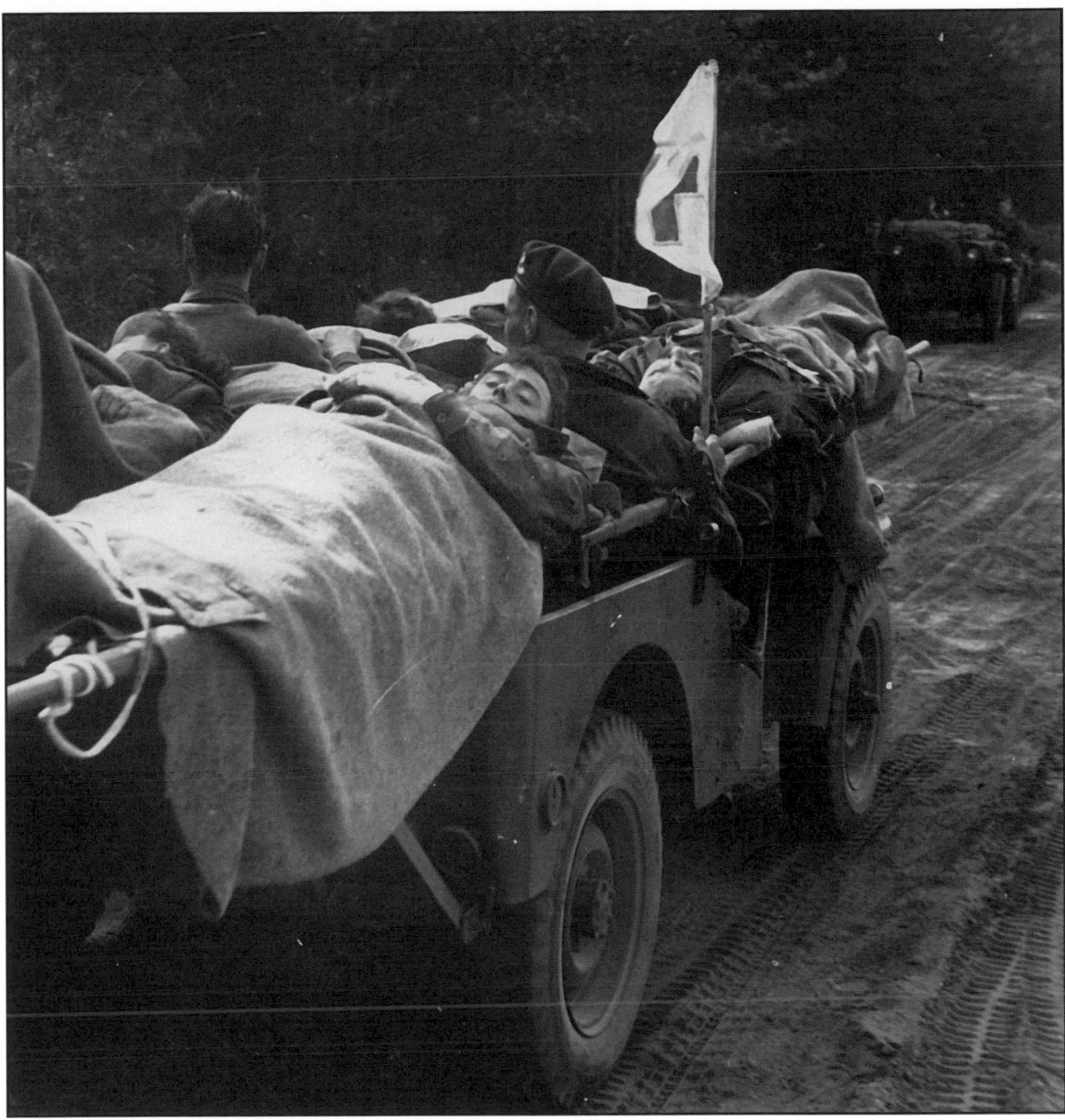

Evacuating
casulties from 6th
Airborne Division.

Lieutenant-Colonel P.W. Strickland could count on medium artillery to neutralize known enemy positions beyond the village. He could also count on the field artillery to keep heads down while his men crossed 1,000 metres of flat open ground. However, the village itself would have to be cleared house by house. Strickland decided to use just one company in the initial attack, seizing the northwest corner of Speldrop and trying to identify the Black Watch positions. Strickland, like other experienced battalion commanders, was convinced it was better to stage attacks across open country with fewer men, reducing the casualties sustained from both friendly and enemy fire. If one company–80

officers and men–could get onto a position and establish a firm base, the rest of the battalion could advance in stages with additional covering fire. This approach worked at Speldrop even though all three platoon commanders were hit. Sergeant Cornelius Reidel inspired a fixed-bayonet charge on enemy positions in an orchard and then led his men to the objective. The rest of the company joined Reidel, who turned over a number of prisoners and three 75-mm guns.

Getting to the edge of the village was one thing, clearing it was quite another. The enemy had moved a troop of assault guns into Speldrop to support the paratroopers so Major J.C. King called for battalion six-pounders and Wasp flamethrowers rather than more infantry. The Highland Light Infantry of Canada used this close support to storm the German position and secure the northern edge of the village. King's Distinguished Service Order and Reidel's Military Medal were two of seven gallantry medals awarded to the HLI in the first two days of combat.

While the HLI fought to clear Speldrop, the Stormont, Dundas and Glengarry Highlanders–the Glens–and the North Nova Scotia Highlanders–the North Novas–bypassed the village moving north towards Bienen where another highland division battalion, the 7th Argylls, was waiting for relief. The Argylls had seized a group of farm buildings 300 metres from the village but could go no further. Lieutenant-Colonel Don Forbes took one look at the terrain and decided to be cautious. He sent Major Don Learment's "A" Company forward to Argyll Farm to secure the start line for an attack on the village. Learment, who had led the North Nova vanguard on June 7, was captured and then escaped from his German captors, took his men single-file along the side of a dike to Argyll Farm. Unfortunately, the 15th Panzer Grenadier Division had arrived to block the advance and when the North Novas attacked the village of Bienen, they had to fight for every house, losing 114 men, including 43 killed. The initial advance had been supported by heavy artillery fire, including a liberal use of smoke, but the companies were brought under heavy enemy fire before the barrage started and the advance took place under conditions of growing confusion. Brigadier J.M. Rockingham ordered a withdrawal and directed the battalion to "start from scratch and do the attack over again, using the two remaining companies."

The second North Nova attack managed to secure the southern half of the village. This was not Rockingham at his best for he had seriously underestimated the extent of German strength. That night, after a 3rd Anti-tank Regiment battery of self-propelled Valentine 17-pounders had beaten off an armoured counterattack, the HLI advanced through the North Novas to complete the capture of the village.

The battles fought by Scottish and Canadian troops in the Rhine crossing were as difficult and costly as any in the experience of the two veteran divisions. The decision to stop and organize a set-piece attack instead of bouncing the Rhine allowed Montgomery time to build up resources so that his armies could race to Berlin once the bridgehead battle was won. This reasoned though debatable command decision placed an enormous burden on the infantry and airborne battalions used to attack an enemy that had ample time to create and camouflage strong defensive positions.

Ironically, Montgomery's plans for a rapid thrust to Berlin were frustrated when Eisenhower decided to advance through the centre of Germany to meet the Soviet armies at the Elbe River. British protests were to no avail. Berlin, already under attack from the east, was well within the Soviet zone of occupation and Eisenhower had no intention of sacrificing men for such an objective.

There were other reasons for Eisenhower's decision, including the growing antagonism of American senior officers towards Montgomery and his methods. Bradley and Patton had long challenged the priority assigned to Montgomery's operations and when the Ninth U.S. Army commander added his voice to the protests, Eisenhower decided to reunite Ninth U.S. Army with Bradley's Army Group. Montgomery, with his British and Canadian armies, were to clear Holland and northern Germany and protect the American flank, a very different task than the thrust to Berlin Montgomery had proposed.

Winning With Reinforcements

Originally published, September/October 2003

This instalment of "Canadian Military History In Perspective" was written in June 2003 just after I received an advance copy of my new book, *Fields of Fire: The Canadians in Normandy*. Regular readers of this series will not be surprised to learn that the book pays tribute to the achievements of the Canadian army and establishes a new balance sheet in which success greatly outweighs failure. The destruction of two German armies in Normandy in just 76 days was one of the greatest victories in the campaign to liberate Europe and the Canadians played a role that was all out of proportion to their numbers.

The same argument can be made for the battle of the Rhineland and for many aspects of the fighting east of the Rhine River in 1945. After 9th Infantry Brigade's struggle to subdue the enemy at Speldrop and Bienen, 7th Infantry Brigade, now commanded by Brigadier T.G. Gibson, was ordered to expand the bridgehead to the north, including the town of Emmerich. Eighth Infantry Brigade would then pass through, seizing the high ground at Hoch Elten. All three brigades were part of 3rd Canadian Infantry Division.

Hoch Elten overlooked the river where Canadian engineers were constructing Blackfriars Bridge, the longest Bailey bridge of the war, measuring 1,814 feet in length.

The Royal Canadian Engineers reported that "work started on 26 March and was complete at noon on 28 March. The construction was done by 29, 30 and 31 Field companies RCE.... The sappers and (British) pioneers toiled by night as well as day using artificial moonlight...when fog set in the searchlight was moved to the bridge and its beam aimed directly along the structure."

Blackfriars Bridge was built by Canadian engineers but it was to be used to support Field Marshal Bernard Montgomery's main thrust to the east. The Canadian advance into Holland required the RCE to build three new bridges, but first there was the matter of Emmerich, a large town, defended by battle groups from Hitler's 6th Parachute and 346th Infantry divisions supported by tanks and self-propelled assault guns. The Sherman tanks of the Sherbrooke Fusiliers, Royal Canadian Artillery anti-tank guns and a squadron of British tanks armed with flamethrowers–the Fife and Forfar Yeomanry–were placed under Gibson's command. As always, the machine-guns and heavy mortars of the Cameron Highlanders of Ottawa were in support, but it was up to the infantry to close with and root out the enemy defending the ruins that were once a town of 16,000 people.

On March 28, Gibson sent the Canadian Scottish Regiment down the main road while the Regina Rifle Regiment advanced along the river.

Historian Reg Roy, who wrote the history of the Canadian Scottish Regiment, described the situation confronting the battalion: "Between the Rhine and the trunk railroad...is a fair-size open field which slopes...up towards the oil refineries, slaughterhouses and other industrial plants in the Emmerich suburbs...only a rubble pile of wrecked buildings remained."

Reports from Dutch civilians suggested the enemy was withdrawing and the lead company decided to cross the Landwehr canal in the city centre on an improvised footbridge, without waiting for the engineers to bridge the obstacle. The Canadian Scottish knew their job and fanned out working their way up the slope. Machine-gun fire forced them to the ground and Major H.F. Bailey sent one of his platoons right, flanking along the railway line. The platoon was soon pinned down and it became clear that the enemy, far from withdrawing, held the town in strength. Well directed German artillery fire prevented the engineers from bridging the canal so the Canadian armour had to stay well back. Lieutenant-Colonel L.S. Henderson decided to expand the battalion bridgehead and borrow "D" Company of the Reginas to help out. After a night "marked by alternate periods of stealthy approaches and sharp, savage firefights" the industrial area was secure and the canal bridged.

The extent of German resistence forced 7th Brigade to pause and allow the armour time to marry-up with the infantry. The Reginas launched the second phase of the attack with the Sherbrookes and tanks with flamethrowers in close support. The battalion broke into the southern sector of Emmerich, but progress was slow. Lieutenant Walter Keith, who commanded the Reginas' 16 Platoon recalls the frustration of a 3rd Anti-Tank Regiment officer who was unable to bring his 17-pounder guns into action because the enemy had blocked the streets with "rubble-filled railway cars."

While the Regina Rifles fought its way into the city, the Canscots staged a two-company attack to clear the area north of the railway line. With adequate time for reconnaissance and a good view of the battlefield for the artillery observer, the attack resembled an exercise. The Royal Winnipeg Rifles then captured the nearby village of Leegmeer and moved west to clear a large wood. The Winnipeg thrust threatened to cut off the forces defending Emmerich and the Germans responded with a wave of counterattacks on both prairie battalions.

The Reginas in the heart of the ruined city had to improvise street-fighting tactics using PIATs (Projector, Infantry, Anti-Tank), six-pounders and flamethrowers to repel the enemy. The Winnipegs dealt with several platoon-sized attacks, one of which began with the enemy "coming at them singing." The German soldier must have known defeat was now certain, but if he was desperate he was still deadly.

LCMSDS

Young Canadians in Germany 1945.

By midday on March 30 most of Emmerich was in Canadian hands. Seventh Brigade was told to secure a start line for 8th Brigade and then go into reserve. The key to a secure start line was a large cement factory on the western edge of the town and the task of taking it was given to the weary Canscots. Reg Roy, who interviewed veterans of the battle, offered this description of the last attack: "Under ordinary circumstances a tank would be driven over tangled telephone wires, broken telephone poles, mounds of brick, rubble and woodwork strewn in the street, past burnt cars, over shell holes.... But Emmerich had been more than battered about. It had been blasted time and time again.... As the Canadian Scottish fought their way forward...the armour could not follow. It was a job for the bayonet and the grenade with sections and platoons covered by machine-guns leap-frogging one another.... The western outskirts of Emmerich were cleared in this fashion by nightfall on March 30." The brigade suffered 172 casualties, including 44 killed or died of wounds in this forgotten three-day battle.

Once past Emmerich there was room to deploy two brigades and their advance was assisted by the arrival of 2nd Division moving on a parallel course into Holland. At noon on March 31, Canadian engineers began construction of Melville Bridge, named after the chief engineer of First Canadian Army, Brigadier J.L. Melville. Measuring 1,373 feet in length, the Bailey bridge was opened to traffic the next morning. Two other bridges soon followed, guaranteeing adequate logistical support for Canadian operations in the Netherlands.

The Canadian victory in the Rhine bridgehead was a remarkable achievement given the strength of the German forces defending the northern flank. Two Canadian brigades fought the equivalent of three German regiments, inflicted heavy losses and forced their withdrawal. The artillery and tactical air force played a vital role in the success of both 9th and 7th brigades, but victory was primarily won by infantry using their own weapons to close with and destroy the enemy.

By early 1945 most battalions had suffered close to 1,000 casualties, more than 100 per cent of their original strength. And so these battles were largely fought by replacements, including conscripts recently arrived from Canada. The western regiments in 7th Brigade had lost 485 men—one third of their rifle company strength—at Moyland Wood in February. By early March, hundreds of new reinforcements had joined the brigade.

Officer and non-commissioned officer casualties had been especially high and most of the original platoon and company commanders had been replaced. Senior leadership had also changed. Gibson was the third officer to command the brigade and all three battalion commanding officers had been appointed after the Battle of the Scheldt during October and November 1944.

Battalion and company commanders had proved themselves in combat and been promoted, but most lieutenants and riflemen came directly from the reinforcement pool. How were those men able to fight so effectively at the Rhine?

When J.L. Ralston, the minister of National Defence, visited front-line units in Italy and Northwest Europe in the fall of 1944, he was told that "the reinforcements received now were green, inexperienced and poorly trained" causing "large numbers of unnecessary casualties...both to the rookie and to older soldiers who have the added task of trying to look after the newcomers." The "green" reinforcements, who had been re-mustered from other branches of the army because of heavy infantry casualties, were singled out for criticism.

Apart from anecdotal evidence we have very little information on the quality of conversion training or the performance of officers and men transferred to the infantry. In November 1944, the Black Watch surveyed the replacements who arrived after the costly battles of October and reported that some had less than a month's infantry training. But many of the officers and men who fought with success in October were themselves reinforcements who joined the Black Watch after Normandy. Combat veterans always complain that the reinforcements are poorly trained and not up to the standards of the unit. After a few weeks in action the newcomers became veterans ready to criticize the next draft of inexperienced kids.

The same problem arises when we attempt to generalize about the 2,463 conscripts who reached field units in 1945. University of Alberta historian Dan Byers, who has studied most aspects of the conscript question, agrees it is difficult to assess their performance since the army did its best to "place them in the reinforcement stream as individuals mixing them throughout the army." What we do know is they had much more extensive training than re-mustered soldiers and proved to be at least the equal of other reinforcements. Byers adds,

"In the end a total of 9,667 NRMA (National Resources Mobilization Act) men reached the front as conscripts...of that number 2,463 saw duty in operational units, 69 were killed, 232 wounded and 13 taken prisoner." Without them many battalions would have been short of men in the last phase of the war.

The evidence from the battlefield suggests the combination of experienced company commanders and non-commissioned officers working with young reinforcements was effective. When the Regina Rifles absorbed more than 100 replacements after Moyland Wood the newcomers included Lieutenant Walter Keith who joined the army in 1941 and served overseas as signal corps officer. After volunteering to transfer to the infantry he attended a six-week junior leaders course and on March 7, 1945, joined the Regina "Johns" in the Rhineland. Keith's memoir, written for Gordon Brown and Terry Copp's book, Look To Your Front...Regina Rifles, relates how he was given command of 16 Platoon, Dog Company, commanded by Gordon Brown and the second in command, Captain Dick Roberts. Brown and Roberts were an outstanding team with experience dating back to D-Day in June 1944, and they did their best to prepare Keith and the other replacements for combat.

On March 8, 1945, Keith's platoon numbered 32 men. Just two, including Sergeant R.S. Tomlison, had fought in Normandy. Two others had been at the Leopold Canal and two more at Moyland Wood for a total of six combat veterans. Keith soon learned that one of the six had been at it too long, but he had hid his fear and was killed-in-action at Emmerich.

The rest of the platoon had joined the Reginas about the same time as Keith so Emmerich was their first battle. "They ranged in age from 19 to 35 but most were in their early 20s," recalled Keith. "Most (19) were from Saskatchewan.... All but one were single.... The veteran section leaders included Homer Adams, a First Nations volunteer who had won the Military Medal at the Leopold Canal, Anatole Turcotte a D-Day

veteran who always refused promotion and Chris Vogt, a Saskatchewan farm boy who had distinguished himself at Moyland Wood."

Keith recalled that he never once had to "cajole or threaten or even encourage them to do the job they were given. The section commanders unhesitatingly led their small group of riflemen where they were told to go and the section followed.... The two-inch mortar men...sited their weapon and delivered bombs where they were needed with no detailed orders from anyone and their accuracy was amazing.... They had a job to do and they did it."

Before he joined, Keith imagined an infantry battalion would be "full of swashbuckling, macho, tough, big fighting men of the Hollywood type. Rather they were mostly fairly small, very young, very quiet and most unwarrior-like."

Keith's memoir describes the small world of the infantry platoon. "We knew nor cared about very little beyond the rifle section or in my case the platoon. In or out of battle we saw only the men in the platoon. (Sergeant) Tommy Tomlison and I occasionally went to company HQ (headquarters) and from time to time we were close to the rest of the company but for the most part the platoon or section was our world and the guys became really close."

In the Rhine bridgehead these young, quiet soldiers and their counterparts in other Canadian and British battalions went about doing their job with enough skill and determination to overcome an enemy still capable of organized resistance. Re-mustered soldiers, conscripts, young volunteers–men who had just turned 19–plus a smattering of veterans did what they had to do: they crossed the Rhine, won the bridgehead and spearheaded the liberation of Holland. Those who gave their lives lie in the Canadian military cemeteries at Groesbeek and Holten where the people of the Netherlands do their best to keep the memory alive.

The Cruelest Month

Originally published, November/December 2003

Canadian military historians have generally paid slight attention to the operations carried out by First Canadian Army in April 1945. It is almost as if the great battles of February and March in the Rhineland exhausted the historians just as they wore down the men who fought there in 1945. April is instead remembered as the month of the liberation of Holland, "the sweetest of springs." But April was also the cruelest month, for if the war was all but won, the killing did not stop. The military cemeteries in Holland contain the graves of 1,191 Canadian soldiers killed in April and 114 who lost their lives during the last five days of the war in May. Their story and the record of the reunited 1st Canadian Army are well worth examining.

On March 27, Field Marshal Bernard Montgomery issued a new directive that began with the words "We have won the battle of the Rhine." Montgomery proceeded to outline his plans for the final phase of the war which focused on operations aimed at Northern Germany and Berlin. Supreme Allied Commander Dwight D. Eisenhower's negative response to this directive created one of the great controversies of the war, which we will examine in a future article, but for the moment we can explore the consequences of the one strategic issue that Ike and Monty agreed upon–Canadian operations to liberate the western Netherlands and establish a supply route through Arnhem and Apeldoorn to support Second British Army's advance into Germany.

Lieutenant-General Charles Foulkes's First Canadian Corps, newly arrived from Italy, took over control of the Nijmegen bridgehead, with 49th British Division under command, on March 15. The Yorkshiremen of the West Riding Division had served in 1st Canadian Army since the previous August and there were no difficulties with the new arrangement. Foulkes accepted the plans prepared by the British division for an attack on the German positions south of the Rhine River and 5th Canadian Armoured Division supported the British advance, forcing the Germans to retreat to the north bank of the river.

The army commander, General Harry Crerar, decided to delay a direct attack on Arnhem until the city and its defenders were cut off by an advance across the Ijssel River to Apeldoorn. This in turn depended upon the success of 3rd Canadian Division in clearing the east bank of the river and the cities of Zutphen and Deventer. As the Canadians prepared for these operations they were confronted with a new set of problems. Reports from the old provinces of Holland, including the cities of Amsterdam and Rotterdam, indicated that the terrible conditions of the "hunger winter" were continuing and the people of western Holland were facing starvation. The Nazi governor, Seyss Inquart, who had deliberately created the food shortage in retaliation for the actions of the Dutch resistance, now threatened to flood much of Holland as a defensive measure. If military action was the answer, all possible speed was required.

First Division, waiting in the Rhineland, was placed under the command of Guy Simonds's 2nd Canadian Corps. Formation patches and divisional signs were removed and the division was brought north to woods in the vicinity of Gorssel while 3rd Division captured Zutphen. Major-General Harry Foster held his "O" group on April 10 and outlined the plan for the first phase of Operation "Cannonshot". Foster selected 2nd Canadian Infantry Brigade, (The Princess Patricia's Canadian Light Infantry, The Seaforth Highlanders of Canada, The Loyal Edmonton Regiment) to make the assault crossing of the Ijssel River.

Each brigade in 1st Division had one battalion from a Permanent Force regiment and two militia battalions. This distinction had been of some importance during training in England but by 1945 very few officers and non-commissioned officers who served in the early years of the war were still around and the battalions were staffed with the products of Brockville and other officer training schools, while many senior NCOs were former privates. This citizen army had acquired a high degree of professionalism, particularly at the staff level and in the supporting arms. Infantry rifle companies suffered such high casualties that the ever-changing mix of officers and NCOs makes generalization about comparative combat effectiveness impossible. A battalion that distinguished itself in 1944 might still carry the same proud name in 1945 but it was made of different men. Sydney Frost, a captain in the Patricias during Operation "Cannonshot", noted that just two officers who had landed with the Patricias in Sicily were still with the battalion in April 1945. Despite the turnover regimental traditions and reputations lived on.

The 2nd Canadian Infantry Brigade had long been considered the outstanding brigade in the Canadian army. During his famous 1942 inspection, Montgomery, who was unimpressed with then divisional commander George Pearkes and most other senior Canadian officers, declared that the 2nd could be the best brigade in all the Commonwealth armies. "The PPCLI," he wrote, "have the best officers, the Seaforths the best NCOs and the Edmontons the best men." After Sicily and Ortona and the promotion of brigadier-generals Chris Vokes and Bert Hoffmeister to divisional commands, the reputation of the 2nd Brigade was set for all time. One result was that it got more than its share of high profile operations.

Brigadier-General M.P. Bogert, a veteran of the Italian Campaign, was now in command and he planned the assault crossing within the framework of a corps artillery plan. The battalions were introduced to the Buffalo, a Landing Vehicle Tracked, which could enter and leave the water on most gradients while providing 30 men with protection from small arms fire. The corps plan called for an elaborate "smoke box" created by smoke generators and concentrations of medium and heavy artillery on prearranged targets with virtually unlimited artillery on call

down to company level. Medium bombers were to hit on prearranged targets and Typhoon aircraft were on call. This was war in a new style for those who had fought in Italy.

In his memoirs, *Once A Patricia*, Syd Frost writes: "The more I saw of the orderly, deliberate way the Canadian Army (in Northwest Europe) went about its tasks, the more I liked doing business with them."

Operation "Cannonshot", after a delay of 24 hours was launched at 3:30 p.m. on April 11. The enemy appeared to be totally surprised. Apparently ignorant of 1st Division's presence they assumed that the attack would come from 3rd Division's at Deventer. The initial opposition came from small German battle groups built around one or two self-propelled guns. The Seaforths and PPCLI used their PIAT (Projector, Infantry, Anti-Tank) guns until the first anti-tank guns got across the river. By 9 p.m. the bridgehead was "snug". German reserves reached the area at midnight and in accordance withtheir doctrine counterattacked immediately.

Military historians have long argued that the German army was particularly effective on the battlefields of World War II because of its training and commitment to mission tactics. The German army's *Instructions On The Command of Troops* insisted that "decisive action remains the prerequisite for success in war. Everybody from the highest commander to the youngest soldier must be conscious of the fact that inactivity and lost opportunities weigh heavier than do errors in the choice of means." In other words, if in doubt, attack. Perhaps this doctrine has merits in the abstract but the Allies had long since learned that German battlefield behaviour was amazingly predictable. That is why competent Allied commanders insisted on digging-in after an assault rather than exploiting their initial success. Why, they reasoned, risk an encounter battle when the enemy will come to you allowing your artillery, mortars and machine-guns to destroy them with observed fire?

This is precisely what happened in the Ijssel bridgehead. The Seaforths and PPCLI repulsed

NAC 4191310

Dutch children greeting Canadian troops, April 1945.

hastily mounted counterattacks, taking more than 200 prisoners and inflicting heavy casualties. The Loyal Eddies joined them, and by dawn the engineers had a bridge in place and the tanks of the First Hussars were across in preparation for the next phase.

The plan now called for Brigadier-General J.D.B. Smith's 1st Canadian Infantry Brigade (Royal Canadian Regiment, 48th Highlanders, Hastings and Prince Edward Regiment) to advance east along the axis of the Apeldoorn-Deventer railway to the airfield at Teague while Brigadier-General J.P.E. Bernatchez's 3rd Canadian Infantry Brigade (Royal 22nd Regiment, Carleton and York Regiment and West Nova Scotia Regiment) was directed south of Apeldoorn to prepare an assault crossing of the canal in the event 1st Brigade ran into difficulty.

With the 48th Highlanders leading, 1st Brigade moved swiftly west. Resistance was spotty but one burst of shell fire struck the command group killing Lieutenant-Colonel D.A. Mackenzie, the Highlanders, commanding officer. The RCRs

(Lieutenant-Colonel D.A. Reid) with C Squadron of the First Hussars took over the lead and by noon on the 13th were less than one mile from Apeldoorn. The plan to pause at the airfield and prepare a co-ordinated attack across the Apeldoorn canal north of the city was abandoned when the Dutch resistance reported that the main road bridge over the canal, in the heart of the city, was intact. At first light on the 14th the RCR-Hussar battle group fought its way toward the bridge which turned out to be well protected by anti-tank guns. The Hussars lost two tanks, including one which tried to smash through a road block. North of the city the bridges were blown and patrols from the Hasty Ps established that the canal was strongly defended.

To the south, 3rd Brigade was held up by a strong enemy position until Bernatchez ordered the lead battalions to bypass the resistance and head for the canal. The Royal 22nd Regiment, as the reserve battalion, was ordered to deal with the enemy and did so by assaulting the woods from the rear. It then joined its sister battalions along the canal two kilometres south of Apeldoorn. It was now the evening of April 15. Operation "Cannonshot", which had begun with such great promise four days earlier, was in danger of deteriorating into a series of costly piecemeal attacks.

Major-General Harry Foster did nothing to help the situation when he ordered 1st Brigade to continue operations to attack across the canal in the centre of Apeldoorn. To the north and south of the city the enemy had created a thin crust of defences based on the western bank of the canal. A set-piece attack with the kind of assets used in the crossing of the much wider Ijssel would bring certain success and force the enemy to abandon the city or risk encirclement. Fighting to clear city streets in a town full of friendly civilians and refugees was not a brilliant idea. No one could use tactical air or serious artillery fire against a Dutch city, so the infantry and tanks would have to do it one house at a time.

The RCRs and 48th Highlanders went about their task carefully. With the BBC reporting that the Red Army was in the suburbs of Berlin and the Germans seeking a truce in western Holland, no one wanted to take unnecessary casualties in what appeared to be the last days of the war. The attack quickly turned into a stalemate. The forward companies were "pinned down by arty, mortar and machine-gun fire" and the supporting tanks were bogged down trying an indirect approach to the canal. A request for Crocodiles to flame the basements of houses along the canal was refused, as none were immediately available.

The best solution seemed to be an assault crossing of the canal south of the city by 3rd Brigade. Bernatchez was warned to plan such an attack but as divisional engineers and artillery prepared to provide support the situation suddenly changed. The army commander wanted bridges across the river at Zutphen, and ordered 2nd Brigade south. The Germans had abandoned the area because 5th Canadian Armoured Division had entered Arnhem and turned east, threatening to cut off the enemy. This manoeuvre allowed 2nd Brigade to do an unopposed crossing of the

Apeldoorn canal and then advance north, turning the enemy positions in front of 3rd Brigade The Germans withdrew as fast as they could run, abandoning equipment and the city of Apeldoorn. Syd Frost recalls that, "The War Diarist of the Loyal Edmonton Regiment could not restrain his envy of the staff cars, vehicles, household wares, food and other loot left behind by the Germans for the Patricias: 'the PPCLI had been busy on our night capturing hundreds of wandering enemy with so much loot that most of the Patricias were offering to resign their positions as privates ad go home to live in a manner befitting their status as millionaires.'" RCR patrols reported the enemy was gone and on April 17 the regiment was in the centre of the city. The joy of the Dutch population knew no bounds. It had appeared as if their garden city was to become a battleground and now almost miraculously the fighting had ended. Canadian veterans who return to Apeldoorn for the anniversaries of the liberation know that memories of 1945 are still warm.

First Division suffered 506 casualties, more than 100 of them fatal, in the six days of Operation "Cannonshot". Most of 1st Brigade's 184 losses came in the fighting for Apeldoorn, a battle which was allowed to continue despite previous experience with the costs of clearing urban areas.

The contrast between the first phase of "Cannonshot" with its careful preparation and full use of the army's skills and resources and the improvised operation in the suburbs of Apeldoorn needs to be underlined.

Granting subordinate commanders wide latitude to devise and carry out their own measures within the overall framework of the commanders intention has enormous appeal for professional soldiers and military theorists, but the experience of both the German and Allied armies in Northwest Europe suggests that success in battle was almost always due to the co-ordinated application of overwhelming force requiring the exercise of command and control at the most senior levels. Operation "Cannonshot" was no exception.

The Spring Of Liberation

Originally published, April 1995

On military terms April was a month of anticlimax. Fourth Armoured Division was involved in a difficult fight at the Twente Canal near Delden on April 2, but 12 days later armoured spearheads reached the

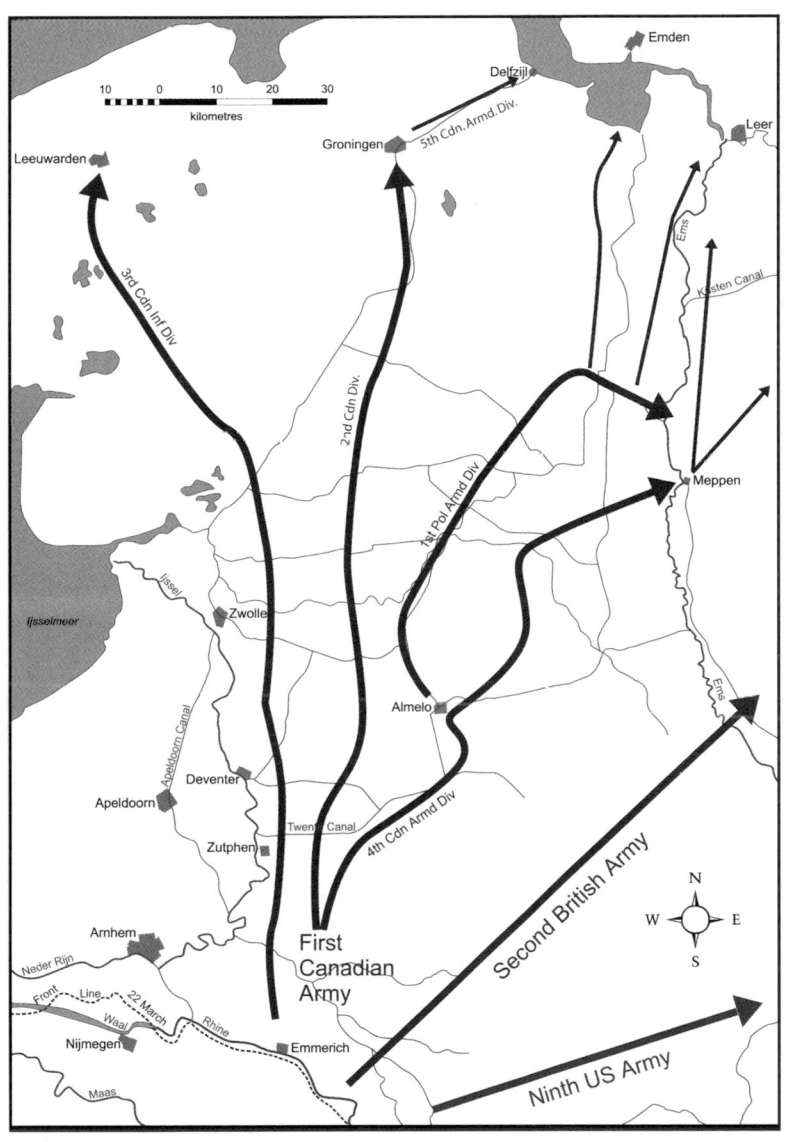

Northern Holland, March 23 to April 22, 1945

Kusten Canal 100 miles inside Germany. On April 13, 2nd Division was on the outskirts of Groningen. Three days later 3rd Division reached the North Sea. In western Holland 1st Canadian Corps, which had arrived from the Mediterranean via Marseilles and the Rhone Valley, began operations on April 11. The veterans of the Italian

campaign fought some tough minor engagements, but famine conditions in occupied Holland required a truce and the halt order was issued on April 19.

If the story of Canadian actions in April contains no great decisive battles, it does include a potent mixture of triumph and tragedy. Fatal casualties are often the best measure of the intensity of combat. For Canadian soldiers in Northwest Europe the worst days during the last year of the war had been June 6, 1944, with 359 fatalities; July 8, 262; July 25, 344; August 8, 290; August 14, 261; and February 26, 1945, 214. On 16 other days, many of them in October 1944, fatalities exceeded 100 men. The last such 100-fatality day was March 10,1945 at Xanten and Veen. In April 1945 more than 50 soldiers were killed on each of seven days; 114 more were killed between May 1 and the surrender on May 5, including 12 on the last day of fighting in Europe.

The Allied air forces also suffered grievous losses. Bomber Command attacked oil targets, U-boat construction and the German navy, while providing direct support to the army. Casualties were not large as a percentage, but each loss was deeply felt. The valour and endurance of bomber crews never ceases to amaze. Flying Officer D.M. Payne was hit in the legs and an arm while flying over Kiel. His Lancaster was struck by heavy flak, but he piloted the plane away from danger and crash-landed in the North Sea. The survivors huddled in a raft for 12 days before reaching land in Germany where they were taken prisoner during the last days of the war in Europe.

Tactical air force pilots flew close support missions from airfields in Germany. Attacks against enemy transport and gun positions helped ease the army's path, but flak was intense and losses continued to the last day of fighting. U-boats continued to seek out targets and HMCS *Esquimalt* was torpedoed and sunk in the approaches to Halifax on April 16. Most of the crew escaped, but 39 men perished from exposure before help arrived. Even the German surrender did not end the losses. One of the new type XXIII subs failed to hear the cease-fire signal and sank two merchant ships off Newcastle on May 7. Men of the merchant marine who had contributed so much to the Allied victory were among the first and last casualties of the war in Europe.

This tragic toll of young lives took place against a background of a triumphant victory over that "most monstrous of tyrannies never surpassed in the dark, lamentable catalogue of human crime."

The Allied armies had developed a battle doctrine that called for the expenditure of massive amounts of artillery shells and, if possible, bombs instead of lives. In the final stages of the war, this doctrine could not be applied to Holland so the battles of April were fought using field artillery regiments and mortars as the main firepower. When 2nd Division reached Holten not far from the site where the last Canadian military cemetery in Europe would be built, the enemy was dug-in along a railway line and in the town centre. Aimed fire from battalion anti-tank guns and the two-inch mortars were used to overcome resistance and limit casualties among a population that rushed out onto the street "dancing jubilantly near the burning buildings."

When the enemy prepared to fight for Apeldoorn, a city swollen with thousands of refugees, 1st Division's plan of attack called for isolating the city and infiltrating infantry without employing artillery. The garrison abandoned Apeldoorn once 5th Armoured Division and 2nd Brigade had pushed beyond the city and the soldiers were greeted by wildly rejoicing citizens instead of

NAC 113697

bullets. The War Diary of the Hastings and Prince Edward Regiment states the battalion's entry in the city was "tough going due to the cheering and crowding of the thousands of liberated Dutch people who showered bouquets of flowers on the troops. A good looking soldier had to use his weapon to beat off the girls, and many a fair maiden's kiss was forced on the boys."

Two German children with pockets turned out to show they are not carrying weapons surrender to Canadian troops, Sögel, Germany, April 1945.

A very different pattern was evident in Groningen where a Dutch SS battalion with little to lose joined miscellaneous German units in determined defence of the city. The Essex Scottish used Kangaroos - armoured personnel carriers - to rush a bridge and penetrate the city's southern edge. The Royal Hamilton Light Infantry then fought a fierce hand-to-hand engagement to gain the railway station. Machine-guns covered the streets and snipers, including SS men in civilian clothes, harassed the Canadians.

Major-General Bruce Matthews sent 6th Brigade into the main battle while using 5th Brigade to attack from the west. The Dutch resistance helped where it could, lashing barges together as an improvised bridge. The Black Watch, directed to clear the houses around a park, fought a pitched battle using Projector, Infantry, Anti-Tank weapons (PIATs) and Brens against an entrenched enemy. Finally the two-inch mortars and a burst from a Wasp flamethrower forced an enemy withdrawal. The division suffered 209 casualties in liberating Groningen.

Across the border in Germany no weapons restrictions applied but resistance was more intense. Young boys, with only an armband for a uniform, were among the civilians found with weapons. One of the most poignant photographs taken in the last phase shows two young lads in Sögel, Germany, with raised hands and pockets turned out to prove they are unarmed.

The German defence of ports was better organized. Third Canadian Division called its attack on Leer Operation "Duck" because once again the Water Rats mounted an amphibious assault. The attack went well, but there were 70 casualties.

These last days of the war in Germany were a miserable period for everyone. Resistance was spotty and prisoners were taken in droves, but the enemy seemed to have plenty of mortar rounds and enough determination to use them. It rained steadily and the tired, soaked men, who were asked to maintain pressure without taking too many chances, collapsed into deep sleep when they were rotated out of action. But pressure had to be maintained to bring the war to an end. When the German capitulation was announced there were few celebrations; the predominant emotion was relief at having survived.

Back in western Holland it was all very different. The truce was extended to allow heavy bombers to drop food supplies to the hostage populations of Amsterdam and Rotterdam. Operation "Manna" delivered tens of thousands of ration packs but the population, verging on starvation, needed much more. On May 3, convoys –one every 30 minutes– began crossing the Grebbe Line. Three days later 1st Division began its triumphal march to Amsterdam and Rotterdam.

Gen. H.D.G. Crerar's message to all ranks summed up the achievement of the nation-in-arms: "From Sicily to the River Senio, from the beaches of Dieppe, to those of Normandy and from thence to Northern France, Belgium, Holland and North West Germany, the Canadians and their Allied comrades in this army have carried out their responsibilities in the high traditions which they inherited... Crushing and complete victory over the German army has been secured. In rejoicing at this supreme accomplishment we shall remember the friends who have paid the full price for the belief they also held that no sacrifice in the interests of the principles for which we fought could be too great."

This was the official view. The ordinary soldier, in a reflective moment, would simply say: "It was the right thing to do."

The Liberation Of Western Holland

Originally published, May/June 2002

The 5th Canadian Armoured Division–Major-General Bert Hoffmeister's Mighty Maroon Machine–began operations in the Netherlands on March 21, 1945 when the Westminster Regiment (Motor) took over a sector of the Nijmegen front from the 12th Manitoba Dragoons. Holland, with "electric light, running water and radios in the forward area," was a new experience for the veterans of the Italian Campaign but cold rain and mud in a flat, flooded landscape was all too familiar to those who had wintered in the Valli di Commachio.

On March 31 the division took over the western part of the "island", south of Arnhem, allowing 49th British Division to concentrate for Operation "Destroyer", the destruction of the last enemy pocket south of the river. The Ontario Regiment, which began its war in Sicily supporting British troops, and the Royal Canadian Artillery's new 1st Rocket Battery were attached to the Yorkshire division for the operation. Fifth Division employed three tank-infantry battlegroups to clear its sector but met little opposition. The Perth Regiment, which liberated Driel, the headquarters of the Polish Parachute Brigade during Operation "Market Garden", reported enemy counterattacks but dealt with them without difficulty.

After that the stage was set for operations intended to liberate western Holland, including Amsterdam and Rotterdam. Operation "Anger", involving 49th British and 5th Canadian divisions was to begin once 1st Division was safely across the Ijssel and on its way to Apeldoorn. Before Operation "Anger" began the decision to negotiate a truce with the enemy and allow relief supplies to reach the people of western Holland was made so once Arnhem was secure, 5th Division started west towards the Grebbe line where military action was to cease.

Sherman tanks of the Governor General's Horse Guards, advance out of Arnhem, April 1945.

Since its arrival in Holland, Hoffmeister's 5th Armoured Division had been offered little opportunity to use its armoured brigade group. The relatively easy conquest of Arnhem had, however, presented the corps commander with an irresistible opportunity to use the 5th Armoured Brigade to cut off the retreat of the Germans still fighting on the Apeldoorn canal line. The British Columbia Dragoons led the way through Arnhem with the 8th New Brunswick Hussars, the Westminster Regiment (Motor) and the Lord Strathcona's Horse close behind. Enemy blocking positions were shot up or bypassed and Otterlo was reached by late afternoon.

Brigadier I.H. Cumberland, who led the 5th Armoured Brigade, was not about to pause. The Strathconas were told to take Otterlo then push northwest to capture Barneveld. If Barneveld was defended they were to bypass it and strike north to cut the Apeldoorn-Amesfort road, the main east-west route of the retreating German forces. The other two armoured regiments were to conform to this thrust, the British Columbia Dragoons to the north and the 8th Hussars to the south. Otterlo was cleared readily enough, but beyond the town's western limits were numerous pockets of infantry, some with Panzerfaust or bazooka men who had to be dealt with by Westminster motorized infantry.

The enemy held Barneveld in strength and the Strathconas lost three tanks on the edge of town. Bypassing was accomplished quickly, but 2,000 yards beyond the north edge of town a well-organized anti-tank gun position, guarded by machine-gun posts, barred the way. The decision was made to stop and organize a proper attack at first light on April 17.

The night of the 16-17 is remembered as the battle of Otterlo. The ferocious attack on the town, which included Hoffmeister's advanced headquarters, was part of a determined attempt by elements of three German divisions to reach the "safety" of western Holland.

The 11th Infantry Brigade had spent two days following the rapidly moving armoured brigade and had seen little action so when the Irish Regiment, the Governor General's Horse Guards and elements of the divisional and corps artillery moved into Otterlo they knew they were well behind the leading troops. The Irish Regiment took up positions on the western perimeter of the village and the tanks of the GGHG found convenient harbours in various corners of the village. Suddenly Otterlo was transformed into a battlefield as hundreds of German soldiers loosely organized into battlegroups stormed through the village throwing grenades and firing at every shadow. One group bumped into the 17th Field Regiment RCA and got a warm reception from the enraged gunners. The regimental sergeant major shot two men with his Sten gun and after it jammed, he used his bare hands.

The officers of the Governor General's Horse Guards were at an "O" group in the church when the attack began and were forced to stay there until the fighting had died down. The regiment's troop sergeants and other NCOs had no trouble organizing the defence of their positions or the mopping up that followed, leading some to question whether they needed officers at all. The next day the Grebbe line was reached and it looked as if 5th Division's war was over.

Field Marshal Bernard Montgomery had other ideas. He told Canadian General H.D.G. Crerar that he needed 2nd Canadian Division to help protect the left flank of the British corps preparing to attack Bremen. Second Division was to move east as soon as Groningen was liberated and it was up to Crerar to find the resources to capture the fortified zone protecting the Ems River estuary and the ports of Delfzijl and Emden. The Canadian commanders must have been reminded of the situation in the fall of 1944 when Montgomery had pressed for immediate action in clearing the approaches to Antwerp, Belgium, while "borrowing" divisions to support his operations in the Arnhem salient.

Before examining the battles for Delfzijl and Emden we need to understand the broad strategic picture in mid-April 1945. The United States 9th Army reached the Elbe on April 11 and secured a bridgehead across the river the next

day. General W.H. Simpson was confident his troops could reach Berlin quickly, it was just 70 miles away, but the Supreme Allied Commander, General Dwight D. Eisenhower was adamant, no lives were to be lost in pursuit of an objective that would have to be handed over to the Soviets.

That night President Franklin D. Roosevelt died, plunging America and the West into heartfelt mourning. Newspapers and radio stations focused on stories about Roosevelt, his successor Harry Truman, the shocking evidence of Nazi death camps–especially Bergen-Belsen –and speculation about an immediate collapse of German resistance.

The war, it appeared, was all but over. On April 16 the Royal Air Force and United States Army Air Force suspended the strategic air offensive and prepared to use their heavy bombers to bring relief supplies to Holland. In Berlin, Hitler, confined to his underground bunker, celebrated his last birthday on April 20 and two days later announced his determination to stay despite the advance of Soviet troops who had all but surrounded the city. Other Nazi leaders, including Heinrich Himmler and Hermann Goring, attempted to arrange a separate surrender in the west while what was left of the German army held off the Russians but these approaches were flatly rejected.

In mid-April Eisenhower believed that two important military operations remained to be carried out. In the south, General George S. Patton's 3rd U.S. Army must continue its advance to reach the Danube so that the Allies would have a postwar role in Austria. In the north, Eisenhower was anxious to see a rapid advance to the Baltic to prevent Soviet forces from entering Denmark. Ike offered to provide Montgomery with a force from his SHAEF (Supreme Headquarters Allied Expeditionary Force) reserve to carry out this task but Montgomery's attention was focused elsewhere.

Montgomery, with full support of the British chiefs of staff, was determined to capture the German north seaports of Emden,

manders to allocate tasks. Major-General R.H. Keefler, now commanding 3rd Division, was told "to prepare for an infantry brigade assault across the River Leda" to capture Leer and then advance to Emden. Hoffmeister's 5th Armoured Division was to clear Delfzijl and the guns of the Ems fortress located in Holland.

Third Division, known since the Rhineland as the Water Rats, assumed that Buffaloes, tracked amphibious vehicles, would be available to make the river crossing. However, Simonds was told that the vehicles were needed at the Elbe. He was also informed that neither Bomber Command nor the medium bombers of Second Tactical Air Force were available. Simonds and his staff were upset at what they saw as the uncooperative attitude of Second Tactical Air Force which insisted that the flak defences of the fortress area and the islands in the mouth of the Ems estuary would exact too heavy a toll on the medium bombers.

By the morning of April 24, 5th Canadian Armoured Division was in position north of Groningen and Brigadier Ian Johnston's 11th Infantry Brigade, the Perth Regiment, the Cape Breton Highlanders and the Irish Regiment of Canada joined by the Westminster Regiment (Motor) began to probe the German defences of Delfzijl. Across the German border, Brigadier John Rockingham's 9th Highland Brigade prepared for the assault crossing of the Ems estuary: "Rocky", who always led from the front, conducted a personal reconnaissance of the German defences. Air photos showed numerous slit trenches along the dikes and having to hit the ground because of small arms fire convinced him the positions were manned. Without the familiar Buffaloes which could handle mud,

Wilhelmshaven, Bremen and Hamburg. Denmark would have to wait. The background of this decision has never been fully explored but its consequences for 30th British Corps, assigned to assault Bremen, and 2nd Canadian Corps, tasked with the capture of Emden, in the last days of the war were enormous. Operations against Bremen began on April 18 and the battle quickly turned into a bitter contest of wills. German resistance was skilful and resolute and casualties to both sides were heavy. Medium and heavy bombers reduced the city to rubble and for the final assault two heavy and four medium regiments supported the field artillery of four divisions. The city finally fell on April 25.

The battle of Bremen was well under way when Crerar handed over temporary command of First Canadian Army to Lieutenant-General Guy Simonds. Crerar felt he was needed in London to deal with repatriation issues and since the only operations under way involved 2nd Canadian Corps, Simonds acted as both army and corps commander, meeting with his divisional com-

climb the river bank and bring the infantry ashore, the attack would have to be at high tide when the storm boats could beach at the base of the dikes.

Rockingham was given enough boats to lift six companies of about 80 men each. He decided on a complex plan that involved simultaneous attacks on Leer from three directions. The North Novas sent one company directly into the town to create a bridgehead. The Highland Light Infantry, with three companies, entered the river well away from the city and under cover of smoke landed in a lightly defended sector east of the built-up area. The Stormont Dundas and Glengarry Highlanders crossed to the west, establishing a bridgehead for the tanks of the Sherbrooke Fusiliers.

Success depended on tactical surprise and the neutralization of the enemy during the assault phase. Typhoons, field and medium artillery and a pepper pot (concentrated fire) orchestrated by the divisional machine-gun and mortar regiment, the Camerons of Ottawa, kept enemy heads down and both the North Novas and HLI were on top of the enemy while they were still under cover. The Glens were confronted with strong enemy positions that wrecked havoc during the build-up, sinking three boats for the loss of 15 men.

With three battalions advancing into Leer, Rockingham was more concerned with confusion and losses from friendly fire than the enemy who quickly surrendered as soon as their own lives were in danger. As darkness fell he ordered a halt to operations turning over the battle for Leer to 7th Brigade which used the darkness to get its battalions into position for a carefully controlled attack at first light. Only the Reginas encountered organized resistance and when this was overcome around noon on April 30 Leer was clear of the enemy. Emden was 30 miles away across flat polder country and any movement brought down shell fire from the coastal guns on both sides of the estuary. At 9:30 p.m. 7th Brigade started north using Wasp flamethrowers to supplement their personal weapons. Movement was slow and when dawn broke everything stopped. Any daylight advance would bring unacceptable casualties.

On the Delfzijl front Hoffmeister and his infantry brigade commander Johnston decided to squeeze the perimeter from two directions. The Perths and Cape Breton Highlanders from the west and the Irish Regiment from the east. The Westminster Regiment (Motor) was dismounted and ordered to take the Termuten battery directly across from Emden. Initially the armoured regiments were used as supporting artillery but 11th Brigade was so thin on the ground that both the British Columbia Dragoons and the New Brunswick Hussars were required to supply troops to fight as foot soldiers. There are no reports of armoured corps personnel subsequently volunteering to transfer to the infantry.

Johnston was trying to compress a 25,000-yard perimeter "in flat country with little cover and a complicated system of ditches and canals that made cross-country movement impossible." His solution was to advance only at night in carefully controlled bounds. The companies were to be dug-in and under cover at first light. The town of Delfzijl fell on the night of May 1 and the next day the last battery position west of the estuary surrendered. This was welcome news to 3rd Division's 8th Brigade which had taken over the advance to Emden. On May 4 as Brigadier J.A. Roberts was negotiating the surrender of Aurich news of a ceasefire reached divisional headquarters.

Casualties in these operations were high, 72 Canadians killed at Delfzijl and about the same number, spread across the three brigades, in the Leer-Emden battles. After-action reports suggest both divisions conducted themselves with a skill and determination maintaining good unit morale to the end. There was much to be proud of and much to regret. It was not easy to understand why such intense operations were ordered in the last days of the Third Reich with the Russians in Berlin and Hitler dead at his own hands. But the army had done its duty and it was now time to celebrate a hard won victory.

LCMSDS

A platoon of Canadian infantry advance into the heart of Germany.

The Fall Of The Reich

Originally published, September/October 2002

Starting a war is easy, the difficult part is ending it. When Churchill, Roosevelt and Stalin met at Yalta in February 1945 they knew the war against Hitler's Thousand-Year Reich was all but won even if much hard fighting remained. Their attention was therefore focused on postwar Europe and plans for the destruction of the Japanese Empire. These discussions were greatly influenced by the military situation in both theatres of war and we need to remind ourselves of what the world looked like in the first months of 1945.

The German offensive of December 1944, remembered as the Battle of the Bulge, consumed the energies of the Anglo-American armies well into January 1945. When it was over, the Allies began preparations for a major offensive that would take them to the Rhine— the objective they had tried to reach at Arnhem in September 1944. The operational challenges confronting the Anglo-American armies were compounded by a shortage of replacements and

the growing differences between the British and Americans over the conduct of the war. Field Marshal Bernard Montgomery's infamous press conference, in which he seemed to claim credit for the defeat of the German Ardennes offensive, was just one of many issues straining Allied unity.

On the eastern front the situation was very different. Stalin had responded to Churchill's request to advance the date of the Red Army's winter campaign and on January 12, 1945, his forces began a 300-mile advance into the heart of Germany. By February 1 they were just 60 miles from Berlin. The contrast between the success of the Red Army and the halting progress in the west was evident to all.

January 1945 was also a difficult time in the Pacific. American General Douglas MacArthur's campaign in the Philippines was behind schedule and both the army and navy were suffering heavy casualties. The battle for Manila was still under way in February when plans for the assault on Iwo Jima—February 19, 1945— and Okinawa—April 1, 1945—were finalized. The horrific human costs of combat in a war of attrition against the Japanese meant that divisions from Europe would be required as soon as possible.

Considering all the circumstances, the agreement reached at Yalta seemed to promise far more than Britain and the United States could have hoped for. Poland, now fully occupied by Soviet troops, was to have new boundaries, a new government, and free elections. The Declaration On Liberated Europe promised a similar future for other countries under Soviet control. Agreement was reached on the structure of the United Nations and the occupation of zones in Germany, including one for France. Most important of all, from the America point of view, was Stalin's commitment to declare war on Japan 90 days after the end of the war in Europe.

If the Soviet Union had lived up to the words of the agreement, Yalta would be hailed as a great triumph, but Stalin had no intention of allowing free elections in Poland or any other country deemed vital to Soviet interests. This became apparent not long after the delegations left Yalta and by the end of March 1945 Churchill was in full cry condemning the Soviet Union. He urged the U.S. to finish the war in Berlin, Prague and Vienna and establish new facts-on-the-ground to counter the Soviet threat.

But Dwight D. Eisenhower—the supreme allied commander—took a very different view. He was determined to withdraw American forces from Montgomery's control and to avoid pursuing political objectives without specific orders. He planned to leave Berlin to the Soviets and to meet the Red Army at the Elbe River while deploying enough forces to overcome German resistance in the so-called Alpine Redoubt.

Eisenhower's decision remains as controversial today as it was in 1945. But leaving politics aside the best way of ending the war was to capture Berlin, force a surrender and avoid fighting for every German city. Instead, with the major U.S. armies stopped at the Elbe, Montgomery committed his forces to a series of costly battles for objectives that would have been bypassed if Berlin had fallen.

Canadian leaders, political and military, were neither consulted nor informed about these strategic debates but Canada's soldiers were soon caught up in the consequences. Eisenhower's decision to avoid Berlin meant that Montgomery's Second British Army was to protect the American flank, clear northern Germany and reach the Baltic, cutting off any Soviet occupation of Denmark. These operations proved beyond the resources of the British Army and Montgomery, determined to avoid asking for American assistance, drew upon the Canadians to help carry out his plans.

On April 5, 1st Polish and 4th Canadian armoured divisions were ordered to provide flank protection for British forces advancing on Bremen, southwest of the German seaport of Hamburg. Montgomery wanted 4th Armoured Division transferred to the 30th British Corps but Canadian General H.D.G. Crerar politely refused. The five-division Canadian Army was at last fighting together and Crerar had no intention of allowing it to be split up. The next day, 4th Canadian Armoured Division crossed into Germany and reached Sögel on April 9. Here the Lake Superior Regiment was counter-attacked by a force that included numbers of very young men in no discernable military uniform.

One of the units caught up in the fighting at Sogel was 12th Canadian Field Ambulance. The unit's war diary records the following: "They (the enemy) pressed an attack (with) approximately 30 men right down the street on which we were situated. Our men had to take up arms. Some of the enemy were killed within 10 yards of the advanced dressing station entrance. Naturally a great deal of excitement ensued. After about one hour a troop of tanks arrived who blasted houses from which enemy sniping (came from). When the attackers were finally wiped out we realized we had been holding a small portion of the front. If we had not taken up arms we would have been shot up and the enemy would have gained access to the main street of town. We had five of our personnel wounded, one seriously. Personnel of an engineer and RCASC (Royal Canadian Army Service Corps) unit who had been overrun in the early dawn were killed or wounded. All ranks of the unit did very

NAC 146287

A signaler with his 18 set relays orders from his company commander, April 1945.

well. Advanced dressing station personnel continued working even with small arms fire coming through the windows. Stretcher-bearers were working under direct fire. Two were wounded."

The soldiers' attitudes towards the enemy hardened in these affairs and so mortars, artillery and—when available—tactical air power were used without any of the restraint evident in the Netherlands. The worst reprisal incident occurred in Friesoythe when rumours that the death of Lieutenant-Colonel F.E. Wigle, commanding officer of the Argyll and Sutherland Highlanders of Canada, was caused by a sniper in civilian clothes. This led to setting the village on fire.

On April 16 the division was confronted with the task of an assault crossing of the Küsten Canal, a water barrier more than 100 feet wide that seemed to be well defended. For 4th Canadian Division this meant a prolonged and costly battle. The Algonquin Regiment, with memories of the Leopold and other canals in mind, got a bridgehead established and were then joined by the Argylls. All through the 18th counter-attacks beat against the perimeter. By the morning of the 19th the exhausted but determined engineers had a bridge in place and a squadron of British Columbia

Regiment tanks sped across to provide sorely needed assistance.

The enemy's determined defence of the Küsten Canal was part of a last desperate attempt to hold parts of northern Germany long enough to allow for the evacuation of soldiers and civilians fleeing the vengeance of the Red Army in the east. Montgomery was equally determined to win control of the area and he committed large resources, including 2nd Canadian Infantry Division which was ordered east to join in the battle for Bremen.

With four Canadian divisions committed to action, the last two weeks of the war produced a large number of casualties, including 490 fatalities. Of these, 114 died in May, including 12 on the last day of the war in Europe. Continuing the advance into northern Germany while the Soviets were in the suburbs of Berlin made little military sense, but the Allies had promised to maintain pressure to prevent the transfer of German units to the east and Montgomery's orders reflected this commitment.

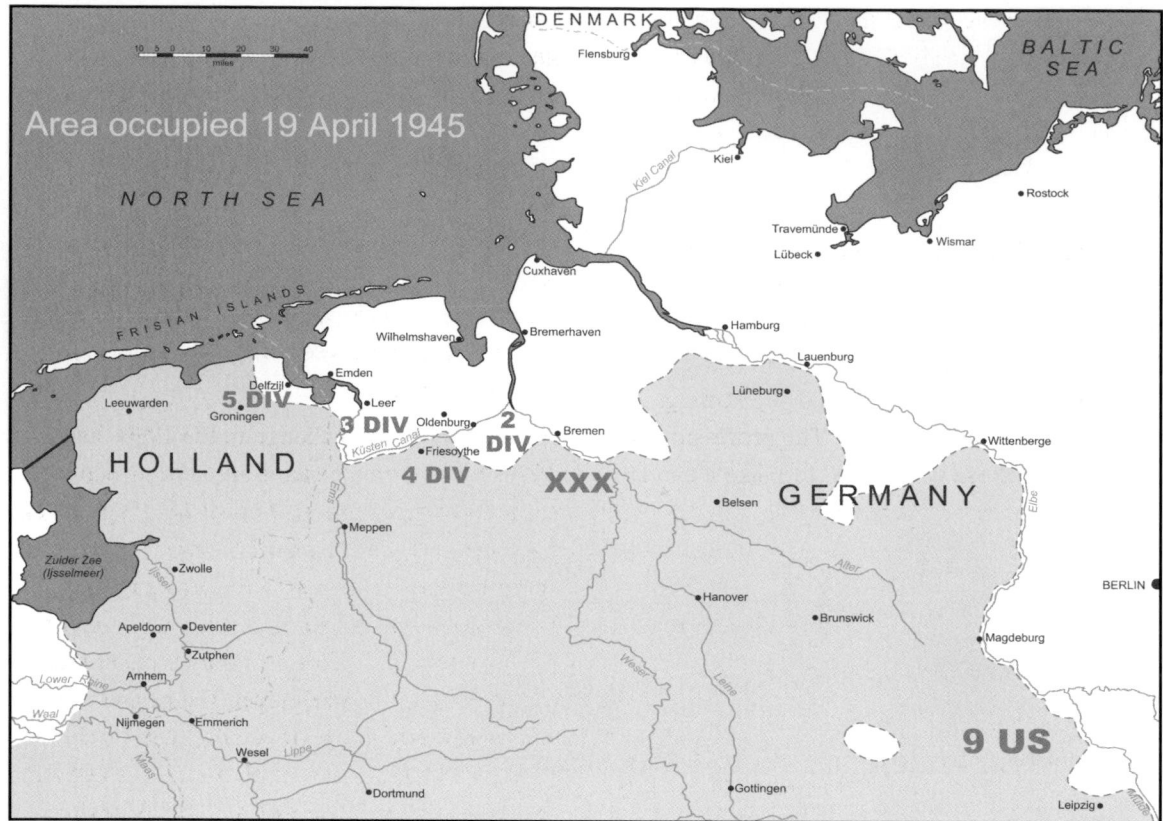

Area occupied 19 April 1945

One last major task remained, the advance to the Baltic to safeguard Denmark. Eisenhower wanted priority for this operation, a request that prompted a last bitter protest from Montgomery, who replied that if the Russians reached Denmark it would be because of Eisenhower's faulty strategy. Montgomery might ignore Eisenhower but when Churchill demanded action, the Field Marshal moved promptly, advancing the date of the dash to the Baltic. This operation was carried out by the 18th U.S. Airborne Corps with 6th British Airborne Division under command. Since Brigadier James Hill's 3rd Parachute Brigade was in the vanguard there was no hesitation and when 1st Canadian Parachute Battalion linked up with the Scots Greys of the Royal Armoured Corps they discovered that tanks could go quite fast even with paratroops clinging onto them.

Hill decided to continue north without pause and the columns raced by thousands of armed German soldiers who, along with masses of civilians, were fleeing from the Russians. The Canadians were in the lead when the Baltic was reached and it fell to Lieutenant-Colonel Fraser Eadie and his men to confront Soviet forces on the outskirts of Wismar. A fine mixture of determination and diplomacy was required to convince the Soviets that Wismar was going to stay in Canadian hands but the tough, experienced paratroopers were the right men for the job. Captain Richard Hilborn, who had jumped into France on D-Day, took on the liaison role with the Russians and managed to smooth over differences with the aid of a generous supply of champagne.

On the morning of May 5, 1945 messages ordering all units to cease offensive operations were issued and the news spread quickly. Lieutenant-Colonel Syd Thompson, the acting commander of 5th Brigade, recalled visiting his battalions to ensure no risks were taken. Their reaction was typical. No one cheered and there were few celebrations. Rumours about a surrender had been circulating for weeks but the fighting had not stopped and the steady drain of casualties had sapped the energy of the men in the rifle companies. The war diaries of combat units portray a mood of deeply felt relief that the killing had ended.

The soldiers now faced a very different future. Some volunteered for service in the Pacific and it was these adventuresome souls wh got home to Canada first. The rest faced the prospect of occupation duties or long periods of waiting for their turn to besent home. The professional soldiers, and those who hoped to make a career in the postwar army, spent time analysing the "lessons learned" in the campaign and developing recommendations for new equipment and doctrine. The vast majority wanted little more than a quick return to civilian life and said so, loudly and often.

Repatriation was organized on a point system, which initially emphasized the principle of early in, early out, so there was a steady exodus from the battalion through the summer of 1945. Those who remained took courses, learned about their options through the Rehabilitation Training Program and went on weekend leaves in the friendly cities of Holland. They also tried to make sense of what they had been through. The Calgary Highlanders published a souvenir issue of their regimental journal, *The Glen*, which included brief histories of each component of the battalion and some reflections on what it all meant. In *The Glen*, as in other regimental publications of the time, Canadian soldiers expressed pride in their achievements, a determination to remember fallen comrades, and hope for a world without war.

In the first decade after 1945, Canadians had little difficulty in giving meaning to the achievements and sacrifices of the men and women of the armed forces. The horrors of the Third Reich were fresh in everyone's mind and no one doubted that Canadians had made a major contribution to the defeat of the "monstrous tyranny" that had threatened the survival of Western civilization.

This view came under attack in the 1960s from a generation influenced by the war in Vietnam and the rise of a new historical nationalism. All wars were suspect and the kind of patriotism that had formed the context for Canadian participation in World War II seemed too closely tied to Britain to be acceptable. History came to be written and taught as though the only important events of the war years were the conscription crisis, the internment of Japanese Canadians and the rise of labour unions.

All of this began to change in the 1980s and 1990s when a new generation, with no active memory of the Vietnam War, came of age. These young people were anxious to learn about the achievements of their grandparents and were quick to recognize that two of the most important chapters of Canadian history were written on the battlefields of Europe. The period was also marked by the retirement of many veterans and a new willingness to tell their story before memories faded. The result was an explosion of popular and scholarly interest in WW II.

For Canadians, the new interpretation centres at Vimy and Beaumont-Hamel are outstanding achievements that present history in an accessible format without any sacrifice of content. The Juno Beach Centre, a marvelous building on a magnificent site, will develop exhibits of similar quality in the years ahead. The Canadian Battlefields Foundation commemorative viewing areas at Point 67/Verrières Ridge and at St-Lambert-sur-Dives offer the opportunity to see and understand two important battlefields. In Belgium, the Canada Museum in Adagem and the Flanders Field Museum in Ypres are must-see sites for Canadians in Europe.

What The War
Was All About

Originally published, May 1995

On May 7, 1945, General Dwight Eisenhower informed the Combined Chiefs of Staff that the mission of this" Allied force was fulfilled at 0241 local time."

Finally, the war in Europe was over.

The fires died slowly, the smoke cleared and millions of hungry and tired people dug themselves out of the rubble. Victory-in-Europe Day was celebrated, but the noise from those celebrations was muted because there was still another enemy to beat. And if the war in the Far East continued for much longer, the soldiers in Europe would have to move to another battlefield. Nevertheless, the taste of victory in Europe was sweet.

It was a victory over one of the most awesome and efficient military machines the world had ever seen. However, WW II was not merely a military contest, it was a war that involved fundamental ideological and political questions. It is important to remember how it started.

During the 1920s and 1930s political philosophies flourished in a number of countries which transformed and exalted nationalism into a racial creed and rejected those concepts - from Christianity to Liberalism-that tried to create value systems that would limit conflict and abolish war. Fascist ideologies – in one form or another-were advocated by men who seized power in Italy, Japan and Germany. These men immediately began to pursue domestic policies that were repugnant to many and deadly to those who opposed them. They adopted foreign policies that were simply reflections of the faith they placed in the virtues of violence.

In contrast to these three states, many countries in which a degree of political freedom existed after WW I had a substantial number of people who swore their country would never again resort to violence. These same people hoped that international organizations, such as the League of Nations, would prevent future wars. The dilemma

was that powers determined to conquer others could only be prevented by the very application of force that so many had vowed never to use again.

When the catalogue of Axis conquests began in Ethiopia, China and Czechoslovakia the other major powers tried to find some compromise, some reasonable, rational way to appease the appetites of the predatory states. At the same time, the lesser powers tried to stay neutral.

There has been much debate about what Arthur Neville Chamberlain should have done during these difficult years, but one should not forget that only France, Great Britain and the British Commonwealth nations went to war in 1939 because they understood that Poland was only the next in a long list of Hitler's probable conquests. The smaller European countries tried to hide behind a paper wall of neutrality that failed to offer the slightest protection when Hitler was ready to conquer.

In Washington, President Franklin Roosevelt nursed a petulant and ignorant Congress towards some understanding of the danger, while in Moscow, Stalin nursed his insane suspicions by killing Russians and selling raw materials to Hitler. America and Russia would be attacked when it suited Berlin and Tokyo.

The nations that declared war against Germany in 1939 - Canada among them- tried to stop Hitler before he conquered all of Europe. This was an act of common sense and self-preservation that came perilously close to failing as Germany and Japan conquered nearly all of Europe and the Pacific basin in two years.

The Allies forged the Grand Alliance in 1942 in response to the arrogance and greed of the Axis powers, which had grown stronger in their conquests, so strong that the road to 1945 was difficult and costly for the Allies, despite their huge manpower reserves and great economic capacity. During that time the leaders of the Axis powers fulfilled the darkest aspirations of their ideologies. They had promised that the world would witness the dawn of a new barbarism and they were right. Tens of thousands were tortured and millions exterminated for the sake of racial purity. Millions

NAC 150931

were enslaved to work and to starve in the factories and jungles of occupied territories. The crimes that were committed were so outrageous that they could not be revealed to their own people, even in the name of military necessity.

An evil stalked the world in those years from which no one could really escape. The war was about the recognition of that evil; the people who fought it understood, perhaps better than we do now, that the ideas of national socialism, of Japanese imperialism and Italian fascism were really only exaggerations of evils that were, and probably are, present in all ideologies. The beliefs of the leaders of the Axis powers filtered out just about everything that was good in mankind and enlarged everything that was evil. The war was about recognizing and defeating this evil.

The victory of May 1945 could not bring everything that was expected or hoped for. The alliance with the Soviet Union did not survive Hitler's defeat. The Cold War came to dominate international relations and the threat of nuclear war overshadowed the achievement of peace. The allied victory did not bring an end to human greed or

lust for power or cruelty, but it did turn back a new form of barbarism and provide the western world with the opportunity to build a new society.

On the battlefield the sudden collapse of German resistance and the announcement of a ceasefire took most people by surprise. The war had been part of everyone's lives for so long that no other context seemed possible. For Canadians the war had been the best of times as well as the worst of times. The casualty tolls were dreadful and the news of what had happened in Nazi concentration and death camps might make people despair for the future of the human race, but the men and women who served in the Canadian forces had other memories.

Canadians had played an important part in a great struggle to preserve humanity from the horrors of Nazi tyranny. They had forged deep and lasting friendships with those who shared their experiences of war. Many had arrived overseas as little more than teenagers. They had grown up together, laughing, crying, praying and relaxing. They had become comrades and now it was over, the brave battalions would soon be just memories.

Some -more than enough- volunteered for the Pacific theatre and it was these adventuresome souls wh got home to Canada first. The rest faced the prospect of occupation duties or long periods of waiting for their turn to besent home. The professionals and those who hoped to make a career in the postwar army, navy or air force, spent time analysing the lessons learned and developing grandiose plans for new equipment and doctrine. The vast majority wanted little more than a quick return to civilian life and said so loudly and often.

Repatriation was organized on a point system that initially emphasized a first-in, first-out principle, giving priority to married men. This meant there was a steady exodus from units throughout the summer of 1945. Those who remained learned about their future options through the Rehabilitation Training Program and went on weekend leaves in friendly Dutch or British towns and cities. They also tried to make sense of what they had been through, expressing simple, even naive hopes for a better future in a world without war.

The Glen, the regimental newspaper of the Calgary Highlanders, published a short message with the heading, The War In Europe Is Over!

We came from all walks of life, from coast to coast, making one of the finest fighting forces in the world. Yes, unity was achieved and victory was the result.

Soon we expect o go home and back to a normal life. Let us not forget. Let us not allow ourselves to fall for lies or propaganda which will have French-speaking Canadians against English-speaking Canadians, Jews against Catholics and Protestants against Catholics, East against West. We must go back and maintain our unity achieved through sweat and blood. We won a great victory for mankind.

Above all we must remember those comrades of ours who gave their lives fighting to make a world which will know no war and in which there will be real happiness for all.

Let us go back together as Canadians to make Canada a happy place for all. We must not fail.

In the first decade after the war Canadians had lit-

tle difficulty understanding the achievements and sacrifices of the men and women of the armed forces. The horrors of the Third Reich were fresh in everyone's mind and no one doubted that Canadians had made a major contribution to the defeat of an enemy that had threatened the survival of civilization. Most Canadians were equally confident that the nation's new role in NATO was a necessary response to abundant evidence of aggressive designs by the Soviet Union. No sensible person believed that isolationism or a policy of appeasement was a rational response to the new world order.

This common-sense view came under attack, with much else, in the 1960s and 1970s. A new generation, which knew only the benefits of postwar prosperity and nothing of the costs, questioned the validity of all wars, because the war they saw on television in Vietnam, seemed to lack legitimacy. This approach reached its climax for Canadians in the CBC/National Film Board series The Valour And The Horror. The producers, steeped in the prejudices of the '60s, portrayed Canadian veterans as the victims of unscrupulous politicians and incompetent or evil commanders. The battles they fought in were portrayed as unnecessary and without purpose.

The programs stirred a deep response among people who remembered the times and the importance of the issues involved. All across the nation veterans gathered to talk to each other and to seek ways of re-establishing an accurate collective memory of the meaning of the sacrifices of war. They discovered that Canadian history texts largely ignored them. The new postcolonial history of the era of biculturalism and multiculturalism avoided the war effort, focusing on issues such as conscription and the internment of enemy aliens. When the military was mentioned it was to highlight Canadian failures, not achievements.

And so as the eyes of the world turn to the ceremonies marking the 50th anniversary of VE-Day, veterans will have a chance to remind Canadians of what the war was all about. A new generation, unsullied by arrogance and cynicism about the war is ready to listen.

Shaping The Future At Home

Originally published, June/July 1995

The men and women who returned to Canada in the summer of 1945 discovered a nation transformed by the experience of total war. First Division veterans who crossed to England in 1939 left a country deep in the throes of the Great Depression, the Dirty '30s. Twenty per cent of the population was on relief and many young people had never held a permanent job. For older workers unemployment was a chronic condition; tens of thousands had been out of work for more than five years. For the majority who still had jobs, life was darkened by the threat of unemployment and fear for the future of their children.

The welfare state, which would offer a safety net to future generations, barely existed. There was a small, means-tested old age pension available to the destitute at age 70 and a mother's allowance for widows with children. Beyond these token measures, ordinary Canadians in trouble had to rely on municipal relief - the dole or private charity.

The government had no plans for altering this situation. It hoped the war would create external demand for Canada's wheat, timber, fish, minerals and newsprint, thus reducing unemployment. In addition, new Canadian industries would be developed to supply ships for the rapid expansion of the merchant marine and Royal Canadian Navy, and aircraft to assist in training aircrews under the British Commonwealth Air Training Plan. The war was to be a limited undertaking without a large expeditionary force likely to suffer the kind of battlefield casualties that had brought about conscription in WW I. But after the fall of France, public opinion forced the government to change its mind about Canada's role and to move quickly to increase war production.

 Industrial expansion was organized by businessmen and civil servants who had little interest in social or economic reform. Parliament had passed the War Measures Act that granted cabinet the powers to regulate the economy for the duration of the war. Canadians quickly learned that in addition to normal laws legislated by the House of Commons or provincial legislatures, a new category of rules known as Privy Council or cabinet orders-in-council also carried the force of law.

The Wartime Prices and Trade Board, established on September 3, 1939, used orders-in-council to control the supply of key commodities, to freeze prices, fix rents and establish food rationing. After 1940 it acted effectively to limit inflation, preventing the rapid price increases that had shocked and destabilized Canada in WW I. Wage control soon followed. In the fall of 1941 the National War Labour Board-with nine regional boards-was created. Henceforth, no change in wage rates could occur unless the board agreed the increase was needed to equal the average income in similar occupations in that region. A cost-of-living bonus was also available.

Hourly workers were not the only ones to be closely regulated. A wartime salaries order froze all salaries, allowing a small cost-of-living bonus for those earning less than $3,000. Promotions were subject to close scrutiny and rarely authorized.

These measures, combined with strong demand for workers of all kinds, produced one of the most efficient war economies in the world. There were jobs for everyone, including married women who entered the labour force in unprecedented numbers. Ordinary Canadians, both rural and urban, had rarely been able to get enough steady work. Most of Canada's industries were seasonal and regular layoffs in mining, forestry, the fishery, transportation and manufacturing were normal. Even if wage rates were frozen, good money could be made through overtime and everyone in the family could contribute. The number of 14- and 15-year-olds granted permits to work full time increased steadily throughout the war.

All of this new purchasing power had to be harnessed or the black market and an inflationary spiral would take hold of the economy. The government's methods of diverting income from spending to saving were the various victory loan campaigns and compulsory war savings. Fortunately, officials in the Finance Department recognized that the long neglected issue of unemployment insurance could also be tackled now that there was little unemployment. The new pro-federalist Quebec government gave its approval and suddenly in 1940 unemployment insurance was a reality.

For the duration of the war employee contributions siphoned off purchasing power but, when a brief postwar recession struck, the fund provided a kind of security and dignity that few workers had previously known. One of the basic foundations of modern Canadian society had been created without conflict or much debate.

Of course the government also recognized the Income Tax Act could be changed to include wage earners. In 1939 a married man with a wife and two children paid no income tax unless he was in the top brackets. At earnings of $3000 - double the average income - the tax was just $10. By 1943 the levy at $3,000 was $334 plus an equal amount in compulsory savings. An unskilled worker who made $1,500 paid $48, half of it refundable after the war. The $10,000 man-there were very few of these-paid $3,346 and a further $1,200 was taken as compulsory savings. This sharply progressive income tax and an excess profits tax helped convince Canadians that everyone was contributing to the war effort.

Rules, regulations, rationing, taxes, long hours of work - it all sounded a bit grim, but the years were anything but that. Wartime Canada was full of energy and excitement. People travelled to take up new jobs, the trains were crowded with soldiers, sailors and airmen on leave or off to a new posting. Rationing did not seriously affect the supply of beer, liquor or tobacco. Tea and sugar were rationed, but coffee sales soared. So did milk consumption. In fact people ate more and better food than had been possible in the 1930s and the overall health of the population improved dramatically.

Relations between the sexes were freer and more open than they had ever been. Women were finally granted the vote in Quebec and there were signs they might find greater equality in the workplace. Unions insisted that when women performed "men's work" they had to be paid at men's rates. Of course most female workers still worked in traditional low-wage jobs, but a new principle with far-reaching implications had been established.

Married women in the workforce meant child care problems and an elaborate network of plant-based day nurseries was created with the co-operation of industry and government. This too pointed to a new future, though with the end of the war federal participation in daycare was abandoned and the program quickly collapsed. By 1945 the authorities were determined to get married women out of the labour force, particularly out of "men's jobs" that were needed for veterans. Once victory was achieved "Rosie the riveter" and her sisters either retrned home to look after children or found a job in traditional women's occupations.

The government and its dollar-a-year business advisers shaped and directed an economy that achieved miracles. The numbers are amazing. From a base of almost zero, production quadrupled and then doubled and then quadrupled again. By the end of 1944, the peak year, more than 300 merchant ships and 368 naval vessels had been launched. Training and service aircraft from the Harvard to the Mosquito and Lancaster were built in the thousands. Armoured vehicles, guns of all sizes and trucks – hundreds of thousands of trucks- were sent overseas for the Canadian, British and Soviet armies. Canadian radar and other electronic equipment was another important contribution and Canada played a significant role in the development of the atomic bomb.

In 1944 Canadians finally persuaded a reluctant government to think about the shape of things to come. In 1942, William Beveridge published his famous report on postwar social security for Britain and almost overnight public debate began about a new society "when the war is

NAC 175793

War brides leaving Liverpool for life in the new Canada of the 1940's.

over". Canadians heard about proposals for health insurance and other reforms in more detail when news of a report on social security for Canada reached the public in 1943. Leonard Marsh, a McGill social work professor who had supervised detailed studies of prewar Canadian society, advocated compulsory health insurance, better old age pensions, and a family allowance system.

Professors could easily be ignored, but no politician could afford to overlook evidence of widespread dissatisfaction with the status quo. The two most important signs of change were the rise of trade union militancy and growing support for the Co-operative Commonwealth Federation. Organized labour was signing up tens of thousands of new members, and pressing for a Canadian version of the Wagner Act-the American New Deal legislation that required recognition of unions and good faith collective bargaining. Labour was also after a new minimum wage of 50 cents an hour.

The CCF had lost ground in the 1940 election because of its half-hearted support of the war, but by 1944 the party had become a major factor. The new Gallup poll tracked the rise of the socialists in British Columbia, Saskatchewan and Ontario. In August 1943 the CCF won 32 per cent of the popular vote in the Ontario election with just four fewer seats than George Drew's Conservatives. Then Tommy Douglas was elected premier of Saskatchewan. Clearly the Liberal government would have to respond to public pressure for major reforms in Canadian society.

The first breakthrough came with the announcement that a family allowance would be paid to 1.4 million Canadian mothers. The monthly payments-six to nine dollars per child - would be especially helpful to poorer families and would also help to stimulate the postwar economy. Organized labour which preferred its 50-cent-an-hour minimum wage plan to "baby bonuses", was offered its own prize in the form of an order-in-council imposing compulsory collective bargaining and union certification on reluctant employers.

Plans were also announced for a Department of Veterans Affairs to administer the Veterans Charter with its wide range of educational and financial benefits. A new department of health and welfare was created as a sign of the government's intent to improve health care. C. D. Howe, the Czar of Canadian war industry, received a mandate to manage the Department of Reconstruction and guarantee "work for all" when peace returned.

The National Housing Act held out promie of home ownership for families who had never imagined such things were possible.

There were also prospects of a new world order. The Charter of the United Nations, with its ringing declaration "to save succeeding generations from the scourge of war" while advancing "human rights and social progress" seemed full of promise for a better future.

There were problems. French Canadian veterans who had played a significant part in the war found that many in Quebec were nursing grievances about conscription and had turned away from co-operation with Ottawa. The behavior of the Soviet Union at the San Francisco Conference and in Eastern Europe suggested it might not be the friendly democratic ally pictured in wartime propaganda. But the summer of 1945 was a time for celebration and hope. Canadians knew they were a people who had done great things together and for the moment that was enough.

The Atomic Question

Originally published, August 1995

The announcement of the Japanese surrender, broadcast to Canadians on the evening of August 14, set off celebrations across the country. Prime Minister Mackenzie King declared VJ-Day a national holiday and he then went for a drive to watch the celebrations. It was he wrote, "a pretty sight to see the crowds, all looking so cheerful, girls without hats-all looking so young."

The simple joy expressed by young and old alike on that day 50 years ago seems strange to many modern observers. The end of the war with Japan is now remembered in terms of the tragedy of Hiroshima and Nagasaki-the beginning of the nuclear age not the end of a long and bloody war.

This approach to August 1945 is entirely understandable. The generations that grew up with the threat of nuclear war tried to understand how that reality happened and what might happen in the future.

Japan, once defeated, was a minor player in east-west confrontations and the struggle to subdue its military power was of marginal interest. Individuals who knew, and cared to know, nothing about the war in the Pacific developed firm opinions about the decision to drop the A-bombs. Military thinkers assumed that warfare had been revolutionized and placed their faith in nuclear deterrence. Critics of American foreign policy insisted that the bombs had been used as atomic diplomacy, a first step in the Cold War. Few were interested in the actual events of the summer of 1945.

The first responsibility of historians is to establish, as best they can, what actually happened. To achieve this they must ask clear questions and search for information from the best sources. Answers will always be incomplete and imperfect but they can be true in the sense that they accurately reflect the available evidence.

Historians have little difficulty in reaching agreement on the answers to clearly stated questions; what they quarrel about is which questions are important. For the men and women involved in the events of 1945, the most important question is what caused Japan to surrender?

Close examination of events in August 1945 reveals that Japanese military and m political elites were sharply divided. A majority, even in the army, was prepared to end the war but sought terms well short of the unconditional surrender demanded by the Allies. The Potsdam Declaration of July 26, 1945 had allowed for retaining the emperor, if that was the freely expressed will of the Japanese people. However, this concession was regarded as insufficient in Japan.

The moderates were trying to use the Soviet Union, still neutral in the Pacific war, as a mediator. Josef Stalin, who intended to attack Japan as soon as it was militarily possible, was not cooperative. The Japanese moderates persisted in assuming that the ongoing sacrifice of Japanese and American lives was a small price to pay - if they could avoid foreign occupation of the home islands, the trial of war criminals by the Allies and the humiliation of the armed forces.

Japanese decision-makers ignored the fire-bombing of Tokyo, which took 130,000 lives, and the subsequent unopposed air attacks on Japanese cities. The loss of civilian lives was regrettable but the army was still powerful and thousands of aircraft, including kamikaze suicide bombers, were available for a last stand. A compromise peace allowing the military to remain in power was thought possible; it was believed the Americans would not want to risk the horrendous casualties they had suffered on Iwo Jima and Okinawa.

War Goes On!.... White House

JAPAN ASKS FOR PEACE; ACCEPTS POTSDAM TERMS

Peace Bid Finds City Unprepared

Council's VJ-Day Committee Calls Special Meeting

The Jap surrender bid caught Vancouver by surprise . . . And Vancouver was not alone.

The entire Allied world was surprised at the sudden capitulation, in spite of the atomic bomb and Russia's declaration of war.

But Vancouver recovered quickly.

Ald. Jack Price, chairman of the civic committee on V-J Day celebration, said:

"With the Japanese surrender right on top of us, the committee will meet at once."

He indicated that plans for Vancouver's official day of celebration will be ready by the time official Allied announcement of V-J Day is made.

Mayor Cornett, Lieutenant-Governor Hon. W. C. Woodward, and Acting Premier Hon. R. C. MacDonald expressed jubilation at the news.

The man on the street was jubilant, too, but he wants to know: "Isn't Nippon now?"

When the word came at 4:30 o'clock Friday afternoon that Japan had taken hold to peace that now reigns in Indiana, all business and traffic conditions were affected.

W. F. Kennedy, chairman of the Liquor Control Board, will not act to close liquor stores or beer parlors until V-E Day.

Beer parlors will remain open both closed for two days—surrender day and V-E Day.

This time, liquor stores will close only if Ottawa declares a holiday.

ARMY READY.

The army was ready—only operations to be ready.

There is to be no consolidation in barracks. The announcement will read out to the troops in Pacific Command army camps.

Observers in each camp will be decided upon by the officer commanding.

There will be army field kitchens for service personnel and their friends.

There will be no parade on the street.

There was no trouble with service personnel in Vancouver on V-E Day, and none is expected on V-J Day.

All army personnel were to be prepared for a short leaving giving service.

Wet canteens will be open when the canteens will have had midnight.

(Continued on Page 2) See CITY.

From The Times:

Today In Europe

Compiled from the news and editorial content of the London Times, and cabled from The Vancouver Times London Bureau, Times Building, London by Hugo Baron.

(Copyright, 1945, by Reuters Co.)

LONDON, Aug. 10.—The acrimonious interchange between King Peter of Yugoslavia and Marshal Tito, who wants to abolish the monarchy, splits the Times editorials, most of our political divisions already allowing that country.

What Yugoslavia requires, like all the Balkans, is to find a firm decision for a peaceful and orderly reconstruction. Through Marshal Tito has promised a political honesty and progress to broaden the basis of political life, King Peter says rather tartly that law has been wiped out, and the proof the plebiscite on the return of the monarchy will take place by peaceful means and under her control.

Yugoslavia is emerging from a condition of chaos due to the German occupation. Before the war there was the democracy, only a police dictatorship, with a "managed" election. A free parliamentary system can not all established.

Inflicts Harm

And King Peter's intemperate statement can scarcely do anything but harm. It can not be said the Yugoslav monarchists are primarily concerned with democracy. On the other side, free elections are not possible where candidates are chosen from a single list that any not nearer than a single party.

Scientists and others are asking in the Times today about developing our security through the community of the atomic bomb's secret should be those secured by the Germans, the Japanese or any other aggressive nation in the next few years.

They advocate that the issue by Council of the United Nations should erect an armament for the safeguard department, aided by international advisers and others, to keep abreast of new inventions flowing from the basic research.

Technical Advances

The second should also have the power to call on any nation to declare its technical inventions in war weapons. As civil police are now equipped with the latest scientific devices to prevent crime, so the function prevents Security Council should be to act likewise.

The future design of airplanes for war purposes will be revolutionized by the atom, insisted the Times scientific correspondent. Since 1935 bombing aircraft have had to be continually increased in order to carry bigger and bigger bombs.

RUSS ARMIES SLASH DEEPLY IN MANCHURIA

Sakhalin, Korea Are Invaded

(Continuing from our dispatches to the Red Army)

MOSCOW, Aug. 10.—The Red Army's tanks, infantry and massed cavalry rolled through numerous gates in Manchuria's defenses with sensational advances today.

(Tokyo announced the broadcasting of the Soviet invasion of Korea and Sakhalin Island.)

(The invasion of southern Sakhalin, known to the Japanese as Karafuto, carried the Soviets into the last of several still available to the enemy.)

Soviet correspondents at several of the Soviet Far East fronts described Russian tanks as whirling along the roads adjoining Manchuria and Inner Mongolia, on the west, and inland war on Japan.

Outer Mongolia, a protectorate of Russia adjoining Manchuria and Inner Mongolia, had not yet declared war against Japan.

THREE MAIN ROUTES.

Moving into Manchuria along three main routes of invasion, the former Chinese Eastern Railway from Lake Baikal, the northward, the Mongolian Caravan Trail from Lake Baikal to the west and the Sungari River Valley from Khabarovsk in the northeast, the Russians had opened up "numerous gates" in the enemy's specially-prepared defenses and apparently were held on a moving offensive.

Gains of up to 25 miles yesterday were being enlarged considerably today.

The first decisive blow was as well prepared that the Japanese were unable to hold a single defensive line along the frontier, one dispatch reported.

The eastern and northwestern vanguards were driving hard for the city of Mulan (Mudan), Japanese forward base on the Chinese Eastern Railway, it was said.

In the northeastern sector, where the Russians struck from the maritime provinces to protect their mainland naval and air base at Vladivostok, they were making steady drive progress from Khabarovsk and captured Fu Yuan toward Harbin, rail heart of Manchuria still distant.

THE TERMS

Here, in brief, is what Japanese acceptance of the Potsdam ultimatum implies:

Unconditional surrender;

Disarmament;

Giving up of all conquered areas;

Return of Manchuria and Formosa to China;

Preparation of independence for Korea;

Withdrawal from Malaya, the Netherlands East Indies and China.

Can Strikers Delay Return To Work

Striking Anstino Can. Co. employees expected to return to work today under Controller James Bell today said they have obtained information as to their contract, the order-in-council set aside with the matter and the settlement of the men involved in the strike, and the end of 10 a.m. today.

ORDERED TO RETURN.

Gordon Bell, senior partner in the Vancouver coal sales firm Ano and Bell, distributed two firms and controller and the strikers ordered to return to work pending the settlement of the dispute.

Mr. Fuller E. E. Richards of Winnipeg, referee arbitration, was ordered to Vancouver to open arbitration hearings to hear the case and the company would decide whether to abide by the recommendations of the referee.

SEVEN POINTS PRESENTED.

They placed seven points before him. They are:

1. Status of a striker's agreement with American Can Company, expiring August 25.

2. A recognition had begun that all men who want to know when will be carrying on work negotiations and with whom the agreement will be signed, the men part of the government.

3. Whether the union after adjustments will comply and how the various steps of arbitration procedure will differ.

4. Copy of the order-in-council passed with the full details and options.

5. If there will be any changes in union against the strikers, or whether workers will all be placed on their usual jobs.

6. Whether the company or the government will define the rights those who placed agents will able while the men management is in effect.

7. How long the conciliation will be in effect, and the scope of the War Measures Act and the termination of the war with Japan.

Cloudy A.M. Sunny P.M. Saturday Setup

Saturday's weather forecast offers a partly cloudy morning to clear in the later afternoon, with moderate winds.

Maximum temperature, at Vancouver airport will be 70 degrees minimum, 56.

Light winds and local fog pockets in the early morning are expected in the Fraser Valley area.

Battle 34 Blazes

NELSON, Aug. 10.—Hitting five fire-fighting crews are busy on 34 small fires in the Nelson forest district.

First Canadian Ship To Fire Shot At Jap, Reaches Nanaimo

Special to The Daily Province.
NANAIMO, Aug. 10.—The H.M.C.S. Uganda, first cruiser in Canada's navy and the first Canadian ship to fire at the now narrow-starting Japanese, docked early after P.a.m. today.

Wartime movement flags were flying and the band of H.M.C.S. Naden was playing as the ship tied up at 8.20.

After a brief stay Uganda went to the Esquimalt dry dock in the afternoon past. For those who remained behind, Victoria plans a welcome tonight.

Ancillary organizations have arranged a series of parties and celebrations.

The Uganda steamed in the harbor escorted by eight Fairmiles. In the outer harbor two frigates, the Matane and the La Salle, saluted the Uganda

dipping their flags and blowing their whistles. The frigates were in the outer harbor on patrol practice.

The 700 men aboard were to come off ship according during the morning. About 200 of them were due to leave for Vancouver in the afternoon past. For those who remained behind, Victoria plans a welcome tonight.

MONTREAL—Four C.P.R. troop special will be on hand at World's Crest, Quebec, on Sunday to meet the S.S. Pasteur and transport the 3500 soldiers westward.

A total of 48 cars will make up the train.

Broadcast Offer Asks Only That Emperor Retain Power

Russian Ambassador in Tokyo Officially Receives Capitulation Bid; Washington and London Anxiously Await Formal Word

WASHINGTON, Aug. 10.—The Japanese Domei Agency announced today that Japan was ready to accept the terms of the Potsdam declaration calling for Tokyo's unconditional surrender, so long as Emperor Hirohito was permitted to retain his prerogatives.

Although the peace offer, which Tokyo said was on its way to all the Allied capitals through neutral sources, had not yet been received officially either here or in London, Moscow radio said Shigenori Togo, Japanese foreign minister, had informed Soviet Ambassador Jacob Malik of Japan's readiness to surrender.

The offer received by Russia seemed to be identical with that broadcast by Domei.

Japan's communication to the Soviet ambassador was reported in a message from Tokyo to the Soviet Tass Agency, whose communications with Japan have apparently not yet been cut off despite Russia's declaration of war yesterday.

Tass said a similar communication would be given to Britain, the United States and China through Sweden.

It appeared that Russia had been the first of the Allied powers to receive the surrender offer formally because the Soviet ambassador has not yet left Tokyo, where the other Allies have no representation except through neutral channels.

The White House made it clear that the offer had not been received officially here and that the war was going on.

The offer was transmitted by the Domei Agency at 4:30 a.m. P.D.T. and picked up in the United States by the Associated Press and government monitors. But it had not come through official diplomatic channels and the White House said at 7:40 a.m. P.D.T. that the United States was continuing to fight.

Despite this, wild celebrations had been set off at Okinawa and at other points throughout the Allied world.

At Behest of Emperor

Domei said the Japanese Government acted in obedience to Hirohito who, it said, "desires earnestly to bring about an early termination of hostilities."

The Domei broadcast was recorded by the Associated Press from an English-language wireless transmission to the United States. The broadcast came shortly after Domei announced that Japan was protesting through diplomatic channels the United States' use of atomic bombs and coincided with new Tokyo reports of Russian advances in Manchuria, Korea and on Sakhalin Island.

The Japanese wireless transmitter went off the air in the middle of a sentence after transmitting 200 words of the announcement of the "desire" to bring about an end to hostilities.

F.C.C. monitors said the transmission ended: "The Japanese Government hope sincerely that this . . ."

Domei waited a moment, F.C.C. monitors said, and then said "stand by."

Through Swiss, Swedes

Domei said Japan was informing the Allies of her acceptance through the Swiss and Swedish governments—neutral intermediaries.

A later Domei broadcast at 6:30 p.m. P.D.T. retransmitted the statement and gave its ending as follows:

"The Japanese Government hope sincerely that this understanding is warranted and desire keenly that an explicit indication to that effect will be speedily forthcoming."

Once the offer is transmitted through official channels, Japan's condition that Hirohito remain in power—may prove a stumbling block to immediate acceptance by all the Potsdam signatories—the United States, Britain and China. The Potsdam declaration itself did not mention the Emperor's status, but broadcasts of the United States Office of War Information have refrained from attacking Hirohito.

If the Domei report is borne out by official communications to the United States and Allied governments, it means that the third member of the Tokyo-Berlin-Rome axis has surrendered three months and one day after the capitulation of Hitler's Germany.

It would mean the end of hostilities that started Sep—

(Continued on Page 2) See JAPAN.

OTTAWA WAITS WORD TO CHANGE PLANS

By TORCHY ANDERSON

(From Daily Province Ottawa Bureau)
OTTAWA, Aug. 10.—If and when Ottawa gets official news that the Japanese war is over, staffs of naval, air and army forces will go into action to modify plans now being carried out for Canadian participation.

While the whole plan must move forward without any delay until the official word of surrender is received, it is known that staffs are considering action that may be necessary within the next few hours.

This morning Ottawa did not appear to have such more information than was available from the news services.

London Cabinet Meets; Awaits Official Word

(By Reuters)

LONDON, Aug. 10.—A meeting of the cabinet was called this afternoon soon after word was received in London of the reported Japanese surrender offer.

No. 10 Downing Street said Britain was consulting with the United States, Russia and China about the Tokyo broadcast.

No official communication from the Japanese Government had yet been received by Britain reporting the broadcast offer to surrender if Emperor Hirohito is allowed to keep his place.

Mr. Attlee has received no official news of the Japanese offer to surrender, the press secretary of 10 Downing street announced.

Emperor Not Mentioned At Potsdam

WASHINGTON, Aug. 10.—(AP)—An official confirmation of Japan's surrender offer was awaited here, specialists pointed out the reported Japanese proposal that the Emperor be permitted to retain his own sovereignty.

There was no mention of the Emperor in the Potsdam ultimatum of July 26 which called for immediate surrender.

Thus, there conceivably could be considerable delay among the Allies before they would give a reply to the conditional Japanese proposal.

The Potsdam ultimatum merely told both establishment in the future of a "peacefully inclined and responsible government."

Contrary to the Japanese contention that the Emperor's status is not specified in the Potsdam declaration, the reported surrender proposal revolved around the Allies' silence over Emperor Hirohito.

"We will not divide from all these lines," he adds, but stuck to give—

These attitudes began to change only after the news that "Hiroshima was destroyed instantly by a single bomb," reached Tokyo. Even then the cabinet was split 3-3 on whether to accept the Potsdam Declaration. The emperor did not insist on capitulation until after the Soviet declaration of war, August 8, and the destruction of Nagasaki, August 9. It was feared Tokyo and Kyoto would be next. Despite last minute attempts to organize a military coup and continue the war the emperor announced the surrender August 15. The A-bombs ended the war in the Pacific.

Few historians would disagree with this summary, but many would argue that we have considered the wrong question. Rather, was it necessary to use the A-bombs to end the war? This is the kind of approach to the past that encourages debate and controversy. The question can not be answered because it is about events that did not happen. Any number of counter-factual arguments may be presented with some plausibility.

Most historians would have no trouble agreeing that Japan had lost the war and would have been forced to surrender sometime in the fall of 1945 or early 1946 without the A-bombs. But there is no agreement on how or when this might have taken place. Some would argue that the Soviet conquest of Manchuria, completed by August 20, would have forced a surrender. This is unconvincing because it was the occupation of the sacred home islands, not Manchuria, that was at issue. However, it is more important to point out that the Japanese army in Manchuria collapsed after the A-bombs were used, we can not possibly determine the outcome of the battle in the absence of the bombs.

Vancouver Daily Province of August 10, 1945.

What can be said is that American plans for ending the war involved continuous bombing of Japanese cities. Indeed, it was expected that all significant urban targets would be destroyed by November 1945. The naval blockade, which had already cut off all shipping with Japan, was slowly starving the population. U.S. battleships were shelling coastal cities while naval aviators attacked the pitiful remnants of the Japanese fleet. Operation "Olympic", the invasion of the southern island of Kyushu, was scheduled for November with an assault on Honshu, the main island set for early 1946.

Canadians would have been affected had the war continued. The desperate plight of the surviving prisoners of war from Hong Kong would have worsened and many more would have died. Elements of the Royal Canadian Navy and the Royal Canadian Air Force would have been drawn into the action, including HMCS *Uganda* slated to return to the Pacific with an all-volunteer crew. Canada's expeditionary force, an infantry division under Major-General Bert Hoffmeister, was to be part of the follow-up force, landing after the planned assault on Honshu. If the war had lasted that long casualties would have been numerous. We can never know what might have have happened but it is clear that the alternative to dropping the A-bombs was not peace but a continuation of a terrible war.

After all this is said there remains the horrific reality of Hiroshima. When the Smithsonian Institute developed its controversial exhibit to mark the 50th anniversary of the bombing, the image of the mushroom cloud and what it meant for the future of humanity led the designers to underplay the harsh realities of 1945. They might have understood the position of the veterans who protested the planned display if any of them had direct experience in the Pacific war or had read a book like, *Quartered Safe Out Here: A Recollection of the War in Burma.*

George Macdonald Fraser, known to many as the creator of the Flashman series, was a 19-year-old volunteer in the Border Regiment when the war ended. His memoirs capture the flavour of life and death in the infantry with an authenticity few authors have achieved. He recalls that the news of Hiroshima evoked "no moralizing and no feeling at all of the guilt which some thinkers nowadays seem to want to attach to the bombing."

Fraser then relates an encounter he had with a man who denounced the bombing as a monstrosity that no civilized person could have contemplated. Fraser responded by asking if the man would give up his life to restore one of the lives lost August 6 and then asked, "By what right then, do you say that Allied lives should have been sacrificed to save the victims of Hiroshima?"

Predictably the moralist insisted that "Japan was ready to surrender anyway and it was only done because (Harry S.) Truman wanted to frighten the Russians." All this talk of 50,000 Allied casualties while stormin the home islands was tommyrot because it never would have happened.

Fraser kept his cool and forced his opponent to admit that some Allied lives – neither mentioned Japanese deaths - would have been lost if the bombs had not been dropped. Unhappy with this admission the moralist demanded to know Fraser's position. "None of your God-damned business," Fraser replied, "but whatever it is, or was, it is somewhere you have never been, among people you would not understand."

But Fraser does offer his readers some personal reflections. The use of the A-bombs he acknowledges was barbaric but the alternative-the death of more Allied soldiers, in a war which was won, against an enemy who would not quit-was simply unacceptable. So the bombing was right. Or was it?

Fraser reveals the complexity and ambiguity of counter-factual arguments in a passage that challenges all our assumptions. He writes, "I have a feeling that if ... Nine section had known all that we know about Hiroshima...and if some voice from on high had said, 'There-that can end the war for you if your want...the alternative is that the war, as you've known it goes on.. .and some of you won't reach the end of the road...it's up to you: I think I know what would have happened. They would have cried' Aw fook that' with one voice...and then they would have been moving south. Because that is the kind of men they were."

Perhaps not every Allied soldier, sailor or airman, and certainly not every prisoner of war suffering in Japanese hands would have been as self-sacrificing as Fraser's comrades. But we should not underestimate the basic decency and humanity of the men and women who went to war on our behalf 50 years ago. At a minimum we should resist the temptation to offer easy judgments about events that took place somewhere we have never been among people we do not understand.

Books Mentioned in the Text

Addison, Paul and Calder, Angus [eds.], *Time to Kill*, London: Pimlico, 1997.

Ambrose, Stephen, *Citizen Soldiers: The U.S. Army from the Normandy Beaches to the Bulge to the Surrender of Germany, June 7, 1944-May 7, 1945*, New York: Simon & Schuster, 1997.

Birney, Earle, *Turvey: A Military Picaresque*, Toronto: McClelland & Stewart, 1976.

Bishop, Arthur, *The Splendid Hundred*, Toronto: McGraw-Hill Ryerson, 1994.

Bowman, Phylis, *We Skirted The War*, Prince Rupert B.C. : Private Press, 1975.

Brown, Gordon and Copp, Terry, *Look To Your Front Regina Rifles: A Regiment at War, 1944-1945*, Waterloo, Ontario: LCMSDS, 2001.

Bruce, Jean, *Back the Attack!: Canadian Women During the Second World War, at Home and Abroad*, Toronto: Macmillan of Canada, 1985.

Buckley, Christopher, *The Road to Rome*, London: 1945.

Calder, Angus, *The Myth of the Blitz*, London: Jonathan Cape, 1991.

Calder, Angus, *The People's War: Britain 1939-45*, London: Jonathan Cape, 1969.

Copp, Terry, *Fields of Fire*, Toronto: University of Toronto Press, 2003.

D'Este, Carlo, *Bitter Victory: The Battle for Sicily, 1943*, New York: E.P. Dutton, 1988.

Dancocks, Daniel, *The D-Day Dodgers: The Canadians in Italy, 1943-1945*, Toronto: McClelland & Stewart, 1991.

Dickson, Paul Douglas, *The Limits of Professionalism: General H.D.G. Crerar and the Canadian Army, 1914-1944*, University of Guelph, Doctoral Thesis, 1993

Douglas, W.A.B...[et al.], *No Higher Purpose: The Official History of the Royal Canadian Navy in the Second World War, 1939-1943, v.2 pt.1*, St. Catharines: Vanwell Publishing, 2002.

English, John A., *The Canadian Army and the Normandy Campaign: A Study of Failure in High Command*, New York: Praeger, 1991.

Fraser, George MacDonald, *Quartered Safe Out Here: A Recollection of the War in Burma*, London: Harvill, 1992.

Frost, C. Sydney, *Once A Patricia: Memoirs of a Junior Infantry Officer in World War II*, St. Catharines, Ontario: Vanwell Publishing, 1988.

Galloway, Strome, *A Regiment at War: the Story of the Royal Canadian Regiment, 1939-1945*, London: Royal Canadian Regiment, 1979.

Galloway, Strome, *The General Who Never Was*, Belleville: Mika Publishing Company, 1981.

Galloway, Strome, *Some Died at Ortona: The Royal Canadian Regiment in Action in Italy, 1943*, London: Royal Canadian Regiment, 1983.

Granatstein, J. L. *Who Killed Canadian History?* Toronto: HarperCollins, 1998.

Granatstein, J.L., *The Generals: The Canadian Army's Senior Commanders in the Second World War*, Toronto: Stoddart, 1993.

Graves, Donald E. with Grodzinski, John R. [et al.], *Fighting for Canada: Seven Battles 1758-1945*, Toronto: Robin Brass Studios, 2000.

Greenhous, Brereton, *The Official History of the Royal Canadian Air Force: The Crucible of War 1939-1945*, Toronto: University of Toronto Press, 1986.

Greer, Rosamond, *The Girls of the King's Navy*, Victoria B.C.: Sono Nis Press, 1983.

Hamilton, Nigel, *Monty*, New York: McGraw-Hill, 3 vols. 1981-1987.

Hayes, Geoffrey, *The Lincs: A History of the Lincoln and Welland Regiment at War*, Alma, Ontario: Maple Leaf Route, 1986.

Hinsley, F.H. *British Intelligence in the Second World War*, London: H.M.S.O., 5 vols. 1979-90.

Hitler, Adolph, *Mein Kampf*, Boston: Houghton Mifflin, 1943.

Holmes, Richard, *Riding the Retreat: Mons to the Marne 1914 Revisited,* London: J. Cape, 1995.

Jarymowycz, Roman *Tank Tactics: From Normandy to Lorraine*, Boulder Colo.: London: Lynne Rienner, 2001.

Keegan, John, *The Battle For History: re-fighting World War Two,* Toronto: Vintage 1995, Barbara Frum Lecture Series

McAndrew, Bill, *Canadians and the Italian Campaign 1943-1945,* Montreal: Art Global, 1996.

Middlebrook, Martin, *Arnhem 1944: The Airborne Battle 17-26 September,* Boulder: Westview Press, 1994.

Milner, Marc, *North Atlantic Run: The Royal Canadian Navy and the Battle for the Convoys,* Toronto: University of Toronto Press, 1985.

Milner, Marc, *The U-boat Hunters: The Royal Canadian Navy and the Offensive against Germany's Submarines,* Toronto: University of Toronto Press, 1994.

Motiuk, Laurence, *Thunderbirds At War: Diary of a Bomber Squadron*, Nepean, Ontario: Privately Published, 1998.

Mowat, Farely, *The Regiment*, Toronto: McClelland and Stewart, 1973.

Nolan, Brian, *Airborne: the Heroic Story of the 1st Canadian Parachute Battalion in the Second World War*, Toronto: Lester Pub., 1995.

Olmstead, Bill, *Blue Skies: the Autobiography of a Canadian Spitfire Pilot in World War II,* Toronto: Stoddart, 1987.

Pierson, Ruth Roach, *They're Still Women After All: The Second World War and Canadian Womanhood*, Toronto: McClelland and Stewart, 1986.

Ritchie, Charles, *The Siren Years: A Canadian Diplomat Abroad, 1937-1945,* Toronto: Macmillan, 1974.

Schull, Joseph, *The Far Distant Ships: An Official Account of Canadian Naval Operations in the Second World War,* Ottawa: Cloutier, 1952, 1950.

Stacey, C.P., *The Victory Campaign: Official History of the Canadian Army in the Second World War,* Ottawa: Cloutier, Queen's Printer 1955-1967.

Swettenham, John, *McNaughton,* Toronto: Ryerson Press, 1968.

Webster, Charles K. and Frankland, Noble, *The Strategic Air Offensive Against Germany, 1939-1945*, London: H.M.S.O., 1961.

Zimmerman, David, *The Great Naval Battle of Ottawa*, Toronto: University of Toronto Press, 1988.

Zuehlke, Mark, *Ortona: Canada's Epic World War II Battle,* Toronto, New York: Stoddart, 1999.

Zuehlke, Mark, *The Gothic Line: Canada's Month of Hell in World War II Italy,* Vancouver, New York: Douglas & McIntyre, 2003.

Zuehlke, Mark, *The Liri Valley: Canada's World War II Breakthrough to Rome,* Toronto, New York: Stoddart, 2001.